Praise for *Animals in Islam*

"*Animals in Islam* shows that in Islam, as in other religious traditions, there is ample material to justify a compassionate view of animals, and in particular, one that is incompatible with treating billions of sentient beings as if they were merely things, to be crowded into factory farms that take no account of their nature and their needs but see them only objects for human consumption."—**Peter Singer**, professor of bioethics at Princeton University, author of *Animal Liberation*

"I had the good fortune to have known the late Al Hafiz Masri in the mid-1980s when he was working on the first edition of this book. I gained much from this relationship in the environmental themes that I was myself developing at that time and his erudition and wisdom is not lost on his grandson, Nadeem Haque, who as editor has produced the second version of this volume. Compassion in World Farming has also much to commend itself for pushing out this volume and is largely responsible for the shape of the final chapter with its emphasis on stunning. Although this volume is meant for a western readership the material is relevant to the Islamic world generally and should be compulsory reading for all those interested in humane slaughter. It also forces people to rethink their dietary habits given the negative impact of high meat consumption on the environment."—**Fazlun Khalid**, Founder of the Islamic Foundation for Ecology and Environmental Sciences, author of *Signs on the Earth: Islam, Modernity, and the Climate Crisis* (Kube Publishing Ltd., 2019)

"A most important book! One of the earliest and very few to offer a comprehensive Islamic perspective on contemporary animal welfare issues. It brings to life and conveys the urgency of a key Qur'anic insight: that our lives and the lives of other animals are inextricably intertwined; that kindness to animals is not a quirk or secondary concern, but an essential part of human virtue.

By all accounts, Masri was an illustrious scholar and the kind of person one meets once and never forgets. May both Muslims and non-Muslims meet Masri through this book and find inspiration in his kindness."—**Rainer Ebert**, PhD; Fellow of the Oxford Centre for Animal Ethics, UK, and International Research Associate at the University of Dar es Salaam, in former Tanganyika, one of the many places Masri called home.

"This new edition of Al-Hafiz B.A. Masri's seminal work is great news for research in Islamic animal theology, especially since it is accompanied by contributions from major authors on these questions. It is an outstanding tribute that the editor Nadeem Haque pays here to the pioneering work of his grandfather."—**Sébastien Sarméjeanne**, translator of the French edition of *Animals in Islam* (*Les Animaux en Islam*)

"As concerns grow for the sustainability of life on our planet, animal welfare has become an issue of increasing relevance and importance. This pioneering book provides an overview of animal welfare through the lens of Islam and encourages the reader to rethink how values of compassion can be implemented."—**Sabrina Sehbai**, Founder and Director of Join Hands

"In the divine revelation of Islam, we see multiple references to animals in different contexts. Clearly the Qur'an alludes to a high level of sophistication (or even development) that some (or many) animals or even insects may have. Masri, in his seminal contribution, sheds light on animals in Islam that extends the debate beyond the question of animals as a source of humans' pleasure or utility. In light of the modern Western culture of extreme excess in everything, and in light of the dominant Muslims' culture that mainly focuses on which animal products are permissible to eat, and in light of the advances in psychology, sociology, and the physical sciences, Masri's book will ignite a broader debate that is highly timely."
—**Omar M. Ramahi**, Author of *Muslims' Greatest Challenge: Choosing Between Tradition and Islam.*

ANIMALS IN ISLAM

Al-Hafiz B.A. Masri, Author

Nadeem Haque, Editor

Lantern Publishing & Media • Woodstock & Brooklyn, NY

2022
Lantern Publishing & Media
PO Box 1350
Woodstock, NY 12498
www.lanternpm.org

Cover design by Rebecca Moore
Copyediting and typesetting by Pauline Lafosse

Printed in the United States of America

Library of Congress Cataloging-in-Publication Data

Names: Masri, B. A. (Basheer Ahmad), 1914- author. | Haque, Nadeem, 1960- editor.
Title: Animals in Islam : Masri's book and scholarly reflections on his work / edited by Nadeem Haque.
Description: Woodstock : Lantern Publishing & Media, 2022. | Includes bibliographical references and index.
Identifiers: LCCN 2022011695 (print) | LCCN 2022011696 (ebook) | ISBN 9781590566800 (paperback) | ISBN 9781590566817 (epub)
Subjects: LCSH: Animal welfare—Religious aspects—Islam. | Animal welfare—Moral and ethical aspects. | Animals—Religious aspects—Islam. | Masri, B. A. (Basheer Ahmad), 1914- Animals in Islam. | BISAC: RELIGION / Islam / General | RELIGION / Islam / Rituals & Practice
Classification: LCC BP190.5.A58 M375 2022 (print) | LCC BP190.5.A58 (ebook) | DDC 179/.3—dc23/eng/20220404
LC record available at https://lccn.loc.gov/2022011695
LC ebook record available at https://lccn.loc.gov/2022011696

Contents

Original Profile: Al-Hafiz B.A. Masri · · · · · · · · · · · · · · · · · · · ix
Foreword to 1989 Edition · x
Original Preface by Al Hafiz B.A. Masri · · · · · · · · · · · · · · · · xi
Preface to New Edition · xiii

Essays on Al-Hafiz B.A. Masri's Influence and Legacy
Masri's Project and Compassion in World Farming - *Joyce D'Silva* · · ·3
Islam and Animals: Masri's Pioneering Contributions
   Concerning Non-human Animals - *Richard Foltz* · · · · · · · · · · · ·8
A Veterinary Bioethical Perspective - *Michael W. Fox* · · · · · · · · · · ·10
Respect and Mercy Towards All Creatures and
   Masri's influence - *Princess Alia Al Hussein* · · · · · · · · · · · · · · · · ·20
Like All Pioneers: Masri's Impact on the Field of
   Animal Ethics in Islam - *Sarra Tlili* ·24
Anymals in Islam - *Lisa Kemmerer* ·33

A Short Biography of Al-Hafiz B.A. Masri - *Nadeem Haque* · · ·49

Animals in Islam:
Chapter 1. Islamic Concern for Animals · · · · · · · · · · · · · · · · · · ·65
Chapter 2. Vegetarianism vs. Meatarianism · · · · · · · · · · · · · · · · ·117
Chapter 3. Pig—A Thorn in the Flesh · · · · · · · · · · · · · · · · · · ·155
Chapter 4. Animal Sacrifice ·193
Chapter 5. Halal Meat—The Bone of Contention · · · · · · · · · · · · ·229
Chapter 6. The Islamic Method of Slaughter · · · · · · · · · · · · · · · ·257

About the Editor
About the Publisher

Original Profile: Al-Hafiz B.A. Masri

Al-Hafiz Basheer Ahmad Masri was born in 1914 in India and graduated with a B.A. (honours) degree in Arabic from the Government College, Lahore, of the University of Punjab. He also attended the Faculty of Arabic at al-Azhar Seminary in Cairo. He was fluent in many languages, including English, classical Arabic, Urdu, Hindustani, Punjabi, Kiswahili . . . (For our non-Muslim readers, we should explain that Al-Hafiz denotes one who has memorized the whole of the Qur'ân).

During the 20 years he spent in East Africa (1941-1961), he was Headmaster of the then-largest secondary school and held secretarial or presidential posts on religious, social, and educational organizations among the African, Asian, and European communities—including animal welfare.

In 1961, he settled in England and studied journalism and was the Joint-Editor of the well-known Islamic monthly magazine for six years—*The Islamic Review*. In 1964, he was the first Sunni Muslim to be appointed as the Imam of the Shah Jehan Mosque in Woking, U.K., which was the European center for Islam at the time. Following his retirement in 1968, in order to gain a deeper first-hand knowledge of Islamic culture, he spent three years touring more than forty, mainly Muslim, countries by car. He became well-known in the U.K. for his lectures, radio and television broadcasts, and published articles as an authority on the wider aspects of Islam.

Al-Hafiz Masri's dedicated and far-ranging study of the practical problems of the Muslim world for over half a century made him one of the few authorities to successfully undertake the writing of this comprehensive book on 'Animals in Islam'.

Publishers

Foreword To The 1989 Edition

The uniqueness of this book, 'Animals in Islam', is that it is possibly the only truly authoritative work on Islamic Concern for Animals. For many years the author, Al-Hafiz B.A. Masri, was the first Sunni Imam of the Shah Jehan mosque (Woking, U.K) when it was the Islamic center of Europe. He is widely respected for the depth of his scholarship in this field. The observations the author makes are supported by a wealth of quotations from the Qur'ân and Hadith.

True to Islamic tradition, Al-Hafiz Masri welcomes Muslim readers and particularly Muslim theologians and scholars, to write to him giving their opinions on what must be one of the most relevant and thought-provoking pieces of literature on animals within Islam, to be released for many centuries.

The publishers and author have decided to use any profits from the sale of the book for the formation of an Islamic Trust for Animal Welfare.

Publishers
[Compassion in World Farming]

Original Preface By Al-Hafiz B.A. Masri

Quite a few of my friends have been surprised to learn that I have chosen 'Animals' as a subject to write on from the Islamic point of view. They feel that I should be more concerned with other multifarious problems which Muslims are facing these days and need help and guidance in solving them. The way I look at it, however, is that life on the earth is so inextricably intertwined as a homogeneous unit that it cannot be disentangled for the melioration of one species at the expense of another.

All human problems—physical, mental, or spiritual—are of our own creation and our wounds self-afflicted. By no stretch of imagination can we blame animals for any of our troubles and make them suffer for it.

There is no paucity of Muslim scholars and theologians who are far more qualified than me to expand theologically all sorts of such problems. Notwithstanding this, I feel that my practical experience of a lifetime in the field of animal welfare, combined with some theological knowledge, lays a moral responsibility on me to express my views candidly on the current spate of cruelties to animals. The learned theologians generally remain blissfully uninformed on this subject, which is generally beyond the pale of their normal responsibilities. Similarly, the general Muslim public is not fully aware of the scale on which the human pecuniary, selfish, and short-sighted interests have started exploiting the animal kingdom and making havoc of the ecological balance.

The most alarming and distressing predicament of this deplorable state of affairs is that our Islamic countries too have started treading the footsteps of the West in the name of commerce and trade. No doubt we have a lot to learn from Western technology and science, but surely animal welfare and environmental conservation is not one of these subjects.

The Islamic instruction and guidance on animal rights and man's obligations concerning them are so comprehensive that we need not go elsewhere for any guidance. As believers in the consummate and conclusive revelation of God we are expected learn from the misconceptions of the past and cast behind us the parochial approach to religion. Fourteen centuries is a long enough period to grasp mentally the fact that the way (Din) to spiritual development does not lie in the ritualistic observance of hair-splitting of the Law (*sharia*), Surely it is a long enough period to liberate ourselves from the pre-Islamic traits of our respective cultures.

Not to be cruel or even to be condescendingly kind to the so-called inferior animals is a negative proposition. Islam wants us to think and act in the positive terms of accepting all species as communities like us in their own right and not to sit in judgment on them according to our human norms and values.

I hope and pray that my Muslim brethren will fully appreciate the points I have touched upon here, after reading the book.

PREFACE TO THE NEW EDITION

Nadeem Haque—Editor

The idea for republishing Al-Hafiz B.A. Masri's original book *Animals in Islam* in its entirety came about as a result of my visit to Harvard University in 2013, for a unique conference on Animals and Islam,[i] the world's first ever conference on this subject at a University, to my knowledge. Here, I met various highly reputable academics who, to my delightful surprise, expressed the sentiment that the book has been indispensable for studies in the area of Islamic studies and animals/ecology. From what I know of the history of this book, one of the reasons Compassion in World Farming (CIWF) commissioned it was to deal with the issue of stunning animals before slaughter for food, apprising Muslims of this method, and elevating the welfare of animals in the nominal Muslim regions of the world.

To put this volume in the proper context, I feel that a few points might be worth mentioning concerning Masri, my maternal grandfather. I had the privilege of visiting and living at his residence on numerous occasions over the years, in Hampton Court, Surrey, England. In my many conversations with Masri, I came to realize that his focus was on the Qur'ân, compassion, practicality, and rationality. He really had a deep concern for animals and was unusually drawn to helping them in practical ways, not only academically. For example, he used to pick up car-injured birds on the busy road that ran past the front of his house (in Hampton Court) and cared for them until they were fully recovered. Then he would set them free. He was against exploitation of any kind from any early age, risking life and limb to defend humans and animals alike.

---

i   Nadeem Haque gave a lecture and spoke on the panel, "Animal Rights & Animal Welfare: Prospects and Challenges," as part of the Fifth Annual Prince Alwaleed Bin Talal Islamic Studies Conference at Harvard University, held on April 5-6, 2013. The theme of the conference was "Communities Like You: Animals and Islam." https://vimeo.com/68147397. Nadeem discussed his "Ecognitions" paper (see reference 3).

Masri had this air of calmness and coolness about him, with an incredibly strong (though kind) personality, and his gaze was at various times keen and shrewd, but also compassionate and friendly. The best way to describe Masri, the older Masri, is to imagine a combination of the screen toughness and coolness of 1960s action heroes (an Eastern version!) with a heavy dose of congeniality: indeed, he had mellowed in his later years and the sternness and aloofness that my mother (Tahera) and uncles (Tahir and Mubarak—his sons) complained about when he was a young man and they were kids, had disappeared. I wonder how much this transformation had to do with his study of Animal Welfare and the attendant compassion that it engenders; I think it had a huge impact in his own growth as a human being. Yet he still retained what one would call an authoritative presence, and everyone who knew or met him would testify to the same. He was also the type of person who, if he met you, would be genuinely interested in what *you* were doing and were interested in. He would give you practical advice for your life, not in a lecture or arrogant way, but as a natural part of the conversation, especially since he had so much life experience and had also been an Imam at the Shah Jehan mosque, where Imams typically serve as counsellors. The 'presence' that he had, was more than anyone I have met since and probably ever will meet. Of the extraordinary people I have been fortunate enough to meet, Masri has certainly been one of the most memorable—and I am not just saying that because he was my grandfather!

Masri and I had many animated discussions on Islam over the years, and he would acquiesce if I showed him to be incorrect (which was rare); he was not arrogant at all, but very humble and accepted an alternate view if a proof was found. On the other hand, I have come to see his wisdom on some issues where we had differed when I was young and brash—such as his nuanced and logical approach to the vegetarianism/Islam issue and his ways of countering "inter-religious" arguments in a sensitive manner, without compromising on the facts. Of course, he was also an extremely skilled public speaker and, as Imam of the Shah Jehan Mosque in Woking, England, he used to give many talks at Speakers' Corner in Hyde Park. In all, he estimated that he had given about 200 public lectures. Just to give you a quick example of his bravery, public speaking skills, and practical problem-solving abilities, as well as the type of person he was: In the 1930s, he was in a car during a deadly riot in India where hundreds of violent protestors gathered in the streets against the government. As luck would have it, he happened to be seated in a government car! The hyper-agitated throng of dissidents was fast approaching the vehicle and the encounter was no doubt going to be deadly. Suddenly, Masri got out of the car, stood on its roof, and began to lecture on the government's initiatives to help the masses. He said he agreed wholeheartedly with their grievances and would try to help them. The threat was averted, and the riot turned into an amicable gathering.

Another interesting example that illustrates his bold character is one pertaining to animals, also from his time in India (est. in 1932). He was probably around 18 years old at the time. As he was crossing the road he saw a horse-drawn carriage approaching the village and in it, visible to all the villagers, was an old, bearded man with a huge lion! Masri explained to me that the whole idea of this scam was to convey to the masses that the Pir (a term used in the Indian Sub-continent) or Sheikh (an equivalent term) was so powerful that he had control of the lion, though "spiritual power." The carriage stopped and almost the whole village gathered around it. They got out, and lion was tied to a tree by the Pir. People were amazed and believed he must be extremely powerful to have such a normally ferocious beast under his total control. Masri, on the other hand, made a beeline for the lion—and the people witnessing this were horrified and anxiously tried to dissuade him from such a foolish action. When he reached the lion, he stroked its mane gently. Much to the surprise of everyone, the lion did not attack him. He then said to the crowd in a loud voice: "Don't you see that this lion is a tame one? How can you be so foolish to believe in this charlatan?" Very soon after having verbally blasted the villagers, Masri was accosted. He had now become a problem to the Pir, who wanted to exert his full control on the village. The Pir sent four of his henchmen to meet Masri and forced him to get into a car. There were too many of them and he did not want to put up a fight, so he went along for a "ride." They drove a long distance and he was dumped in a forested area—totally isolated. Then they hastily left. Masri made his way towards the village. After walking for several hours, he alighted upon a hut in the middle of the forest. He knocked on the door and an old saintly-looking man—the proverbial hermit—invited him into his humble abode. Masri relayed the whole story to this kind soul, who exclaimed: "You know what? *You* are the one with the 'spiritual power!'"

I was with Masri for a few days in 1992 to help him type the chapter for a series on religions and ecology, published by Cassels (*Islam and Ecology*). Although he was on his death bed with an oxygenator—terminal *fibrosing alveolitis*, the doctors had given him three months to live—he enthusiastically, though with great physical discomfort, continued to expand and edit his work. It was published just before his death. My uncle Mubarak Masri, his son, suspects that Masri had damaged his lungs working in the mines in East Africa during his youth.

To his last day, Masri continued to be a source of inspiration and ideas for me. He was serenely at peace because he was sure of a life beyond death in another form. I know this not only because, as a Muslim, he was supposed to be convinced of this, but because he consoled his wife Salima (1920-2011, my grandmother) concerning this eventuality. He stated to her in a relaxing manner that this life was only a passing phase to another world. In fact, as I was told by my late grandmother, that he was mentally very at ease during his last days at the hospital: He advised some relatives who had come to visit him on practical matters and maintained his typical witty, self-effacing humor with the hospital staff.

Masri's last words to me were: "Keep strong and continue your [Islamic] research." I knew that I would not be seeing him again, at least not in this life, and departed for Canada with great sadness. He died just three months later in 1992. His last words resonated with me and have stayed with me ever since, inspiring me to continue my scholarly-activist pursuits. In 2011, I wrote the article "The Principles of Animal Advocacy in Islam: Four Integrated Ecognitions" which was a continuation of my research into the essence of the Islamic view on animals—its core teachings and principles. I combined some of Masri's unpublished writings with my own work, trying to blend them seamlessly. This article was published by the top peer-reviewed journal *Society and Animals*.[ii] And it was this article that brought me to the attention of Harvard University and their conference on the subject of Islam and Animal Welfare and eventually to a re-issuing of this book in its entire form!

I really believe that Masri's reflection on animals through his formal and pioneering study of the Qur'ân and Hadith has contributed greatly towards widening and deepening our scope of understanding—for *both* humans and animals and their equitable interrelationships. His writing, in the pre-internet age on a 1960s typewriter, were initially posted after the internet's advent, helping to spread this aspect of Islam; now there are a plethora of websites with basic information on this subject, influenced by his pioneering and foundational work. He was also influential in the establishment of the environmental organization IFEES, based in Britain. He had wanted to start an organization called IMAAN (International Muslim Association for Animals and Nature), a clever acronym, where the word 'Imaan' in Arabic means: confirmation, verification, security, and belief (commonly translated as 'faith' or 'belief').

When we extend our compassion towards all living things, we feel empathy for all beings as Creatures of God. In re-publishing the book, I have, as editor, added the updated version of the missing chapter on animal stunning, excluded from the 2007 version of the book.[iii] I have also included the chapter on pig meat consumption, with additional footnotes. Furthermore, I have edited some Qur'ânic translations to increase their accuracy. However, most significantly, I have benefitted from the graciousness and kindness of eminent scholars/activists in the field who were influenced to various degrees by Masri's pioneering work; hence, their contributory essays on Masri's influence on their work, herein. My co-authored work on the environment and Islam (*Ecolibrium: The Sacred Balance in Islam*), which had been begun with Masri in 1992, has recently been

---

ii Nadeem Haque and Masri, Al-Hafiz Basheer Ahmad. "The Principles of Animal Advocacy in Islam: Four Integrated Ecognitions" *Society and Animals*, 19 (2011): 279-290.

iii Masri, Al-Hafiz Basheer Ahmad Masri. (2007). *Animal Welfare in Islam*, The Islamic Foundation, Leicestershire.

published by Beacon Books in Manchester, U.K.[iv] My only regret is that Masri is not here with us to see the final product.

The issue of both Animal Welfare and Islam are among some of the most pressing issues in today's world. I do hope that by re-issuing the book with minimal editing, it will inspire and instruct human beings to understand and implement the best policies for humankind, animals, and nature. With the approach suggested by Masri, espousing the true tenets of Islam, we can wade through the precarious waters of the present century and beyond in the least harmful way. It is indeed a world filled with uncertainty. But at the same time, the advancement of information brings hope: If properly connected it facilitates the flow of knowledge into implementation for the benefit of humans, flora, and fauna, and indeed, nature in general. Having lived in England for so long, during his final months, Masri conveyed to me in very British terms: "I feel that I have put in a good innings in this life." I would definitely agree that he had indeed put in a good innings, with several good sixes in the process!

Nadeem Haque

---

iv *Ecolibrium,: The Sacred Balance in Islam*, published by Beacon Books, Manchester in 2021, co-authored by Nadeem Haque, Al-Hafiz. B.A. Masri and Mehran Banaei.

Essays On Al-Hafiz B.A. Masri's

Influence & Legacy

Masri's Project and Compassion in World Farming

Joyce D'Silva, D.Litt., D. Univ. (Hons).

Soon after I began to work for Compassion in World Farming in 1985, I was introduced to "Mr. Masri"—or, as I discovered his full title, Al-Hafiz B A Masri. Compassion's founder, Peter Roberts, had asked him to write a book about Islam and Animal Welfare and we were already publishing the first chapter as a separate booklet, "Islamic Concern for Animals," in both English and Arabic. The final book was published in 1989 as "Animals in Islam" and was distributed internationally over the next few years.

As a result of this book, Mr. Masri built up a huge correspondence with Muslims all over the world—I remember him showing me supportive letters from Muslims as far afield as Turkey and Argentina. It seemed that his careful reading of the holy books of Islam, and his publicizing of all they had to say on caring for animals as part of Allah's creation, had struck a chord with compassionate Muslims everywhere.

Not that his book was universally welcomed. He had decided that the correct interpretation of Islamic teaching on kindness to animals at the point of slaughter meant that it was right to use some modern stunning methods to cause the animals immediate unconsciousness (but not death) before the actual slaughter. In this way, they would be spared the pain of throat-cutting and distress as they bled out.

However, this is an issue that still causes disagreement within the Islamic community, and it was no different a quarter century ago. He was asked to address it while attending a packed meeting at a mosque in Birmingham. Some agreed with him; some did not.

The wonderful thing about Mr. Masri was that he was such a gentle man. He seemed to hold no aggressive feelings or antagonism, even for those who might vehemently disagree with him. I got to know him well over the years and never heard him raise his voice. Mrs. Masri obviously supported his work. Often when he would visit our offices, he would bring a box of delicious vegetable samosas which she had made for us.

Of all the major faiths, the holy books of Islam appear to contain the most about how wonderful animals are and how we should have compassion for them. The Qur'ân tells us that animals prostrate themselves to Allah (Qur'ân 22:18), that they are communities like humans and that they will share in the resurrection (Qur'ân 6:38). Indeed, Allah knows about the lives of every creature on Earth (Qur'ân 11:6). So, animals are in an intimate relationship with Allah, where they worship Him and He cares for them. No species of animal is excluded from these verses in the Qur'ân.

But what about the relationship between humans and animals? Several Hadith of Prophet Mohammad record how, after a prophet of the ancient days (prior to Prophet Mohammad) was bitten by an ant, he destroyed the ants' nest and was rebuked by Allah, who said "Because one ant stung you, you have burned a whole community which glorified me" (Bukhari and Muslim).

Some Hadith go further, emphasizing the importance of respect for animals. When the prophet's companions took some fledgling birds from the nest, whilst their mother bird hovered nearby in an agitated manner, Mohammad scolded them saying "Who has injured this bird by taking its young? Return them to her" (Muslim).

The Prophet Mohammad is recorded as feeling great compassion and empathy with animals. There is more than one hadith account of when he came upon an overworked camel in a terrible state. He asked the camel's owner "Don't you fear God with regard to this animal, whom God has given to you? For the camel complained to me that you starve him and work him endlessly." (Sunan Abu Dawud 2186, and Musnad Ahmad 1654 and 1662 (similar)).

This fine example should surely inspire all followers of Islam to be kind towards animals. In fact, the hadith record how such kindness may well be rewarded. When the Prophet had told his companions that the man who had given water to a thirsty dog was blessed by Allah for showing such kindness, his companions asked if they would be rewarded for assisting animals. The Prophet said,

"There is the possibility for a reward for helping each living being" (*Bukhari*, Hadith 168, 2190, 2286; *Ibn Hajar* Vol 2, Hadith 173).

Of course, the holy books accept meat-eating. However, it is interesting that the Qur'ânic verse "And the grazing livestock He has created for you; in them is warmth and (numerous) benefits, and from them you eat" (Qur'ân 16:5) refers only to grazing animals, such as sheep, cattle, and goats. Chickens will forage in a pasture, but grass is not the main component of their diet—they could not be included in a list of "grazing animals."

Today most of the world's chickens are raised indoors in giant sheds and fed on a diet of grain, soya, and additives, often including antibiotics. This hardly qualifies them as "grazing animals!"

Indeed, Muslims eating US-produced beef may wish to consider that although the average steer will have enjoyed several months grazing on pasture, his last few months will most likely have been spent in a barren feedlot, where there is no grass and the food provided is, once more, a concoction of grain and soya. The steer is not a grazing animal by the time of slaughter then.

There is another question for Muslims to consider when choosing what or how much meat to eat. The Qur'ân (2:168) says that one should eat what is lawful (halal), and good (tayyib). How can a modern Muslim define "tayyib" in the context of today's industrial farming? Those chickens who don't go outside (the vast majority) are also victims of selective breeding to make them grow ever faster and meatier. The end result is frequently a gamut of health and welfare problems for the chickens such as widespread lameness, with the skeleton unable to support the greatly increased muscle mass. The fast growth rates can also lead to increased demand for oxygen, resulting in ascites, where the abdominal cavity fills with fluid, leading to heart failure, and Sudden Death Syndrome, where the birds simply fall over and die. Although Muslims will not be eating the birds that died in the shed, they will almost inevitably be eating parts of chickens who have suffered from painful leg conditions. Can such meat be considered "tayyib"? Maybe the only solution for conscientious Muslims is to eat only chickens that are of a slower-growing breed and are kept in organic or free-range farms, where they can live a more natural life.

Sadly, this scenario also applies to turkeys. In fact, the modern industrialized turkeys have been bred to be so huge and meaty, unlike their recently wild ancestors, that breeding has to be done by artificial insemination, as the males are too heavy to mount the females. This sounds like the very opposite of "tayyib." Mr. Masri was very opposed to such factory farming methods, writing, "Like human beings, animals also have a sense of individuality . . . how right is it to deny these creatures of God their natural instincts so that we may eat the end product."

The question of humane slaughter exercised Mr. Masri greatly. He looked at every new stunning method to see if it could be acceptable to Muslims. Since writing the original book, many developments have taken place in the effort to find a humane and efficient stunning method for animals. The final chapter of the book has been updated to incorporate mention of these and to update the legal situation. Although this book may be read in many countries with different legal requirements, nearly every country in the world belongs to the World Organisation for Animal Health (OIE) and these countries have endorsed the Organisation's guidelines on the slaughter of animals ("Slaughter of animals" in *Vol. 1, Terrestrial Animal Health Code: General provisions*, 2021).

From personal conversations, I know Mr. Masri was unhappy about the massive sacrificial slaughter for the Eid-ul-Adha festival. He felt that a donation of money to the poor would be a better way to show one's desire for sacrifice in these modern times. Although this is a controversial view, it is shared by some modern scholars, such as Gamal al-Banna (1920-2013), the Egyptian Islamic scholar and brother of the founder of the Muslim Brotherhood, Hassan al-Banna. Banna said one should not have to sacrifice an animal at the festival:

> in today's modern world, ideas and religion change and Islam is no different. We must not remain rigid in our understanding of faith to mean the blind acceptance of anything, killing living beings included. There is no obligation to kill.[i]

---

i http://www.theguardian.com/commentisfree/belief/2010/aug/26/meat-islam
-vegetarianism-ramadan

This book does not preach to Muslims as to what they should or should not believe or practice. But it does earnestly call for Muslims everywhere to reflect upon the teachings of care and compassion so obvious in their holy books and to consider how these teachings, which display such respect for animals and such a desire to see their wellbeing protected, can be put into practice in daily life.

Joyce D'Silva has an MA from Trinity College Dublin and two Honorary degrees from the universities of Winchester and Keele. Joyce taught in India before becoming Head of Religious Education at a school in England. She has worked for Compassion in World Farming since 1985, including fourteen years as Chief Executive. Joyce played a key role in achieving the UK ban on sow stalls in the nineties and in getting recognition of animal sentience enshrined in the European Union Treaties. Joyce co-edited, with Professor John Webster, the book *The Meat Crisis: Developing more sustainable and ethical production and consumption* (Earthscan, 2017). Joyce worked with Al-Hafiz B.A. Masri and was instrumental to publishing *Islamic Concern for Animals* and the first edition of *Animals in Islam*, as well as updating and editing this version.

Masri's Pioneering Contributions Concerning Non-human Animals

Richard Foltz

B. A. Masri's bold and ground-breaking book was, as far as I know, the first of its kind to be written by a Muslim in modern times. To say that it was the inspiration for my own book on the same subject, however, would not be exactly right. In fact, if Masri's book had been in print ten years ago I doubt I would have written mine. As I wrote then in my preface, I undertook that project reluctantly, and for the sole reason that at the time there was not a single book on Muslim attitudes towards non-human animals available in the English language which I could assign to my students. Masri's book was so hard to find that I had to assign photocopies of photocopies; even my attempts to discover who owned the copyright for it were unsuccessful. Yet reading Masri had convinced me beyond any doubt that Islam had much of value to say about our relations with other species, and I found it shameful—even scandalous—that none of it was readily available in print.

At first I used some of my contacts amongst Islamic scholars to try to persuade someone with better credentials than me to write the sort of updated and expanded work on Islam and non-human animals the subject deserved. Alas, none could spare the time for such a project, the demands of Islamic Studies today being so desperately pressing in so many domains. So, I brought to the task what I could, and have been humbly gratified that so many readers have found it to be of some use. There is an essential difference between Masri's work and mine, however: Masri's credentials enable him to speak with authority to an audience of Muslim believers, whereas mine do not. Here is part of what I said about Masri in my book:

> Masri's voice is a pioneering one in the domain of
> Islamic values and animal rights, but it will have to be

8

joined by many others if the attitudes and behaviors of Muslims toward animals is to change.[i]

...in pushing the limits of Islamic tradition, teachers like Masri and Nursi go further even than any of today's self-proclaimed Islamic environmentalists who have mentioned the rights of non-human animals.[ii]

After Masri, not until Sarra Tlili's recent study of non-human animals in the Qur'ân, did any Muslim writer attempt to seriously engage this audience in a significant scholarly way. Many more such studies are called for; in the meantime, decades after it was written Masri's book continues to challenge Muslims to re-assess their own attitudes towards non-human animals to a degree no other writer has dared.

Dr. Richard Foltz is Professor in the Department of Religions and Cultures at Concordia University in Montréal, Canada. His book *Animals in Islamic Tradition and Muslim Cultures* (Oneworld, 2006) was the first scholarly survey of how Muslims have viewed the importance of non-human animals. He has also written on environmental ethics and animal rights in Zoroastrianism.

---

i   Foltz, Richard, (2006). *Animals in the Islamic Tradition and Muslim Cultures*, Oneworld, p. 94.

ii   Ibid. p.99.

Islam and Animals: A Veterinary Bioethical Perspective

Michael W. Fox

I started to write this contribution during America's July 4th Independence firework celebration in 2013. Victims of post-traumatic stress disorder—including many veterans of war—along with countless wild animals, in-home dogs and cats and stabled horses, suffered the trauma of percussive incendiaries of this nation-wide pyrotechnic human indulgence. The previous winter several flocks of roosting birds were reported being killed, flying blindly into the night and colliding with trees after being terrified by New Year's Eve fireworks. What is it about human nature that we continue to indulge ourselves without concern for the consequences, and especially to the potential harm to fellow creatures?

I recall the first time that I met Al-Hafiz B.A. Masri in the early 1980s at a conference in London where he quipped to me that "All animals are true Muslims because they are obedient to their Creator." I later read that a bee is a Muslim precisely because it lives and dies obeying the *sharia* (a word whose meaning is: the proper path to sustaining life) that God has prescribed for the community of bees. Native American cultures, notably the Ojibwe, see animals, such as the wolf in particular, as exemplars of such obedience, for in being true to their natures they are following their "original instructions."

To hear the choral songs of one dawn-sprung, sunset-haloed birds in my own garden or in Africa, India, or wherever your feet and your heart may have taken you, is a very different kind of celebration. Perhaps you may feel the glory and joy this living Earth can birth, and celebrate a natural, if not unconventional, communion. Perhaps too, you might glimpse the *mysterium tremendum* of this cosmic realm: And then ask yourself why you are here, for what purpose. Then perhaps, you may choose to be a One who strives to harm no other One.

This simple state of wild bird appreciation and empathic One-mindfulness is the antithesis of the rationalized egocentrism of Ayn Rand's sanctified Objectivism and competitive individualism (see *Atlas Shrugged*, Penguin, in 2004, first published in 1957), which is embraced by many transnational corporate and political followers. Objectivism and materialism limit our awareness of the interconnected nature of the reality of which we are co-inhering participants. Realization of Self-in-Other was accomplished by more civilized societies in times past through the vision quest, as with the Anishinaabe or Native American tribes, and various spiritual teachings and rites of initiation into responsible adulthood. Where are these practices today?

Persian Muslim poet Farid ud-Din Attar, in his narrative poem *The Conference of the Birds*, captured their sanctity and dignity, as well as the numinous and transcendental nature of reality, through his communion with the birds as subjects, not objects. Objectivism turns animals into things, and in the famous words of the late Father Thomas Berry: "The universe is not a collection of objects but a communion of subjects" (*The Dream of the Earth*, San Francisco Sierra Books, 1988). As it says in the Qur'ân 6:38 "There is not an animal (that lives) on the earth, nor a being that flies on its wings, but (forms part of) communities like you. Nothing have we omitted from the Book, and they (all) shall be gathered to their Lord in the end".

Human insensitivity and objectivism make the world insensate. We all have sufficient senses to save the birds and the Song of the Earth, and to be sensible and sensitive to hear the silence of the birds when they are gone after we have destroyed their forests and poisoned the land. But in order to adapt to the human-Earth condition we turn off our senses to the holocaust of the animals, becoming increasingly insensate, unaware when the birds are singing and deaf to their silence.

It is with these thoughts in mind that I believe it is more important than ever to examine the truths, values, and perceptions by which we choose to live—and bring to light those basic moral codes and ethical principles concerning our relationships with animals and the natural environment. These lie at the heart of the world's major religious traditions. This is because animals, domesticated and wild, are caught up in a holocaust of suffering and extinction which for all people of conscience is a call to action, be they atheists and theists, followers of Islam, Judaism, Christianity, Hinduism, Jainism, and Buddhism in particular, as well as indigenous animists. Any and all actions to reduce, prevent, and prohibit animal suffering and environmental harms—moving in the direction of planetary CPR (conservation, preservation, and restoration)—are in our own enlightened self-interest. When we demean or harm animals and the environment, we do no less to ourselves. This is because human health and well-being (physically, mentally, spiritually, socially, and economically) are dependent upon environmental and animal health and well-being (as detailed in my book *Healing Animals & The Vision of One Health*, CreateSpace, 2011).

Now when we look at the excerpts identified, translated, and interpreted by scholars of various religious texts, we find a scarcity of citations relevant to our treatment of animals and the natural world. Such omissions may speak more to the concerns and focus on human behavior and moral conduct, than on the anthropocentric worldview and andromorphic conception of god/divinity. But one ethical principle, which I see as the spiritual core of religious doctrine developed during the "axial age" (900 BCE to200 BCE) and incorporated into all the world's major religions is the Golden Rule: do not do to others what you would not have them do to you. (See Karen Armstrong's *The Great Transformation: The Beginning of Our Religious Traditions*).

This is the first injunction awakening empathy or fellowship toward other beings. It put the spark to conscience which ignited the moral sensibility of compassionate right action and relationship, the duty of care and the sense of fairness and justice. An indirect affirmation of the benefit of extending the Golden Rule to include other sentient beings is captured in the Hadith of the Prophet: "Whoever is kind to the creatures of God is kind to himself," Mohammad taught. "A good deed done to a beast is as good as doing good to a human being; while an act of cruelty to a beast is as bad as an act of cruelty to a human being."

With the willpower to disobey, moral codes and ethical principles had to be acquired epigenetically for human communities to survive and thrive. But while the human species may arguably be less biologically constrained from causing harm and of being subject to the laws of nature than most other species, there is clear evidence in many other species of varying degrees of prosocial empathy and moral/ethical sensibility, (see M. W. Fox *Animals & Nature First*). It is when we violate the Golden Rule because of an individual or collective lack of self-constraint and mindfulness concerning the rights, interests, and intrinsic value of fellow beings that we demean and harm our own humanity; unless, that is, we chose to re-define being human as being a global predator or parasitic infestation rather than Earth's compassionate custodian and protector—which is stated both explicitly and implicitly in the Qur'ân, according to Masri and others. For example, Mohammad opposed recreational hunting saying: "Whoever shoots at a living creature for sport is cursed." (*Encyclopedia of Religion and Nature*, entry *Islam, Animals, and Vegetarianism.* Bron Taylor, Ed., Continuum, 2005).

Suppose the Qur'ân had been written a decade ago, or the Torah of Judaism, or New Testament of Christianity. Would they instruct that we give equal consideration to our relationships with and responsibilities for animals and the environment as to our own kith and kin, and to our neighbors regardless of race, tribe, and belief? Religious skeptics and some historians might contend that religions have done more to promote separation and conflict than unity and respect, and until recently I would have said that this is certainly true when it comes to our relationships with and responsibilities for animals and the broader life community of Earth. Secularization of religious beliefs in civic, judicial, legal, and business affairs is claimed to be the hallmark of civil society and a sane and humane civilization. (See John B. Cobb Jr *Spiritual Bankruptcy: A Prophetic Call to Action*, Abingdon Press 2010). But secularism, according to Prof. Cobb, seeks to exclude the wisdom of the core teachings of the world's great religious traditions from being incorporated into society as an antidote to materialism and rationalized selfishness.

Justice—just treatment based on compassion and the Golden Rule—must be extended voluntarily to all species if such a secular society is to remain viable and human civilization to progress. To honor and respect all of God's creatures and creation is the basic creed of all current monotheistic traditions. But religious fundamentalists generally oppose such secularization and extension of spiritual and ethical values to embrace animals and the environment. In 1989, for instance, Dominican priest Fr. Matthew Fox, (see his book *Original Blessing: A Primer in Creation Spirituality*), an advocate of Earth-centered or Creation-centered spirituality (on the heels of the Liberation theology movement) was silenced for one year by the future Pope and Vatican doctrine enforcer, Cardinal Ratzinger, on the grounds of promoting paganism. But the panentheism Fox envisioned (see also Michael W. Fox, *The Boundless Circle: Caring for Creatures & Creation*) is quite different from animistic paganism and pantheism. For me, this event underscores the vital importance of separating the religious from the secular and of saving the spiritual and ethical truths of every religious tradition from the politics and prejudices, vested interests, and the harmful perceptions and values of archaic religious dogma and law.

Masri, in his book *Animals in Islam* and in his life's work, sought to rectify these "sins" of omission and commission by focusing the spotlight of relevant Qur'ânic teachings and aphorisms on the plight of animals in the modern age, addressing ritual slaughter in particular. This is also an issue for the followers of Judaism and Sikhism, and an example of where—under the impetus of sound science and reason, and in the name of compassion—religion-based practices can either be made more humane or abandoned. For religionists to resist such secular progressive influences, which do not undermine belief or faith, is to resist the very essence of human evolution; a resistance which can make religious belief and praxis archaic, cruel, and irrelevant anachronisms rather than an ethically relevant spiritual light guiding the concerns of the human heart toward a community of compassion governed by the Golden Rule.

I have witnessed ritual slaughter in Canada, the U.S., Tanzania, and India, often being executed with neither skill nor reverence, the absence or presence of which makes little or no fundamental difference to the helplessness and terror of the animal. Either way, the Golden Rule is broken. I saw it in the eyes of the animals, the abject fear, the betrayal and disbelief; and heard it in the voices of kids (young goats) crying with the voices of human children while being dragged in tied-up bunches of fives and sevens across the slaughterhouse floor to the flashing knife. And I saw it in the eyes of the slaughtermen, laboring in an arena of our own consumptive making, fit for neither man nor beast: an emptiness of cold resolve and protective indifference which harmed the souls of both.

Muslim and other communities have suffered from cynophobia, fear of dogs, for millennia. This is, in part, due to the threat of dogs suffering from hydrophobia (the primary symptom of rabies) which is transmitted to other animals and humans in the community when, in the "frenzy" stage of this viral brain disease, they bite whomever they can reach before becoming paralytic and dying in all-consuming seizures. Such infected dogs were thought to be possessed by evil spirits. Cynophobia is also associated with the belief that dogs (along with pigs) are unclean because they eat carrion, including human corpses. A Bantu Muslim in Tanzania told me that "Our people look down on the Hehe tribe because they will eat dog meat. If you eat dog meat you could be eating one of your relatives or ancestors." Yet no such dog-eating taboo is evident in some regions of China and the Far East, or for ritual purposes in some Native American tribes. Cultural relativity in human regard for and treatment of animals must be discarded for a more unified, bioethical sensibility.

The majority of both Sunni and Shi'a jurists consider dogs to be ritually unclean, but outside their ritual uncleanness, individual Islamic *fatawa* or rulings have expressed that dogs must be treated kindly or else be freed (see *Aalim Network: Dogs* online).

Great strides are needed to improve the health and welfare of dogs in urban and village communities, Muslim and other, around the world through public education, vaccinations, anti-mange and other parasite treatments, and spay/neuter for much needed population control rather than using poison bait and periodic roundups for mass extermination. For example: Afro-American Muslims in St. Louis, among others in poor Black communities, continue to work with Stray Rescue, in collaboration with city police and the FBI, to stamp out dog fighting and other animal abuses.

As a first-year British veterinary student visiting Tangier, Morocco in 1957, I happened on a dying kitten who had been placed on a roadside shrine. While examining the poor creature and deciding on the best course of action, an Imam miraculously walked by. I asked him where the nearest veterinary clinic or animal shelter might be. He said "What can be done? It is the will of Allah," and walked on. I euthanized the kitten with a rock when he was out of sight. I find such fatalistic acceptance of animals' suffering incompatible with the spirit of compassion and loving kindness implicit in the Golden Rule.

To end suffering is an act of compassion, yet I faced this same attitude of fatalistic non-intervention decades later working with my wife Deanna Krantz at her animal refuge and veterinary clinic in south India. It was more prevalent in the Hindu and Jain communities than in the Muslim, where the opinion was frequently voiced that one should not interfere with another's fate or karma. Hindus and Jains were also averse to mercy killing because it violated their principle of *ahimsa*, of non-harming. To violate this principle would make them spiritually impure, a belief which put self-interest before compassion. Muslims and members of India's lower castes, who were not averse to killing animals for food, I found were more receptive to mercy killing. But this Jain and Hindu aversion has resulted in centuries of suffering for India's "sacred" cows (*India's Holy Cow: The Sacred & the Suffering*, www.drfoxvet.com).

Mahatma Gandhi, no doubt with the best intentions from his religious and socio-political perspective, opposed the British colonial authorities during their end of Raj era exodus and attempts to smooth a democratic transition for India's "independence", on two significant ethical and economic concerns. The British sought to abolish the caste system, which Gandhi contended would destroy Hinduism, as would the British proposal to set up cow, calf, and spent working ox slaughter facilities that would be as humane and hygienic as possible, throughout the country. Muslims and members of the "scheduled" castes, who had no religious taboo against eating meat, such as cow beef in particular, would engage in the slaughter and marketing of the byproducts of the dominant Hindu and Jain cow-economy (of accepted milk consumption and use of oxen for pulling carts and ploughs). But because of such opposition, to the grave detriment of cow welfare, cattle slaughter was outlawed in all states across India, with the exception of the states of Kerala and West Bengal, where to this day these poor animals are force-marched and crowded into trucks and railroad cars—many collapsing and dying in transit, as my wife and I have documented—on their way to ritual slaughter.

Today, hundreds of thousands of unwanted male calves—which are born in the process of bringing cows into milk—are slaughtered by Muslims and others in clandestine facilities across India, using operators with insufficient funds to bribe the police and politicians while being routinely prosecuted in waves of enforcement against such "illegal" slaughter. By being forced underground, sanitation and humane standards are often lacking in these backyard operations. Their legalization, upgrading, and decentralization for cattle slaughter in India would do much to help reduce the suffering of India's most revered animal. Reverence as ritual or sanctimonious rhetoric is hypocrisy when there is no compassionate action.

A clarifying distinction must be made here: India, with an estimated 46% of children being physically and mentally stunted from chronic malnutrition, is now the world's leading exporter of "beef". But this meat is from buffalo which are not held sacred, unlike the cow/cattle species, by Hindus or Jains. So decentralized, local slaughter of this species is permitted. The same can be said for sheep, lambs, goats, kids, and poultry, and the pigs being killed for consumption by tourists, Christians, and the lowest and poorest in the caste system.

As a spiritual discipline of exemplary moral conduct, self-discipline, and ethical sensibility, Islam (liberated from its internal conflicts) has much to offer the secular world; not through totalitarian or absolutist, doctrinal imposition, but through applying the core teachings in the Qur'ân, as Imam Masri sought to accomplish, to our regard for and treatment of animals. Most urgently, the more affluent and influential members of this religious tradition need to help improve the health and well-being of domestic animals in poor communities, setting up shelters, veterinary, educational, legal, and inspection services to address and rectify the plight of the beasts of burden and free-roaming community dogs, in addition to improving the husbandry, handling, transportation, and slaughter of farmed animals.

Since from an Islamic perspective all creatures are the children of God, then I see no reason why all wild animals should not be treated with the same devotion as a cherished trained falcon; or why any informed Muslim would support the cruel methods of livestock and poultry factory farm production, or the harmful aquaculture practices of the modern transnational food industry.

In addition to the arts, mathematics, poetry, philosophy, and music, reflective of the depth of aesthetic and indeed visionary powers that are the hallmark of a highly evolved civilization, the Persian/Arabian followers of Islam have given the world the most magnificent of horses which bear their name, Arabian. Now in the name of compassion and gratitude I call upon this affluent equine community to help prevent the needless injury, killing, and abandonment of racehorses who, in the East and West alike, have become slaves and victims of a profit-driven industry at far too young an age. They are put into races before their skeletal structure has fully developed, to avoid serious injury when racing at the dangerously high speeds for which they have been selectively bred and trained. In too many instances, they are even medicated to continue racing after injury. Crippled horses are abandoned in the streets in some countries, or slaughtered for the French, Japanese, and other consumer markets or else processed into a manufactured pet food ingredient under the ubiquitous label, "animal protein" or "meat byproducts".

In conclusion, and with all respect to Muslims and followers of other religious traditions, I urge that we consider the aphorism attributed to the Buddha: that the hallmark of true religion is *maitri*, a loving kindness toward all beings. And as addressed in my book *Animals & Nature First* (CreateSpace, 2011), in these difficult times both locally and globally, we all have an opportunity to serve the greater good and to put into practice in our daily lives and in our spheres of professional activity and aspiration, the Golden Rule.

Afterthought

We are spirits experiencing life in human form. Other creatures are spirits experiencing life through different forms of being, but in essence there are no significant differences between them and us except with regard to our capacity to choose to cause great harm or good. This means that we should give all living beings equal and fair consideration and acknowledge their sentience, their capacity to suffer, to be harmed, as well as their individual fears and joys, and their entitlement, when under our care, to be given a quality of life in accord with their physical and emotional needs. They are not lesser beings but kindred spirits sharing the travails of life and enriching our own as companions, totems, teachers, and healers, and in the wild, serving to maintain the dynamic integrity, beauty, and vitality of ecosystems and a healthy environment for all. In this vein, Masri's works, especially during the latter part of his fascinating life and through his book *Animals in Islam*, have helped foster the true Islamic view on nature and animals, which coincides with reality and universal compassion. We have surely reached the beginning of the end and must now chose to either evolve or continue along the path of suffering, destruction, and extinction of the life and beauty of our planet. In particular, the blind-spots of individual egocentrism and collective anthropocentrism in every afflicted religious tradition and political ideology must be removed to help achieve a more eco-centric, empathic perception and way of life. I hope that this re-publication will continue to be influential in this respect.

Dr. Michael W. Fox is a graduate of the Royal Veterinary College, London, and holds doctoral degrees in medicine and ethology/animal behavior from the University of London, England. He is author of over 40 books, writes the nationally syndicated newspaper column *Animal Doctor*, is a member of the British Veterinary Association, American Holistic Veterinary Medical Association, and Honor Roll Member of the American Veterinary Medical Association. His website is www.drfoxonehealth.com

RESPECT AND MERCY TOWARDS ALL CREATURES AND MASRI'S INFLUENCE

Princess Alia Al Hussein

I am so pleased that a new edition of Mr. Masri's seminal book is being published. The first one was invaluable to me as I am sure it was to many others. Mr. Masri was a wonderful, *humane* person who has, and surely (*inshallah*) will continue to have enormous positive influence on animal welfare through the wisdom and honesty with which he presented the issue of animals as sentient beings—an issue which is of such deep relevance and yet so often ignored or not even acknowledged.

In Islam, man's duty on Earth is to act as Vice Regent, and his mission is to strive to represent and to reflect to his best ability the directives and qualities of our Creator in the perfect balance. This is clearly extremely hard, for while other living beings behave fundamentally in accordance with their nature and instincts (and are not expected to do otherwise) humans have the responsibility of surpassing their baser instincts and striving to develop their higher nobler ones, in a constant struggle to achieve the *right* balance.

Respect for and mercy towards all creatures, as well as respect for and appreciation of the inanimate natural world around us, are basic and essential necessities if we are to be truly human. The fact that Islam considers all creatures as sentient is clear in the Qur'ânic verse which refers to them as "Communities like unto yourselves." We are told that they all are aware of and praise God, but that we do not understand their manner of praising Him. Thus, we are the ones who in this earthly life are to some extent blocked or lacking in awareness while the rest of Creation—even the mountains and inanimate world—are conscious of God.

Examples of the depth of other creatures' intelligence and awareness abound in the Qur'ân. In Surat Al-Naml (The Ant) we are told of an ant advising her fellows to hide "lest Solomon and his army trample us unawares." The ant is not only anticipating what harm could come to them but also aware of the fact there is no harm *intended* by Solomon or his army (an army which included animals and birds as full members of its ranks) and this proved to be correct, as we are told that Solomon heard her and diverted the course of the whole army. The ant incident is followed by reference to the hoopoe bird—a scout in Solomon's army—which was thought to have deserted but in fact returned bringing tidings not only of the queen of Sheba and her magnificent court but also of their wrongful practice of worshipping other than God—in this case the sun.

The incident of the army of Solomon altering its course to protect an ant colony is beautifully paralleled in the incident of the Prophet Mohammad (peace be upon him (PBUH)) and his great army 's march to take Mecca. The prophet noticed a dog who had recently given birth to a litter of puppies by their path, and he posted a sentry to stand guard until the whole army had passed, ensuring that nobody would bother her or her litter.

This incident is particularly worthy of mention as Islam's image has become "anti-dog," which is due to subsequent scholars making ever narrower pronouncements on interaction with dogs. However, the only confirmed (certain) Hadith of the Prophet Mohammad on the matter is that if one is going to eat from a dish from which one has fed a dog, the dish should be scoured with earth and not just rinsed. This implies that one would be feeding a dog from a household dish, and as dogs' saliva does leave residue if not properly wiped, the directive to scour the dish as well as rinsing it is valid advice to avoid rabies.

Furthermore, in the Qur'ân, we have the tale of "Ahl al Kahf" (The people of the Cave) who were young people being persecuted for their belief in God (as Unitarians) and who God enacted a miracle upon by having them sleep for many years and awaken to find their world totally changed. We are told that people debate their number, but that the miracle included a dog who slept on the threshold with them and was one of their number.

The Messengers of God in Islam each had significant incidents with creatures and nature: Christ's first miracle (aside from the immaculate conception and speaking from the crib) before healing the sick and raising the dead was to create (with God's permission) a clay bird into which he then breathed life.

Moses spoke to God through a burning bush and his staff became a snake which devoured the illusory snakes conjured up by the magicians in Pharaoh's court, proving to them that his snake was real and from a Power far beyond their illusions. From that point on, they dutifully followed Moses' message—despite the threat of torture by Pharaoh.

The prophet Mohammad (PBUH) not only defended the rights of all creatures from trees to animals to humans in many incidents, but had full confidence in the sense of his camel, Qaswa, by having her select the place where he would first stay upon arrival in Medina.

The topic of animals in Islam is too wide to be addressed adequately here, but a major and extremely pressing concern is that of Halal slaughter. In brief most people eat what is killed in Muslim countries or abattoirs assuming it is halal—but halal does not just mean the severing of certain arteries and pronouncing the basmallah over the creature: halal as described by the prophet (PBUH) means that the creature should stress (never mind suffer) as little as possible, not be aware of the blade (which must be sharp and kill with one stroke), not be aware of impending death, and not see any others killed before or near it. The severing of the arteries was to ensure the fastest possible loss of consciousness—and lack of blood in the meat. It is not a bloodlust! Furthermore, *non-invasive* stunning is perfectly acceptable, the injunction being to relax the creature—not to beat and bully and stress—but to "*lead it to death in a beautiful way.*" The prelude to the killing must be equally stress-free.

Today with animals shipped and trucked in horrible conditions, arriving terrified and exhausted, killed often in abattoirs with no real regard for (nor even comprehension of) what "halal" insists upon, we need to make enormous and serious efforts to stop these horrific trends.

We know that "Whosoever shows no mercy shall receive no mercy", and we need to understand that our current carelessness and abusive practices open the door to concrete negative consequences to ourselves. The meat from stressed animals is filled with toxins and carcinogens (adrenaline and noradrenaline), has destroyed protein composition and vitamin content, and poor mineral absorption potential.

Our further disregard for nature has resulted in loss of biodiversity everywhere—oceans and waterways filled with waste, dying reef life, and sea creatures filled with plastics and mercury. The very air we breathe is losing quality and yet we blithely focus on making money and forget that we threaten our very existence. What a far cry from being God's Vice Regents on Earth!

Princess Alia Al Hussein, born 13/2/1956, is the eldest child of the late King Hussein of Jordan (and Queen Dina Abdul-Hamid). She studied at schools in Jordan and the UK and graduated with Honors from the University of Jordan in 1977 with BA in English Literature. She worked as a volunteer with the British School of Archaeology in the Amman from 1978 to 1982. She is also Director of the Royal Stables of Jordan, President of the Royal Jordanian Equestrian Federation, Board Member of the World Arabian Horse Organization, and Member of the Spanish Riding School. She is also a patron of The Brooke Hospital and of Compassion in World Farming, an Honorary board member of IFAW, on the Honorary Committee for Good Will, and an ambassador for Four Paws International

Alia is the founder and CEO of the Princess Alia Foundation, which is an NGO whose message is "Compassion and Respect for All Creation" and whose main projects to date have involved slaughterhouse reform, improving school environment through renewable energy, and stray and feral dog control through spay, vaccinate, and release procedures. This is a joint project with Four Paws International which protects the natural forest, provides jobs for local community, and offers shelter to animals confiscated as victims of illegal trade or rescued from conflict zones or other unsuitable situations. Raising awareness on these and other related issues is a large part of their work.

LIKE ALL PIONEERS: MASRI'S IMPACT ON THE FIELD OF ANIMAL ETHICS IN ISLAM

Sarra Tlili

Although Basheer Ahmad Masri's work is part of a longstanding scholarly tradition on animal ethics in Islam, to my knowledge, it is the first to address problems unique to our time from an Islamic standpoint. Likely triggered by the fact that he resided in the West, where largescale and institutionalized animal cruelty inspired profound debates on the status and welfare of nonhuman creatures, Masri's work ponders Islam's position on various animal products and uses, both old and emerging. The exercise has yielded fresh insights, but as is the case with all pioneering work, it is not without problems. While offering original and invaluable perspectives, Masri also reinforces questionable notions pertaining to nonhuman animals. This mixed legacy is not without precedent. Conflicting views about animals are common in Islamic tradition and require critical scrutiny, not only because they detract from the tradition's otherwise remarkable approach to the subject, but also because they pose serious theological problems and can hinder or diminish Muslims' commitment to the wellbeing of fellow creatures. Thus, in this article I wish to highlight aspects of Masri's mixed legacy, but my larger aim is to offer a critical assessment of prevalent attitudes toward animals in Islamic tradition and to invite contemporary Muslims to rethink many assumptions they tend to hold about nonhuman animals and religious teachings about them. To this end, I will first point out and analyze Masri's egalitarian insights, especially the way he destabilizes human exceptionalism through his simultaneous affirmation of similarity and difference between humans and other creatures. Second, since Masri also claims that "Both science and religion assert that man is the apex of creation"(4),[i] I will try to show why such affirmation is problematic. Throughout my reading I try to situate Masri's work in the larger Islamic context and to assess his impact on Western academic research so as to rethink not only this pioneer's work, but also the larger field of animal ethics in Islam.

Egalitarian Outlook

Drawing on the Qur'ân, science, and personal experience, Masri often assigns nonhuman animals great complexity and places them at the same level with humans. "Animals are not inferior to us because they have a different vocal apparatus," he writes, "nor does the fact that they cannot make articulate speech, like we can, means they are 'contemptible dumb animals.'" Indeed, Masri affirms that animals possess "articulate communication" and seems to blame our failure to grasp other species' articulations on the fact that we, humans, are no longer in tune with nature.[ii] Similarly, from the Qur'ânic theme of God's address to the bee,[iii] Masri derives the conclusion that animals "have a sufficient degree of psychic endowment to understand and follow God's messages—a faculty which is higher than instinct and intuition" (21). He also affirms that the "emotions of animals and of human beings are, no doubt, the same, even though we may differ in our respective needs and in degree" (43).

This simultaneous affirmation of similarity and difference is one of the strengths of Masri's approach. With remarkable dexterity, he establishes interspecies kinship without erasing individuality and particularism. Nonhuman animals are not completely incomprehensible aliens to us: The various features we have in common with many species allow us to relate to and to empathize with them. On the other hand, nonhuman animals' skills and capacities need not replicate those of humans to count as such. Animals possess articulate communications, but their articulations

---

i These are page numbers from *Animal Welfare in Islam*, by Al-Hafiz Basheer Ahmad Masri, published in 2007 by the Islamic Foundation, U.K.

ii Al-Hafiz Basheer Ahmad Masri, *Animal Welfare in Islam* (The Islamic Foundation, 2007), 16.

iii "And your Lord inspired the bee, saying: "Choose habitations in the hills and in the trees and in that which humans have built." 16/al-Naḥl: 68.

need only be decipherable to their own fellow species members, not necessarily to humans. In other words, humans are not the measure of all things and deviation from their ways does not constitute failure. Masri goes so far as to suggest that inability to grasp other creatures' articulations can be symptomatic of human shortcomings (the fact that humans are no longer in tune with nature) rather than of other animals' limitations. This approach, which disrupts humans' privileged status and resituates them within the realm of creation, is one important step toward a sound animal ethic.

The same egalitarian outlook can be discerned from Masri's assertion that "every individual species, including the human one, has been endowed with a potential nature to *serve the whole creation as a homogeneous unit*" (15, emphasis added). Again, this approach depicts humans as one member among a community of subjects, something that many animal ethicists consider foundational for a sensible animal ethic.[iv] Furthermore, this egalitarian stance has concrete egalitarian outcomes. For Masri, the fact that "each species is a 'community'" entails that "every creature on earth has, as its birthright, a share in all the natural resources." Each animal "is a tenant-in-common on this planet with human species" (21). This is a clear departure from the assumption, prevalent among the members of many philosophical schools and faith traditions, that the world belongs to or is created for the sake of humans and that nonhuman creatures are there merely for the service of humankind. Creatures serve one another and are to share God's bounties. These insights subvert the principle of human exceptionalism by situating nonhuman animals at the same level with humans. Humans and other animals may have different skills, needs, and habits, but difference does not imply that one species is better, superior to, or more important than the others.

These insights are not without precedent in Islamic tradition. From the Qur'ânic affirmation that nonhuman animals form communities,[v] earlier exegetes derived the same conclusion that

iv See Paul Waldau and Kimberly Patton; *A Communion of Subjects: Animals in Religion, Science, and Ethics* (Columbia University Press, 2006).

v "There is no creature that moves on earth and no bird that flies with its two wings save that they are communities like yourselves. We have neglected nothing in the Book. Then to their Lord they will be gathered" (6/al-Anʿâm: 38).

animals share important faculties with human beings without becoming identical replicas to them. The early exegete Ibn Jarīr al-Ṭabarī (d. 310/923),[vi] for example, writes, "They (nonhuman animals) have knowledge as you (humans) do (*taʿrifu kamā taʿrifūn*) and they manage that for which they have been created as you do (*tataṣarrafu fīmā sukhkhirat lahu kamā tataṣarrafūn*)."[vii] This indicates that in al-Ṭabarīs' view human and nonhuman species have comparable, though unidentical, skills. Similarly, in their commentaries on verse 10 in sūrat al-Raḥmān (55), which states "And the earth, He (God) set it for all beings," many exegetes write that God has laid down the earth for all animals. These commentaries do not privilege humans over other creatures. Masri not only reiterates these age-old insights, but also reframes them in modern language and situates them in the modern context. In so doing, he breathes much-needed new life into the subject of animal ethics in Islam.[viii]

Human exceptionalism

While contributing these invaluable insights, however, Masri also uncritically reproduces and even reinforces prevalent stereotypes. As noted earlier, he affirms that both "science and religion assert that man is the apex of creation" (4). Indeed, although subscribers to the principle of human exceptionalism often appeal to science to justify their claims, scientific epistemology is not qualified to issue such judgments. Science can perhaps provide objective insights into the psychological and physical makeup of humans and other animals (though its ability to account for other animals' psychological states is debatable), but any scientific attempt to rank various features or abilities is destined to be shaped by human subjectivity. Similarly, although mainstream religious traditions generally assign to humans a privileged status, many have argued that this bias is more

---

vi Al-Tabari was an influential scholar, polymath, historian, and commentator of the Qur'an, originating from Amol, Tabaristan, in present day Iran, Mazandaran Province. He is best known for his Qur'anic exegesis.

vii Abū Jaʿfar Ibn Jarīr al-Ṭabarī, Jāmiʿ al-bayān ʿan taʾwīl āy l-Qur'an (Dār ibn al-Jawzī, 2008), 11:344.

viii See, for example, ibn ʿAṭiyya al-Andalusī, al-Muḥarrar al-wajīz fī tafsīr al-kitāb al-ʿazīz (Dār al-Kutub al-ʿIlmiyya, 2001), 5:225.

the result of human interpretations of religious doctrines than of what the founders of these religions might have intended.

Science and human exceptionalism

The main "scientific" argument invoked in support of the theme of human exceptionalism is the Aristotelian principle of cognition and rationality. As Margo DeMello explains, according to this principle "not only are humans endowed with rationality and thus superiority over animals, but animals themselves are superior to plants because they possess consciousness."[ix] However, the prevalent idea that humans are the only animals that have cognition, whereas other species behave mechanically and follow their raw instincts, has been challenged as untenable. As Edward A. Wasserman and Thomas R. Zentall write, closer scrutiny shows that

> Humans are far from unique in exhibiting cognition. … [I]nvestigative methods have disclosed that nonhuman animals also exhibit complex and flexible behaviors that most observers would confidently conclude disclose cognition if members of our own species had displayed the same behaviors in the same circumstances.[x]

Indeed, although some scientists and science advocates continue to insist that humans and other animals are separated by an unbridgeable gulf, a growing body of scientific research points in the opposite direction. Ethologists have demonstrated that innumerable animal species, including apes, elephants, and dolphins, have elaborate mental and emotional capacities and rich lifestyles. The work of entomologists has shown the same about many insect species. In view of this, the gulf that presumably separates humans from other species does not seem as unbridgeable as some tend to believe. In fact, the more researchers learn about the richness of the

---

ix Margo DeMello, Animals and Society: An Introduction to Human-Animal Studies (Columbia University Press, 2012), 378.

x Edward Wasserman and Thomas Zentall, "Comparative Cognition: A Natural Science Approach to the Study of Animal Intelligence" in *Comparative Cognition: Experimental Explorations of Animal Intelligence*, edited by Edward Wasserman and Thomas Zentall (Oxford University Press, 2006), 5.

lives of certain animal species, the more they become inclined to question human exceptionalism.

Furthermore, researchers in the field of animal cognition recognize the challenges surrounding their field. By observing the behavior of other animals, we can certainly infer some ideas about their psychological and mental states, but such inferences are also shaped, and in fact limited, by our human nature and knowledge. Since we can know the world only from the human standpoint and based on human experience, it is difficult, if not impossible, to perceive all details about the psychological states of other creatures in the absence of developed interspecies communication systems. Because of this, we are less likely to understand, or even to take note of, behaviors and features that bear little or no resemblance to our own. As a result, full and reliable knowledge of other animals' mental and psychological capacities probably lays outside the human scope.

It should also be noted that even the questions that we ask about other animals are ultimately human questions. One of the dangers of this fact is that we ask questions that are relevant to us about what we tend to value. For example, humans, particularly in modern cultures, tend to overvalue rationality at the expense of other human skills and to treat rational faculties as an objective criterion in measuring psychological sophistication and richness of experience. In view of this, the question of whether and to what extent other animals are rational is not as simple as it may appear on the surface. Generally, its aim is not only to improve our understanding of other animals, but also to measure them against us. It goes without saying that by adopting the feature that we are presumably best at (i.e. rationality) as the ultimate criterion for assigning status it can hardly be surprising that we see ourselves as the apex of creation. By setting the rules of the game in our favor winning the game becomes the only natural outcome and any difference from human ways becomes a deviation or a failure. This human bias leads not only to the conclusion that nonhuman animals have no or little mental capacities simply because they cannot do the things that we can do, but also that their lives are impoverished and less worthy of being lived than the lives of humans.

Religion and human exceptionalism

Can human exceptionalism be founded on religious doctrines, particularly within monotheisms and more specifically Islamic tradition? Masri adduces several Qur'ânic doctrines to establish this theory. First, he invokes the Qur'ânic notion of "*khalīfa*" (supposedly, vicegerent) to state not only that Islam appoints humans as God's representatives among other creatures, but also to affirm that "Islam declares man *as the best* of God's creation"[xi] (4, emphasis added). This is a flawed argument because, contrary to the prevalent understanding, the word *khalīfa* does not mean "vicegerent" or "representative." Solid and ample scholarship using philological, contextual, and historical methods of study has demonstrated that the Qur'ânic word "*khalīfa*" means only "successor," "follower," "replacement," or "substitute" (of a former party). Therefore, this word cannot apply to a relationship between God and any creature, including humankind or any human individual, unless one intends it in the sense of "a successor that *belongs to* God" or "a substitute with which God replaced a former creature."[xii] The more immediate meaning that this phrase conveys (a successor who succeeds or replaces God) is unthinkable and blasphemous by every Islamic standard, as it would imply that God is either absent or dead. The earliest Qur'ân exegetes, as Wadad al-Qadi explains, understood God's address to angels in the Qur'ân, "I (God) am about to place a *khalīfa* on earth" (2/al-Baqara:30) in the sense that God was about to replace the species of jinn with that of humankind, not that he was about to appoint someone as his representative.[xiii]

---

xi Masri is far from alone in this case. Innumerable other scholars before and after him subscribe to the same misconstrued definition of the qur'anic word "*khalīfa*."

xii On this point, see Fritz Steppat, "God's Deputy: Materials on Islam's Image of Man," *Arabica* 36, no. 2 (1989): 163-72; Wadad al-Qadi, "The Term 'Khalīfa' in Early Exegetical Literature," *Die Welt des Islams* 28, no. 1/4 (1988): 392-411; Rudi Paret, "Significations coranique de *halīfa* et d'autres dérivés de la racine *halafa*," *Studia Islamica* 31 (1970): 211-17; Jaafar Sheikh Idris, "Is Man the Vicegerent of God?" *Journal of Islamic Studies* 1 (1990): 99-110; Sarra Tlili, *Animals in the Qur'an* (Cambridge University Press, 2012), 115-123.

xiii Al-Qadi, "The Term 'Khalīfa'", 399-400.

Conclusions

Despite these exceptionalistic views, *Animals in Islam* is a valuable work not only because it is the first to explore the ethicality of emerging practices in the treatment of fellow creatures, but also because of its tone and style. Masri for example poignantly asks, "would the Prophet Muhammad approve of factory farming?" (44) and "If [animals'] Divine Creator gave them legs, is it not a blasphemy to shut them in crates where they are unable to walk?" (41). This approach evokes what Hussein Keshani describes as *"adab-*centred" ethic. It goes beyond the legalistic approach that seems to dominate the Islamic ethical discourse and cultivates "a more engageable form of Islamic discourse." The book therefore should be assessed not only or primarily for its academic quality, but also for its actual or potential concrete impact on Muslims' attitudes toward other animals.[xiv]

Sources

Callicott, Baird J. *Earth's Insights: A Multicultural Survey of Ecological Ethics from the Mediterranean Basin to the Australian Outback.* Berkeley, CA: University of California Press, 1994.

DeMello, Margo. *Animals and Society: An Introduction to Human-Animal Studies.* New York: Columbia University Press, 2012.

Haque, Nadeem and Masri, Al-Hafiz Basheer Ahmad, "The Principles of Animal Advocacy in Islam: Four Integrated Ecognitions" *Society and Animals* 19 (2011): 279-290.

Ibn ʿAṭiyya al-Andalusī, *al-Muḥarrar al-wajīz fī tafsīr al-kitāb al-ʿazīz.* Beirut: Dār al-Kutub al-ʿIlmiyya, 2001.

Idris, Jaafar Sheikh. "Is Man the Vicegerent of God?" *Journal of Islamic Studies* 1 (1990): 99-110.

Kemmerer, Lisa. *Animals and World Religions.* New York: Oxford University Press, 2012.

Keshani, Hussein. "Engaging Islamic Views on Human-Animal Relations: Towards an Adab-centred Approach" *Worldviews* 14 (2010) 6-25.

Masri, Al-Hafiz Basheer Ahmad. *Animal Welfare in Islam.* Leicestershire, UK: The Islamic Foundation, 2007.

---

xiv Hussein Keshani, "Engaging Islamic Views on Human-Animal Relations: Towards an Adab-centred Approach" *Worldviews* 14 (2010), 6.

Paret, Rudi. "Significations coranique de *ḫalīfa* et d'autres dérivés de la racine *ḫalafa*," *Studia Islamica* 31 (1970): 211-17.

Al-Qadi, Wadad. "The Term '*Khalīfa*' in Early Exegetical Literature," *Die Welt des Islams* 28. 1/4 (1988): 392-411.

Al-Qurṭubī, Abū ʿAbd Allāh Muḥammad. *al-Jāmiʿ li-aḥkām al-Qurʾan* (Beirut: Muʾassasat al-Risāla, 2006).

Steppat, Fritz. "God's Deputy: Materials on Islam's Image of Man," *Arabica* 36, no. 2 (1989): 163-72.

Al-Ṭabarī, Abū Jaʿfar ibn Jarīr. *Jāmiʿ al-bayān ʿan taʾwīl āy l-Qurʾan*. Cairo: Dār ibn al-Jawzī, 2008.

Tlili, Sarra. *Animals in the Qurʾan*. New York: Cambridge University Press, 2012.

Waldau, Paul and Kimberly Patton, editors; *A Communion of Subjects: Animals in Religion, Science, and Ethics*. New York: Columbia University Press, 2006.

Wasserman, Edward A. and Thomas R. Zentall, "Comparative Cognition: A Natural Science Approach to the Study of Animal Intelligence" in *Comparative Cognition: Experimental Explorations of Animal Intelligence*, edited by Edward Wasserman and Thomas Zentall. Oxford: Oxford University Press, 2006. 3-11.

Dr. Sarra Tlili is Associate Professor of Arabic literature at the University of Florida, Department of Languages, Literatures, and Cultures. Her main areas of research are animal and environmental ethics in Islam, Qurʾânic stylistics, and tradition and modernity in Arabic literature. Her publications include *Animals in the Qurʾan*, "All Animals Are Equal, or Are They? The Ikhwān al-Ṣafāʾs Animal Epistle and its Unhappy End," and "From Breath to Soul: The Quranic Word *Rūḥ* and Its (Mis)interpretations."

Anymals in Islam

Lisa Kemmerer

I approach the world of Islam as an outsider. I am a professor, a scholar of anymal[i] ethics and comparative religions, and the author of *Animals and World Religions*, a book that explores the many ways that religions support anymal liberation. It is in this capacity that I come to this anthology, and this chapter is indebted to research done for *Animals and World Religions*. (The word "anymal" is a contraction of *any* and *animal*, which includes human beings).

In the course of my studies on anymals and Islam, I discovered powerful sacred texts, inspiring religious exemplars, and dedicated contemporary activists in the Muslim world, including Masri—and Masri's grandson, Nadeem Haque, whom I have stayed in touch with across time, and who has invited me into this updated collection of writings.

As with all religious traditions, one can find teachings that are negative and harmful to anymals. But in my research and writing on the topic, I have repeatedly been impressed with the teachings of the Islamic tradition where anymals are concerned. This essay explores some of my favorite Islamic teachings, including sacred nature, the Prophet as moral exemplar, the expectations of vice regency, anymal rights, and dietary choice with regard to *halal* and *tayyib*.

---

i   **Editor's note:** Anymal is a term coined by Lisa Kemmerer and is a contraction of "any" and "animal," pronounced as "any" and "mal." Anymal indicates all individuals from all species other than that of the speaker/author. In other words, if a human being uses this term, all species except Homo sapiens are indicated, but if a chimpanzee signs "anymal," they reference all species (including human beings) except chimpanzees. Using the term "anymal" avoids the use of

  • "animal" as if human beings were not animals;
  • dualistic and alienating references such as "non" and "other"; and
  • cumbersome terms such as "nonhuman" and "other-than-human" animals..

Nature and Anymals

I begin with the big picture—creation, and Allah's commitment to the larger world of life. According to the Qur'ân, the universe exists by divine power as "the personal creation" of Allah (Marshall 128). Nature is "a form of divine revelation" (Foltz, *Animals* 96), and "whichever way you turn there is the face of Allah" (Qur'ân 2:115). Contemporary Muslim Turkish scholar, Ibrahim Ozdemir, writes: "Muslim thinkers regard nature as a sacred book . . . [J]ust like the Qur'ân; the universe reveals to us the existence of a Sustainer and Creator" (Ozdemir 21). Anymals are, of course, part of nature—all that exists is part of divine creation.

The Qur'ân teaches that Allah did not create the universe for humans, but for all living beings: "And the earth He has spread out for all living beings" (Qur'ân 55:10). As but one part of Allah's creation, humans are to "have a moral feeling of obligation" to Allah and all that has been created (Ozdemir 10).

The Qur'ân invited the pagan Arabs, who were illiterate, to ponder nature and the universe for at least two purposes: first, to have an idea about God's existence and His presence through whatever He creates; and second, to have a moral feeling of obligation toward a transcendental being, God . . . To infuse the natural world with transcendent (revealed) ethics is the main purpose of man according to the Qur'ân. (Ozdemir 10)

Sufism,[ii] the mystical branch of Islam, is distinct from the larger Islamic tradition, but very much a part of the world of Islam: Sufism is "an expression of Islamic spirituality"—not a separate faith

---

ii **Editor's note:** Many Muslims who stick to the clear Qur'ânic methodology of rationalism believe that many adherents of Sufism fall outside the pale of Islam, because of the blind following of their Masters (Pirs/Sheikhs). It is a plain fact that Sufism was partially responsible for the collapse of the scientific trend in Islam, and its systems' view of the world, covering all areas of life. This has indelibly left odious harmful ramifications of which the nominal Muslim world is still reeling from today. Masri did not pay much heed to Sufism; he once told me that he did not really like the separation of 'spirituality' from practical life solutions. He also felt that those who followed Sufism often lost their grounding of reality. However, it is true that many Sufis have spoken about nature/animals and there are instructive lessons therein. One of my colleagues, has recently authored a book that goes into depth in the depiction of the problematic nature of 'Sufism', see: Joel Winter, *A Critique of Sufism: A Rational Look at Sufism's Claims*, published in 2022.

(Stoddart, 61). The most well-known Sufi in the Western world, the Persian (Iranian) poet Jalal al-Din Rumi (1207–73), writes: "I am the servant of the Qur'ân as long as I have life. I am the dust on the path of Muhammad" (Divan-I, quatrain 1173, quoted in Seker, 4). Sufi traditions permeate "everything Islamic—philosophy, Qur'ân commentary, economic life, and popular institutions" (Cragg and Speight 64).

In particular, Sufi traditions have influenced Muslim understandings of the natural world and of human relations with nature. Sufis tend to view the environment as "a revelation of God," finding "beauty and wisdom" in every aspect of creation (Marshall 135). Rumi's poetry is filled with imagery of nature, revealing his connection to Allah through the natural world. His *Mathnawi* states that all of the "forms and the creatures have a purpose" because they make Allah known to us (IV, 3028). Rumi's *Mathnawi* states that all of the "forms and the creatures" make Allah known to us (IV, 3028, Barks translation). For Sufis, the "whole creation is one great mirror, or a large number of mirrors, reflecting God's overwhelming beauty" (Schimmel 382)—eighteenth century Sufi poet Mir Taki Mir (Northern India) writes: "Rose and mirror and sun and moon—what are they? / Wherever we looked, there was always Thy face" (Schimmel 289).

Mountains and rivers, dogs, and chickens—all point back to their Creator and are thereby of moral concern. Humans and anymals are mutually dependent on one another and wholly dependent on the Creator; anymals are graced with "moral corollaries, requiring on the part of humans due regard for the rights of nature, understood in light of the rights and purposes of God" (Said 163). Put simply, Allah is "Lord of All creatures" (Qur'ân 69:28–52), and every living being is due "watchfulness, gratefulness, and respect" (Ozdemir 21).

Creation has "intrinsic value" through the Creator (Ozdemir 21). Every aspect of creation is precious because it is inseparable from the creator (Stoddart 42). Because Allah can be found in every leaf and lizard, the natural world is "an avenue both of sacred experience and sacred responsibilities—nature has rights that must be respected, rights which are due the Creator" (Kemmerer, *Animals and World Religions* 243). Any privileges that humans have been given by Allah "follow and do not precede responsibilities" and human beings will be held accountable for our treatment of Allah's creation—all of it (Nasr 97).

Prophet Mohammad, Moral Exemplar

Mohammad is the quintessential moral and spiritual exemplar; humans are encouraged to imitate the life of the prophet (J. Smith 403). Remembered by his followers and collected by scholars, *Hadith* ("traditions") preserve the life and words of Mohammad. They are the most authoritative Muslim texts after the Qur'ân.

Hadith reveal Mohammad to be compassionate not only toward suffering and downtrodden people, but also toward suffering and downtrodden anymals, including small insects (Berry 244–45). Mohammad is reported to have said, "he who is devoid of kindness is devoid of good" (Friedlander 65). He "loved animals and displayed great kindness to them and encouraged other Muslims to do likewise" (Nasr 97). *Hadith* indicate that Mohammad sought to mitigate anymal suffering and to protect the lives of anymals (Haq 147). *Hadith* denounce "hunting or killing for sport or amusement," as well as killing for "vanity," such as for ivory, fur, or feathers. He discouraged the use of skins, target practice on living creatures, and the pitting of anymals against one another as a means of sport (Masri, *Animal* 46). *Hadith* reveal killing anymals without justification as "one of the major sins" (Masri, *Animal* 46).

Hadith remind us, through the life of the Prophet, that we are *required* to provide for anymals and to treat them with compassion (Haq 148). For example, Mohammad reprimanded a man who neglected his horse (Masri, *Animal* 36), and on seeing the same man handle his camel roughly, the Prophet responded, "it behooves you to treat the animals gently" (*Sahih Muslim*, 4:2593. He encouraged camel riders to allow their camels to stop as needed, and to travel by night, when it was cooler (*Muwatta Malik* 54:15:38). He forbade branding and hitting anymals in the face (*Sahih Bukhari* 67 67:449); hadith indicate that the Prophet discouraged the collection of eggs, noting that such theft was distressing for mother birds (*Sahih Bukhari* referenced on *Jamaat*).

Mohammad taught that how we live, and how we treat anymals, matters spiritually (Haq 150), that acts of kindness and charity to anymals are rewarded by Allah. One of the sayings of the prophet in the *Mishkat* (a secondary source of *hadith*) states: "If anyone wrongfully kills [even] a sparrow . . . he will face God's interrogation" (Haq 149). Another saying from the prophet notes that a good deed done for an anymal "is as good as doing good to a human being; while an act of cruelty to a beast is as bad as an act of cruelty to a human being" (*Mishkat al-Masabih* Book 6, Chapter 7, 8:178.). In one much retold story, a woman is *condemned* for cruelty because she confines and starves a cat, while a prostitute who "saw a dog panting, dying of thirst, on top of a well . . . removed her boot, tied it to her head covering and drew water for the dog . . . was forgiven on this account" (Friedlander 63).

Vice Regency and Compassion
"Islam" means to "surrender to God's law" (Esposito 69). In the Islamic worldview, "humankind has no rights, only duties" and the correct relationship between people and Allah "is that of slaves to master" (Denny 8). Muslim holy books place humans as vice regents, servants of Allah working in and through creation. The Qur'ân describes humans as Allah's vice-regents, a role requiring "commensurate humility and sensitivity, predicated upon respect and reverence for the divine purpose in every created thing" (Said 164). Humanity is to respect the rights of the Creator in creation— to be humble and compassionate, to serve the Creator and not their own interests. Allah's creation has been designed for the benefit of all—not just for humanity (Ozdemir 23). Vice-regency can only be understood in light of "Islam"—in light of a life surrendered to an invested, compassionate, righteous Creator.

As Vice Regents, compassion lies at the core of our expected service to the Creator—"Islamic teachings have gone to great lengths to instill a sense of love, respect, and compassion for animals" (Masri, *Animal* 45). Those who are cruel to anymals— "It is not their eyes that are blind, but their hearts" (Qur'ân 22:46). Humans are to tenderly care for Allah's magnificent creation—preventing or avoiding "physical cruelty is not enough" (Masri, *Animal* 48). And the emotional state of other creatures must also remain in our sights— "mental cruelty is" forbidden (Masri, *Animal* 48). Allah created the universe with the "breath of compassion" (Bakhtiar 16-17), and as vice regents, Allah beseeches humans to exhibit patience and mercy (Qur'ân 90:18-19), for Allah "observes all things" (Qur'ân 67:16-24) and any "act of cruelty toward animals is strongly forbidden" (Siddiq 455).

Islamic stories of saints, mystics, and holy people reveal that those who are closest to God are also close to anymals, sharing compassionate, companionable, and peaceful relations with the many creatures of Allah. For example, stories from the life of Sahl ibn Abd Allah al-Tostari (9th century Sufi who died in what is now Iraq), tell how "lions and other wild beasts" came to him as visitors and he would "feed and tend them" (Attar 158). The prolific mystic, Ibn 'Arabi (born in present-day Spain in 1165), wrote: "My heart has opened unto every form: it is a pasture for gazelles, a cloister for Christian monks, a temple for idols, the Ka'ba of the pilgrim, the tables of the Torah, and the book of the Qur'ân. I practice the religion of Love" (Stoddart 51). Rumi tells of a man who failed to show love for anymals—who kept but did not feed a dog. To claim to be a Muslim while starving a dog, Rumi notes, might cause even "the infidels [to] strike thee down with their very looks when they hear the reading of the Koran" (Rumi, *Mathnawi* 228, Whinfield translation). Compassion is a critical expression of devotion to Allah (Schuon 9) and a moral requirement (Muttaqi 2).

Islamic Law and Anymal Rights
The Qur'ân and *hadith* shape Islamic law, or *sharia*. Stemming from an Arabic word meaning "way" (as in direction), *sharia* is "God's ordaining of the right way for his faithful creatures," providing "the ideal social blueprint for the 'good society'" (Esposito 75). *Sharia* provides guidelines that inform Muslims of what they may and may not do, regulating day to day Muslim life for centuries (Denny 8).

Organized advocacy on behalf of anymals in Islamic communities pre-dates European animal welfare societies (Foltz, *Animals* 88). Early European visitors sometimes noted with astonishment that Turks had alms and hospitals for anymals (Foltz, *Animals* 5). That is because, unique among religious traditions, Islamic law includes anymal rights that regulate human behavior (Ozdemir 22). Humans are expected to "respect and pay what is due to each creature," because "each creature has its rights accordingly" (Nasr 97), and those rights are rooted in one no less than the creator, who "desires no injustice to His creatures" (Qur'ân 3:105–10).

Anymal rights in the *sharia* are intended to be followed and enforced: "all animals have legal rights which must be enforced by the state" (Foltz, *Animals* 88). *Sharia* explicitly outlines that which humans *owe* anymals, and these rights "are so comprehensive" in Islamic law that there would likely be no need for secular regulation protecting anymals, were we to implement *sharia* law (Masri, *Animal* xi). According to Islamic texts, wild anymals "should be allowed to live their lives unmolested . . . Birds should be allowed to fly free and not kept in cages" (Foltz, *Animals* 33). With regard to laboring anymals, humans are required to provide for them even after their days of service have ended, exactly as one would provide for younger anymals (Foltz, *Animals* 34). Most fundamentally, Islamic law protects the earth's varied creatures from cruelty and exploitation at the hand of humanity (Llewellyn 233). Islamic laws, were they followed, would put an end to much that is wrong in our relations with anymals—factory farming, hunting, and trapping (except if truly needed for survival), the ivory trade, exotic anymal trade, and contrived "sport" fights such as dogs vs. cocks and dogs vs. bears, or the infamous dogfighting and cockfighting.

With regard to factory farming, under Islamic law, Muslims are required to satisfy the basic needs of all domestic anymals. Humans may not house domestic anymals in ways that might cause injury, or "imprison" anymals "in unsuitably cramped conditions" (Foltz, *Animals* 34). A *sharia* jurist in the 13th century wrote a legal treatise titled *Rules for Judgment in the Cases of Living Beings*, which requires Muslims to keep anymals in quarters that are cleaned regularly, including separate spaces that hold "resting shelters and watering places" (Foltz, *Animals* 34). We are required to feed and water anymals who are under our care (even before we satisfy our own hunger or thirst) (Foltz, *Animals* 34-35). Islamic law sets a high bar for our relationships with and care for domesticated anymals. So high, in fact, that it would seem impossible to purchase flesh, dairy, or eggs at any market in the industrialized world, even in local markets in villages, and remain faithful to Islamic law.

At Cairo's much esteemed Al-Azhar seminary, founded over a thousand years ago, jurists have tremendous power and authority. In 2004, this venerable institution hosted a conference on anymal rights, "scholars of Islamic law, history and philosophy, government officials, veterinarians, and animal rescue workers," determined that serious improvements were needed in our treatment of anymals, particularly in the areas of scientific research and food production, "encouraging further elaboration of concern for animals from an Islamic perspective" (Foltz, *Animals* 45).

In the 10th century, the "Pure Brethren" of Iraq (Muslim philosophers), expressed their understandings of Islamic anymal rights, and the human failure to uphold these rights, in a story titled *The Case of the Animals versus Man before the King of the Jinn*, in which anymals put humans on trial for unjust treatment. Anymals remind humans that they roamed the earth in peace and harmony before humans were created and complain bitterly of how humans have exploited and destroyed the earth and anymals. They accuse humanity of "injustice, oppression, and usurpation" as they lay out their case (*The Case of the Animals* 108):

> Each kind looked after its own, absorbed in raising our broods and rearing our young on the good food and water God allotted us, safe and unmolested in our domain. Night and day we praised and hallowed God, and God alone, assigning Him neither rival nor peer.
>
> Ages later God created Adam, the ancestor of humankind, and made him His vice-regent on earth. His offspring reproduced, and his seed multiplied, spreading over the earth, land and sea, mountain and plain. Humans encroached on our ancestral lands. They captured sheep, cows, horses, mules, and asses from among us and enslaved them, subjecting them to the exhausting toil and drudgery of hauling, ploughing, drawing water, turning mills, and being ridden. They forced us to these tasks with . . . every kind of duress, torture, and chastisement throughout our lives.

Some of us fled to deserts, wastes, or mountain-tops,
but the Adamites pursued us, hunting us with every kind of
wile and device. Whoever fell into their hands was yoked,
haltered, caged, and fettered. They slaughtered and flayed
him, ripped open his belly, cut off his limbs and broke
his bones, tore out his sinews, plucked his feathers or
sheared his hair or fleece, and set him on the fire to cook,
or to roast on a spit, or put him to even harsher tortures,
torments ultimately beyond description. Even so, the sons
of Adam are not through with us. Now they claim this is
their inviolable right, that they are our masters and we
their slaves. They treat any of us who escapes as a fugitive,
rebel, and shirker—all with no proof or reason beyond
main force. (*The Case of the Animals* 107)

In response, humans malign anymals, but the beasts ably defend themselves, and the text vividly describes the fine qualities and special merits of anymals. *The Case of the Animals versus Man before the King of the Jinn* portrays anymals as just and rational, while humans are exposed as arrogant, selfish, narrow, and irrational. The story (rightly) accuses humans of failing to understand or live up to Allah's expectations of vice-regency. The Muslim philosophers who composed this text shows remarkable empathy for exploited and slaughtered anymals—and an understanding that humans are failing in their God-given role as vice-regents.

Halal and Dietary Choice

Muslims are only permitted to consume *halal* ("permissible") flesh. *Halal* flesh is from the body of an anymal who has been kept, tended, killed, and prepared according to the requirements of Islamic law, which reflects the moral importance of compassion: *Halal* flesh can only come from anymals who have been kept and tended according to "clearly established Islamic principles of compassion" (Foltz, *Animals* 126). *Halal* requirements also regulate slaughter. Islamic law reminds Muslims that killing ought to be avoided (Foltz, *Animals* 33, 125), and if they are to be killed and consumed, then *halal* flesh—most fundamentally—comes from an anymal that has been killed humanely (Llewellyn 233).

Undercover footage from nations around the world has repeatedly demonstrated that "humane" does not apply to any aspect of industrialized anymal agriculture. (It would follow that "humane" does not apply to any kind of anymal exploitation short of that essential to survival that is carried out as humanely as possible.) Not only are anymals raised, kept, transported, and killed without compassion; they are subjected to the cutting off of beaks, tails, horns, toes, teeth, and testicles without anesthesia. Contemporary Muslim scholar, Tariq Ramadan, comments that Mohammad "required animals to be treated in the best possible way and spared needless suffering" and in animal agriculture (and any other form of exploitation) this requires respecting "their dignity as living beings" and "sparing them unnecessary suffering." (Ramadan n.p.) Islamic theologian Al-Hafiz Basheer Ahmad Masri, the focus of this book and pioneer in the realms of animal rights and Islam in contemporary society, looks to Allah and the Prophet Mohammad to highlight moral concerns entailed in consuming anymal products in industrialized nations: The basic moral question is: How right is it to deny these creatures of God their natural instincts so that we may eat the end product? For Muslims, these questions pose the additional question of a fundamental moral pertinence—would our Prophet Mohammad have approved of the modern methods of intensive farming systems if he were alive today? His overwhelming concern for animal rights and their general welfare would certainly have condemned (*La 'ana*) those who practice such methods, in the same way he condemned similar cruelties in his day. He would have declared that there is no grace or blessing (*Barakah*)— neither in the consumption of such food nor in the profits from such trades. These are not just hypothetical questions. The cruel and inhumane methods of intensive farming are being practiced in most Islamic countries these days, even in countries where indigence is no excuse (Masri, *Animal* 44).

Masri asserts that informed Muslims ought to refuse flesh on *religious grounds*. By extension, Muslims also ought to refuse dairy and eggs. In a world where compassion lies at the core of ethics, opting for a plant-based diet is ideal—a diet where anymals are "allowed to live their natural lives" without cruel exploitation, and without "having their throats slit" (Masri, *Animal* 56).

Tayyib and Dietary Choice

According to the Qur'ân, Muslims must not only limit themselves to the consumption of foods that are *halal* but also to foods that are *tayyib*. *Tayyib* foods are "wholesome, pure, nutritious and safe" and must be "healthy, free of disease, hormones, antibiotics, and chemicals" ("Halal versus Haraam"). *Tayyib* requirements indicate that, "unless proven to be safe," items sold for consumption "should be kept out of [the] halal food chain" ("Halal—Into the Future"). Even if one switches to organic milk, eggs, and flesh to avoid antibiotics, hormones, and chemicals—and even if one could get around the moral requirement of compassion—animal products pose a threat to human health, including increased risks for heart attack, stroke, diabetes, obesity, and several types of cancers: "Research suggests that [a non-anymal] diet can improve heart health, protect against cancer, and lower the risk of type 2 diabetes" (A. Smith n.p.). Not just any diet either: "On average, vegans have lower cholesterol levels and blood pressure, a greatly reduced rate of type 2 diabetes, and a reduced risk of cancer" ("Ensure Optimal Nutrition" n.p.).

The consumption of anymal products also harms humanity by contributing to food shortages and chronic hunger (Kemmerer, *Eating Earth* 9-10). Cows exploited for nursing milk consume a particularly large quantity of grain: A lactating cow eats 56 pounds (24.5 kg) of grain every day (Grant and Kononoff). In comparison, a person in India consumes roughly 440 pounds of grain annually (Brown, "Feeding the World" n.p.): In the course of one year, one adult in India eats less grain than a lactating cow eats in eight days. Other farmed anymals are also fed large quantities of precious grains. Calves in feedlots consume more than one ton (2000 pounds) of grain in a handful of months before they are slaughtered (Kemmerer, *Eating Earth* 9). A family of five could live on that quantity of grain for a year, with plenty to spare (Kemmerer, *Eating Earth* 11). Factory farmed fishes (fish farms) also consume grains (as well as other fishes), and like land anymals, they consume much more than their little bodies yield in the at the dinner table ("Do All Farmed Fish" n.p.). For most people, eating meat is a choice—a choice that privileged people enjoy at the expense of the poor, who starve for want of staples that have been fed to cattle, pigs, chickens, and turkeys at a net loss of calories and nutrients. Each day, 18,000 children die "from hunger and related causes" (L. Brown, 46).

Food energy is wasted when we cycle grains through anymals. Rather than breed hungry cattle and chickens to consume grains, we should *stop breeding anymals* and feed these precious grains to those who are already starving. *"If we did not breed and consume anymals, billions of tons of grains could be redirected to feed hungry human beings, alleviating and/or preventing starvation worldwide"* (Kemmerer, Animals and World Religions 286).

Dietary choices that harm the earth also harm those who live on the earth, and thereby fail to meet *tayyib* requirements. Anymal agriculture is the number one cause of every major environmental threat (Kemmerer, *Eating Earth* 41). "Modern animal agriculture is linked to a truly staggering number of environmental problems: natural-habitat destruction, greenhouse gas emissions, soil degradation, aquifer depletion, and various kinds of pollution—including the creation of dead zones" (Halley 158). As it turns out, *"[f]ood choices are the number one determinant of an individual's environmental footprint"* (Kemmerer, *Eating Earth* 144) and this is as true of vegetarians as it is for carnivores:

> From an environmental point of view, if one is concerned about deforestation and species loss, we ought to seriously reduce our consumption of animal products—not only meat but all animal products. Merely moving towards a diet rich in non-meat animal products (dairy and eggs) achieves virtually nothing. Thus the environmentalist is led to a conclusion similar to the animal activist: removing meat from one's diet is not enough; it is much better to be quarter-vegan than 100 percent vegetarian. (Halley 159)

As vice-regents, humans are to care for the Creator's splendid planet, not destroy Allah's good works. "Adopting a plant based diet is the most important choice we can make on behalf of the environment" (Kemmerer, *Eating Earth* 144). Sincere, informed Muslims who are fortunate enough to have a choice as to what they eat will opt for a diet that protects creation, people, and anymals—a vegan diet.

Conclusion

Returning to the world of Islam for insights on ethics and anymals and the ethics of diet reminds me why I was so impressed with Islam when I began my studies in the realms of animals and Islam—when I first read Masri's writings. Is it not easy to see why Islamic teachings on the topic of anymals have made a strong and positive impression on me, as an outsider studying the tradition? Islam expects human beings to see nature (including anymals) as sacred creation, to treat the compassionate Prophet as a moral exemplar, to engage with our care-taking responsibilities as vice-regents, to honor the God-given rights of anymal, and to uphold the expectations carried by the concepts of *halal* and *tayyib* with regard to dietary choices. These teachings are not peripheral to Islam—they lie at the very core of the tradition. Collectively, these teachings encourage not only anymal rights but anymal liberation.

Sources

Attar, Farid Al-Din. *Muslim Saints and Mystics: Episodes from the Tadhkirat al-Auliya'*. Tr. A. J. Arberry. NY: Arkana, 1990.

Bakhtiar, Laleh. *Sufi: Expressions of the Mystic Quest*. NY: Thames and Hudson, 1987.

Berry, Rynn. *Food for the Gods: Vegetarianism and the World's Religions*. New York: Pythagorian, 1998.

Brown, Lester R. "Feeding the World Means Hogging Less Grain." Web. Nov. 10, 2010. Accessed Jan. 13, 2018. <http://grist.org/article/2010-11-09-improving-food-security-by-strategically-reducing-grain-demand/>

The Case of the Animals versus Man Before the King of the Jinn. Trans. Lenn E. Goodman and Richard McGregor. Oxford, Oxford U.P., 2009.

Cragg, Kenneth, and R. Marston Speight. *The House of Islam*. Belmont, CA: Wadsworth, 1988.

Denny, Frederick M. *Islam and the Muslim Community.* Harper San Francisco, 1987.

"Do All Farmed Fish Eat the Same Thing?" *NOAA Fisheries: National Oceanic and Atmospheric Administration.* Web. Accessed Jan. 6, 2018. <http://www.nmfs.noaa.gov/aquaculture/faqs/faq_feeds.html#1what>

"Ensure Optimal Nutrition." *Vegan Outreach.* Web. Accessed March 13, 2021. <https://veganoutreach.org/why-vegan/>

Esposito, John L. *Islam: The Straight Path.* Oxford: Oxford U, 1988.

Foltz, Richard C. *Animals in Islamic Tradition and Muslim Cultures.* Oxford: Oneworld, 2005.

Friedlander, Shems. *Submission: Sayings of the Prophet Muhammad.* NY: Harper Colophon, 1977.

Grant, Rick and Paul J. Kononoff. University of Nebraska-Lincoln. "Feeding to Maximize Milk Protein and Fat Yields." Feb. 2007. Accessed Dec. 28, 2018. <http://extensionpublications.unl.edu/assets/pdf/g1358.pdf>

"Halal—Into the Future." *Halal Food Authority.* Online. Internet. Oct. 19, 2010. http://www.halalfoodauthority.co.uk/seminars-halalfoodexhibit.html

"Halal V/s Haraam Food in a Non-Muslim Country." *ShiaChat.com: Forums.* Web. Oct. 19, 2010. <http://www.shiachat.com/forum/index.php?/topic/234916013-halal-vs-haraam-food-in-a-non-muslim-country/#top>

Halley, John. "So You Want to Stop Devouring Ecosystems?" *Animals and the Environment: Advocacy, Activism, and the Quest for Common Ground.* Ed. Lisa Kemmerer. NY: Routledge, 2015.

Haq, S. Nomanul. "Islam and Ecology: Toward Retrieval and Reconstruction." *Islam and Ecology: A Bestowed Trust.* Ed. Richard C. Foltz et al. Cambridge: Harvard U, 2003. 121-54.

Kemmerer, Lisa. *Animals and World Religions.* Oxford: Oxford University Press, 2012.

___. *Eating Earth: Environmental Ethics and Dietary Choice.* Oxford: Oxford U. Press, 2014.

Llewellyn, Othman Abd-ar-Rahman. "The Basis for a Discipline of Islamic Environmental Law." *Islam and Ecology: A Bestowed Trust.* Ed. Richard C. Foltz et al. Cambridge: Harvard U, 2003. 185-248.

Marshall, Peter. *Nature's Web: Rethinking our Place on Earth.* London: Cassell, 1992.

Masri, Al-Hafiz Basheer Ahmad. *Animal Welfare in Islam.* Leicestershire: Islamic Foundation, 2007.

Mishkat al-Masabih. Islam, the Modern Religion. "Animals in Islam II." Web. Oct. 19, 2010. http://www.themodernreligion.com/misc/an/an2.htm

Muttaqi, Shahid 'Ali. "The Sacrifice of 'Eid al-Adha': An Islamic Perspective against Animal Sacrifice." IslamicConcern.org. 29 June 2004. <http://www.islamveg.com/sacrifice01.asp>.

Muwatta Malik. *Guided Ways: Hadith.* Web. Oct. 19, 2010. <http://www.guidedways. com/book_display-book-54-translator-4-start-30-number-54.12.31.htm>

Nasr, Seyyed Hossein. "Islam, the Contemporary Islamic World, and the Environmental Crisis." *Islam and Ecology: A Bestowed Trust.* Ed. Richard C. Foltz et al. Cambridge: Harvard U, 2003. 85–106.

Ozdemir, Ibrahim. "Toward an Understanding of Environmental Ethics from a Qur'anic Perspective." *Islam and Ecology: A Bestowed Trust.* Ed. Richard C. Foltz et al. Cambridge: Harvard U, 2003. 3-38.

Qur'ân. Trans. N. J. Dawood. Harmondsworth: Penguin, 1956.

Ramadan, Tariq. "The Unethical Treatment of Animals Betrays the Spirit of Islam." *ABC Religion and Ethics.* Oct. 2013. Accessed March 13, 2021. <https://www.abc.net.au/religion/the-unethical-treatment-of-animals-betrays-the-spirit-of-islam/10099574>

Rumi, Jelaluddin. *Mathnawi.* Trans. Coleman Barks and John Moyne. *This Longing: Poetry, Teaching Stories, and Letters of Rumi.* Putney: Threshold, 1988.

___. *Mathnawi.* Trans. E. H. Whinfield. "Story II: The Building of the 'Most Remote Temple' at Jerusalem." *The Spiritual couplets of Maulana Jalalu-'D-Din Muhammad Rumi, Book IV.*

Sahih Bukhari. Guided Ways: Hadith. Web. Oct. 19, 2010. <http://www.guidedways.com/searchHadith.php>

Sahih Bukhari 67. Guided Ways: Hadith. Web. Oct. 19, 2010. <http://www.guided-ways.com/book_display-book-67-translator-1-start-60-number-442.htm>

Sahih Bukhari referenced on *Jamaat e Islami Hind, Kerala.* "10. The Religion of Compassion." Online. Internet. Oct. 19, 2010. <http://www.jihkerala.org/htm/english/RELIGION/10.html>

Said, Abdul Aziz, and Nathan C. Funk. "Peace in Islam: An Ecology of the Spirit." *Islam and Ecology: A Bestowed Trust.* Ed. Richard C. Foltz et al. Cambridge: Harvard U, 2003. 155-84.

Schimmel, Annemarie. *Mystical Dimensions of Islam.* Chapel Hill: U of N Carolina, 1975.

Schuon, Frithjof. *Sufism: Veil and Quintessence.* Bloomington: World Wisdom Books, 1979.

Seker, Mehmet. "Rumi's Path of Love and 'Being Freed' with the Sama." In *Rumi and His Sufi Path of Love,* edited by Fatih Citlak and Huseyin Bingul, 1–8. Somerset, NJ: Light Incorporated, 2007.

"Selected Comments on Islamic Teachings." ReligiousTolerance.Org. Web. Oct. 19, 2010. <http://www.religioustolerance.org/tomek14.htm>

Siddiq, Mohammad Yusuf. "An Ecological Journey in Muslim Bengal." *Islam and Ecology: A Bestowed Trust.* Ed. Richard C. Foltz et al. Cambridge: Harvard U, 2003. 451-62.

Smith, Amy. "What to Know About Vegan Diets." *Medical News Today.* April 27, 2020. Accessed March 3, 2021. <https://www.medicalnewstoday.com/articles/149636>

Smith, Jonathan Z. et al., ed. *The HarperCollins Dictionary of Religion.* New York: Harper San Francisco, 1995.

Stoddart, William. *Sufism: The Mystical Doctrines and Methods of Islam.* New York: Paragon P, 1985.

Lisa Kemmerer is the founder and director of the educational non-profit, Tapestry. Internationally known for work on behalf of anymals, the environment, and disempowered human beings, professor emeritus Lisa Kemmerer earned a BA in International Studies at Reed College, a Master of Theological Studies in Comparative Religions at Harvard, and a PhD in philosophy at Glasgow University in Scotland. She has published more than 100 articles and anthology chapters and 10 books, including *Animals and World Religions*; *Sister Species: Women, Animals,* and *Social Justice; and Eating Earth: Environmental Ethics and Dietary Choice.* For more information, visit lisakemmerer.com and lisakemmerer.com/tapestry.html.

A SHORT BIOGRAPHY OF
AL-HAFIZ B.A. MASRI

B. A. MASRI, JULIUS NYERERE, SHAFIQ ARAIN, TOM MBOYA, AND UNKNOWN

AL-HAFIZ B. A. MASRI[i]

MUSLIM, SCHOLAR, ACTIVIST—REBEL WITH A JUST CAUSE

Nadeem Haque

In a game park in the middle of Africa in the 1950s, three aggravated Masai tribesmen were arguing with the principal of a local school. Apparently, the school overlapped with Masai tribal grounds; if they wanted to stay on those lands, the principal would have to physically defeat the tribesmen. The principal was willing to take on the Masai—three against one—on behalf of the students. The savannah became a gladiatorial arena for a full-contact stick-fighting contest. Somehow the principal defeated his challengers. The tribesman ran away, claiming that the principal was a magician—so skillful in battle that they were not able to land a single blow.

The principal was Al-Hafiz B. A. Masri (1914–1992). By any standards, Masri was an outstanding man. The sense of justice that motivated him to take on three Masai tribesmen was part of a core attitude that shaped Masri's life and drew him to the interchange between human beliefs and animal welfare/rights. This chapter explains how Masri came to be the first twentieth-century thinker to demonstrate that Islam has both the theoretical and practical power to protect nonhuman animals.

India: The Land of Masri's Birth

Masri was born to a saintly father and a strict mother in Punjab, India, in 1914. His father, the learned Shaikh Abdul-Rahman Misri, was born to an upper caste (*Kshatriya*) Hindu family. Changing religions, especially from Hinduism to Islam, was considered worse than someone being infected with a highly contagious disease. Nonetheless, Abdul-Rahman embraced Islam at the age of eighteen,

---

i   This section is a chapter from the book *Call to Compassion*, by Lisa Kemmerer and Anthony J. Nocella II, Editors, Lantern, New York (2011), pp. 185-196. Only minor modifications have been made.

and was promptly excommunicated from his family, receiving none of the property that a Hindu son would normally have inherited. In fact, his father threatened to kill him with a sword if he did not revert back to Hinduism. Abdul-Rahman replied: "My body may belong to you, but my soul belongs to God!"

In time, Abdul-Rahman became both scholarly and spiritual, traveling to Egypt to study Islam (Al-Azhar Seminary). On his return to India, he married and started a family; Basheer Ahmad (Al Hafiz B.A. Masri) was his first son. To fulfill a promise, he set about teaching Masri the Qur'ân, and five years later, at age thirteen, Masri had memorized the entire text, earning him the title Al-Hafiz—one who has memorized the whole Qur'ân verbatim.

Masri got married in 1935 to Salima, but because of his opposition to the Qadiani Movement (followers of Mirza Ghulam Qadiani), they immigrated from India to East Africa (in 1941) with a price on Masri's head. Before he could get away, a henchman tried to assassinate Masri; in the process, one of his colleagues was killed and another injured. Masri landed a blow to the assailant's head with a cudgel, but the culprit ran away, leaving a blood-dripped trail that led the police to his door. He was tried and executed (Masri 1988).

Politics in East Africa
In East Africa, Masri's sense of justice led him in a variety of directions. He became vice-president of the Uganda SPCA (Society for the Prevention of Cruelty to Animals), and secretary of the Tanganyika SPCA. (Tanganyika, was an East African territory between the Indian Ocean and the largest of the African great lakes, which eventually became part of Tanzania.) Africa was teeming with wildlife at the time, and Masri gained tremendous practical knowledge of the local flora and fauna. He had a unique way of working with African wildlife, and it served him well. Once, when Masri and two friends were out hunting for food, they came across three male lions. Rather than succumb to fear, Masri took a huge step forward and roared like a lion. He wanted the lions to believe that *he* was defending his territory, that *they* were encroaching on his area. It worked, and the lions went their way.

Masri moved to Uganda from Tanganyika in 1952, and like the Argentine Marxist revolutionary, Che Guevara, sought African socioeconomic emancipation from colonialism. With Milton Obote, who eventually became prime minister of Uganda, Masri co-founded the Uganda People's Congress, which the two men hoped to build into an enlightened political party. The British, who were ruling East Africa at the time, pursued Obote, intent on blocking his efforts to create an independent Uganda. Masri protected Obote in his home, but ultimately the two men broke ties and went their separate ways. Masri headed for England with his family, where he became prominent both in the Muslim world, and in the animal welfare/rights movement of the mid to late twentieth century.

Animal Welfare/Rights in England, Egypt, and Beyond

In England, Masri studied journalism, and between 1963 and 1967 he served as the joint editor of the prestigious *The Islamic Review*, published by Shah Jahan Mosque, built in Woking in 1889. *The Islamic Review* carried articles from the world's pre-eminent Islamic thinkers/scholars, such as Mohammad Marmaduke Pickthall, Syed Qutb, and Malik Bin Nabi. In 1964, Masri was the first Sunni imam (worship leader) to be appointed at Shah Jahan Mosque, and three years later, Masri wrote and delivered a speech to 500 delegates from Western nations at the International Association for Religious Freedom, in London. In his talk, "Islam: Precursor of the Intellectual Age," Masri noted that Islam calls the faithful to rethink their conception of and relationship with the Creator, who gifted humanity with a message of peace and justice that prophets had expounded for hundreds of years, culminating in the voice of Prophet Mohammad. Masri, imam of Europe's main mosque, made a name for himself as a thinker and a lecturer.

As time passed, Masri's reputation grew, and sometimes his *khutbas* (sermons) were broadcast by British television. One of Masri's most well-received talks, a presentation that reached hundreds of thousands of British viewers, he corrected common misconceptions about Islam. Now at the forefront of Islamic affairs, Masri met such famous Muslims as Malcolm X (at the London

School of Economics) and Muhammad Ali (at the Shah Jahan Mosque after his Olympic win). Some of Britain's most famous personalities sought Masri to learn more about Islam, such as Lord Hugh Dowding, commander-in chief of the Royal Air Force, who was responsible for winning the "Battle of Britain" during World War II. Dowding became one of Masri's closest friends, and in later years the two men shared a common concern for animal welfare; Dowding put Masri in touch with various animal welfare organizations and animal activists.

In 1967 Masri's three children—Taher, Mubarak, and Tahera (my mother)—had reached adulthood, and Masri resigned as imam of the Shah Jahan Mosque to undertake a three year, forty-five-nation car-and-caravan tour with his supportive wife Salima. Masri and Salima traveled through Western and Eastern (Communist) Europe, North Africa, Turkey, Iran, and Pakistan. They stayed in Egypt for a year, where Masri studied Arabic at Al-Azhar Seminary. It was during this period of time, as a traveler in foreign Islamic nations, that Masri was confronted with animal cruelties that he could not ignore, and which he recognized as contrary to Islamic teachings. One of these pivotal moments was at Al-Azhar, when he heard one of the leading lecturers curse pigs. According to the Qur'ân, Muslims are not supposed to eat swine flesh because the Qur'ân states that such "meat" is harmful and unhealthy. Masri begged to differ, and politely referenced Hadith, noting that there was nothing wrong with pigs—that pigs are not intrinsically evil. Scavenging pigs, Masri explained, help to maintain ecosystems, and they have an important role, for which they were designed by the Creator.

Animal Welfare and Islam

In the 1980s, Masri began to ponder animal welfare and Islamic teachings with great zeal. He was in "early retirement," but people remembered his knowledge of Islam, and his eloquence in English, and continued to invite him to talk on various subjects relating to Islam. Consequently, when the International Association Against Painful Experiments on Animals (IAAPEA) wanted a definitive Islamic view on the subject, they contacted Masri. Masri's first paper on animal welfare and Islam was presented in 1984 at the IAAPEA conference on animals and religions (later published in this anthology: *Animal Sacrifices: Religious Perspectives on the Use of Animals in Science* (Regan, 1986)). In this paper, Masri posed the following fundamental questions:

(i) Can human beings rightly claim to be the apex of value in the world?

(ii) If such a view is religiously justified, what moral implications does this carry for other life forms, particularly with regard to nonhuman animals? (Regan 1986, 171)

To answer these questions, Masri quoted extensively from the Qur'ân and Hadith. He discussed the importance of the preservation of species, noting that other animals are owed their legitimate share of the planet, and noting that the Qur'ân states that God created animals to live in communities like our own. He also demonstrated that the position of humans who choose to do evil is "lower" than that of any other animal:

> In the words of [William] Hazlitt: "Man is the only animal struck with the difference between what things are, and what they ought to be." Animals don't possess this freedom of choice. That's why the Qur'ân characterizes those humans who fall short of this endowment as the "lowest of the low" (Regan 1986, 177).

Masri noted that Islamic "laws strongly deprecate all direct or indirect acts of cruelty to animals" (Regan 1986, 185). He lists six acts that are common in animal experimentation (as well as in other forms of contemporary animal exploitation), which are forbidden under Islamic law:

1. subjecting animals to pain,
2. killing animals for luxuries,
3. enclosing animals in cages,
4. breeding animals in confined and unhygienic conditions, and
5. using traps that cause lingering death. (Regan 1986, 185)

He concludes:

> The basic and most important point to understand about using animals in science is that the same moral, ethical, and legal codes should apply to the treatment of animals as are applied to humans. (Regan 1986, 192)

Masri then recounts Hadith quoting Prophet Mohammad, stating: "Anyone who kills even a sparrow or anything smaller than that, without proper justification, will be held accountable to God" (Regan 1986, 192).

Based on his work for IAAPEA, Compassion in World Farming (CIWF) commissioned Masri to write a book, which resulted in his short work, *Islamic Concern for Animals*. This book became the first chapter of his later work, *Animals in Islam*, which presents his definitive position on animal welfare and Islam. At the very outset, he writes:

> Quite a few of my friends have been surprised to learn that I have chosen "Animals" as a subject to write on from the Islamic point of view. . .. The way I look at it, however, is that life on this earth is so inextricably intertwined as a homogenous unit that it cannot be disentangled for the melioration of one species at the expense of another. (Masri 1989, vii)

In *Animals in Islam*, Masri discusses, with great analytical depth—for the first time in the modern era—key issues with regard to animal welfare/rights and Islam. This definitive work focuses on basic Islamic principles, derived from the Qur'ân, such as animals as members of communities like our own, and also discusses key Hadith (Masri 1989, 4–5). Through these sacred writings Masri examines factory farming, and the consumption of flesh. He also discusses animal sacrifice, demonstrating that this practice has nothing to do with appeasing God, and that Islam does not permit such superstitious, ritualistic practices (Masri 1989, 114). He speaks out against such waste and meaningless ritualism, especially the waste from the mass slaughter of animals for the Hajj. He suggests that wealthier pilgrims offer cash to the poor, rather than kill innumerable animals.

Diet and Islam

Masri accepted meat consumption under certain conditions. In Chapter 6 of *Animals in Islam*, "The Islamic Method of Slaughter (*Dhabh*)," Masri explores *halal* meat using Hadith and the Qur'ân, noting that it's almost impossible to be certain that flesh bought in local markets is *halal*. Nonetheless, he concludes that flesh might be considered *halal* in non-Muslim countries so long as no name other than the name of God has been invoked during the time of slaughter. (In truth, of course, it is impossible to know what has been uttered over an animal during slaughter.) He adds that one who chooses to consume flesh should invoke the name of God just before eating meat (Masri 1989, 131–140).

Masri argues in *Animals in Islam* that pilgrims from Western countries ought to slaughter animals for food by proxy, allowing meat distribution among the poor in distant nations. (This suggestion was acknowledged favorably by the Saudi Arabian government (Masri 1989, 124).) While Masri accepted the eating of flesh, he also accepted—even encouraged—other options, such as a vegan or vegetarian diet:

> The spirit of sacrifice lies in offering the animal as charity to the indigent IN THE NAME OF GOD AND NOT TO GOD . . . It needs to be repeated here, especially for the benefit of general Muslims, that Islam neither recommends nor forbids the eating of meat (Masri 1989, 157).

This leaves the dietary choice of vegan, vegetarian, and omnivore to individual Muslims according to place and time, provided one maintains a healthful diet. This responsibility requires Muslims to apply other Islamic ideas to our dietary choice—such as the requirement for compassion—and that Muslims know how animals are treated on factory farms, and in slaughterhouses, and not remain blissfully ignorant.

By way of curbing ignorance, *Animals in Islam* discusses pre-slaughter stunning, and Masri concludes that Qur'ânic principles only permit captive-bolt stunning. Electric stunning, gas stunning, and mechanical stunners fail to pass the crucial Islamic requirement for blood flow. Furthermore, Masri notes that captive-bolt stunners (applied just before the ritual slaughter method) cause the least pain and are therefore a considerable improvement over "ritual slaughter" (in which the jugular vein is cut without stunning) (Masri 1989, 157–196). In addition, Masri emphasizes that Muslims who eat flesh must *know* how the animals whom they consume are killed. After analyzing nutritional factors, the anatomy of humans, the economics of food, protein levels, and a comparative analysis of various major world religions, Masri concludes:

> Our moral responsibility toward the rest of the species demands that we employ all our scientific knowledge to acquire as much of our nutrients as possible from sources other than the flesh of those animals whom God has created and who are at our mercy. (Masri 1989, 46)

Masri also created a video, *Creatures of God*, stemming from his most fundamental and critical understandings of Islam. Cruelties inflicted on cattle exploited for their milk and hens exploited for their eggs, from a Qur'ânic viewpoint, cannot be justified—and the vegan diet is therefore more meritorious in the eyes of the Creator. Masri emphasized that the ideal Islamic diet—most consistent with the Qur'ân, avoids factory farmed flesh. Were he alive today, he would surely have extended his comments to protect hens and cows enslaved in the egg and dairy industries. The cruelties of factory farming have greatly increased animal suffering since Masri's time, and even then he was concerned for the welfare of farmed animals.

That said, I think Masri would *not* have required contemporary Muslims to adopt a vegan diet *if* farmed animals were treated compassionately, and he would definitely require Muslims to purchase foods from farms devoid of animal cruelty—but such farms simply do not supply today's supermarkets. Consequently, Masri would doubtless have emphasized the need for a vegan diet. Masri's ideas on vegetarianism, and by extension veganism, would include the following factors:

1. The Creator who designed this dynamic universe has infinite knowledge and wisdom. The Creator allowed humans the choice of whether or not to eat certain animals, but requires that we minimize psychological and physiological suffering in our choice of foods.

2. If one can obtain the proper diet without causing suffering, then one ought to do so. It is currently possible for many of us to choose a balanced diet, but this diet is still not possible for many people around the world.

3. Because animal products are permitted in the Qur'ân, it is difficult to convince Muslims to reconsider their dietary choices.

4. A healthful vegan diet places Muslims on a higher spiritual plane because such a diet reduces pain and suffering, and engenders compassion. Furthermore, such a diet is healthier for our bodies and our environment, and allows more people to have access to essential food and water. Choosing a vegan diet is in perfect consonance with Qur'ânic teachings and the Creator's expectations.

Muslims are called to engage in sustainable practices that eliminate or at least minimize ecosystem damage, strive for compassion, and maintain nature's dynamic balance (*mizan*). All point to a vegan diet as preferable, when possible—or at least a diet with reduced consumption of all animal products.

Last Days and Legacy

Over time, Masri's ideas evolved from a human sociopolitical focus to a broader perspective, in which he recognized that all life is interconnected, and that nonhuman animals must be treated with respect and compassion. Masri espoused a vibrant, non-relativistic ecumenism, requiring believers to rise above doctrinal irrationality, ritualism, and parochialism, to embrace a universal worldview:

> My humble and sincere advice to those who are trying to seek spiritual guidance through literalism of their scriptures is to pay more regard to the spirit of the

messages . . . The Qur'ân calls upon us over and over again to rack our brains and use our common-sense in grasping the quintessence of the Divine messages (Masri 1991).

Masri remained an advisor to the World Society for the Protection of Animals, and maintained connections with the World Wildlife Fund, until his death in 1992. He told me, a few months prior to his death, that he believed he would be remembered most for his work in the area of animal welfare/rights and Islam. Indeed, Masri's ideas continue to spark interest in the area of animals in Islam. For example, in 2005 Masri's "bold statements on animal cruelty and the required Muslim response have been used by PETA . . . in a campaign against cruelty to animals occurring in Australia, where sheep are being exported to Muslim countries" (Haque 2007, 550). One of God's fundamental messages for humanity, according to the Qur'ân, is that we are to be compassionate and just. Masri's influence is likely to continue as humanity seeks religious support for sustainable, compassionate lifestyle choices.

Fearless when standing up for the rights of others, whether schoolchildren in Africa, Indians or Africans under colonial rule, or factory-farmed animals in England, Masri's devotion to a singular God, coupled with his determination to take action on behalf of justice, inspired Masri's fascinating and rewarding life. His simple tombstone at the Shah Jahan Mosque is emblazoned with Prophet Mohammad's maxim: "Whoever is kind to the Creatures of God, is kind to himself" (Amin 1965, 200).

Sources

Amin, Muhammad. 1965. *Wisdom of Prophet Mohammad*. Pakistan: Lion Press.

Haque, Nadeem. 2007. "Book Review: Animals in the Islamic Tradition and Muslim Cultures," by Richard C. Foltz. In *Journal of Agricultural and Environmental Ethics*. Vol. 20, Issue 6.

Masri, Al-Hafiz B. A. 1991. "An Islamic Viewpoint on Animal Protection." In *ANIMALS International*. Vol. XI, Issue 36.

____. 1989. *Animals in Islam*. Petersfield: The Athene Trust.

___. 1988. *The Bane of Mirzaiyat*. South Africa: Young Men's Muslim Association.

___. 1986. "Animal Experimentation: The Muslim Viewpoint." In *Animal Sacrifices: Religious Perspectives on the Use of Animals in Science*, ed. Tom Regan, pp. 171–98. Philadelphia: Temple University Press.

Qur'ân. 2008. Trans. M. A. S. Abdel Haleem. U.K.: Oxford University Press.

ANIMALS IN ISLAM

ILLUSTRATION BY NADEEM HAQUE

SOME MUSLIM SAGES
THE AFFINITY BETWEEN MAN AND BEAST

In the region of existing matter, the mineral kingdom comes lowest, then comes the vegetable kingdom, then the animal, and finally the human being. By his body he (man) belongs to the material world but by his soul he appertains to the spiritual or immaterial. Above him are only the purely spiritual beings— the angels—above whom only is God: THUS THE LOWEST IS COMBINED BY A CHAIN OF PROGRESS TO THE HIGHEST. But the human soul perpetually strives to cast off the bonds of matter, and, becoming free, it soars upwards again to God, from whom it emanated.   (Al-Hazen).[1]

⊷······———◆———······⊷

Dying from the inorganic, we developed into the vegetable kingdom:
Dying from the vegetable, we became men.
Then what fear that death will lower us?
The next transition will make us angels.
From angels we shall rise and become what no mind can conceive;
We shall merge in affinity as in the beginning.
Have we not been told, 'All of us shall return unto Him'?   (Rumi).[2]

1

ISLAMIC CONCERN FOR ANIMALS

PREAMBLE

CRUELTY TO ANIMALS HAS existed throughout the ages. It takes various forms and guises, from cockfighting to cat burning, from sheer overloading of beasts of burden to downright neglect and abuse. Animals have died, and are dying, harsh deaths in traps and snares to provide fur coats and ornaments for the wealthy, and they have been hunted throughout the world for the sheer sport and morbid pleasure of man. However, until very recently the acts of cruelty were on a smaller and individual scale. What has changed now is the nature and extent of the cruelty, which is practiced on a much subtler and wider scale. The most alarming aspect of the current streak of cruelty is that it is being justified in the name of human needs and spurious science. Scientific and pharmaceutical experiments on animals are being done to find cures for diseases most of which are self-induced by our own disorderly lifestyle.

To satisfy his ever-increasing demands and fads, man has begun to use his technological might and scientific prowess to transform increasing numbers of animals into food products. In laboratories, scientists are producing new genetic variations that may be amenable to low-cost intensive methods of rearing. Many stockkeepers are more concerned with finance than the moral principles of animal husbandry, and look upon their livestock as meat and milk machines.

Even the once proud farmers have started yielding to temptation. The medieval sport of the feudal nobility to chase and kill animals for fun is still in vogue. Anglers hook up fish and throw them back into the water maimed—just to while away their time. All kinds of denizens of the forest are fair game for the trophy-hunters. There is a large-scale carnage of fur-bearing animals. All this, and much more, is being done to satisfy human needs, most of which are non-essential, fanciful, wasteful and which can be satisfied by alternative humane products which are easily available.

In this foul climate, the protests of animal welfarists are only just beginning to be heard. The politico-economic pressures of international balance of power and monetary balances of payment give little scope to state-legislators for moral considerations: and so, millions of helpless animals go on suffering torture.

Why is it that human attitudes towards animals are so tardy in changing? The organised religious institutions could have played an important role in educating the general public. Almost ninety percent of the world's population owes allegiance to one or other of the major religions. Each of these religions has the benefit of platforms wherefrom it could influence and educate captive audiences. But one seldom hears from their pulpits any sermons preaching the word of God about animals or respect for nature. Perhaps the clerics of our religions are too busy preparing their respective laities for the Life Hereafter to spare any thought for the so-called 'dumb beasts' and the ecology which sustains us all.

Human greed and self-indulgence needed some excuse, however flimsy, to exploit animals; and the institution of religion offered them that excuse by disseminating the creed of man's unconstrained dominion and domination over the rest of God's creation. It is true that all religions have tried in their respective ways to strike an equitable balance in the mutual rights and obligations between man and the rest of the species. The Scriptures of all religions contain expostulations on all kinds of cruelty to animals, but they have ceased to be taken seriously—either by theologians or the public.

The religious institutions are supposed to be there to give guidance to their respective followers in all kinds of moral problems. If all the churches and temples, all the mosques and synagogues were to make a concerted effort to bring their moral influence to bear, it would not only educate their laities, but would also put pressure on the politicians and the economists of the world—most of whom are sitting on the fence. Perhaps some religious leaders, though, still suffer from the misconceptions of the Middle Ages when they believed that their only business was to deal with the human soul. Since animals are thought to have no soul, they are not considered to be the responsibility of organised religion.

Let us hope a day will dawn when the great religious teachings may at last begin to bear fruit; when we shall see the start of a new era when man accords to animals the respect and status they have long deserved and for so long have been denied.

MAN'S DOMINION OVER ANIMALS

Both science and religion assert that man is the apex of creation. Science bases this claim on man's physiological superiority over the rest of the animated world, while religion bases it on man's psychical excellence and potential. Islam too, declares man as the best of God's creation and designates him as His viceregent (*khalifah*) on earth. So far, it all sounds very flattering, but is this position of pre-eminence unconditional? Let us see how the Islamic concept of viceregency is meant to work. A conscientious study of this concept involves a study of issues such as: Who is this man who has been appointed as God's representative on earth? Does anyone who possesses human features qualify for this exalted rank, or are there any qualifying conditions attached to this office? If there are any qualifying conditions, what are they?

Islam's corroboration of man's claim of superiority over the other species is circumscribed by mental, moral, and physical limitations in the exercise of this power. Man should use animals out of necessity and with compassion, humility, and loving care rather than with malevolence, avidity, or greed for the satisfaction of creature-comforts, luxurious pleasures, and self-indulgence. All the major religions have taught compassionate and humane treatment of animals. It is neither feasible nor necessary for a religion to lay down in its scriptures detailed rules and regulations covering every aspect of life. Each religion has tried in its own way to lay down the basic principles and to nurture in man a sense of responsibility as the custodian of nature. In our age of ever-increasing human mastery over nature, this responsibility has also increased proportionately.

The Qur'ân, while declaring man's viceregency, makes it clear in the following verses, that the appointment is not unconditional:

> He [God] it is Who made you viceregents on earth;
> he who disavows, the burden of disavowal will be on
> him. . . ." (Qur'ân 35:39).

The Qur'ân also states that:

> Certainly, we created man in the best make:

However, in the very next sentence the Qur'ân makes it clear what happens to those who fail to conform to the conditions, in these words:

> then We reduce him to [the status of] the lowest of
> the low. (Qur'ân 95:4,5).

Man is the only species[i] which has been endowed with the ability to differentiate between evil and virtue and to exercise his freedom of choice. Animals are capable of differentiating between 'good and bad' in the material sense, but not in the moral and ethical sense. In the following verses, the Qur'ân tells us about those humans who misuse their freedom of choice and transgress—they lose the status of human beings in the spiritual sense and are reduced to the status of animals:

> . . . they are those whom Allah has rejected and whom
> He has condemned and has turned into [the nature of]
> apes and swine, because they served evil. Such people
> are even worse than them and farther astray from the
> right course." (Qur'ân 5:63).[3]

No doubt such people still possess human features, as distinct from those of animals, but their moral status is degraded even lower than the status of animals for not making use of their faculties in the way expected of human beings. The Qur'ân explains this further in these words:

---

i   **Editor's Note:** Masri is referring to only carbon-based beings, excluding the Jinn, who are made of a more exotic energy form, according to the Qur'ân.

. . . they have hearts wherewith they fail to comprehend, and eyes wherewith they fail to see, and ears wherewith they fail to hear. They are like cattle; nay, even less cognizant of what is right. Such [humans] are far astray from the right path. (Qur'ân 7:179).

Again, the Qur'ân urges in remonstrance:

And be not like those who say, 'we have heard', while they do not hearken. Verily, the vilest of all creatures, in the sight of Allah, are those deaf and dumb ones who do not use their rationality." (Qur'ân 8:21,22).

The above verses occur in the Qur'ân in a context not directly related to animals vis-a-vis man. Nevertheless, they do lay down a very relevant principle that 'it depends on the conduct of man whether he maintains his privileged position as a human being, or gets himself degenerated to a status lower than that of animals'. While elaborating man's responsibilities as the viceregent of God, the Qur'ân lays great emphasis on the development of Godly attributes which have been imbued in man's incarnation. These attributes are eternal and unchangeable. Compassion, love, mercy, justice, charity . . . are some of the Divine attributes which form the pedestal of that musnud (raised seat) on which God has seated man as His viceregent to establish His Kingdom on earth, in harmony with His laws of nature. This Kingdom of God is not meant to be only a human domain. God's suzerainty encompasses all creation, including the Animal Kingdom. How, then, can man as His Minister on earth administer justice and grace over the whole of His Kingdom without nurturing in himself the Godly attributes and a tender conscience? This is how the Qur'ân explains this moral philosophy: "Direct your face toward the upright way of life. . . ."

The spontaneous question arises here as to what is implied by 'upright way of life (religion)'. The answer is given in the lines of the same verse that follow:

Direct your face towards the upright way of life— the nature of God upon which He has instituted the innate nature of humankind. No change is permissible in God's creation; this is the proper way of life and yet, most people do not even know of this. (Qur'ân 30:30).

Man's superiority over other species does not lie in his physique. As a matter of fact, physically, man is inferior to animals in many respects. Muslims have often been advised by their mentors to learn lessons from some species of animals. For example, the Imam Hazrat Ali gives this piece of advice: "Be like a bee; anything he eats is clean, anything he drops is sweet and any branch he sits upon does not break."[4]

The real criterion of man's superiority lies in his spiritual volition, called in the Qur'ân 'taqwa'. This spiritual power bestows on a man a greater measure of balance between the conscious and the unconscious elements of mind, thus, enabling him to make the best use of his freedom of choice. He is considered the best of God's creation only because of this distinction. Without the power of spiritual volition, this distinction is rendered superficial.

Man's dominion over animals, in the true Islamic sense, is a patriarchal authority—an arrangement under which the paterfamilias rules the family with discipline and paternal love. The Prophet Mohammad puts it in these words: "All creatures are like a family [ayal] of God: and He loves the most those who are the most beneficent to His family".[5] This Hadith has been interpreted by some scholars in the sense that the word 'creation' (khalq) means here human species only. The writer however is convinced, both philologically and theologically, that the word khalq in this context stands for makhluqat and comprehends all species of creation. Imam Raghib, the great classical authority, agrees with this interpretation. (See: Mufredat-e-Imam Raghib 157). The Prophet used to say: "Whoever is kind to the creatures of God, is kind to himself".[6]

The Qur'ân puts this analogy in tribal or communal terms in these words: "There is not an animal on earth, nor a two-winged flying creature, but they are communities like you. . .". (Qur'ân 6:38). According to the learned commentators of the Qur'ân, the word 'communities' is used here in the sense of 'animals' and 'flying creatures' of all types: vertebrates, quadrupeds, mammals, crustacea, reptiles, worms, insects, and the like. They all live a life, individual and social, like members of a human commune. In other words, they are communities in their own right and not in relation to human species or its values. These details have been mentioned to emphasize the point that even those species which are generally considered as insignificant or even dangerous, deserve to be treated as communities; that their intrinsic and not perceptible values should be recognized, irrespective of their usefulness or apparent harmfulness.

To define further what it means by 'communities of animals', the Qur'ân explains:

> Allah has created every animal from water: of them there are some that creep on their bellies; some that walk on two legs; and some that walk on four..." (Qur'ân 24:45).

The first category includes all kinds of worms, reptiles, centipedes, insects, and all kinds of creeping creatures. The second category includes birds and human beings; and the third category covers most species of mammals. The significant point to note is that, physically, man has been put in the same bracket as all other species. The following *Hadith* leaves no ambiguity in the sense in which the Qur'ân uses the word 'communities':

> Abu Huraira reported the Prophet as telling of an incident that happened to another prophet in the past. This prophet was stung by an ant and, in anger, he ordered the whole of the ants' nest to be burned. At this God reprimanded this prophet in these words: "Because one ant stung you, you have burned a whole community which glorified Me."[7]

The Islamic laws (*sharia*) concerning the rights of animals are very elaborate and explicit. In the case of the ants' nest, the following Juristic Rule would apply: "Any damage or a damaging retaliation for a damage is forbidden" (*Lâ zarara wa lâ zirar*).[8]

There are parents in this world who are cruel to their children, and rulers who exploit their subjects. Similarly, there are, and will always be, people who take the concept of man's dominion over animals as a licentious freedom to break all the established moral rules designed to protect animal rights. The Imam Hazrat Ali has this to say about such people:

> The worldly-minded people are like barking dogs and wild beasts; some of them roar on others, the strong ones eat the weak and the big ones hurt the small." And again, writing of those who misuse their authority over the weak, he writes: "A savage and ferocious beast is better than a wicked and tyrant ruler."[9]

The following verses of the Qur'ân apply verbatim to those people of our age who are exploiting wastefully the resources of nature and are wreaking havoc in the animated as well as the inanimate world, while defending their actions with clever and seemingly convincing arguments:

> And of mankind there is he whose glibness on the mundane life may dazzle thee, [especially] when he calls on God to witness the verity of his statements, because he is very skillful in his arguments.
> But, whenever he comes to power, he goes about in the land trying to create disorder by destroying tilth and progeny.
> And when it is said to him, 'fear God', his vainglory seizes him in his sin. So, Hell shall be his reckoning—verily, it is a vile abode. (Qur'ân 2:204-206).

In the context of these verses, the expression 'destroying tilth and progeny', means the 'resources of nature'. Literally, tilth means flora and progeny means fauna.[10]

ANIMALS' PLACE IN NATURE

The question of man's responsibilities towards animals cannot be studied without discussing the reasons for man's ill-treatment of animals. At the same time, the problem has to be understood in the perspective of the inter-relationship between man and the rest of the animated world as well as their inter-dependence upon each other. This relationship is primarily influenced by man's concept of the status of animals, which man gives to them in the hierarchy of various species. To establish in our minds the status of animals is as important a postulate as is the assessment of our fellow human beings for determining our mutual relationships.

We owe a great deal to modern naturalists who have sifted quite a few facts from fallacies, myths, and superstitions about animals. The pioneers in this field were mostly the members of the Christian Holy Order in the 17th century who were enthusiastic and bold enough to re-interpret the Biblical chronology of creation, in spite of being accused of and censured for puritanical leanings as naturalists. Notwithstanding the fact that some of their observations and theories have been found to be fallacious, it has been mostly due to their pioneering work that research in Natural History and Science has been given respectability and scholastic interest. As a result, we now know so much more about the animal world, its behaviour, its classification, and categorization—most of all, its correlative status vis-a-vis the human world. The Naturalists have also helped us a great deal in understanding better those parts of our scriptures which deal with subjects, such as:

1. Balance in Nature.
2. Conservation of Species.
3. Animals' Faculty of Speech.
4. The Utility-value of animals.
5. The Metaphysics of Animal Mind.
6. Animals' Right to the Resources of Nature.

The Qur'ân and *Hadith* have discussed all the above subjects in great detail. However, until recently, few scholars felt any need to study them seriously. Some of those who did, were not interested enough to comprehend their full significance. It is only now, when modern scientific research has started corroborating the Qur'ânic statements, that Muslim theologians have begun to give serious thought to the current problems related to animals.

1. BALANCE IN NATURE

All the sources of Islamic instruction, especially the Qur'ân, lay great emphasis on Nature Study in order to understand life as one homogeneous organism. The Qur'ân is full of verses exhorting man to study nature—the planetary system; the terrestrial elements; the fauna and flora on earth. The real purport of this repeated appeal in the Qur'ân is to give credence to the existence of Godhead as the primeval originator of the universe; but the point that concerns us here is that the creation of animals takes a very prominent place in such citations as His portents. Here are a few of the numerous such verses:

> Human beings and the wild and domestic animals are too, comprised of various colours. Thus, only those among His creatures who humble themselves unto God, are truly the people of knowledge. (Qur'ân 35:28)
>
> Verily! In the Heavens and the Earth, there are portents for the believers. And in your own creation, as well as in the creation of all the animals pervading the Earth, there are portents for those who believe. (Qur'ân 45:3,4)
>
> Behold! everything We have created is in due measure and proportion." (Qur'ân 54:49)
>
> Allah knows what every female bears and by how much the wombs may fall short [of gestation], and how much they may increase—for with Him everything is in due measure and proportion." (Qur'ân 13:8)

Two words in the last verse are significant. The Arabic word 'untha' denotes a female of any species, whether human or animal. Secondly, the Arabic word for measure is 'miqdar', which is used in all such verses. It means 'in accordance with the particular purpose for which a thing has been created, the exigencies and the role which it is meant to play within God's plan of creation.[11]

> And the Earth—We have spread out its expanse and cast on it mountains in stable equilibrium, and caused life of every kind to grow on it, justly weighed. (Qur'ân 15:19)
>
> And do not spread corruption on the Earth, after it has been put in order. . . . (Qur'ân 7:56)

We created man, and gave him the faculty of speech. The sun and the moon rotate in ordered orbits, the plants and the trees, too, do obeisance. The firmament—He raised it high, and set the balance of everything, so that you may not upset the balance. Keep up the balance with equity, and fall not short in it. And the Earth—He spread it out for all living beings: with its fruits, blossom-bearing palms, chaff-covered grain, and fragrant plants. Which, then, of the bounties of your Lord will you deny?" (Qur'ân 55:3-13)

The following saying of the Prophet Mohammad shows how much importance was attached to the conservation of nature:

[Even when the world is coming to an end] on Doomsday, if anyone has a palm-shoot in hand, he should plant it.[12]

2. CONSERVATION OF SPECIES

Thanks to modern scientific research, we have started appreciating the fact that the ecological and environmental balance of our planet is of paramount importance for life on earth. This balance rests on very complex and interwoven laws of nature. The denizens of the forest, if left on their own, generally adapt themselves to those laws and learn to abide by them. One never sees environmental damage being done by animals living in their natural habitats, such as in the tropical forests. It is only the human species who have the idiosyncrasy to flout those laws and to upset the balance of nature. And it is the humans, of all the species on earth, who need to have religious and secular education to make them realize that they are here to harness nature instead of leaving behind them a trail of wanton destruction for posterity.

Contrary to certain scientific theories, the Islamic concept is that, in this Divine design of animated nature, there are some fine differences providentially created and preserved in the origin of species to keep them distinct one from the other. Territorial, climatic and other such evolutionary processes may change their ethological characteristics or anatomical structures. In their struggle for existence, animals may learn how to camouflage themselves to distract attention or to deceive by impersonation and manipulation of their environment; but no species can transgress beyond the orbit of its genetic origin.

The Qur'ân speaks of creation, it speaks of it in terms of opposite pairs. According to the Qur'ân, not only animal life, but also every kind of flora has been created in male and female sexes. We know it scientifically now that plants, like animals, possess generative organs, i.e. male stamens and female pistils—comprising ovary, style and stigma. Botanical definitions explain stigma as that part of the style or ovary-surface that receives pollen in impregnation. Style is defined as the narrowed extension of the ovary which supports the stigma.

Keeping in mind that the Qur'ân was revealed more than fourteen centuries ago, it could not have been clearer in expression on such scientific subjects. The following verses emphasize the salient point that each species has been conditioned biologically to procreate in order to continue its heterogeneity and, thus, to go on playing its assigned part in the theatre of nature. Our scientific dexterity can bring about genetic mutations, but we shall never be able to CREATE even one germ-cell. Once a particular species is exterminated, its germ-cell is launched into eternity—as dead as the dodo—and no human skill can re-create it. Recently some scientists have expressed hopes that they might be able to bring back to life those extinct species whose dead bodies still contain some live tissues. Even if they do succeed in doing that, the fact still remains true that the re-generation of those extinct species would be dependent on the tissues containing the DNA which was originally created by God. The following verses of the Qur'ân bring out the significance of the law of parity in nature and, hence, the significance of an uninterrupted sequence of species:

> Glory be to Him Who created all the progenitive pairs of that which the earth grows; and of themselves [human beings], too; and of that which they do not know [yet]. (Qur'ân 36:36)

> And all things We have created in pairs, that you may reflect. (Qur'ân 51:49)

[My Lord is He] Who spread out for you the earth like a carpet; and made paths therein for you, and sent down water from the cloud. Then, thereby, We have produced diverse pairs of plants—each distinct from the other." (Qur'ân 20:53)

And We cause flora of every kind to grow as spouses." (Qur'ân 31:10)

And it is He who spread out the earth. . . and of all fruit He produced therein, as spouses of two and two. . . ." (Qur'ân 13:3)

[God is] The Originator of the heavens and the earth. He has created mates for you from among yourselves, and mates of the cattle too, multiplying you thereby. . . ." (Qur'ân 42:11)

And He did create in pairs. . . . (Qur'ân 53:45)

The story of Noah's Ark is well known. The Qur'ân tells it in Chapter 11, Verses 36-48:

When the deluge came and the flooding of the whole *regional* area was imminent, there was the danger that some of the species of animals and birds might be exterminated. Even at such a time, God showed His concern to save at least one pair of each species, along with the faithful followers of Noah by giving him the following instructions: ". . . load in the Ark two of all species—one male and one female of each kind. . . ." (Qur'ân 11:40)

All these observations of the Qur'ân lay down two basic principles. Firstly, that the preservation of species is of paramount importance. Secondly, that the Divine scheme of regeneration works through the opposite, but complementary, forces of nature—not only in animals and plants, but also in inorganic matter. In the elements of nature, for example, we find that every atom possesses a positively charged nucleus of protons and negatively charged electrons. We also see the existence of particles and anti-particles.

The underlying message in the following verses seems to be that 'every individual species, including the human species, has been endowed with a potential nature to serve the whole creation as a homogeneous unit':

> Behold! In the celestial systems (star-systems, galaxies, etc.) and the earth there are portents for the believers. And in your own animated nature, as in that of the beasts which He has dispersed about, there are portentous messages for a people who would accept the truth." (Qur'ân 45:3,4)

> And among His portents, is the creation of the celestial systems (star-systems, galaxies, etc.) and the earth, and all the beasts that He has dispersed therein; and He has [also] the power to gather them to Himself whenever He wills." (Qur'ân 42:29)

The Arabic word 'Dâbbatun' used in this verse comprehends all breathing creatures on the protoplasmic basis of life—carbon-based life, in other words. In various other places also the Qur'ân has placed all kinds of beasts, amphibians, vertebrates, invertebrates, and primates (including human beings) in one bracket and mentions the creation of all of them as one of the portents of God. This shows the importance that God attaches to life as a whole.

3. FACULTY OF SPEECH

Animals are not inferior to us because they have a different vocal apparatus; nor does the fact that they cannot make articulate speech, like we can, mean that they are 'contemptible dumb animals'. Science has proved now that they do communicate not only with each other but also with humans—at least enough to express their social interests and biological needs. Those of us who enjoy the privilege of a loving and caring relationship with our pets will bear witness to this fact. Modern scientific research by naturalists has discovered quite a few interesting facts in this field. The honey-bee's buzzing dance is not just an outburst of merriment. It is meant to convey to other bees the location of the nectar—with the exact details of direction, distance and, perhaps, the quality and quantity of the find. The insignificant ants' well-organised and industrious social life could not be run without intelligent communication among them. The sonic vibrations made by marine mammals, generally called whale-songs, are articulate communications. Animals and birds in the wild can pass on different kinds of information to each other by slight modulation of voice. The very accentuation in the 'mew' can tell the owner of a cat whether it is 'requesting', 'complaining', or saying 'thank you'.

There are numerous legends about the Muslim saints and other holy men who could talk to animals. However, for lack of authentication, they are taken generally as mere fables. There is one statement in the Qur'ân, though, which proves that man had acquired the lore of speech with animals as early as the time of King Solomon. Perhaps in those days human civilization was more in tune with nature than it is today. The Qur'ân verse runs like this:

> And Solomon was David's heir, and he said: 'O you people! We have been taught the speech of birds. . . ."
> (Qur'ân 27:16)

4. THE UTILITY-VALUE

The Qur'ân and *Hadith* also plead for the cause of animal rights by repeatedly citing their utility-value and worth. Their status vis-a-vis human beings has already been discussed. The plea on the ground of their utility is, perhaps, addressed to those people whose values are determined more by benefit motives than by moral conscience. Here are some of many such quotations:

> And He has created cattle for you: you get from them your warm garments and other benefits, and you eat of their produce.
> And you pride yourselves on their beauty as you drive them home in the evenings, and as you lead them forth to pastures in the mornings.
> And they carry your heavy loads to places where you could not otherwise reach save by laborious strain to yourselves. Verily! Your Sustainer is most kind—a dispenser of grace.
> And [He has created for you] horses, mules and donkeys for riding as well as for adornment—and He

will yet create things of which you have no knowledge now." (Qur'ân 16:5-8)

And surely there is a lesson for you in cattle: We provide you with a drink out of that [substance] which is in their bellies—coming from a conjunction between the contents of the intestine and the blood—milk which is pleasant for those who drink it." (Qur'ân 16:66)

The Arabic word *'fars'* means that glandular protoplasm which is filled with particles of secretions no longer needed by the metabolism, which is secreted out by the body. It has been established by scientists now that milk is a mixture of those particles and lifeblood. The messages of some of the above verses are repeated below for emphasis:

And surely there is a lesson for you in cattle. We provide you with a drink out of their bellies; and there are numerous other benefits in them for you; and out of them you derive your food. And on them, as on ships, you make your journeys. (Qur'ân 23:21,22)

It is God Who provided for you all manner of livestock, that you may ride on some of them and from some of them you may derive your food. And there are other uses in them for you to satisfy your heart's desires. It is on them as on ships, that you make your journeys. (Qur'ân 40:79,80)

While enumerating the wonders of God's creation, the camel— the ship of the desert—is pointed out conspicuously in these words:

Do they not reflect on the camels, how they are created (designed)? (Qur'ân 88:17)[ii]

5. THE METAPHYSICS OF THE ANIMAL MIND

Unfortunately, modern scientific research has been confined mostly to the behaviour and physiology of animals. Until recently, in the field of consciousness research, most scientists attributed animal learning purely to instinct. Research work in this field tends to

---

ii **Editor's note:** Amazing discoveries about the camel have been made on its 'design'; refer to Camel—Wikipedia

state that no creature other than humans has been endowed with a conscious mind and, hence, has no faculty for higher cognition. This presumption is based on the misconception that even rudimentary spiritual awareness can emanate only from a consciously analytical mind as opposed to the organic life of a body which can exist and grow without the help of apprehensive senses. What is overlooked in this hypothesis is the fact that the quantum of balance in the conscious and the unconscious elements is of varying degrees in each species. Our scientific research has not yet been able to define the lines of demarcation between the conscious, the unconscious, and the subconscious elements of mind, nor have we heard the last word on how these elements interact—hence the confusion about the psyche of animals which ranges from one extreme to the other in the hierarchy of species.

Some creeds have raised them to the sublime position of being capable of receiving human souls; others have deified some animals to a status worthy of worship; while for some, all creatures other than humans are nothing more than food-parcels of flesh and bone, neatly wrapped up solely for the benefit of man. The last view is accepted mainly by those who conveniently find in it a licentious freedom to exploit the defenceless creatures for sadistic pleasure, or for gain.

According to the Qur'ânic theology, all living creatures possess a non-physical force of spirit and mind which, in its advanced form, we call 'psyche'. This concept should not be confused with the concepts of 're-incarnation' or 'transmigration' of souls, which doctrines are based on postulations different from those of Islam. Although animals' psychic force is of a lower level than that of human beings, there is ample evidence in the Qur'ân to suggest that animals' consciousness of spirit and mind is of a degree higher than mere instinct and intuition. We are told in the Qur'ân that animals have a cognisance of their Creator and, hence, they pay their obeisance to Him by adoration and worship. Out of the many verses on this proposition, the following few must suffice here:

> See you not that it is Allah whose praises are celebrated whoever is in the heavens and on earth, and

by the birds with extended wings? Each one knows its
prayer and psalm, and Allah is aware of what they do.
(Qur'ân 24:41)

It is worth noting the statement that 'each one knows its prayer
and psalm'. The execution of a voluntary act, performed consciously
and intentionally, requires a faculty higher than that of instinct
and intuition. Lest some people should doubt that animals could
have such a faculty, the following verse points out that it is human
ignorance that prevents them from understanding a phenomenon
like this:

> The seven heavens and the earth and all things therein
> declare His glory. There is not a thing but celebrates His
> adoration; and yet you mankind! You understand not
> how do they declare His glory. . . ." (Qur'ân 17:44)

It is understood that the inanimate elements of nature perform
the act of worshipping God without articulate utterances. They
do it by submitting themselves (*tasleem*) to the Divine Ordinances
known as the Laws of Nature. The following verse tells us how
all the elements of nature and all the animal kingdom function in
harmony with God's laws; it is only some humans who infringe
and, thus, bring affliction on themselves. The Qur'ân dwells on this
theme repeatedly to emphasize the point that man should bring
himself into harmony with nature, according to the laws of God—
as all other creation does:

> See you not that unto Allah pays adoration all things
> that are in the heavens (the celestial systems) and on
> earth—the sun, the moon, the stars, the mountains, the
> trees, the animals, and a large number among mankind?
> However, there are many [humans] who do not and
> deserve chastisement. . . . (Qur'ân 22:18)

The laws of nature have respect for no one and "time and tide
wait for no man." Even the most unruly and the unsubmissive have
to submit to those laws, whether they like it or not—as the Qur'ân
tells us:

And unto Allah prostrate themselves [in submission] whosoever are in the heavens and on earth, whether willingly or unwillingly, as do their shadows in the mornings and evenings." (Qur'ân 13:15).

The analogy of shadows is employed here to emphasize the point that man's submission should be like that of their shadows, which fall flat on the ground in the mornings and evenings—the times of the day when shadows are at their longest. In the case of animals, however, the Qur'ân tells us that God actually communicates with them, as the following verse shows:

And your Lord revealed to the bee, saying: 'make hives in the mountains and in the trees, and in [human] habitations'. (Qur'ân 16:68)

It is anybody's guess what form God's communication with animals takes. We know only this, that the Qur'ân uses the same Arabic word 'wahi' for God's revelation to all His Prophets, including the Prophet Mohammad, as it uses in the case of the bee. It is obvious that the connotation of God's revelations to His Messengers would be different from that of His revelations to animals. This is a serious theological subject which cannot be dealt with here. Nevertheless, it proves the basic fact that animals have a sufficient degree of psychic endowment to understand and follow God's messages—a faculty which is higher than instinct and intuition.

According to a great Confucian sage, *Hsun-Tzu,* who lived in the third century B.C., all living creatures between heaven and earth which have blood and breath must possess consciousness.[13] Similarly, the very cognizance of human relationship with the rest of the species in Buddhist literature and the Hindu Vedanta is based on the premise that all living creatures (*jiva*) possess the faculties of thinking and reasoning (*Manas*).

6. RIGHTS IN THE RESOURCES OF NATURE

Once it has been established that each species of animals is a 'community' like the human community, it stands to reason that each and every creature on earth has, as its birthright, a share in all the natural resources. In other words, each animal is a tenant-in-common on this planet with human species. Let us see now why some human beings do not act according to the terms of this joint tenancy. The inequitable attitude of some people towards animals seems to be a legacy from the early ages when man had to compete with them for food in order to survive. Man has always been in competition with animals for food, and the problem has been aggravated in the current world-situation, especially because of modern agrarian mismanagement. The Qur'ân has tried to allay this fear of man by reassuring him that God is not only the Creator but also the Sustainer and the Nourisher of all that He creates.

> And [God] bestowed blessings on the Earth, and measured therein sustenance in due proportion . . . in accordance with the needs of those who seek. (Qur'ân 41:10)

The conditions laid down in the above two verses for human beings to work for their food seems to be conveniently ignored by some people. Some tend to rely solely on God's beneficence—lying down on their backs with their mouths open and waiting for the manna from heaven to fall therein. Others have invented dubious ways and means to get more than their share by as little work as possible. Some of those who do work, muscle in to poach on others' preserves—and who can be an easier prey for exploitation than the poor defenceless animals who cannot fight back for their rights?

Those who expect to be fed by God, the Sustainer, without working for their bread fail to understand the real sense of the doctrine of 'pre-destination', or 'fate' (*Qaza wa Qadr* or *Qismat*). The literal meaning of 'pre-destination', in the Islamic sense is: "pre-fixing the fate of someone or something" in the sense of determining the capacity, capability, endowment, function and other faculties. The Qur'ân uses the Arabic word '*taqdir*' meaning 'destiny' not only for the decreed orbits of the planetary motions, but also for inorganic substances as well as for animated creatures including human beings. Within those pre-fixed limitations, however, conditions could be changed for the better: suffering could be avoided or lessened by human effort and skill.

Unlike some human beings, animals are quite capable of satiating their hunger and of procuring all their necessities of life, if man would only let them do so without interference. The Qur'ân repeatedly hammers home the fact that food and other resources of nature are there to be shared equitably with other creatures. Below are just a few of the numerous such verses:

> Then let man look at his food: how We pour out water in showers, then turn up the earth into furrow-slices and cause cereals to grow therein—grapes and green fodder; olive-trees and palm-trees; and luxuriant orchards, fruits, and grasses. . . . (Qur'ân 80:24-32)

Let us stop at this point of the quotation and ask ourselves the question: 'what for and for whom has this sumptuous meal been laid out?' The last line of the verse tells us that all these bounties of nature are there as "Provision for you as well as for your cattle".

Again, in the following verses, the bounties of nature are enumerated with the accent on animals' share in all of them:

> And He it is Who sends the winds, as glad tidings heralding His mercy. And We send down pure water from the clouds, that We may give life thereby, by watering the parched earth, and slake the thirst of those We have created both the animals and the human beings in multitude. (Qur'ân 25:48,49)

In numerous passages the Qur'ân explains the reason for everything, such as: the cosmos as an ordered whole; the dark nights and the bright days; the Earth with its immense expanse, shooting forth its moisture and its pastures; the stable mountains—all this, we are told, has been created for the benefit of man and animals. Below are some of such verses:

> And do they not see that We meander water to a barren land and sprout forth from it crops, whereof, their cattle, as well as they themselves, eat? Will they take no notice of it? (Qur'ân 32:27)
>
> We [God] brought forth from it [the earth] its waters and its pastures, and established the mountains

firm—as a source of provision for you and for your animals." (Qur'ân 79:31-33)

One could get the impression from these verses that they refer only to the livestock in whose welfare we have a vested interest. After reading the whole of the Qur'ân in this context, there remains no doubt that the message comprehends all animals, and not only domestic livestock. The following verses support this view:

> There is no moving creature on earth, but God provides for its sustenance. . . . (Qur'ân 11:6)
>
> And the Earth: He [God] has assigned to all living creatures. (Qur'ân 55:10)

In the words of Moses, as recorded in the Qur'ân: "Surely! The Earth belongs to God; He bequeaths it to whosoever He pleases of His servants. . . ." (Qur'ân 7:128).

The Qur'ân recounts the history of past nations to show how they fell into error and perished. There is an incident mentioned in the Qur'ân which is relevant to the subject under discussion. The tribe of Thamûd were the descendants of Prophet Noah. They have also been mentioned in the Ptolemaic records of Alexander's astronomer of the 2nd century A.C. The people of Thamûd demanded that the Prophet Saleh show them some sign to prove that he was a prophet of God. At that time the tribe was experiencing a dearth of food and water and was, therefore, neglecting its livestock. It was revealed to Prophet Saleh to single out a she-camel as a symbol and ask his people to give her a fair share of water and fodder. The people of Thamûd promised to do that but, later, killed the camel. As a retribution, the tribe was annihilated. This incident has been mentioned in the Qur'ân many times in different contexts (Qur'ân 7:73; 11:64; 26:155; 54:27-31).

This historic incident sets forth the essence of the Islamic teachings on 'Animal Rights'. Depriving them of their fair share in the resources of nature is so serious a sin in the eyes of God that it is punishable by punitive retribution. In the case of Thamûd, this retribution was so severe that the whole tribe was annihilated for this and other iniquities.

The Servitude Of Animals

Almost all religions allow the use of animals for necessary human needs. Man has always used them and their labour, just as human beings take each other in service. There seems to be nothing wrong in this arrangement, except that the animals are not capable of protecting their rights as human labour unions can do. The protection of animal rights is left mainly to human conscience, social censure, and government legislation; though the last does not count much, as the legislation always follows the trends of public opinion. Political leaders and reformers are two different species.

All religions have tried to regulate the use of animals humanely and with equity and justice. There are many laws in the Scriptures which cover specific cases; but the problem is that human needs and social conditions are constantly ringing the changes. Modern scientific and technological revelations, the current interlacing of global cultures, international and politico-economic pressures and numerous other influences are demanding modulation in our respective lifestyles. Our social and moral values are changing so fast that an average man is no longer sure how to act.

In this section the following subjects will be discussed from the Islamic point of view: Medical and other experiments on animals; Modern Hunting and Fishing for sport; Animal Fights; Beasts of Burden and other similar controversial fields.

The Islamic Juristic Rules

Most of the above-mentioned issues did not exist about fourteen centuries ago and, therefore, there was no occasion to pass any specific laws about them. It was felt sufficient to lay down general principles as guidelines. In cases like these, Islamic jurisprudence (*fiqh*) has left it to the Muslim Jurists (*fuqaha'a*) to use their judgement by inference and analogy. The first source of Islamic law (*sharia*) is the Qur'ân. The second source is Tradition (*Hadith*). The third is inference by analogy, called *Ijtihâd*. Since the law by analogy or *Ijtihâd* will be quoted in many cases below, a brief explanatory note is called for here.

With the expansion of Islam into vast empires there grew the need for law and justice by inference and analogy in cases which were not mentioned specifically in the Statutory Law of the Qur'ân and *Hadith*. During the early period of this development, the Muslim jurists were greatly influenced by Latin terms: *'jurisconsults'* or *'prudents'* were named in Arabic *'fuqaha'a'* (plural of *faqih*): the *'responsa prudentium'*, meaning 'answers to legal questions' were named *'qiyas'* in the sense of 'legal opinions' based on analogical deductions from the Qur'ân and *Hadith*. Some such 'opinions' by the jurists came to be accepted as 'canons' (*fatawa*, plural of *fatwa*)—similar to what is known in Roman law as *'jurisprudentia'* or *'responsa'* or 'case law' in the West. The Roman freedom of 'opinion' based on equity, in spite of the rescript of Hadrian, had originated from secular concepts and did not meet the theological requirements of Islam. It was, therefore, found necessary to codify the Islamic law by speculation (*qiyas*) into a reliable system which would be more in line with the spirit and intention of Qur'ânic and *Hadith* law. This system is known in Islam as 'law by *ijtihâd*'. *Ijtihâd* literally means 'to try hard to do or achieve something'.

The Islamic law by inference and analogy (*ijtihâd*) has long been a controversial issue among Muslims. This controversy is mainly due to the fear that the admissibility of the *ijtihâd* law could be used by some unconscientious theologians to take liberties with the spirit and intention of the law of *sharia* to suit their convenience and transitory exigencies. Others, however, feel strongly that a total rejection of analogy (*ijtihâd*) would close the doors for Muslims to make the necessary adaptations according to the changing conditions of life. This whole disputation could be resolved without much fuss if a fundamental principle of Islamic jurisprudence were to be understood. It is that: the law by analogy and inference (*ijtihâd*) is subordinate to the intrinsic spirit and intention of the laws of the Qur'ân and *Hadith*—just as the *Hadith* is subordinate to the Qur'ân. In fact, the jurists of the early Islamic era followed this principle and built-up juridical miscellanea which have been used for centuries and have been called case-law or 'Juristic Rules' (*qwâidatul-fiqhiyah*).

Any juristic opinion which does not conform to the *sharia* law, or even does not conform to its spirit and intention, would be rejected on the grounds of the above-stated principle. One example of such a case was the suggestion made by a Turkish leftist newspaper, *Cumhuriyet*, that the Islamic prohibition of pork-consumption be rescinded in modern Turkey.[14]

EXPERIMENTS ON ANIMALS

To kill animals to satisfy the human thirst for inessentials is a contradiction in terms within the Islamic tradition. Think of the millions of animals killed in the name of commercial enterprises in order to supply a complacent public with trinkets and products they do not really need. And why? Because people are too lazy or self-indulgent to find substitutes. Or to do without. It will take more than religious, moral, or ethical sermons to quell the avidity and greed of some multi-million/billion corporations and their willing customers.

Many of the experiments that are being done in the name of research and education are not really necessary. This kind of knowledge could easily be imparted by using charts, pictures, photographs, computer simulations, dummies or the corpses of animals that have died their natural death. In other spheres animals are poisoned, starved, blinded, subjected to electric shocks, or similarly abused in the alleged interests of science. Scientists generally scoff at religionists as sticklers for convention. Are scientists themselves doing any better by sticking to their primordial practices even when there are so many alternatives available now? It is very sad to see that even in the Islamic countries where Western curricula have to be followed in science subjects, similar unnecessary and inhuman experiments are being performed on animals. Those Muslim students are perhaps in ignorance of the fact that such experiments are in violation of Islamic teachings. Even if they were aware of it, it is doubtful whether they would have any sway in the matter.

Some research on animals may yet be justified, given the Traditions of Islam. Basic and applied research in the biological and social sciences, for example, will be allowed, if the laboratory animals are not caused pain or disfigured, and if human beings or other animals would benefit because of the research. The most important of all considerations is to decide whether the experiment is really necessary and that there is no alternative for it. The basic point to understand about using animals in science is that the same moral, ethical, and legal codes should apply to the treatment of animals as are applied to humans.

According to Islam, all life is sacrosanct and has a right of protection and preservation. The Prophet Mohammad laid so much emphasis on this point that he declared:

> There is no man who kills [even] a sparrow or anything smaller, without its deserving it, but God will question him about it.[15]

> He who takes pity [even] on a sparrow and spares its life, Allah will be merciful on him on the Day of Judgement.[16]

Like all other laws of Islam, its laws on the treatment of animals have been left open to exceptions and are based on the criterion: "Actions shall be judged according to intention."[17] Any kind of medical treatment of animals and experiments on them becomes ethical and legal or unethical and illegal according to the intention of the person who does it. If the life of an animal can be saved only by the amputation of a part of its body, it will be a meritorious act in the eyes of God to do so. Any code of law, including religious law, which is so rigid as not to leave a scope for exceptional circumstances, results in suffering and breeds hypocrisy.

According to all religions, all life, including animal life, is a trust from God. That is why, in the case of human life, suicide is considered to be the ultimate sin. The animals, however, do not possess the freedom of choice wilfully to terminate their own life and have to go on living their natural lives. When man subjects an animal to unnecessary pain and suffering and thus cuts short its natural life, he figuratively commits a suicide on behalf of that animal and a spiritual part of his own self dies with the animal. Most problems and wrangles about the use of animals in science as well as about their general treatment would become much easier to solve if only we could acknowledge the realism of nature and learn to treat all life on earth homogeneously without prejudice and selective standards.

Take, for example, a high-security jail where cut-throats, murderers, rapists, and other hardened criminals are imprisoned and compare it with a so-called research laboratory where innocent and helpless animals are cooped up in cages. By what stretch of imagination can we justify the difference in the living standards of these two places? What moral or ethical justification is there for the difference in their treatments? In the case of human prisoners, you are not allowed even to prick a pin in their flesh; while the animal captives are allowed to be lacerated and hacked by surgical knives in the name of science and research most of which is for futile commercial purposes. These and many other such disparities are being allowed in our human and so-called humane societies only because of the double standards of our moral and ethical values. The real and ideal approach to this problem would be to set forth for ourselves the criterion that any kind of medical or scientific research that is unlawful on humans is unlawful on animals.

HUMAN NEEDS AND INTERESTS (AL-MASÂLIH)

It has been mentioned earlier that certain kinds of cruelties which are being inflicted on animals these days did not exist at the time of the Prophet Mohammad and, therefore, they were not specifically cited in the law (*sharia*). Commercially motivated scientific experiments are one such case. We have to seek guidance on such issues by analogy and inference which is the third source of law, i.e. the Juristic Rules, based on *ijtihâd*. One of the main excuses for all kinds of artful cruelties to animals is selfish interest or human needs. Let us see how Juristic Rules define 'needs' and 'interests' and judge these cases according to those definitions. The basic Juristic Rule (*qâidatul-fiqhiyah*) that would apply to pecuniary experiments is: "One's interest or need does not annul other's right" (*al-idtirâru lâ yabtil haqqal-ghair*). The question arises that there are certain needs that deserve to be regarded as realistic and that the use of animals to fulfil such needs should be legitimate and justifiable. The Juristic Rules are well defined for such cases.

To begin with, needs are classified as follows:

(1) The necessities (*al-Masâlih ad-darûrîyah*); i.e. the essential needs or interests without which life could be not sustained.

(2) The requisites (*al-Masâlih al-hâjîyah*); needs or interests that are required for comfort from pain or any kind of distress, or for improving the quality of life.

(3) The luxuries (*al-Masâlih at tahsîniyah*); needs or interests that are desirable for exuberance, enjoyment, or even for self-indulgence.

It should be kept in mind that each of the above categories differs in degree, according to circumstances. These Juristic Rules can be applied to various situations of life; but, for the present, they concern us only in relation to the use of animals in science or otherwise.

Under the category (1) come the experiments which are absolutely essential for the well-being of both humans and animals and are done genuinely for medical research. The basic principles under which such experiments could be permissible are the following Juristic Rules (*qwâidatul-fiqhiyah*):

(a) "That without which a necessity cannot be fulfilled is itself a necessity."[18] This rule only states an exception, and underlines the importance of making sure that the experiment is really a necessity (*wajib*). However, after leaving the door open for the unavoidable necessary cases, all sorts of restrictive and prohibitive conditions have been imposed by the following Juristic Rules:

(b) "What allures to the forbidden, is itself forbidden."[19] This rule implies that material gains, including food, obtained by wrongful acts, such as unnecessary experiments on animals, become unlawful (*harâm*). The following verse of the Qur'ân supports this stand when it condemns those who fulfil their needs by illicit means, in these words:

> Why do not their learned men and doctors of law prohibit them from saying sinful things and from eating food gained by dishonest means? Certainly it is evil what they do." (Qur'ân 5:66)[20]

(c) "If two evils conflict, choose the lesser evil to prevent the bigger evil."[21] According to this rule, even genuine experiments on animals are allowed as an exception and as a lesser evil and not as a right.

(d) "Prevention of damage takes preference over the achievement of interests or fulfilment of needs."[22] This rule lays down the principle that the advantages and the disadvantages of an experiment should be weighed from all angles.

(e) "No damage can be put right."[23]

(f) "No damage can be put right by a similar or a greater damage."[24] When we damage our health and other interests by our own follies, we have no right to make the animals pay for it by inflicting similar or greater damage on them, such as by doing unnecessary experiments to find remedies for our self-induced ailments.

(g) "Resort to alternatives, when the original becomes undesirable."[25] This rule has a great bearing on the current controversy about the use of alternatives for animals in experiments, such as tissue-culture and other substitutes. Muslim experimenters should take this Juristic Rule seriously. It places a great moral responsibility on them, as well as on Muslim medical students, to find alternatives.

(h) "That which was made permissible for a reason, becomes impermissible by the absence of that reason."[26]

(i) "All false excuses leading to damage should be repudiated."[27]

The above two rules leave no excuse for Muslims to remain complacent about the current killings of animals in their millions for their furs, tusks, oils, and various other commodities. The excuse that such things are essential for human needs is no longer valid. Modern technology has produced all these things in synthetic materials and they are easily available all over the world, in some cases at a cheaper price. In olden days, for example, furs and skins were a necessity. Even the Qur'ân mentions the animals as a source of warm clothing (Qur'ân 16:5). However, this refers only to the skins and furs of domesticated cattle which either die their natural death or are slaughtered for food. There are millions of wild animals which are being killed these days commercially just for their furs and skins, while their carcasses are left to rot. Fourteen centuries ago, Islam realized the absurdity of this wasteful and cruel practice and passed laws to stop it in the following *Ahadith*:

> The Holy Prophet Mohammad prohibited the use of skins of wild animals."[28]
>
> The Holy Prophet forbade the skins of wild animals being used as floor coverings.[29]
>
> The Holy Prophet said: 'Do not ride on saddles made of silk or leopard skins.'[30]

It is important to note that the first *Hadith* covers all wild animals. The reason why leopard skins have been mentioned specifically could, perhaps, be that the Prophet might have seen someone using a saddle of leopard skin. Similarly, the specific mention of floor-coverings and saddles does not mean that they could be used for other purposes.

VIVISECTION

Given the practical approach of Islam to human imperfections and inadequacies, as said before, some research on animals and the concomitant surgical operations may yet be justifiable provided that they are carried out without pain and under anaesthetics; provided that the subject animal is put to sleep before it regains consciousness; provided that the animal is not disfigured; provided that it is done honestly and truly for knowledge and not for the promotion of commercial interests; provided that the operations are done by conscientious and qualified scientists; and provided that there is no alternative to it. It is comparatively easier to keep under control professionally qualified scientists and educational institutions, although experience shows that even some of them could be tempted to abuse their professional privilege. In view of the prevailing conditions in this field, a more uncompromising legislation would not be amiss.

According to the spirit and the overall teachings of Islam, causing avoidable pain and suffering to the defenceless and innocent creatures of God is not justifiable under any circumstances. No advantages and no urgency of human needs would justify the kind of calculated violence which is being done these days against animals, especially through international trade of livestock and meat. One of the sayings of the Prophet Mohammad tells us: "if you must kill, kill without torture".[31] While pronouncing this dictum, he did not name any animal as an exception—not even any noxious or venomous creature, such as scorpions and snakes. People are allowed to kill them only if they become a threat to life or limb, and even then, without torture.

Luckily, on this theme, there are quite a few of the Prophet's sayings. During the pre-Islamic period, certain pagan superstitions and polytheistic practices involving acts of torture and general cruelties to animals used to be common in Arabia. All such practices were condemned and stopped by Islam. The following few sayings of the Prophet will serve as an example: "Jabir told that God's Messenger forbade striking the face or branding on the face of animals."

The same companion of the Prophet reported him as saying, when an ass which had been branded on its face passed him by: 'God curse the one who branded it.'[32] This *Hadith* is concerned with causing pain to the animal on sensitive parts of its body, as well as with the disfigurement of its appearance.

When the Prophet migrated to Medina from Mecca in 622 A.C., people there used to cut off camels' humps and the fat tails of sheep. The Prophet ordered this barbaric practice to be stopped. The temptation for the people to perform this sort of vivisection on the animals was that the juicy humps and fatty tails could be eaten while the animal remained alive for future use. To remove this avidity, he declared: "Whatever is cut off an animal, while it is still alive, is carrion and is unlawful (*harâm*) to eat."[33]

To make sure that no injury was inflicted on an animal while there was even a flicker of life in it, it was forbidden by the Prophet to molest the carcass in any way, for example: by breaking its neck, skinning, or slicing off any of its parts, until the body was dead cold. One of his sayings on this theme is. "Do not deal hastily with a 'being' before it is stone dead."[34] Hazrat 'Omar ibn al-Khattab used to instruct repeatedly: "Give time to the slaughtered 'being' till it is dead cold."[35]

Many other Muslim authorities have also given juristic opinions (*fatâwa*) to the effect that, after slaughter, time should be given for the *rigor mortis* to set in before cutting up the carcass.[36]

Another malpractice in Arabia in those days was stopped by the Prophet in these words: "Do not store milk in the dugs (udders) of animals, and whoever buys such animals, has the option to keep them or return them."[37] Storing of milk in the dug was perhaps done to preserve milk longer, or to beguile the prospective buyers.

Not only physical but also emotional care of animals was so much emphasized by the Prophet that he once reprimanded his wife, A'ishah, for treating a camel a bit offhandedly. Hazrat A'ishah herself narrates: "I was riding a restive camel and turned it rather roughly. The Prophet said to me: 'it behoves you to treat the animals gently'."[38]

The Prophet himself was once reprimanded by God for neglecting his horse, as the following *Hadith* tells us: "The Prophet was seen wiping the face of his horse with his gown (*jullabiyah*). When asked why he was doing that, he replied: 'Last night I had a reprimand from Allah regarding my horse for having neglected him."[39]

The following *Hadith* forbids the disfiguration of the body of an animal. "The Prophet said: 'Do not clip the forelock of a horse, for a decency is attached to its forelock; nor its mane, for it protects it; nor its tail, for it is its fly flap'."[40]

There are many *Ahadith* forbidding blood sports and the use of animals as targets, some of which are as follows:

> The Prophet condemned those people who take up anything alive as a mere sport.[41]
>
> The Prophet forbade blood sports, like the Bedouins.[42]
>
> The Prophet said: 'Do not set up living creatures as a target.'[43]
>
> The Prophet condemned those who use a living creature as a target.[44]

The Prophet forbade an animal being made a target.[45]

The Prophet was reported as saying: 'Do not make anything having life as a Target.'[46]

Ibn 'Umar happened to pass by a party of men who had tied up a hen and were shooting arrows at it. When they saw Ibn 'Umar coming, they scampered off. Ibn 'Umar angrily remarked: 'Who has done this? Verily! Allah's Messenger has invoked a curse upon one who does this kind of thing.'[47]

The Prophet passed by some children who were shooting arrows at a ram. He told them off, saying: 'Do not maim the poor beast.'[48]

The fact that these *Ahadith* repeat the same sayings of the Prophet in slightly varying wordings show that he took the matter very seriously and repeated them again and again on different occasions in the presence of different people. Another significant point to note in this respect is that, to stop the use of animals as targets or in blood sports, the Prophet did the same as he did in the case of camel-humps (*harâm*) for consumption, according to the following *Hadith*:

God's Messenger forbade eating a *mujaththema* [carrion] of a bird or animal set up and shot at as a target for shooting.[49]

One might also appeal to the Islamic law (*sharia*) to oppose animals in military research in general and in the so-called wound laboratories in particular. The above-quoted *Ahadith*, as well as the Juristic Rules, would seem to support the view that our wars are our own problems and that we have no right to make the animals suffer for them.

There is no doubt that the Islamic prohibition against the cutting or injuring of live animals, especially when it results in pain and suffering, does apply to modern vivisection in science. We are able to support this interpretation of the Islamic teachings by referring not only to the above-quoted representative Traditions (*Ahadith*), but also to the Qur'ân. In the verses quoted below, we find expressed the principle that any interference with the body of a live animal, which causes pain or disfigurement is contrary to the Islamic precepts. These verses were revealed in condemnation of the pagan superstitious custom that the she-camels, ewes, or nanny goats which had brought forth a certain number of young ones in a certain order should have their ears slit, be let loose and dedicated to idols. Such customs were declared by the Qur'ân as devilish acts, in these words:

> It was not God who instituted the practice of a slit-ear she-camel, or a she-camel let loose for free pasture, or a nanny-goat let loose. . . ." (Qur'ân 5:106)

> "God cursed him [Satan] for having said: 'I shall entice a number of your servants, and lead them astray, and I shall arouse in them vain desires; and I shall instruct them to slit the ears of cattle; and, most certainly, I shall bid them—so that they will corrupt God's creation'. Indeed! He who takes Satan as a friend rather than God, ruins himself manifestly." (Qur'ân 4:118,119)

Animal fights, such as bull- and cockfighting, are another kind of vivisection. The only difference is that, in this case, man does not do it himself—he makes the animals tear each other apart to provide amusement for him. Those who seek entertainment in such scenes of violence and if the sight of blood warms their own blood, would do better by watching more television. All kinds of animal-fights are strictly forbidden in Islam. Out of the numerous such injunctions, one would suffice here:

> God's Messenger forbade inciting animals to fight each other.[50]

It is interesting to note that, like the camel-humps, fat-tails of sheep and target-animals (*mujaththema*) as stated above, the meat of animals which die as a result of fights is also declared in Islam as unlawful to eat (*harâm*). For example, the Spaniards hold fiestas on special occasions to eat the bull killed by a matador. There is no room here to give the gruesome details of such bullfights. Suffice it to say that the meat of such animals is *harâm* (forbidden) for the

Muslims. One wonders how and why, in this day and age, such cruelties to animals are being tolerated by the civilized world. Even in England some revoltingly cruel dogfights have been brought to light, some of which have resulted in prosecutions.

FACTORY-FARMING

Man's exploitation of animals and the resources of nature is spreading like an epidemic. The contagious influence of the West has started affecting the character and destiny of the developing countries. Formerly, in those countries, cruelty to animals used to be inflicted mostly through individual ignorance and the lack of veterinary facilities. Now it is becoming a mammonish creed of rapacious grabbing by fair means or foul. The agrarian mismanagement, referred to above, is particularly of concern to the environmentalists because of the change in our attitude to nature which has characterized the last forty years or so. This concern for nature becomes deeper when it applies to farm animals and wildlife, whose dependence on ecology is absolute. Those developing countries which have started copying the current methods of agriculture and animal husbandry should try to learn from the mistakes of the West.

Ever since the enclosure of commonly owned land, an ecologically sound system of farming had been developed in the West, based on the beneficial interaction between the animal and the soil. Thus, in the simplest rotation called the Norfolk four-course rotation, a quarter of the farm would be down to root crops such as the cattle food called mangolds or mangels and swedes or turnips; a quarter to barley; a quarter to clover-grass mixture and a quarter to wheat. Each year the fields would be rotated, so that the exhausting and the restorative crops would alternate for the benefit of fertility. As a field never had the same crop growing on it for two years in succession, crop weeds and pests, as well as fungus diseases were prevented from building up.

Sheep, not without cause called the golden hoof, grazed over at least half the farm each year and enriched the soil. Flocks would graze the barley and wheat stubbles as well as the clover leys after the hay crop had been taken. They were also to be seen arable-folded during the wintertime on turnips. All the crop and animal by-products such as straw and manure were jealously conserved and had to be returned to the soil. A tenant-farmer could be dispossessed if he burned even a small amount of straw, or sold hay off the farm. In the rotational mixed farming system, animals were related to the land and to the benefit of both. The "rules of good husbandry" were written into every tenancy agreement and no one considered breaking them.

Today this cyclic system has been displaced by a straight-line system on many farms in the Western so-called developed countries, and the costs are only now being realized, with a consequent trend to reintroduce many of the old techniques. Let us look at what happened.

Increasingly, the animals were taken off the land and reared intensively, tightly packed together in the windowless houses of factory farms. They were not allowed straw to lie on because this would mean extra labour and would in any case block the pumps that deal with the slurry effluent. The fields, devoid of live-stock, were brought back into large hundred-acre blocks by the removal of hedges and trees and the filling in of ditches. Instead of a variety of cropping, the most profitable crop—barley—was grown continuously and each year an embarrassing bulk of straw burned in the field where the combine harvesters had left it. The soil structure started to deteriorate, and fertility could only be maintained by ever-increasing doses of artificial high nitrogen fertilizers until the soil, devoid of micro-life, became addicted to chemicals. Plant diseases and pests proliferated like the plagues of ancient Egypt and could only be controlled by recourse to the agricultural chemist's skill in devising toxic sprays. Weeds also were able to pose a challenge to the spray manufacturers. The weeds of old that the harvester knew—poppies, charlock, and thistles—used to be kept in check by through-cultivation methods. Herbicides quickly eliminated these weeds, and a new spectrum of more troublesome weeds arose, such as Shepherd's Purse and Pierts Parsley. Wildlife disappeared from the cultivated areas, retreating to woodlands and motorway (highway) banks.

Now a host of new troubles are being studied. Scientists are asking whether there is a link between some of the diseases of modern life, particularly cancer, and forced-growth crops and forced-growth animals. In some parts of the country the water supply has been so contaminated with nitrogen run-off from fields that it is considered unsafe for life in general, and for babies in particular. Rivers and streams have become septic where no aquatic life can survive. Concern about the deterioration in wildlife, especially insects, is making itself felt in the same way as the deterioration of frogs in some of the developing countries. Added to all this catalogue of concern is the growing pressure on politicians and economists from some scientists and the lay public about the welfare and protection of animals. Even the religious institutions are starting to murmur that the "Covenant" was not made with man alone, but with the non-human species also.

The politicians and economists of those Islamic countries which have started following blindfold in the footsteps of the West should ask themselves a few pertinent questions at this stage before they get their countries entangled inextricably in the Western system of farming and animal husbandry. Do these animals, upon which man has always depended for his food, have certain basic rights? For instance, the right to the companionship of their own kind, the right to an appropriate diet to keep them in health, and the right to a natural life and a painless death? If their Divine Creator gave them legs, is it not a blasphemy to shut them in crates where they are unable to walk? Are we perhaps forcing them back upon their own evolution by taking them from the fields and the hills and putting them in rows, unmoving—like rows of vegetables? In so doing, are we perhaps reversing our own evolution and becoming more bestial ourselves, unable to know right from wrong? Let us look at some of these areas of concern.

The patient dairy cow is now forced by genetics and nutritional science to yield many times more milk than her forbears did only a few years ago, and to such an extent as to shorten her productive life to about three years. Her calves, which bring her into milk with their birth, are taken from her at one or two days old, artificially fed and then put into the market, probably to be bought by veal farmers. Such is the stress and trauma of the market that many of the calves pick up enteric diseases during this stage and so need medication with antibiotics on the receiving farm.

Some veal farmers rear the calves in communal pens on beds of straw, but there are still others who put the calves into narrow crates as soon as they are brought onto the farm. There they stay unable to walk, gambol or even turn round until they are ready for slaughter at about 16 to 20 weeks old. Although calves are highly social animals, they cannot touch one another and can scarcely see each other in their restrictive crates. They lie on bare wooden slats so that the dung and urine can be cleared away mechanically as slurry. Although ruminant and having a strong urge to chew the cud, they are denied any sort of roughage and so pluck the hair from their own shoulders and flanks to satisfy their appetites. Any slaughterman will tell you that the stomachs of these calves contain indigestible hairballs.[iii]

There is a biological similarity between the veal calves and swine. Like swine, they are cloven-footed but do not chew the cud. Are they therefore unclean in terms laid down in Leviticus 11:7, prohibiting the Jews from eating pork? This question will be dealt with later in the book.

Chickens kept for egg production are packed tightly into wire cages and kept there all their productive lives crouching on a sloping wire floor. The sole purpose of their existence is supposed to be to lay eggs, and they are denied any other inherited behaviour. They cannot stretch their wings out. Indeed, the wingspan of a battery hen is 76 cm or thereabouts, yet five or sometimes even six are crowded into a cage. In the European Union each hen is given only 550 square centimetres of floor space, in many countries each hen has even less than this. In neither case has she enough space to spread her wings. The hens cannot scratch the ground, searching for seeds or grubs; they cannot dust-bathe; they cannot even flee from a more aggressive cage mate.

---

iii **Editor's Note:** Although this cruel method of rearing calves for veal has recently been phased out in the European Union, it is still in widespread use elsewhere. Despite the fact that the EU ban came into place by the year 2007 A.C., veal crates continue to be used in other countries such as the U.S.A.

Perhaps the most offensive aspect of all this is the contempt for life which is bred into the modern farmer. Even cattle are no longer individuals but numbers in a herd. Poultry flocks are not numbered in hundreds these days but in tens of thousands. Will this contempt affect our sensibilities and eventually be extended to others of our own species? Even from the spiritual point of view, meat of such animals is unhealthy to eat. Our dieticians do not lay enough stress on the point, but the history of nations bears out the fact that there is a strong ethological link between diet and character formation. Animals reared under unnatural and inhumane conditions become frustrated, morose, and cantankerous. Such characteristics are passed on to those who eat their meat, though it may take many generations to show. The biological laws of nature are the same for the human species as for other animals. Their diet, environment and general living conditions affect all of them alike. Like human beings, animals too have a sense of individuality. The Qur'ân repeatedly confirms this fact. Even chickens are individuals and, if given the chance, will demonstrate their own characters peculiar to each individual.

The writer knows of a hen who is six years old. A farmer friend of his bought her with a dozen of her sisters from a battery farm some years ago—poor, featherless, demented things. They then were unable to perch and stared vacantly at the new experience called 'grass'. It was something out of this world for her, until taught by other freer cousins the joys of free-range. This hen, called 'One-tail', because she only ever did grow one feather in her tail, now enters the house through the cat-flap and challenges the cat to its dinner.

The emotions of animals and of human beings are, no doubt, the same, even though we may differ in our respective needs and in degree. They feel pain and joy, they fear and feel relief, they experience an advanced sense of fun—just as human beings do.

We have to ask ourselves all these and many more questions. The basic moral question is—how right is it to deny these creatures of God their natural instincts so that we may eat the end product? For Muslims these questions pose the additional question of a fundamental moral pertinence—would our Prophet Mohammad have approved of the modern methods of intensive farming systems if he were alive today? His overwhelming concern for animal rights and their general welfare would certainly have condemned (la'ana) those who practice such methods, in the same way as he condemned similar other cruelties in his day. He would have declared that there is no grace or blessing (barakah)—neither in the consumption of such food nor in the profits from such trades. These are not just hypothetical questions. The cruel and inhumane methods of intensive farming are being practiced in most Islamic countries these days, even in countries where indigence is no excuse.

For some years, the developing countries, including the Islamic countries, have been importing high technology farming systems from the West, and the trend is growing fast. According to figures published in the "World Poultry" gazette for October 1984, European firms have developed special projects of high technology farming units for the Middle East. One of their laying houses in Egypt is producing 25 million eggs per year. According to the same gazette, similar projects have been installed in Saudi Arabia, Libya, Morocco, Tunisia, Oman, and other Middle Eastern States. Pakistan, Indonesia, and other Islamic countries are following suit. Under the intensive farming system, a hen lays on average over 300 eggs a year. One can imagine from the above figures how many millions of hens are being subjected to the un-Islamic methods of food production in all these Islamic countries put together.

Most of these un-Islamic businesses are flourishing in Islamic countries due to the ignorance of the consumer public. People do not know how meat chickens are being reared, how they have been bred to grow excessively fast and how they are being fed on diets to fatten them even faster to produce more meat, more quickly. Fowls and other food animals are no longer creatures of God; they are numbers in computers. After all, computers can give the breeders up-to-the-minute figures of profit and loss at the touch of a button, while God's reckoning is a long way off in the Hereafter. If only the average, simple and God-fearing Muslim consumers of such food-animals knew the gruesome details about the Westernized meat industry in their own Islamic countries, they would become vegetarians rather than eat such sacrilegious meat. The least that the Muslim 'Ulamā' can do is to inform the lay public how their food is being produced, so that people can—with knowledge—decide what to do about it. Some may decide that the products of intensive factory farms are not suitable, both from religious and health points of view, and seek more naturally produced eggs and meat such as free range or organic; or give up eating meat altogether.

General Reforms Of Islam

The Islamic teachings have gone to great lengths to instil a sense of love, respect, and compassion for animals. As already mentioned, some of the cruelties to animals which used to be practiced during and before the time of the Prophet were stopped by him. However, we come across many cruel practices these days which, though not mentioned in the Islamic law, are obviously against the very spirit of the teachings of Islam. It is sad to see that most of these cruelties are taking place in so-called civilized Western countries. However, it is encouraging to see that the protest of the Western animal welfarists against all kinds of cruel exploitation of animals is well organized and, hopefully, will prevail.

From the Islamic point of view, however, the worrying thing is that the developing countries, including most of the Islamic countries, have started emulating their Western preceptors in practices such as intensive farming methods; use of insecticides which are harmful to human and animal health and do more damage to the environment than good to crops; and export of animals in millions for exotic foods, or for profit-motivated experiments to manufacture cosmetics and other such luxuries. Better and quicker returns, plus the feeling that civilized Western society has given its tacit approval to these and many other cruel methods of making money, are corroding the moral ethos of the underdeveloped as well as the affluent nations of the East. Islam's directive teachings in cases like these are very helpful and educational, as the few examples given below will show:

The Moral Appeal Of Islam

Most of the sermons from our pulpits are admonitions against sin. If someone were inclined to choose a subject pertaining to animal welfare, there is enough material in every scripture to choose from.

For example, here are two sayings of the Prophet Mohammad which could make very appropriate themes for such sermons. In the following sayings, the Prophet has placed the killing of animals without a justifiable reason as one of the major sins:

> Avoid you the seven obnoxious things [deadly sins]: polytheism; magic; the killing of breathing beings, which God has forbidden except for a rightful reason.[iv & 51]

> The baneful [sinful] things are: polytheism; disobedience to parents; the killing of breathing beings.[52]

The Prophet has even tried the 'Punishment and Reward' approach in the following *Ahadith*:

> The Prophet told his companions of a woman who would be sent to Hell for having locked up a cat; not feeding it, nor even releasing it so that it could feed herself.[53] (This *Hadith* has been recorded by almost all the authentic books of *Hadith*, as Ref. No. 53 will show).

> The Prophet told his companions of a serf who was blessed by God for saving the life of a dog, by giving it water to drink, and quenching its thirst.[54]

> The Prophet was asked if acts of charity even to the animals were rewarded by God. He replied: 'Yes, there is a reward for acts of charity to every beast alive.'[55]

> "Mishkat Al-Masabih" concluded from "Bukhari" and "Muslim" to the effect that: 'A good deed done to a beast is as good as doing good to a human being; while an act of cruelty to a beast is as bad as an act of cruelty to human beings' and that: 'Kindness to animals was promised by rewards in Life Hereafter.'[56]

---

iv The Arabic word for 'breathing beings' is '*nafs*'. Until recently it used to be taken as meaning 'human beings' only. All the Arabic dictionaries give the meaning of '*nafs*' as '*rûh*' (soul), and since they are breathing creatures, there seems to be no reason why the Qur'ânic verses No. 6:151,152 and others should not comprehend all 'breathing beings', i.e. all species of animals. These verses should be read in conjunction with other verses of the Qur'ân and numerous *Ahadith* which speak of the sanctity of life as a whole, declare animals as possessing soul (*rûh*) and place animals physically on a par with human beings.

BEASTS OF BURDEN

The following *Ahadith* lay down the principles that animals in the service of man should be used only when necessary and for the purpose for which they are meant, and that their comfort should not be neglected:

> The Prophet once saw a man sitting on the back of his camel in a market place, addressing people. He said to him: 'Do not use the backs of your beasts as pulpits, for God has made them subject to you so that they may take you to places you could not otherwise reach without fatigue of body.'[57]

> The Prophet once passed by a lean camel whose belly had shrunk to its back. 'Fear God' he said to the owner of the camel, 'in these dumb animals and ride them only when they are fit to be ridden, and let them go free when it is meet that they should rest.'[58]

About taking care of animals during travelling, the Prophet used to give the following advice:

> When you journey through a verdant land, [go slow to] let your camels graze. When you pass through an arid area, quicken your pace [lest hunger should enfeeble the animals]. Do not pitch your tents for the night on the beaten tracks, for they are the pathways of nocturnal creatures.[59]

Saying daily prayers (*salat*) is one of the five most important obligations of the Muslim religion. In the following *Hadith*, one of his companions tells us that the Prophet and his fellow travellers used to delay even saying their prayers until they had first given their riding and pack animals fodder and had attended to their needs:

> When we stopped at a halt, we did not say our prayers until we had taken the burdens off our camels' backs and attended to their needs.[60]

> Hazrat Imam Ali's[v] general advice about pack-animals is: "Be kind to pack-animals; do not hurt them; and do not load them more than their ability to bear."[61]

---

v   **Editor's note:** The Prophet's close companion, third Caliph after the Prophet, and his cousin, and son-in-law.

MENTAL CRUELTY

Islam's concern for animals goes beyond the prevention of physical cruelty to them which, logically, is a negative proposition. It enjoins on the human species, as the principal primates of the animated world, to take over the responsibility for all creatures in the spirit of a positive philosophy of life and to be their active protectors. Prevention of physical cruelty is not enough; mental cruelty is equally important. In this age of scientific research and knowledge, it should not be difficult to comprehend that these so-called 'dumb animals', too, have feelings and emotional responses. Dogs, cats, and various other animals that have become part of human society as pets were originally untamed brutish animals. It was only love and care that won their confidence in man; and it is only their ill treatment and neglect by man that brings back the beast in them.

The incidents of the Prophet Mohammad's personal grooming of his horse; his wife A'isha's rough handling of her camel; the Prophet's prohibition of cutting forelocks, the mane or tail; the condemnation of striking and branding on the face or ears—all these and many other such *Ahadith* show that this great man Mohammad had realized even fourteen centuries ago that animals have a sense of adornment and sensitivity. In the following incident, a bird's emotional distress has been treated as seriously as a physical injury:

> We were on a journey with the Apostle of God and he left us for a while. During his absence, we saw a bird called *hummara* with its two young and took the young ones. The mother-bird was circling above us in the air, beating its wings in grief, when the Prophet came back and said: 'who has hurt the FEELINGS of this bird by taking its young? Return them to her'.[62]
>
> It is reported by the same authority that: "a man once robbed some eggs from the nest of a bird. The Prophet had them restored to the nest."[63]

Slaughter Of Food Animals

One wonders why Islam, with all its concern for animals, has allowed its followers to consume their meat and has not asked them to become vegetarian, like some other religions. The question of vegetarianism and meatarianism will be discussed later. Let us accept the fact that Islam has allowed the slaughter of animals for food and see what instructions it gives us to ensure humane slaughter, with as little pain to the victim as possible. The following *Ahadith* are self-explanatory:

> God's Messenger was reported as saying: 'Allah Who is Blessed and Exalted, has prescribed benevolence towards everything [and has ordained that everything be done in a good way]; so, when you must kill a living being, do it in the best manner and, when you slaughter an animal, you should [use the best method and] sharpen your knife so as to cause the animal as little pain as possible'.[64]
>
> The Messenger of Allah was heard forbidding to keep waiting a quadruped or any other animal for slaughter.[65]
>
> The Prophet forbade all living creatures to be slaughtered while tied up and bound.[66]
>
> The Prophet said to a man who was sharpening his knife in the presence of the animal: 'Do you intend inflicting death on the animal twice—once by sharpening the knife within its sight, and once by cutting its throat?'[67]
>
> Hazrat Iman Ali says: "Do not slaughter sheep in the presence of other sheep, or any animal in the presence of other animals".[68]
>
> Hazrat Omar[vi] once saw a man denying a sheep, which was going to slaughter, a satiating measure of water to drink. He gave the man a beating with his lash and told him: 'Go, water it properly at the time of its death, you knave!'[69]

---

vi **Editor's Note:** The second Caliph, after the Prophet.

It is reported that Hazrat Omar once saw a man sharpening his knife to slaughter a sheep, while he was holding the cast sheep down with his foot placed on its face. He started lashing the man until he took to his heels. The sheep, meanwhile, had scampered off.[70]

CONCLUSION

There seems to be no better winding up of this chapter than by quoting a great Muslim theologian of the 20th century—Sayyid Abû A'la Maudadi (1903-79 A.C.). This is what he says about the rights of animals and their general treatment in the light of the teachings of Islam:

> God has honoured man with authority over His countless creatures. Everything has been harnessed for him. He has been endowed with the power to subdue them and make them serve his objectives. This superior position gives man an authority over them and he enjoys the right to use them as he likes. But that does not mean that God has given him unbridled liberty. Islam says that all the creation has certain rights upon man. They are: he should not waste them on fruitless ventures nor should he unnecessarily hurt or harm them. When he uses them for his service he should cause them the least possible harm, and should employ the best and the least injurious methods of using them.
>
> The law of Islam embodies many injunctions about these rights. For instance, we are allowed to slaughter animals for food and have been forbidden to kill them merely for fun or sport and deprive them of their lives without necessity. . . . Similarly, killing an animal by causing continuous pain and injury is considered abominable in Islam. Islam allows the killing of dangerous and venomous animals and of beasts of prey only because it values man's life more than theirs. But here too it does not allow their killing by resort to prolonged painful methods.
>
> Regarding the beasts of burden and animals used for riding and transport, Islam distinctly forbids man

to keep them hungry, to take hard and intolerable work from them and to beat them cruelly. To catch birds and imprison them in cages without any special purpose is considered abominable. What to say of animals: Islam does not approve even of the useless cutting of trees and bushes. Man can use their fruit and other produce, but he has no right to destroy them. Vegetables, after all, possess life, but Islam does not allow the waste of even lifeless things; so much so that is disapproves of the wasteful flow of too much water. Its avowed purpose is to avoid waste in every conceivable form and to make the best use of all resources living and lifeless.[71]

REFERENCES AND NOTES (CHAPTER 1)

1. Hasan bin Haitham, a famous Muslim philosopher and scientist (Cir. 11th century A.C.), the father and pioneer of Optics and Experimentalism, known in Europe as 'Al-Hazen'. He belonged to the first school of Scholasticism called the 'Academy of Science and Philosophy' which was founded by Abu Huzaifa Wasil in the early 8th century A.C. as quoted in *The Spirit of Islam*; Syed Amir Ali; 10th Edition; Chatto & Windus, London; June 1964; p.424.

2. Maulana Jalal-ud-Din Rumi—one of the most eminent 'orthodox' Muslim theologians and sages (1207-1273 A.C. = 585-651 A.H.). (As quoted in the same Ref. No. 1); p.425.

3. cf. *Tabari's Commentary*, 2:65; *Manar*, 6:448; for *Taghut* in the sense of evil. Also see Razi.

4. *Maxims of Ali*; translated by Al-Halal from *Nahj-ul-Balagha* (in Arabic); Sh. Muhammad Ashraf, Lahore, Pakistan; p.436. (Hereafter referred to as *Maxims.*) The Imam, Hazrat Ali bin Abi Talib was the son-in-law of the Prophet Mohammad, and the fourth Caliph (644-656 A.C.—22-34 A.H.).

5. Narrated by Anas. *Mishkat al-Masabih*, 3:1392; quoted from *Bukhari*.

6. *Wisdom of Prophet Muhammad*; Muhammad Amin; The Lion Press, Lahore, Pakistan;1945.

7. *Bukhari* and *Muslim*.

8. Juristic Rules serve as legal maxims in the Islamic jurisprudence (*Fiqh*).

9. *Maxims* (see Ref. No.4); pp.203,381.

10. cf. *Razi* and *Al-Azhari*, as quoted in *Manar II* (in Arabic); p.248.

11. *The Message of the Qur'ân*; Muhammad Asad; Dar al-Andalus, Gibraltar; 1980; footnotes 18,19; p.359.

12. *Musnad of Ahmad*, 5:440 and 3:184. (Hereafter referred to as Musnad).

13. *Basic Writings of Husn-Tzu*; Burton Watson; Colombia University Press, New York; 1963; p.106.

14. *Arabia*—The Islamic World Review; Vol.4, No.49, September 1985; Slough, England; p.11.

15. Narrated by Ibn 'Omar and by Abdallah bin Al-Âs. *An-Nasaî*, 7:206,239, Beirut. Also recorded by *Musnad al-Jami—Ad-Darimi*; Delhi, 1337. Also *Mishkat al-Masabih*: English translation by James Robson, in four volumes; Sh. Muhammad Ashraf, Lahore, Pakistan; 1963 (hereafter referred to as 'Robson').

16. Narrated by Abu Umama. Transmitted by *Al-Tabarani*.

17. In Arabic: "*Al-A'amâlo binniyah*".

18. In Arabic: "*Mâ lâ yatimmu al-wajib illâ behi, fahuwa wajib*".

19. In Arabic: "*Mâ ad'â ela al-harame, fahuwa haramun*".

20. *The Meaning of the Glorious Qur'ân*; English translation by Marmaduke Pickthall; George Allen & Unwin Ltd., London; 1957; verse 63, chapt.5.

21. In Arabic: "*Idhâ ta'ârada mafsadatani ru'iya â'zamahuma dararan be irtikabe akhfa-huma*".

22. In Arabic: "*Dar'ul-mafâsid muqaddamun 'ala jalb-ul-masâlih*".
23. In Arabic: "*Ad-dararu lâ yuzâlu*".
24. In Arabic: "*Ad-dararu lâ yuzâlu be mislehi au be dararin akbaro minho*".
25. In Arabic: "*Iza ta'zuro al-aslu, yusaru ila-l-badle*".
26. In Arabic: "*Mâ jaza le uzrin, batala be zawalehi*".
27. In Arabic: "*Sadduz-zarae al-mua'ddiyate ela-l-fasâd*".
28. Narrated by Abu Malik on the authority of his father. *Abu Dawûd* and *Tirmidhi* as recorded in *Garden of the Righteous—Riyad as-Salihîn* of Imam Nawawi; translated by M.Z. Khan; Curzon Press, London, 1975; (hereafter referred to as *Riyad*); Hadith No. 815, p.160.
29. id.
30. Narrated by Mu'awiah. *Abu Dawûd*; (see Riyad, Ref. No. 28); Hadith No. 814, p.160.
31. In Arabic: "*Lâ taqtolu bi'l-îdhâ'i*".
32. Narrated by Jabir bin Abdullah. *Muslim*, Vol. 3, Hadith No. 2116. Also *Awn al-Ma'bûd Sharh Abu Dawud* (hereafter referred to as *Awn*); 7:232, Hadith No. 2547. Also *The Lawful and Unlawful in Islam* (in Arabic); Yusuf el-Kardawi; Mektebe Vahba, Cairo; 1977; p.293. Also '*Robson*' (Ref. No. 15); p.872.
33. Narrated by Abu Waqid al-Laithi. *Tirmidhi*; Hadith No. 1480, Ch. on *Al-At'imah*. Also '*Robson*'. (Ref. No. 15) p.874.
34. "*Kitab al-Muqni*", 3:542. Also "*Al-Muhallâ*", 7:457; Ibn Hazm; (both in Arabic).
35. "*Al-Muhallâ*", 7:457; Ibn Hazm; (in Arabic). Hazrat 'Omar ibn al-Khattab was the second Caliph (634-644 A.C. = 12-22 A.H.).
36. *Kitab al-Nîl wa Shifâ' al-Alîl*", 4:460; (in Arabic).
37. *Muslim* and *Bukhari*. Also *Holy Traditions*; 1st Edition; Vol.1; Muhammad Manzur Ilahi; Ripon Press, Lahore, Pakistan; 1932; p.149.
38. Narrated by A'ishah. *Muslim*, Vol. 4, Hadith No. 2593. Also *Awn*, 7:155, Hadith No. 2461; (Ref. No. 32).
39. Narrated by Yahya bin Saîd. "*Malik bin Anas al-Asbhahî.*" Also *Al-Muwatta*, (in English); Divan Press, Norwich, England; 1982; p.205.
40. Narrated by 'Utbah ibn Farqad Abû Abdillah al-Sulamî. *Abu Dawûd*. Also *Awn*, 7:216, 217, Hadith No. 2525; (Ref. No. 32).
41. Narrated by Abdullah bin 'Omar. *Muslim*, Vol. 3, Hadith No. 1958.
42. Narrated by Abdulla Ibn Abbas. *Awn*, (Ref. No. 32); 8:15, Hadith No. 2803. Also '*Robson*'; p.876. (Ref. No. 15, but it does not mention 'Bedouins').
43. Narrated by Abdullah bin Abbas. *Muslim*, Vol. 3, Hadith No. 1957. Also '*Robson*'; p.872; (Ref. No. 15).
44. Narrated by Abdullah bin 'Omar. *Bukhari* and *Muslim*. Also '*Robson*'; p.872. (Ref. No. 15).
45. Narrated by Anas. Recorded by Riyad. (Ref. No. 28); Hadith No. 1606; p.272.
46. Narrated by Ibn Abbas. *Sahih Muslim—Kitab-us-Saîd Wa'dh-Dhabâ'ih*"; Ch. DCCCXXII, Vol. III; Sh. Muhammad Ashraf, Lahore, Pakistan, 1976; Hadith No. 4813; p.1079; (hereafter referred to as *Kitab-us-Saîd*).

47. id. Narrated by Saîd bin Jubair.

48. Narrated by Abdallah bin Ja'far. *An-Nasaî*, 7:238.

49. Narrated by Waqid al-Laithi. *Abu al-Darda. Tirmidhi*, Hadith No. 1473, Ch. '*Al-At'imah*'. Also '*Robson*' (Ref. No. 15); p. 874.

50. Narrated by Abdullah bin Abbas. *Bukhari, Muslim, Tirmidhi* and *Abu Al-Darda*; recorded in *Riyad* (Ref. No. 28); Hadith No. 1606; p.271. Also '*Robson*' (Ref. No. 15); p.876.

51. Narrated by Abu Huraira. *Sahih Muslim—Kitab-ul-Iman* (Ref. No. 46); Ch. XXXIX, Vol. I; p.52. *Bukhari*, 4:23. Also Awn, (Ref. No. 32); Hadith No. 2857.

52. id. Narrated by Abdullah Ibn'Amr.

53. Narrated by Abdullah bin 'Omar. *Bukhari*, 4:337; recorded in *Riyad* (Ref. No. 28), Hadith No. 1605; p.271. Also *Muslim*, Vol. 4, Hadith No. 2242. English translation by Abdul Hamid Siddiqi; Sh. Muhammad Ashraf, Lahore, Pakistan; 1976; Vol. 4, Hadith No. 5570; p.1215. (According to the English translation, this Hadith was also narrated by Abu Huraira and by Naqi who had heard it from Abdullah); Hadith No. 5573; p.1215.

54. Narrated by Abu Huraira. *Muslim*, Vol. 4, Hadith No. 2244. Also *Bukhari*, 3:322. Also *Awn* (Ref. No. 32); Hadith No. 2533 and others.

55. Narrated by Abu Huraira. *Bukhari*, 3:322. Also *Muslim*, Vol. 4; Hadith No. 2244. Also *Awn* (Ref. No. 32), 7:222, Hadith No. 2533. Also *Mishkat al-Masabih*; Book 6; Chapt.6.

56. *Mishkat al-Masabih*; Book 6, Chapt.7, 8:178.

57. Narrated by Abu Huraira. *Awn* (Ref. No. 32); 7:235; Hadith No. 2550. Also *Traditions of Islam*; Alfred Guillaume; Khayats Oriental Reprinters, Beirut, Lebanon; 1966; pp.106, 107. (Hereafter referred to as '*Guillaume*').

58. Narrated by Abdullah bin Ja'far. *Awn* (Ref. No. 32); 7:221; Hadith No. 2532.

59. Narrated by Abu Huraira. *Sahih Muslim—Kitab-ul-Iman* (Ref. No. 53); Vol. III; Ch. DCCCVII; Hadith No. 4724; pp.1062, 1063.

60. Narrated by Anas. *Awn* (Ref. No. 32); 7:223; Hadith No. 5234. Also '*Guillaume*' (Ref. No. 57); pp.106,107.

61. *Maxims* (Ref. No. 4).

62. Narrated by Abdul Rahman bin Abdullah bin Mas'ûd. *Muslim*. Also *Awn* (Ref. No. 32) Hadith No. 2658. Also '*Guillaume*' (Ref. No. 57); p.106.

63. id.

64. Narrated by Shaddad bin Aus. *Muslim*; Vol. 2; Ch. 11; Section on '*Slaying*'; 10:739; verse 151. Also '*Robson*' (Ref. No. 15); p.872. Also recorded in *Riyad*. (Ref. No. 28); Hadith No. 643; p.131.

65. *Bukhari*. Also *Muslim*; Vol. 2; Chapt.11; Section on '*Slaying*'; 10:739; verse 152. Also '*Robson*' (Ref. No. 15); p.872.

66. id. (Ref. No. 46); Hadith No. 4817; p.1079.

67. *Al-Furû 'Min-al-Kafi Lil-Kulini* (in Arabic); 6:230.

68. id. (for Hazrat Ali see Ref. No. 4).

69. Reported by Ibn Sîrîn about Hazrat 'Omar and recorded in *Badâe al-Sanâe* (in Arabic); 6:2811.

70. id. 6:2881.

71. *Towards Understanding Islam*; Sayyid Abû A'lâ Maududi; English translation by Dr. Khurshîd Ahmad, a Muslim of renown in the literary and religious circles in the West; Islamic Publications Ltd., 13-E Shah Alam Market, Lahore, Pakistan.

2

VEGETARIANISM VS MEATARIANISM

PREAMBLE

WE HAVE DISCUSSED IN the previous chapter the Islamic exhortations for kindness to all living creatures. As a matter of fact, Islam is so concerned about compassion for animals that one wonders why it has allowed us to kill them for food, and why it did not enjoin on us to become vegetarians. To find an answer to this question, one has to understand and appreciate the overall approach to the Islamic laws regulating human behaviour in relation to other animals and the environment. These laws do not lay down categorical imperatives irrespective of man's biological necessities of life, food being the most important of them.

Unfortunately, the limited scope of this book does not permit a detailed discussion of the respective points of view of both vegetarians and non-vegetarians. From the humanitarian point of view, it would be an ideal situation if all the world were to become vegetarian and all the animals were allowed to live their natural lives. Perhaps a time may come, sooner or later, when this will happen. Meanwhile the poor animals shall go on having their throats slit.

Before discussing the subject from the Islamic angle, it will help to mention briefly other points of view, including those offered by other religions as well as the current scientific view that meat is not as essential and as healthy a diet as people generally consider it to be. At the same time, the writer's moral responsibility demands that the reader should know at the very outset what his personal feelings are and what to expect from this chapter.

The writer was born into a meat-eating family some 74 years ago. In those days the general impression used to be that meat was the best source of nourishment, and a child was weaned from milk to a meat diet right from the cradle. Modern information about the properties of vitamins, proteins, carbohydrates, and minerals found in vegetables etc. was not available then. The concept of balance in diet was not fully understood. It was natural, therefore, that the writer's metabolism got so used to meat that a complete change over to a vegetarian diet has now become very difficult. Otherwise, at heart, he has become a vegetarian by conviction.

Those who are traditionally habituated to and indoctrinated into believing from an early age that meat is more nutritious than vegetable food find it more difficult mentally than physically to give it up. In some cases, this indoctrination even takes on cultural overtones, as if meat-eating had some ethnological advantage. Then there is the problem of life-long acquired taste for meat which works as a drag even on those who wish to give it up. Very few meat-eaters realise that man's natural food is vegetables, fruit, and nuts. Even his body is not equipped with the tools required for killing and eating flesh. Why then has he ended up as the most ferocious and devastating of the carnivores and a sadist—killing not only for food but for pleasure and fun as well? How has the unnatural diet of meat affected not only his own health but also the environmental equipoise of the planet which he hopes he will inhabit through the generations until eternity? What has his religion to say about this physical as well as mental pabulum and spiritual sustenance—or is he using his religion to peg on it his perverted sense of power over the rest of the species?

It is not possible in this short chapter to deal at any length with the multifarious aspects of these and other questions. The following few pages are just a laconic explanation, from biological, economic, and mainly moral points of view of why the writer has come to believe that a well-balanced herbivorous diet is more nutritious, healthier, and tastier than that of meat—for those who heed Cicero's advice: "Thou shouldest eat to live; not live to eat."[1]

THE DIALECTICS OF DIET AND HEALTH

We are fortunate in our age that scientific research in dietetics has enabled us to eat a much more balanced diet than our ancestors did. We are much better informed about the properties of foodstuffs, such as proteins, vitamins, carbohydrates, and other nutrients, which we can measure now in terms of calories. We know now the difference between saturated (animal) and unsaturated (vegetable) fats and their comparative cholesterol levels.

Both vegetarians and meatarians (meat-eaters) have no bone to pick with each other on the fundamental point that diet should be such as to supply adequate nutrition to the body to keep it functioning healthily. The controversy starts between them only when it comes to the choice of sources from which man can derive the nutrients. The old school of dieticians still believes that these sources of nutrition are not distributed equally in the various foods available and, therefore, a mixed diet of vegetable and meat is more likely to provide a balanced amount of all bodily needs. However, apart from moral and ethical considerations of cruelty to animals which the current meat-eating habits entail, scientific opinion is shifting more and more, for physiological reasons, towards a purely herbivorous diet. It is being claimed now by reliable authorities that man can lead a healthier life purely on a plant-based diet, establishing this claim by scientific evidence and statistical data—provided the diet is a well-balanced mixture of vegetables, fruit, nuts, cereals, and lentils etc.

Normally, vegetarians add dairy products to the above list, including milk, butter, cheese and sometimes eggs. They are called 'lacto-ovo-vegetarians'. Those who abstain from dairy or any other kind of animal products are called 'vegans'. For meat-eaters, the writer has taken the liberty of poetic licence by coining the term 'meatarians' for lack of any other single word in English. It has always been taken for granted that man is in any case a meat-eater and, therefore, the word 'carnivore' has become solely associated with animal meat-eaters.

It is an established fact now that meat, with all its ingrained saturated fat, is not an ideal diet. Medical evidence shows that cholesterol is produced much more by animal fats than by polyunsaturated vegetable oils. Let us try to understand in simple words why animal fats are harmful for our health. The function of the heart is to pump about 5,000 gallons of blood every twenty-four hours. With every beat of the heart, all the arteries in the body, especially the large ones, shrink and expand (pulsate) to circulate the blood. Too much fat causes swellings in the layers (plaques) of the smaller vessels and makes the arteries less elastic. This interferes with the supply of blood to the various parts of the body. In order to keep the flow of blood normal through the swollen arteries, the heart has to work so much harder and goes on becoming weaker. All the diseases associated with the circulation of the blood and the coronary arteries are generally called 'rich man's diseases' because rich people eat more fatty and richer food. Diseases such as the following are more common in wealthy countries than in the poor: high blood pressure, angina, or thrombosis in the coronary vessels of the heart, circulatory disturbances in the legs, diabetes, gout, and cerebral haemorrhage.

The major controversy used to be over sources of protein, as only meat was considered to be the first-class source of it, containing all the ten essential amino acids. In fact, research has shown that by combining the various types of non-meat foods—such as pulses, beans, cereals, lentils, all kinds of vegetables, fruits, and nuts—in a suitable balance and rotation, all the essential amino-acids can be ingested. Many of the old concepts of protein have now been found to be fallacious. For example, the idea that meat contains 'first-class' and vegetables 'second-class' protein has been proved to be wrong. Protein should be measured in terms of the ten essential amino acids. It is true that no one item of plant food contains all ten kinds of amino-acids; that is why dieticians recommend a mixture of plant-foods so that jointly they would make up for each other's deficiencies and produce the required balance of protein. For that matter, even meat on its own does not contain all the essential nutrients. Examples will be given later of people who live on animal products alone and, as a result, are suffering from degenerative diseases.

THE IMPORTANCE OF VITAMINS

In order to appreciate fully the importance of vitamins, especially of Vitamin B, one has to study their function in the body. It will not be easy for a layman to understand the medical terms in which it is generally explained by scientists. Still, it is hoped that he would be able to get a general idea from the following explanation:

Enzymes are organic substances in a body, formed by living cells. They are capable of effecting a chemical change (by catalytic action) in other bodies without undergoing any change in themselves. The Vitamin B coenzymes function in the enzyme systems which transfer certain groups between molecules. The very life of the molecules depends on the Vitamin B enzymes.

In terms of their functions, vitamins are distinct from carbohydrates and proteins. Owing to the insufficiency of data available so far, medical opinion is not unanimous on various dietetic matters. It is, however, agreed that an inadequate supply of any one vitamin may lead to a condition known as 'hypovitaminosis' which affects the physiological functions of the body and hampers its growth. A deficiency of vitamins due to diet is called 'primary' deficiency and it is a known fact that some of the harmful effects of this type of deficiency cannot be put right.

Until a few years ago, it was generally believed that the only dependable source of Vitamin B was animal flesh. However, it has now been discovered that all the different kinds of Vitamin B, as well as protein, minerals, carbohydrates, and fats which the human body needs, are also found in plant foods. For example, yeast, bran (separated husks of grain) and germs of cereals and pulses contain them in the form of thiamine, riboflavin, niacin etc. The only kind of Vitamin B for which the major source is meat is B12. However, although animal products are the major source of it, it is not exclusively the only source. An appreciable amount of B12 is contained in yeast, soya beans, wheatgerm, eggs and in sea-kelp and spirulina (types of algae or seaweed) and can be bought in powdered form. It is significant to know that the recommended daily dose of it is so small—only 3 to 5 micrograms—that it could easily be obtained from non-meat sources.

Careful studies have shown that the most likely deficiencies of Vitamin B12 and iron are not found even in strict vegans who do not eat any kind of animal products. The incidence of pernicious anaemia is no more prevalent among them than among meatarians. On the contrary, statistics show that meatarians suffer more from Vitamin B12 deficiency than vegetarians and vegans. It is not only the lack of vitamins that causes such illnesses—there are other nutritional deficiencies too which could cause them and prevent the body from utilising the vitamins, especially B12, such as the failure of the lower part of the intestinal tract (ileum) to absorb it. Normally, vegans and vegetarians enjoy long and healthier lives. Even if it is true that meat-abstinence causes deficiency of Vitamin B12, it could always be augmented by other supplements—as happens in other cases of deficiencies. Many vegan foods (such as yeast extracts) are supplemented with B12. The killing of animals to obtain Vitamin B12 or other nutrients is not the only remedy.

It is paradoxical that man consumes the flesh of those animals which are vegetarians themselves, such as cows, sheep, and goats, to obtain vitamins in general and B12 in particular. If B12 is obtainable only from meat, where do these animals, who do not eat flesh, get their supply of Vitamin B12? Elephants develop the strongest physique and live longer than most animals by deriving their nutrients and vitamins from a kind of grass which is the poorest of all grasses. The life-expectancy of elephants is 60 years. It is not generally known to lay-people that there are certain kinds of vitamins, such as C, A, E and K which are non-existent in meat but can be obtained from vegetables or dairy products. The best source of Vitamin D is God's gift to his creation—the sun's rays.

The additional advantage of vegetarian food is that plant-protein contains much lower levels of cholesterol which has been implicated in various arterial and heart diseases. As early as 1961 a medical survey in America, published in *The Journal of the American Medical Association*, revealed that: ". . . a vegetarian diet can prevent 90 percent of our thrombo-embolic disease and 97 percent of our coronary occlusions." The current hedonistic philosophy in the rich West and America is guided by the doctrine that pleasure is the chief good, as William Gilmore puts it: "Eat, drink and be merry, for tomorrow we die." The choice of food is no longer dictated by the chemistry of our bodies, but by the taste of our tongues—which more often than not is perverted. This trend of faddishness for unnatural food is costing man, especially in the opulent West, much more than is printed on the menus of candle-lit restaurants—the real price he pays is in the currency of his health.

Too many deaths in these countries are premature and are caused mostly by unnatural and bizarre carnivorousness. The 'hidden persuaders' engaged by the multi-million-pound international meat business have succeeded in changing man into an omnivore. The chemical hormones on which animals and birds are fed in the modern intensive factory farms carry various kinds of poisons. Even fish in rivers and lakes are no longer safe. Statistics show that in the United Kingdom, for example, about 80 percent of food-poisoning cases are caused by meat. Both physical and nervous diseases, such as coronary thrombosis, blood-pressure, diabetes, cancer, and various other ailments, are on the increase. Excessive consumption of red meat and some types of char-grilled meat has been associated with some particular cancers. According to the medical science dealing with children's health (paediatrics), our modern unnatural diet is having still greater adverse effect on the younger generations.

It would be wrong to generalise the effect of diet alone on health and the longevity of life from individual cases. One does occasionally come across individuals who have been eating meat, smoking, and playing ducks and drakes with the hygienic principles of health all their lives and still manage to live long and uninfectious lives. On the other hand, there are some lacto-ovo-vegetarians and vegans who are not sound in body. In spite of the fact that food is the most material factor, there are various other factors too which influence one's health—such as genetic heredity and variations, salubrity of the environment, mental disposition, and general lifestyle etc. It is only from an empiric study, based on long-term observation and experiment of a class of people, that logical inferences can be drawn.

Take for example the Masais of East Africa among whom the writer has lived for many years. Their diet is blood, milk, and meat. Or the Inuit who live mostly on meat and fish. It is an anthropological fact that both these people are now suffering from an increase in various degenerative diseases. As opposed to that, there are vegetarian races who live much longer and healthier lives. The Hunzakuts of Kashmir are known to be one of the healthiest people on earth with a naturally long span of life. Their diet is mainly vegetarian. The writer has personally met some Hunzakuts and was greatly impressed by the simplicity of their taste and lifestyle. It is not that the climate of Kashmir is the only reason. The climate of the Andes in South America is no better than the rest of that part of the world. Not so long ago an Andean tribe was discovered in a remote part of the Andes which had so far escaped contact with our so-called civilized world. It was discovered that in one of their villages with a population of 400, there were many over the age of 100 years, 38 over the age of 75 and one over 121 years. Their medical examination showed that only two old people had any signs of heart disease. The diet of these people consists basically of plants, herbs, and wild fruit.[3]

THE ANATOMY OF MAN

The secret of health lies in eating what the chemistry of the body needs and for which its anatomy is structured. All the anatomical evidence of the human body shows that the organs and limbs of man have not been designed to obtain food by predacity. He has no claws to tear the prey with; the flimsy little nails he has are not retractable. His teeth are non-canine and he has no fangs and cutters; they are not sharp and strong enough to gnaw, crush bones or to flay a carcass. The munching movement of his jaws is like that of the herbivorous animals. Unarmed, he cannot fight tooth and nail even a wild cat. The fact that he cannot perform such functions without the aid of tools confirms the point that God did not design his body to kill for food, otherwise He would have equipped it with tools as He did the other beasts of prey. Even his internal organs and whole digestive system is not designed for a fleshy diet. His stomach does not secrete enough hydrochloric acid to liquate bones and other indigestible matter, as the stomachs of all carnivorous animals do. Since the excreta of carnivores is much fouler and noxious, nature has provided them with much shorter alimentary canals for rapid emptying of the bowels after they have eaten flesh, so that it does not remain in the body longer than necessary; the canals of herbivores are longer. Man's digestive system in this section also follows more closely to the pattern of herbivores. Uric acid in the body has a poisonous effect and causes various kinds of diseases. Human kidneys cannot convert the uric acid into *urea-glyoxal*, as do the kidneys of all carnivores.

Whatever way you look at it, it becomes obvious that man belongs to the herbivorous order of species. The nearest animals to man, biologically, are the genera of anthropoid apes. Everything anatomical between them and man is almost the same, except that they are arboreal (living in trees) while man is terrestrial (living on the ground). The differences of intellectual and spiritual capacities do not warrant a discussion, as we are dealing here with physical food and not with mental or spiritual pabulum. The blood of apes is essentially identical to that of man. The menstrual cycle in chimpanzees and gorillas has the same phases as in human females. The gestation period (between conception and birth) of nine months is the same. The organ which is attached to the foetus by the umbilical cord and falls out after birth (placenta) is alike. In spite of all these anatomical and biological similarities, almost all apes have remained basically vegetarian, without suffering from deficiencies of any kind of vitamins including B12, while man has become a meatarian. Nobody knows exactly at what stage of evolution this change occurred in man, because all the anthropological evidence shows that man started life on Earth as a herbivore. It should not go unnoticed that we in our time are witnessing another phase in human evolution. Man is changing fast into an omnivore, i.e. he has started eating anything and everything that is on offer.

THE ECONOMICS OF FOOD

The current use of agricultural land for food-animals does not make any economic sense. It is proving to be a miscomputation as well as amoral. There are highly specialised people in this field who are much better qualified than the writer to advise on this subject. However, the writer looks at this problem more from moral and ethical points of view than the mundane pros and cons of the modern agricultural scenario. But, to give the devil his due, the subject has to be discussed from the earthly point of view in the light of the current unfortunate trend in the developing countries to follow the Western plough and to warn them of the disaster they are heading for by depleting their exhaustible natural resources, irrespective of economic as well as ecological exigencies. The spade-husbandmen in the developing countries are too busy working and scraping their meagre fare, as best they can, to know what is happening in the rest of the world. For example, it never crosses their minds that, if the present agrarian outrage is allowed to continue, sooner or later the world will have to become vegetarian by force. Perhaps the following facts and figures will make them think twice before they allow themselves to fall into the same trap as the short-sighted Western farmers have fallen.

At present approximately one quarter of the world's total land area is being used for grazing livestock and 30% or more of the global cereal harvest and most of its soya harvest is fed to farm animals, while millions of human beings go hungry or starve to death. If the available land and all its resources were to be utilised for sensible agriculture, it could feed far more mouths than the present human population of the world. We need 100 acres of fertile land to pasture enough food animals to feed 20 people. The same 100 acres could produce enough maize to feed 100 people; or wheat to feed 240 people; or beans to feed 610 people. In Great Britain, for example, we consume about 850 million animals every year. To feed these animals we import cereals from countries where the general populace is suffering from malnutrition and wasting diseases.

Famines in various parts of Africa should be read by economists as the ominous writing on the wall. There are various reasons for such famines, but the root of this sorry plight is the short-sighted policy of the developed countries to tempt the under-developed regions of the world to grow cash-crops for export, instead of their indigenous food. Most of these cash-crops are seeds and cereals for livestock. If a small country such as Britain were to utilise all its land for growing human food instead of herbage for animals, it would be able to feed more than four times its present population of about 56 million people.

This is what a prominent writer on this subject, Jon Wynne-Tyson, has to say about the current state of affairs:

> ... think for a moment what the habit of meat-eating involves in terms of the world's food supplies ... About four-fifths of the world's agricultural land is used for feeding animals, and only about one-fifth for feeding man directly. This fact, shocking in its implications, has been examined by nutritionists Frank Wokes (editor-in-chief of *Plant Foods for Human Nutrition* and chairman of the Plant Foods Research Trust) and Cyril Vesey (University Department of Clinical Neurology, London) in their paper 'Land, Food and the People', Part One of the series "*Perspectives in Nutrition*":
>
> At the beginning of this decade there were about 35 hundred million people in the world ... The Rich Western nations, occupying half of the world's agricultural land, amounted to only about two-sevenths of the world's population; whereas the poor, mainly Eastern, occupying the other half of the world's agricultural land, amounted to about five-sevenths. Moreover, the poor Eastern people live mainly in the tropics where the yields of crops are often less than a quarter of those in the Western countries. Multiplying the yields factor of about 4 by the population density factor ... we get a differential of about 10 between the average food crop production of the average Westerner and that of the average Easterner. The average Westerner does not, of course, eat 10 times ... as much food as the average Easterner. But he consumes much more animal food, about five times as much animal protein and animal calories as the Easterner. He is able to do this only because he has two-and-a-half times as much agricultural land on which to produce his food, and this on the average is several times more fertile. But because the people in Western countries consume much more animal food, he even needs to import materials to feed his animals as well as himself.

When we consider the work and cost and wastage that goes into stockbreeding in order that the world's affluent minority can indulge in so unnecessary a luxury, the sheer extravagance and foolishness of it all is staggering. We read in our newspapers about the starving and under-fed millions, and all the time we are feeding to meat-producing animals the very crops that could more than eradicate world food shortage; also, we are importing from starving nations large quantities of grain and other foods that are then fed to our animals instead of to the populations who produce them.

In our greed to profit from the under-developed world, we have already gone to great lengths to popularise meat-eating among nations whose diet was previously largely or wholly meat-excluding.

Most of the fertile land devoted to cattle—which eat cereals, root and green crops and various seeds for improved milk production—could show a much quicker and more economical return if used for crops suitable for direct feeding to human beings. . . .

It is to our shame that such revelations are far from new. Much further back Sir John Russell, FRS, and others before him, made similar estimates showing incontrovertibly that plant foods, if fed directly to man rather than after processing through animals, can increase the yield per acre by up to ten-fold. As an example, soya beans yield seven times as much amino acid per acre as milk production and eight times as much as egg production.

Plant foods create protein from water, carbon dioxide and nitrogen, which is why they are the primary source of protein today . . . This above all is why governments, economists, industrialists, and international welfare organizations have begun to realise that the sooner the cow, the chicken, and other victims of our prodigal way of life are replaced by food made from plant proteins the better for the world at large.[4]

All this absurd extravagance and waste is being perpetuated in spite of modern scientific evidence that the human body can derive all its nourishment from a fibrous diet exclusive of meat and other animal products. Almost all kinds of edible nuts—such as peanuts, walnuts, almonds, cashew-nuts, Brazil nuts—give more calories, protein, and vitamins pound for pound than meat, in addition to having many other advantages over meat. The argument that nuts and fruit work out more expensive than meat for a family of average means is just a lame excuse. There is no part of the world where meat is cheaper. In these days of inter-continental means of transport, all kinds of vegetables, fruits and nuts are available in places where they cannot be grown. The reason why fruit and nuts are comparatively dearer is because they are not grown in enough quantities. Why? Because they have not yet become regular items of the daily diet. The law of supply and demand does not justify their cultivation other than on purely economic grounds. The writer (during his travels by car in the East, mainly through Islamic countries, covering about 70,000 kilometres over a period of about three years) often passed through miles and miles of hilly country where various kinds of fruit and nuts could easily be grown. The only signs of life which he and his wife used to see in such expanses of virgin hills were a few rambling flocks of sheep and goats.

Horticulture of fruit and nuts has many positive advantages over the breeding of food-animals. Once a tree has taken root, it does not need much attention, unlike livestock which demand constant—daily chores as well as the cost of fodder. Dried fruit and nuts do not need any contrivances such as refrigerators to keep them longer or chemical additives to preserve them as meat does. There is little danger of their getting putrefied and becoming a health hazard, as meat sometimes does with its poisonous chemicals. Without doubt they are much cheaper to grow and would be much cheaper to buy, once the increase in demand starts encouraging the supply.

Soya beans require one acre of land to produce as much nutrition as milk would through cows using five or six acres. There is no animal or plant food which can beat the humble soya bean in nutritional value. It contains Vitamin A, B1, and B2, has a high calorie count, iron, calcium, phosphorous, 23 percent unsaturated fat, and a high content of the amino-acid lysine, but it is low carbohydrate and has almost no starch. Milk, for which cows are subjected to great physical and emotional cruelties, contains almost no iron. The cycle of their yearly pregnancies has to be kept uninterrupted for the regular supply of milk. Calves are separated from their mothers as early as possible and are fed on such stimulative foods for rapid growth as to make them ready for their own cycle of pregnancies before reaching the age of two years.

Just to take a few more examples: a banana gives as much energy as the same weight of beef. Recent experiments have succeeded in extracting protein and fat from leaves—about 20 percent protein and about 25 percent unsaturated fat. In order to grow 3 million calories through animal products, 20 acres of grazing land is needed; while walnut trees on only one acre would produce the same amount of calories. The following chart shows the comparative properties of almonds and beef:

COMPARATIVE FOOD-VALUES OF BEEF AND ALMONDS

100 grams (5.5 ounces)	Calories	Protein	Energy KCAL	Value KJ	Carbo-Hydrates	Calcium	Fat	Water Content
Lean Beef Steak	242	14.8%	313%	1,311%	0%	8mg	28.2%	59%
Almonds	580	20.5%	580%	2,430%	4.3%	247mg	53.5%	59%

This book is not meant to be a dietary manual. Those interested in the subject should get more authentic information from the books listed in Reference No. 4 at the end of the Chapter. The above Chart has been prepared by the writer from the same books.[5]

The moral and ethical principles in the issue are even more complicated than the biological aspects of it. If and when people are convinced that adequate sources of nutrients other than meat are available, it should not be difficult to make them change their bill of fare. However, deep-rooted immemorial traditions and some religious rituals are beyond the domain of reason. Right through the ages of cave-dwellers to the present jet-set day, the scenario of animal plight has been the same. All religions, including the most primitive disciplines, have been trying to strike a sensible and equitable balance in the relationship between man and animals, but man's greed and self-indulgence have always tempted him to circumvent those disciplines. During the early stages of man's spiritual evolution, even the voodoo priests and oracles tried to bring man into harmony with nature through animism, spiritualism, and various other kinds of fetishism. Later on, the scriptural religions laid down elaborate laws to define the mutual rights and obligations of man and beast. While it is true that some religious disciplines have made the mistake of over-reaching themselves by imposing constraints and self-denial beyond the limits of practicability, the obverse of the coin these days presents a picture of opposite extremes in the shape of exploitation of animals by the disciples of Mammon.

As mentioned earlier, this chapter is meant to discuss the question of meat eating from the moral, and hence the religious, point of view. The point cannot be over-emphasised that apart from considerations of the physical and material advantages of a vegetarian diet over meat, the real concern of humane human beings should be their conscientious responsibilities towards the weaker species. The true altruistic spirit is that which engenders a sense of regard for others as a principle and not for the ulterior motive of gain or the expectation of advantage. It is time that civilised man should rise above "The Charters for HUMAN Rights" and start thinking in terms of Rights of ALL CREATURES. Morality within the circumscription of human species alone remains a misnomer unless it becomes all-embracing, including the tiniest of God's creatures in the comprehensive connotation of ecological morality. It is this all-absorbing kind of sublime morality to which all the divinely-inspired religions have been trying to edify man; while man has persistently been fighting shy of that edification in his self-indulgent gratification of fleshly pleasures and appetites.

There is no doubt that both hygienic and economic factors are in favour of a vegetarian diet, but the issue goes beyond these mundane considerations. Our moral responsibility toward the welfare of the rest of the species demands that we employ all our scientific knowledge to acquiring as much of our nutrients as possible from sources other than the flesh of those animals whom God has created and who are at our mercy. Let us see how some of our religions have endeavoured to solve this moral problem.

CONFUCIANISM

Classical Confucianism does not throw any light on the question of meat-eating. The code of morality taught by Confucius, on which the Chinese, Korean, and Japanese cultures were developed and which ultimately became the State religion of China, does not concern itself directly with the welfare of animals. The Analects (551-479 B.C.), however, mention some anecdotes about Confucius which depict him as a man of high moral principles (*chun-tzu*) who would kill animals only if necessary, but would not take undue advantage of them. For example, he caught fish by hook and bait and did not use a net, nor did he hunt a roosting bird.[6] Another anecdote throws a different light on his character. Once, his stables were burnt down. On hearing the news, his only concern was to know if any human beings were hurt. He was not interested in knowing about the fate of the horses.[7]

However, such stories are often misleading and should not be taken seriously, especially when one is seeking an insight into the character of such a great and highly moral personality as Confucius who gave the world a great religion. We know, for example, that he gave the people of those olden days a new concept of heaven (*Tien-li*) which accommodated not only human beings but also animals and plants.

There is one incident recorded and repeatedly discussed in Confucian literature which throws light on the psychology of meat-eaters and which could be applied even in the modern context. People buy their meat at butchers' shops without giving it a thought that the neatly wrapped-up joints were once parts of the body of an animal which would still be alive and kicking but for the butcher's knife. The story runs as follows: A king once saw a man leading an ox to the altar and ordered him to release it. The man remonstrated, explaining that the slaughter of the ox was by way of a sacrifice. The king did not want to interfere with the ritual of a sacrifice but, at the same time, he was moved with pity for the ox. He, therefore, ordered the man to replace the ox with a sheep. The great Confucian sage, Mencius (*Meng-Tzu*)[8] while discussing the incident with the king analysed his behaviour in these words: "Your conduct was an artifice of benevolence. You saw the ox and had not seen the sheep. So is the superior man affected towards animals that, having seen them alive, he cannot bear to see them die; having heard their dying cries, he cannot bear to eat their flesh."[9] One wonders how many people would still relish their Sunday joints if they ever happened to watch the slaughtering of animals in an abattoir.

The spiritual and cultural influence of Confucianism and Neo-Confucianism notwithstanding, most of East Asia has ended up as heterodox in the choice of food in the real sense of omnivorousness. Vegetarianism as a creed has no place in their cuisine. Although their overall meat consumption is far lower than in the West, it is rapidly increasing. It is believed by some that the Japanese used to be vegetarians until some 250 years ago.

HINDUISM, JAINISM AND BUDDHISM

The Sanskrit word 'Veda' means knowledge. The Vedas are the most ancient sacred literature of Hindus (Cir. 1500 to 1000 B.C.), comprising more than one hundred books, which have been collected in four Vedas, namely: Rig Veda, Yajur Veda, Sama Veda, and Atharva Veda. They advocate vegetarianism throughout their teachings. Based on such teachings, the *Manu Samhita*, which is the ancient Indian code of law, states: "Meat can never be obtained without injury to living creatures, and injury to sentient beings is detrimental to the attainment of heavenly bliss; let him [man] therefore shun the use of meat." In another section, it warns: "Having well considered the disgusting origin of flesh and the cruelty of slaying of corporeal beings, let him entirely abstain from eating flesh." It goes on to say, "One whose flesh I eat will eat my flesh in the next life." Similarly, the *Annu Shasen Perva Mahabharat* gives the verdict: "Undoubtedly all those human beings who prefer meat to several other forms of food are like vultures." According to the Vedas, all living beings possess a soul and, hence, they all are equal in that sense, although they have different bodies and different levels of intelligence.

It is generally believed that Hindus have been vegetarians from the beginning. Their early records, however, put some doubt on this claim. There is some evidence that they used to fish and hunt, and also killed domestic animals for food. Many historical records could be quoted, but the following few examples would suffice here:

> Formerly, in the kitchen of the beloved of gods, King Priyadarsin [Emperor Asoka, 274-232 B.C.], a hundred thousand animals were killed every day for the sake of curry. But now after Asoka had embraced Buddhism when this *Dharma-script* [the Buddhist decree or custom] is written, only three animals are killed. . . .[11]

It must, however, be understood that the conduct of a lay person such as Emperor Asoka should not be taken as an exemplification of the Hindu doctrine. What used to happen in his court is just a reflection on the social life of that period.

A Brahmin belongs to the highest sacerdotal or priestly caste of the Hindu society which is divided into four hereditary hierarchical grades. According to an anecdote recorded in the Encyclopaedia of Buddhism, a rabbit once coming upon a hungry Brahmin, lighted a fire and jumped into it to be roasted so that the Brahmin could eat him.[12] The fact that, according to the story, the hungry Brahmin was the god Indra who had appeared to the rabbit in the guise of a Brahmin makes no difference to the inference that the Brahmins in those days did eat rabbits.

The ancient Vedic literature repeatedly narrates stories on the theme of mutual feelings of sacrifice between man and animals, even to the point of the ultimate sacrifice of life for each other. Such stories are not meant to be fairy tales for children. They are taken in the literal sense by millions of Hindus, even these days, and have been influencing the attitudes of the Hindu laity towards animals for about the last three thousand years. The following story, for example, is meant to transfuse a sense of the doctrine of re-birth:

A Brahmin was once about to kill a goat as a sacrifice when the goat started laughing and crying alternately. When asked why, the goat explained: "I was laughing out of happiness because this time I shall be reborn as a human being, after having passed through 500 rebirths as a goat; I was crying out of pity for you because the same is going to happen to you as happened with me. I was originally condemned from Brahminhood to 500 lives as a goat for sacrificing a goat. If you kill me, you too shall be condemned to a similar fate." The story has a happy ending: the Brahmin did not kill the goat and continued to live as a human being, while the goat was struck by lightning and was reborn as a human.[13]

It was only at a later stage, perhaps under the influence of Jainism and Buddhism, that meat-eating became sacrilegious for Hindus. Vegetarianism in the West is practised mostly out of compassion for animals. The Hindu abstinence from meat, however, is based on the pantheistic philosophy or wisdom (*Vedanta*) leading to non-violence and re-birth. The doctrine of non-violence (*ahimsa*) cannot be explained better than in the following words of *Acaranga Sutra*:

> Injurious activities inspired by self-interest lead to evil and darkness. This is what is called bondage, delusion, death, and hell. To do harm to others is to do harm to oneself. Thou art he whom thou intendest to kill . . . ! Thou art he whom thou intendest to tyrannize! We corrupt ourselves as soon as we intend to corrupt others.[14]

The doctrine of rebirth is very relevant to the subject of animals' welfare in general and meat-eating in particular. We are not concerned here with the theological intricacies of this doctrine. Nevertheless, it must be appreciated that it has played a significant role in influencing the behaviour towards animals of millions of people throughout the various parts of the sub-continent of India as well as in East, South, and Central Asia. The moral aspect of this influence can be appreciated only after getting some idea of the theological fundamentals on which the concept of reincarnation, and hence rebirth, is based, which can be summarised as follows:

a. All the 'animals' and the so-called 'inanimate' beings (*sat*) pass through a continuous succession of changes. In the case of the 'inanimate' beings (*ajiva*), the changes take place through metamorphoses, i.e. changes of form or condition by natural development; in the case of human and other 'animate' beings (*jiva*), the process of change is through metempsychosis, i.e. the transmigration of soul at death into a new body belonging to the same or a different species.

b. The highest grade in the hierarchy of the 'animate' beings is that of humans; next comes the grade of animals; and so on down.

c. The inherent propensity of each 'animate' is to try to rise to a higher status in each incarnation, by gaining merit through good deeds, with the proviso that each individual creature is responsible for its salvation through its deeds or *Karma*.

d. Some succeed in improving their lot, while others get demoted by way of punishment for bad deeds. The vilest of such deeds is considered to be violence, harm, or injury (*hims*) in any form.

e. The final haven of rest, after a long struggle of 'action' (*karma*) and successive states of flux (*samsara*), is the state of 'inaction'—a state of bliss, purity, and freedom, called *Mukt*, *Moksha*, or *Nirvana*.

Admittedly, the above is a feeble attempt at the simplification of very elaborate concepts of theology but, hopefully, it will serve to make a few relevant points.

To give credence to the concept that an animal could have been one's close relative in the previous incarnation or that one could become an animal in the next incarnation is daunting enough to inhibit the killing and eating of animals. How could one swallow the flesh of an animal who, according to the *Lankavatara Sutra*, could have been anyone of the following:

> In the long course of 'samsara' (successive incarna-
> tions), there is not one among living beings with form
> who has not been mother, father, brother, sister, son,
> daughter, or some other relative. Being connected with
> the process of [repeated] births, one is kin to all wild
> and domestic animals, birds, and beings born from the
> womb.

According to the *Brahmajala Sutra* of the Buddhists: ". . . all the living beings of the six *gati* [categories of beings] are our parents; and if we kill them, we kill our parents and also our former bodies. . . ."[15]

As mentioned before, some believe that the emphasis on vegetarianism in Hindu thought came from Jainism and Buddhism. Jainism is a reform movement within the spectrum of Hinduism. The origin of this movement, as of Buddhism, can be traced back to the late 6th or early 5th century B.C. Both believe in vegetarianism; strongly condemn the Hindu practice of animal sacrifice; reject quite a few of the dogmas associated with Vedas; and both deny the existence of a personal and a creative God.[i]

Jainism is claimed to have been started by some pre-historic Jain monks, but the one who has been recorded in history as the founder is called Rusabhdev. However, Vardhamana Mahavira (599-527 B.C.) is also given a very prominent place by historians. He was the 24th *Tirthankara* in the line of succession. Like the Gautama Buddha, he also came from a princely family. The founder of Buddhism was Buddha (the wise sage) Gautama Sidhartha or Sakya Sinha or Muni (563-483 B.C.).

Although Jains are still counted as Hindus, they have earned for themselves a distinct identity as a religion within a religion. Originally, in line with the Hindu prejudice against crossing the waters, they too had remained confined within the shores of India, but now they have settled in many parts of the world. In spite of being less than one percent (about 4/5 million), they wield a great influence on overall Hindu thought. They are mostly centred in Ahmedabad, the famous city of India where Mahatma Gandhi spent twelve years of his life and became greatly influenced by Jainism.

Like the Confucians, Jains too believe that all creatures are equal and possess a soul. Their doctrines, such as non-injury to animals in the general sense of *Ahimsa*, and successive rebirths, are no doubt very benedictory to animal welfare. However, some of their idealistic interpretations are perhaps too far stretched and difficult to practise. Let us take a few examples:

---

i **Editor's note:** As interpreted by most Buddhists, but there is a view among some Muslims, based on new Qu'ânic evidence, that Buddha was one of the four Greatest (in terms of influence) Prophets of God, the other three being: Moses (Musa), Jesus (Isa), and Mohammad. See Haque, Nadeem, 2017, "Buddha: A Prophet in Islam", *Quranicosmos: An Interdisciplinary Journal of Quranic Thought*, Volume 1, Issue 1, August 2017, p. 3-20.

For fear of killing germs and insects, Jains are not supposed to eat root vegetables such as potatoes, or to pulp and grind grains. One of the five tenets of *Ahimsa* is that one should eat only during day-time, before sunset. From a health point of view it is a very wise proposition. Even modern dieticians recommend that it is not healthy to retire for the night on a heavy stomach. However, the reason given in the religious sources of this tenet is that, after dark, there is a greater possibility of insects in the air getting in the mouth along with the morsels of food.[16] One should not travel far from home lest one should cause harm to 'beings' in an unfamiliar place.[17] Worms and insects in the soil get injured by digging or ploughing, therefore farming is considered as one of the contra-ahimsa occupations.[18] One Jain sect, called the Digambaras, denounces even activities such as bathing, use of fire, wearing of clothes, farming etc., for fear of hurting the creatures in air, water or earth.[19]

The early Buddhists, in general, were more liberal than the Jains in meat-eating, but gradually vegetarianism became the norm. Many Buddhist sects these days are staunch vegetarians although other Buddhists take the view that one should eat what one is offered, even if it includes meat. Buddhists in south-east Asia are often fish-eaters too. Some Buddhist teachings have gone to the opposite extremes of non-violence against animals by recommending that human beings should offer their bodies to the animals as food. One such text reads as follows: "One should be willing to forsake one's entire body, one's flesh, hands and feet as an offering to starving tigers, wolves, lions and hungry ghosts."[20]

Many of the stringently moral and ethical standards, as laid down in the above disciplines of Jainism and Buddhism, were beyond measure for an average person. It was therefore, right from the beginning, found necessary to chalk out two separate codes of practice—one for the layman (*anuvrata*); and one for the monks (*dhikhu* or *mahavrata*). The monks are to observe the laws of *Ahimsa* to the letter while the laity is allowed some leeway in matters of detail. The monks, for example, are to confine themselves in their monasteries during the monsoon season, because the insects and worms which come out of their holes in the rain could get crushed under their feet.[21] They are to be abstemious not only in food, which would naturally be vegetarian, but also should suppress all fleshly appetites including sex.[22]

Notwithstanding all this priestly code, the Buddhist monks (*Blama*) living in the bleak Tibetan and Mongolian mountains eat meat, as they say, to survive. Their excuse that meat is a necessity for them is belied by the presence of the Zanskar Buddhists amongst them in the same mountains who are strict vegetarians. However, the meat-eating Buddhists derive some consolation from the fact that they do not hunt or kill the animals themselves—they engage others to do it for them.

It is a very sad fact that dogmatism invariably ends up in defeating the very purpose for which the related doctrine was originally laid down. If the purpose of *Ahimsa* (non-injury) is to spare all living creatures any pain and suffering, then some believe the Jains are guilty of neglecting the spirit of that principle. Basing their code of practice on the theory that deeds (Karma) and suffering follow the natural course of 'cause and effect', they may allow sick and injured animals (that cannot be cured, or whose pain cannot be alleviated) to die a lingering death instead of putting an end to their suffering by 'mercy-killing'. Once Mahatma Gandhi allowed a suffering calf to be killed by euthanasia and was strongly criticised by the Jains.

It must be mentioned here that the writer has always believed in the intrinsic and altruistic philosophies based on the original teachings of the Jain, Buddhist, and Hindu prophets (may God bless all of them). The above criticism is not against these religions as such; it is meant to point out the greatest of all priestly weaknesses, namely to play God in trying to uplift man above the laws of nature, and put so much stress on his physical capabilities that, instead of bending, he, the layman, breaks, or opts for the easy way out and tells the priests to 'go to hell'.

It seems very appropriate to end this section of the book with a few words of wisdom from a Buddha who is amongst us, living as an exile in India—His Holiness Tenzin Gyatso the fourteenth Dalai Lama:

Even the lowest insect strives for protection against dangers that threaten its life. Just as each one of us wants happiness and fears pain, just as each one of us wants to live and not to die, so do all other creatures.[23]

CHRISTIANITY

There is very little to be said about Christianity in respect of vegetarianism or meatarianism. Jesus Christ has not been recorded as saying anything definitive on this subject, and his silence is taken by Christians as leaving the decision on diet to individual choice.

Jesus, personally, has been mentioned in the Gospels (*Injîl*) about sixteen times as eating meat. However, some Biblical scholars take the view that the Greek word translated into the English Bible as 'meat' actually means 'food' and not necessarily the flesh of an animal. Even in the Old Testament the word 'meat' has often been used in the sense of food in general, which includes vegetables, fruit, and cereals. In the Third Book of Moses[24] the word 'meat' is used for flour. Again, after explaining how to offer bullocks, sheep, and fowls, it reads: "And when any will offer a meat offering unto the Lord, his offering shall be of fine flour . . ."[25]

Modern English also uses the word 'meat' as a figure of speech for any kind of solid food in the form of flesh as well as the edible parts of vegetables, fruits, and nuts. To say 'before or after meat' used to mean 'before or after a meal'. Although there is no conclusive historical evidence for it, it is believed by some that Jesus was born in a Jewish community called Essenes who used to lead a monastic type of life and were vegetarians. Basing their argument on that, some Christians have started believing that Jesus himself was a vegetarian. There are still many Essenes living in Israel these days and they are vegetarians. It is estimated that about 4—12 percent of Israelis are vegetarian. According to the *Essene Gospel of Peace*, which is based on the original Aramaic text, Jesus is recorded to have said: ". . . For I tell you truly, he who kills, kills himself, and who so eats the flesh of slain beasts, eats the body of death." The Essenes claim that their version of the Bible is the most authentic one, free from the later alterations and revisions. For example, according to their records, the parents of Jesus, Joseph, and Mary, did not sacrifice a lamb during the feast of Passover, that Jesus himself replaced the Passover meal of the sacrificed lamb with 'bread and wine', and that John the Baptist (Yahya) and his disciples were vegetarian. The famous miracle of Jesus when he fed about four thousand people with 'loaves and fish' was, according to their version, 'loaves and fruit' and not fish.

Some Christian theologians infer from verses 1-4 of St. John's Gospel that Christ as the Logos of God (the Word of the Second Person of the Trinity) confirms the above inference. Those who give credence to this doctrine must also believe that Christ could never have eaten the flesh of the same animals whom he created as a co-creator with God.[26] One wonders how much difference it would have made to the fate of all those millions of animals who are being killed for consumption in the Christian world, if it were to be established that Jesus was a vegetarian. Some Christian theologians earnestly believe that, according to the Bible, God intended man to be vegetarian. In the words of the philosopher Karl Barth: "Whether or not we find it practicable or desirable, the diet assigned to man and beasts by God the Creator is vegetarian."[27]

JUDAISM AND ISLAM

The issue of vegetarianism versus meatarianism in the light of the Islamic concepts has to be discussed in conjunction with those of Judaism, not so much because of similarities between these two concepts, but because of dissimilarities. Both religions allow the use of animals for food in their respective scriptures, but the moral philosophy underlying this Covenant between God and them is not the same. In some cases, the two concepts are discordantly incompatible with each other.

There is ample evidence in the Torah to support the claim of some Jews that God intended man to subsist on vegetables and abstain from meat. In the following verse, while describing the principles of those whose moral code of life is: "Let us eat and drink; for tomorrow we shall die", God mentions that such people derive their "joy and gladness" by "slaying oxen, and killing sheep, eating flesh, and drinking wine." Isaiah (the greatest of the Hebrew prophets,

740-701 B.C.) prophesies about such people: "And it was revealed in mine ears by the Lord of Hosts, surely this iniquity shall not be purged from you till ye die."[28] At the same time a ray of hope radiates in prophecies such as: "For, behold, I create new heavens and a new earth; and the former shall not be remembered nor come into mind. But be ye glad and rejoice for ever in that which I create . . . The wolf and the lamb shall feed together, and the lion shall eat straw like the bullock: and dust shall be the serpent's meat. They shall not hurt nor destroy in all my holy mountain, saith the Lord."[29] "The wolf also shall dwell with the lamb, and the leopard shall lie down with the kid; and the calf and young lion and the fatling together; and a little child shall lead them."[30]

The real difficulty, however, in seeking guidance from the Hebrew Bible for the practical conduct of life is that there are so many contradictory statements in it. There is so much confusion in the amalgam of Rabbinical appendages and the originally revealed version that one can find in it support for one's views ranging from sublime thought to the anomalous as well as to the ridiculous.

It must be pointed out here that Jewish vegetarians infer from verses 29 and 30, Chapter 1, of Genesis, that the Hebrew Bible does not permit food based on meat or any other kind of animal product. They interpret these verses as specifically suggesting a vegan diet. They read as follows:

> And God said, Behold, I have given you every herb bearing seed, which is upon the face of all the earth, and every tree in which is the fruit of a tree yielding seed; to you it shall be for meat . . . and I have given every green herb for meat. . . . [i.e. as food].

Jewish vegetarians, like many other Jewish scholars, believe that: in the Noahtic laws, as in the consequent Hebrew laws given on Mount Sinai . . . , permission granted to eat flesh . . . was as a compromise"; that: "the sixth commandment, 'Thou shalt not kill' seals the general teachings relating to carnivorous habits"; that the phrase in Genesis: "To man and all creatures wherein is a living soul" proves that the prescribed diet of all living creatures, including human beings, is vegetarian.[31]

It has always been the general impression that the dietetic laws of both Judaism and Islam are the same. Even some Muslims have come to believe in this misconception. We are concerned here with the sanction of meat as food. This, however, cannot be explained or understood without reference to the historical and theological links between the two religions. Judaism has influenced the Muslim attitude so surreptitiously that most Muslims are not even conscious of it. The interactions between the two have influenced not only Muslim thought but also their general deportment. This susceptibility of Muslims is becoming increasingly notable in matters of *Halal* (lawful) and *Harâm* (unlawful) food; in the method of slaughter; and in the concept of animal sacrifice. This situation has stemmed from the impression among them that the Jewish dietetic laws are in accord with those of Islam in every detail. One of the reasons which has prompted such misconceptions is the Islamic concurrence with some of the theologies of the previous revealed religions in general and Judaism in particular.

Muslims believe that Islam is not a new religion. Rather it is a continuation of all the previous monotheistic religions whose teachings it incorporates *mutatis mutandis*. The Qur'ân, for example acknowledges all the Biblical prophets as the true Messengers of God and goes further by vindicating their character from the imperfections which the Old Testament has ascribed to some of them. This kind of theological affinity with Judaism was based on monotheism—a link which is still strong and valid.

In the verse below the Qur'ân puts a formal proposal for an alliance between all the monotheistic religions, which has been rendered into a free translation by the late Maulana Abul Kalam Azad, the famous leader of the Indian National Congress and a great Muslim scholar, as follows:

> O Prophet [Mohammad]! Say to the Jews and the Christians: 'O people of the Book! Let us not wrangle over what may be regarded as controversial subjects. Let us at least agree on that which is recognised alike by you and by us, i.e. that we worship none but God and associate nothing with Him, and take not each other as Lord to the exclusion of God . . .'. (Qur'ân 3:64)[32]

The Prophet Mohammad sent letters containing the text of this verse to the Heads of various kingdoms, such as Heraclius, in 627 A.C. A copy of this letter, sent to Al-Muqawkis—the ruler of Egypt, was later discovered and found to be a verbatim copy of the version as recorded in the book of *Hadith, Sahih Bukhari*.[33]

It was in the same spirit of promoting goodwill and social intercourse among the monotheistic religions that the Qur'ân declared:

> This day [all] good and pure things have been made lawful for you, and the food of the heritors of previous Scriptures is lawful for you, and your food is lawful for them. And eligible for you are the chaste women both from among those who believe in Islam and those who are the heritors of the previous Scriptures [provided they do not associate anyone with God], provided that you give them their due dowers—not committing fornication nor keeping them clandestinely as paramours." (Qur'ân 5:6)[34]

One feels sadly disappointed that historically the Jews did not respond favourably to this, and similar other overtures of Islam. It seems that their traditional attitudes towards mingling with other religions has often been guided by the following and similar commandments of the Old Testament:

> And when the Lord thy God shall deliver them [the seven nations mentioned in the previous verse] before thee; thou shalt smite them, and utterly destroy them; thou shalt make no covenant with them, nor shew mercy unto them; neither shalt thou make marriages with them; thy daughter thou shalt not give unto his son, nor his daughter shalt thou take unto thy son.[35]

The Qur'ânic ethics of war are based on an integral body of laws which are beyond the scope of this book. Most fundamentally, Muslims are allowed to fight only defensive wars and are expressly forbidden to initiative the offensive.[36] Hazrat Abu Bakr, the first Caliph after the death of the Prophet Mohammad (632-634 A.C.) addressed the Muslim army at a place outside Medina, called Jorf, before sending them off for the battle of Muta. Among the ten instructions he gave to the soldiers, the following throw some light on the Muslim ethics of war during a period when no mercy used to be shown to the defeated people. He ordered them not to mutilate anybody's limbs; not to kill old men, women, or children; not to cut down fruit trees; not to slaughter animals except for food; and not to molest those living in monasteries. It is not only the residences of monks which Islam has declared as sacrosanct during a war. One of the reasons given in the Qur'ân which justifies a war is to protect the Jewish synagogues and the Christian churches—not only the Muslim mosques but all places of worship as well. It is noteworthy in the above instructions of the Caliph Abu Bakr that even the trees (environment) and the animals have been included in that list of protected things.[37]

The pivot on which this tripartite relationship between Judaism, Christianity and Islam oscillates is the personality of Prophet Abraham, although Christians generally do not accord to him a status higher than that of one of the prophets. For the Jews, he is the patriarch and the founder of the Hebrews, while for the Muslims the very religion, or belief system of Islam is the religion/belief system of Abraham.[38] Prophet Abraham is thus a strong sentimental as well as theological link between Judaism and Islam—a link which has been expressing itself in the form of many common beliefs and practices. The tradition of animal sacrifice and the method of slaughter are the two spheres of influence which are generally supposed to be analogous between the two religions, but in fact they are not.

There is no suggestion in the Qur'ân, or in any other of the Islamic sources, that eating of meat is good for physical or spiritual health. Islam's approach in this matter is neutral; it has left the choice to the individual to be a vegetarian or a meatarian. There are many devout Muslims in the world who do not eat meat and no one ever doubts their faith. Even those who opt to eat meat are urged in the Qur'ân to eat in moderation.[39] Furthermore, there are elaborate and stringent laws governing the overall treatment of animals—their rearing and breeding; the pre-slaughter, during and after-slaughter handling—which are very different from the Judaic laws. It is a sad thing to see that the education of Muslim masses in Islamic countries in such laws leaves much to be desired. One cannot blame non-Muslims for not knowing the details of the Islamic teachings in this respect; in fact, even some Muslims themselves do not know enough about them. This lack of knowledge has resulted in some serious misunderstandings about Islam in the West, as well as misconceptions among Muslims themselves.

Islam has given all sentient creatures a status much higher than is generally conceded to them. There are so many verses of the Qur'ân and so many *Ahadith* on this theme that it would take a voluminous work to cover all of them. Some aspects of this subject have already been discussed in Chapter One. Some stipulations laid down by Islam to the method of slaughter and the pre-slaughter treatment are the essential pre-requisites of permission to eat meat. Religious discipline, like any other discipline, defeats its purpose if those who profess to accept it fail to grasp the essence of its spirit which is meant to influence the mental and moral aptitude. Such people need better education in their religion. Then, there are those who are mentally capable of grasping the spirit of the discipline and do profess to accept its principles, but start picking and choosing parts of it to suit their personal convenience. However, the most censurable are the ones who, knowingly and wilfully, ignore or stretch the law for monetary gain. Even in some Islamic countries these days conditions pertaining to the pre-slaughter handling of animals and the act of slaughter are far from satisfactory. In some cases, they are even in open violation of the dictates of Islam. Of course, the stipulation of invoking the name of God (*tasmiyah* and *takbir*) is being meticulously carried out in Islamic abattoirs, but not enough attention is paid to the rest of the details. Even some of the professional slaughtermen are not given adequate instruction in the code of the Islamic laws in this respect.[40] Comparatively, conditions in Jewish abattoirs are much better organised than in Islamic ones.

The important point to note is that Islam has left the option of eating meat to one's discretion, subject to the limits of one's realistic needs and genuine circumstances. Had Islam laid down a categorical imperative prohibiting meat consumption, it would have gone beyond the bounds of practicability for some. However, this consideration of Islam for human physical needs goes only as far as the consumption of meat is concerned; it does not apply to the rules governing the treatment of animals during their rearing and general handling, nor does it apply to the strict laws and regulations governing the humane method of slaughter. All such injunctions are obligatory and must be carried out in every detail before the flesh of the animal becomes lawful and pure (*halal* and *tayyib*) for consumption. The Islamic permission to eat meat does not mean that one must eat it. It simply means that it may be eaten. There are many things which have not been forbidden by Islam as food, yet we have stopped eating them because modern scientific know-how has discovered better alternatives.

The real problem is that general members of the Muslim public who buy their meat from the shops in their countries never get a chance to see for themselves the un-Islamic and inhumane scenes within some of their slaughterhouses. If they knew what was happening there, they would either stop eating meat or, at least, start lobbying the powers that be to have the Islamic rules implemented.

The Qur'ân allows Muslims to eat meat slaughtered by Jews, as mentioned earlier. Both religions invoke God's name before slaughter; both have been prescribed a method of slaughter with a view to allowing the blood to drain out; and both have been charged with the moral responsibility of not taking the life of an animal except for the legitimate and imperious necessities of life. It all sounds very well in theory, but how it is being worked out in practice is a different matter.

According to the Hebrew Bible, all mankind and all species of animals were vegetarians to begin with.[41] The first recorded permission to the Israelites to eat meat was given through the Prophet Noah (Nûh) after the Flood when God told him: "Each living animal is given to you [to eat] like the grass is given to you."[42] Some Jewish scholars suggest that permission to eat meat was granted to the Israelites as a concession and a compromise to their weakness and that, after the advent of the Promised Messiah, the Jews would be made to become vegetarians again.[43] During their Exodus from Egypt under the conduct of Moses the Israelites were forbidden to eat meat, except those portions of the sacrificed animals which were not offered to God at the altar. After travelling for fourteen years, they entered Israel or Yisrael in Hebrew—a name given to this region after Jacob (Yaqub), according to the Biblical story, wrestled with an angel.[44] After Jacob's encounter with the Angel, they were given permission again to use animals for food, including domestic animals. This time, however, the permission was qualified with the condition that the animal must be slaughtered 'ritually'.[45]

What Muslims understand from this condition of 'ritual slaughter' is that the Israelites were told to keep in mind, while cutting the throat of a creature of God, that permission to do so had been granted as a special Covenant in which God has laid down certain conditions to be fulfilled by man. The invocation of God's name before slaughter is to remind oneself of those conditions. The same thing applies to the invocation of Allah's name as *takbir*. The main reason for this condition was that, in those days, it was a common practice among the idolatrous pagans to kill animals in various cruel ways and to leave the carcasses at the altars for the deities. The monotheistic concept of God becomes meaningless if the name of a deity or any other name were to be invoked instead, especially at the most pensive moment of taking the life of a creature of God. Except for this moral consideration, there is no ceremonial or rubrical service involved in the act of slaughter. Through the passage of time, however, the Rabbinical adjuncts to the law have changed this simple act into a complex mysterious sacrament whose sacredness is liable to be broken by the slightest modification to the traditional method of slaughter. Unfortunately, some Muslims too are making this clerical error in their approach to this problem.

From the Islamic point of view there is no ritual to be observed in the slaughter of an animal. It is just a simple and straightforward, albeit a very serious, act performed to satisfy the physical need for food. The method of slaughter prescribed by both these religions was in those days, and still is, the most efficacious way to draw out blood from the body of the victim. The question whether or not pre-slaughter stunning interferes with the methods of religious slaughter is undoubtedly an important subject for discussion. Blood has been forbidden to both Jews and Muslims simply because it is unhygienic as food. We are concerned that some Muslims are falling into the same habit of adherence to the letter of the law, at the cost of its spirit.

One could give numerous examples of how some Muslims have bandied dialectic niceties in their law (*fiqh*) to make minute distinctions without a difference. However, the matter in hand is to see how far the ardent followers of these two great religions are conforming to the humane laws of slaughter; and more consequently, how far they are conforming to the spirit of these laws instead of the letter.

Muslims should consider themselves lucky that the Qur'ân was written down by scribes during the lifetime of the Prophet Mohammad in toto and that there is no possibility of a variant reading in its text. Throughout the 23 years' period of its revelation in Mecca and Medinah, the Prophet used to follow the practice of dictating every fresh recitation to the scribes, who used to remain in attendance in the adjoining mosque, with instructions where to collate the new verse. These scribes were called *Ashab al-suffah*.[46] In addition to writing it down, people started to memorise the Qur'ân not only to recite it among other local Muslims, but also to convey it to people abroad during their travels. They were called *Qurra'a* (plural of *Quari*), or *Huffaz* (plural of *Hafiz*). As a further precaution to preserve the purity of the text, it was enjoined that portions of the Qur'ân be recited by the Imams during the daily prayers. Thus, even today, we hear the recitation in millions of mosques throughout the world.[47]

While all these measures have succeeded in making sure that the original words of the text remain immutable and invariable, some of our theologians have succeeded in confusing the sense of even simple verses by their micrographic glossaries. The simple, straightforward, and practicable dietary laws too have not escaped the flourishes of their pens. There is a prophecy of the Prophet Mohammad to the effect that a time would come when the followers of his faith would no longer remain in touch with the spirit of the Qur'ân.[48] It is high time for the general Muslims to give this prophecy a serious thought and for Muslim theologians to do some introspection.

The issue of vegetarianism and meatarianism in the Jewish scriptures is so involved that one becomes confused whether or not one should eat meat at all. We have given earlier the views of some Jewish authorities that Israelites were given permission to eat meat as a concession to their weakness. This view begs the assumption that the weakness for which this concession was made is still persisting among Jews. If not, then the concessive clause becomes nullified and they should stop eating meat. We have also mentioned earlier the view of some Jewish theologians that one of the reforms which shall be made by the Promised Messiah would be to abolish the malpractice of meat eating. If the Jews do believe that it is a malpractice, why not start purifying themselves now for the Advent of the Messiah by stopping meat-eating? Some Jewish theologians have put the point in much stronger terms. They assert:

> If the Torah (the books of Moses in the Hebrew Bible) allows the use of meat, it is only for people whose spirit is lost any way. [49]

> Killing of animals in order to consume their meat causes damage to the human spirit.[50]

At the same time, there are other paradoxically conflicting views:

> Meat should be consumed especially by people who are engaged in spiritual work.[51]

Or:

> ... [meat] should be used at times when people work with their spirit such as Sabbath [Saturday] and holy days.[52]

> The use of meat is a positive thing. ... it brings the protein of the animal from the lower level of animal protein to a higher level of human protein.[53]

There are people in this world who kill animals by subjecting them to protracted torture to make palatable relishes and patties. There are those who exploit them commercially; or others who put them on the rack in the name of pecuniary science and other ostensible stakes. From the religious point of view, all such people are committing sins; but more sinful than all of them are those who commit an act of cruelty to animals in the name of God and start quoting His scriptures to justify their iniquities.

Muslims are supposed to have a greater responsibility towards animals and are more accountable for their wrongs to them, because the Qur'ân and the teachings of the Prophet Mohammad have left them with far more detailed instructions on animal rights and on man's moral obligations towards them than any other scripture. Islam has tried to free its adherents from all sorts of rites, rituals and ostentatious ceremonies associated with animals or their slaughter for food. Islam's extraordinary emphasis on animal welfare should have made the Muslims more capable of critical judgement and discernment in their treatment of animals—free from heresy and affected puritanism. Instead, some of them have started looking up to other religions for guidance.

This and other associated attitudes need further discussion on subjects, such as: The method of slaughter; pre-slaughter stunning; the lawful (*halal* and *haram*) concepts of food; sacrifices of animals. All these subjects shall be discussed, next in the sequel.

REFERENCES AND NOTES (CHAPTER 2)

1. Marcus Tullius Cicero, Roman philosopher, politician, and writer; (143-106 B.C.).

2. Avogadro: An Italian chemist famous for his findings about molecules known as Avogadro's 'hypothesis' or 'law' which he announced in 1811 A.C.

3. These and other such examples have been cited by Jon Wynne-Tyson in: *Food for a Future*; Centaur Press, England, 1979. (Hereafter referred to as Wynne-Tyson).

4. Wynne-Tyson; (see Ref. No. 3 Ch. 2.); pp. 16-19, 22, 23, 36, 145.

5. In addition to Wynn-Tyson's book mentioned in Ref. No. 2, the interested reader would find the following books informative:

(1) *The Civilised Alternative* (see Ref. No. 2.).

(2) *The Composition of Foods*; R. A. McCance and E. M. Widdowson; HMSO; 1973.

(3) *Food Fit for Humans*; Frank Wilson; Daniel; 1975.

(4) *Eating for Life*; Nathaniel Altman, Theosophical Publishing House; 1973.

(5) *Abstinence from Animal Food*; Porphyry; Centaur Press, England; 1965.

> Editor's Note: A recent summary of statistical information on this subject can be found in 'The Global Benefits of Eating Less Meat' published CIWF Trust, 5a Charles Street, Petersfield, Hampshire, UK. See www.ciwf.org.uk or www.eatlessmeat.org

6. cf. *The Analects of Confucius*; Arthur Waley; New York; 1938; p.128.

7. id; p.150.

8. Mencius (372-285 B.C.) is considered to be the greatest exponent of the teachings of Confucius: the Neo-Confucian Movement which was started in the 13th. century B.C. drew its inspiration from his teachings.

9. *Meng-tzu, The Four Books*; James Legge; Chinese Book Co., Shanghai; 1930; p.453.

10. cf. *Encyclopaedia of Buddhism*; Government Press, Ceylon; 1965.

11. *Rock Edict I*; Amulayachandra Sen; The Institute of Indology; 1956; p.64.

12. id. Malalasekara; (see Ref. No. 9).

13. *Jataka Tales*; H. Francis & E. T. Thomas; Cambridge University Press; 1916; pp. 20-22.

14. *Studies in Jaina Philosophy*; *Acaranga Sutra*; Wathmal Tatia; Jain Cultural Research Society, Banaras; 1951 p.18.

15. *Ancient Buddhism in Japan*; N.V. De Visser; Leiden; E. J. Brill; 1935; p.198.

16. cf. *The Conception of Ahimsa in Indian Thought*; Koshlya Wadia; Varanasi, Bharata Manisha; 1974.

17. cf. *Purusartha-Siddhyupaya*, 140.

18. *P. S. Jaini*; p.171.

19. cf. *Jaina Sutra*; Herman Jacobi; Motilal Banarsidas, Delhi; 1973.

20. *The Buddha Speaks the Brahma Net Sutra*; Buddhist Text Translation Society, Talmage, California; p.150.

21. *Vinaya Texts*; T. W. Rhys-Davids & Herman Oldenberg; Motilal Banarsidas, Delhi; 1974.

22. id. (see Ref. No. 10.).

23. *Universal Responsibility and the Good Heart*; Tenzin Gyatso, the 14th Dalai Lama, Library of Tibetan Works, India; 1980; p.78.

24. *Genesis*; 1:29, 30.

25. *Leviticus*; 2:1.

26. *Christ in Christian Tradition*; Aloys Grillemier; Mowbrays; 1965.

27. *Church Dogmatics*; Karl Barth; Vol. III, Part One, T & T Clark; 1958; p.208.

28. *Isaiah*; 22:13, 14.

29. *Isaiah*; 65:17-25.

30. *Isaiah*; 11:6.

31. For detailed views of Jewish vegetarianism, refer to *The Prophecy of Vegetarianism and Peace* by Rabbi Hochen-Knock—the first Chief Rabbi of Israel. Also contact the Jewish Vegetarian Society, "Bet Jeva", 855 Finchley Road, London NW11. There have been three vegetarian Chief Rabbis in Israel during the last 25 years.

32. *The Qur'ān*; 3:64; Free translation by: Maulana Abul Kalam Azad; *Tarjuman al-Quran*, Vol. 2; Asia Publishing House; London; 1967.

33. Hadith *Al-Sahî Bukhari*: 1:1 Al-Imam Abd-Allah Muhammad bin Ismail al-Bukhari; Krehl & Juynboll, Leiden; 1908.

34. *The Qur'ān*; 5:6 (some translations, 5:5).

35. *Deuteronomy*; 7:2, 3.

36. *The Qur'ān*; 2:190; 8:61, 62; 22:39.

37. *The Qur'ān*; 22:40. (For the details of Caliph Abu Bakr's instructions to the army cf. *Tabari*, III, p.123).

38. *The Qur'ān*; 3:66.

39. *The Qur'ān*; 7:31; 5:87; and other verses.

40. The writer is basing this statement on his personal visits to about 45 countries, most of which were Islamic.

41. *Genesis*; 1:29, 30 & Isaiah; 11:6-9.

42. *Genesis*; 1:29,30.

43. Rabbi Abraham Kood, the Chief Rabbi of Palestine before the establishment of the State of Israel.

44. *Genesis*; 32:28.

45. See Reference No. 49.

46. (1) Hadith: *Kitab al-Sunan*, 2:123; Abu Dawûd Sulaiman.

    (2) Hadith: *Al-Jami al-Musnad al-Sahih al-Bukhari*, 66:4; Al-Imam Abd-Allah Muhammad bin Ismail al-Bukhari.

    (3) id. 65:19, 20.

    (4) Imam Ibn Hajar Asqualani has mentioned many scribes by name, including the first four Caliphs: Hazrat Abu Bakr (632 A.C.—11 A.H.);

Hazrat Omar bin al-Khattab (634 A.C.—13 A.H.); Hazrat Osman (644 A.C.—23 A.H.); Hazrat Alli bin Abi Talib (656 A.C.—35 A.H.) in his book of Hadith: *Fath al-Bari fi Sharhe Shih Bukhari.*

47. Hadith: *Al-Sahih Bukhari,* 3:27; 66:21-23, 25, 33. (see Ref. No. 33).

48. Hadith: *Al-Jami,* 39:5; Abu Isa Muhammad bin Tirmidhi.

49. cf. *Abarbanel* 1610; as quoted in *Jewish Attitude Towards Slaughter;* I. M. Levinger; Department of Life Sciences, Bar Ilan University, Ramat Gan, Israel; Animal Regulation Studies, 2, (1979) 103-109, Elsevier Scientific Publishing Co., Amsterdam.

50. *Albo,* 1425. (see Ref. No. 49).

51. *Talmud;* (see Ref. No. 49).

52. *Maimonides,* 1150 b; (see Ref. No. 49).

53. *Machmanides,* 1250; (see Ref. No. 49).

3

PIG—A THORN IN THE FLESH[i]

PREAMBLE

THE RECENT INCREASE IN the Muslim immigrant population in the Western countries has brought certain aspects of their cultural and religious disciplines into conflict with the Western way of life. The question of the Muslim dietetic practices and rules, particularly the distinction between the lawful (*halal*) and the unlawful (*haram*) meat, has been a subject of constant controversy. The purpose of this chapter is to discuss the reasons why Islam has prohibited the consumption of pork; other aspects of lawful and unlawful foods will be discussed in Chapter 5.

Pork has been chosen for the discussion only as an example. If one had the time and means to discuss all the other animals which have been prohibited as food by Islam, it should not be difficult to prove scientifically that they are not good for health. We have passed through those dark ages of science-phobia, when religion used to feel itself under attack by secular scholars and science. On the contrary, today, we feel that secular know-how and science are rendering a great service to Islam by corroborating in facts and figures quite a few Qur'ânic statements which the believers had been accepting on 'blind' faith for the last fourteen centuries.

However, some of our young people, especially those born and brought up under the influence of Western culture, need reassurance that the Islamic discipline is based on logical and realistic principles of life, and not on dogmatic prejudices or

---

i The information and opinions expressed in this publication are those of the author. Minor corrections have been made to this chapter to reflect scientific advances since its original publication.

ritualistic conventions. The very word 'discipline' means a system of rules for conduct backed by the necessary instruction for self-control. The Islamic discipline is a system of rules which an individual chooses to obey voluntarily. The Qur'ânic principle that "there shall be no compulsion in religion" denotes that the Islamic discipline should emerge from within and not be imposed by means of coercion, whether physical or psychological.

The Islamic approach to mental, spiritual, and physical education of mankind is through gentle persuasion by way of moral conviction of direct responsibility to God. The only censor of one's actions is one's own conscience. The Muslim theologians and the learned Ulama can help in one's religious instruction and give guidance, but they are not allowed in Islam to play the part of ministerial intermediaries between man and God. That is why professional priesthood is forbidden in Islam. In order to understand why compulsion or undue pressure is forbidden in religious matters, it is necessary to quote the above verse in full. After explicitly stating that "there shall be no compulsion in religion", the Qur'ân goes on to explain that

> true guidance has now been made distinct from error. He who resists evil and puts his faith in Allah indeed takes hold of the most trustworthy support that will never fail him—for Allah hears and knows all. (Qur'ân 2:256)

The verse quoted above, and many other such passages in the Qur'ân, lay down the dictum that is up to an individual to look after their moral, spiritual, and physical health. The function of religion is to show the way (din)—those who follow the way benefit from it and reach the destination; those who do not, get themselves lost. There is no denying the fact that our diet does affect not only our physical health but also influences our mental and spiritual development. This action and reaction of cause and effect may not become perceptible in one's lifetime; it might involve a long chain of causes and might take generations or even centuries to show. The New Testament points out the relationship between body and soul in these words:

> Know ye not that ye are the temple of God, and that
> the Spirit of God dwelleth in you? If any man defile the
> temple of God, him shall God destroy; for the temple of
> God is holy, which temple you are.[1]

Anthropology is the science of the physiological entity of man as an animal while ethology is the science of his character formation. A study of both these sciences reveals that the ethos or characteristic spirit of an individual and, hence, of a community is influenced more by diet and lifestyle than by geographical or other factors such as climate. We see the same law of nature at work with the animals living in the wild—not the domestic animals whose diet has been adulterated and tampered with by man. The carnivorous animals who feed on flesh and the animals who live on a purely vegetarian diet are poles apart in physique and in nature. Tigers, leopards, lions, and other members of the cat family are ferocious and aggressive in nature while elephants and other herbivorous animals are not usually disposed to aggression except in self-defence. Most of the carnivore species never get tamed even after life-long captivity, while most of the vegetarian species are so docile that it does not take long to tame them. If the word could be used on animals, it could be said that they come out of barbarism and become 'civilised' in the true sense of the word. Lions, tigers, and other such carnivores never develop a sense of rapport with man and return back to the bush, whenever they get the chance. The domestic cat still retains its character of aloof detachment even after being domesticated by man for thousands of years. Of course, there are other numerous biological factors which play their part in the formation of the characteristic spirit of a species, but there is ample scientific evidence to conclude that diet is one of the most potent factors.

Perhaps human beings, as one of the animal species, are no exception to this law of nature. Religious instruction aims at covering not only mental and spiritual disciplines but also physical discipline for the simple reason that all these three aspects of human life are interdependent and complementary to one another in the formation of ethos. The comprehensive code of Islamic laws is based on truism of nature and is called *din-al-fitrah*. Its laws are practical and practicable. According to verse 185 of Chapter 2 and many other such verses of the Qu'ran, the Islamic law is for the well-being of man and is not meant to be a source of hardship.

Before concluding this Preamble, another theme of the Islamic teachings needs to be pointed out here. According to a saying of the Prophet Mohammad: "All creatures are like family (ayal) of God, and God loves the most those who are the most beneficent to the members of His family."[2]

While speaking of "all creatures" in this Hadith, no exception has been made of any species of animals—not even pigs. This Chapter has been devoted to explaining that pigs are unclean in the sense that they are unsuitable for human consumption. However, in the light of the above and many other similar Ahadith, our rejection of pigs should be confined only to the eating of their flesh. The true Islamic spirit of animal rights demands that we should accept this animal as one of the species created for some purpose according to the Divine scheme of creation. According to the Qu'ran, Allah has not created anything but for a purpose; and surely, He has not created pigs for the purpose of being hated. The pig is what God's nature has meant it to be and it is entitled to as much compassion and humane treatment as any other animal in the world. Its flesh, no doubt, is forbidden as food like the flesh of many other animals, but surely it is un-Islamic to hate it or to treat it cruelly.

It is very unfortunate that the feelings of hatred for this animal are very deep-rooted among some of the Muslims, as if it were an evil. Such Muslims fail to realise that this sort of attitude against pigs, or against any creation of God, is one of those prejudices and superstitions which owe their origin to the pre-Islamic susceptibilities. The Qu'ran and the Ahadith are so full of behests and admonitions regarding the humane treatment of all animals that it would need hundreds of pages to discuss them all. The Islamic sanction of using animals as food cannot be understood without understanding the true Islamic concept of relationship between human beings and the rest of the animals. However, before trying to explain why Islam has prohibited the consumption of pork, it will help to mention briefly what some other religions have to say about pork; and then, lastly, what modern science tells us about it.

THE ANCIENT ASIAN RELIGIONS

The ancient Chinese, representing the Confucian religion and culture, were not vegetarians in principle. However, the overwhelming majority of them have always been agriculturists. Even these days many are agrarian and can rarely afford to eat pork, except on certain feast days such as New Year's Day, the fifth day of the fifth moon, or the fifteenth day of the eighth moon. The main food of the peasants has been a curd made of soya beans, called Tofu. However, with the growth of the urban middle class in recent years in China, pork has become a popular food and now around half of the world's pigs are farmed in China. As mentioned in the previous chapter, neither the prophet Confucius nor the great sage Mencius were non-vegetarians. In spite of that, pork was considered during their time as unhealthy food. Most of the literature, based on the Confucian "Book of Rites" (Lee-Chi) which is more than 3,000 years old, condemns pork as food. For example, it says: "A gentleman does not eat the flesh of pigs and dogs."[3]

Lee Shih Ch'en was a great authority as a physician during the Ming Dynasty. The very name means an 'oracle in medicine'—a subject on which he wrote a book comprising 50 volumes. He says: ". . . pork has a pungent smell and gives concentrated gravy. It has poisonous ill effects . . ." Another Chinese physician of renown during the Tang Dynasty—Sun See Mao—says: "pork encourages the revival of old ailments, leads to sterility, fosters rheumatism and asthma."[4] In general, the verdict of the other Chinese physicians is that "all flesh is nourishing, except pork" and their advice is not to eat it.[5]

Hindus are not supposed to eat any meat at all. However, even those who do, shun pork. Like the Zoroastrian Zend-Avesta, the Hindu Vedas also do not mention pork specifically except for one passage which records the following incident:

> One day when Manikavasagam was worshipping Siva, he offered him, after his prayers, the meat of a wild boar he had just hunted. Suddenly he saw blood oozing from the eyes of the deity and then he heard a voice saying: "you who eat this meat have sinned."[6]

The Jains and the Buddhists, too, are not allowed any kind of meat including pork. It has been explained in Chapter Two of this book that they are forbidden to kill any creature for food or for any other purpose. Ahimsa being the first of the Buddhists' commandments of the Mahayana, known as the 'Great Vehicle'. Since their prohibition of meat is in toto and purely on religious grounds, the question does not arise in their scriptures as to which meat is more or less hygienic.

JUDAISM

The law of Moses contains the first categorical prohibition of eating in these words:

> And the swine, because it divideth the hoof, yet cheweth not the cud, it is unclean unto you; ye shall not eat their flesh, nor touch the dead carcase.[7]

Again in Leviticus the prohibition is repeated in similar words.[8]

Before commenting on the verses, it is important to understand the sense in which the word 'unclean' has been used in the English translations of the Bible. The original Greek word is koinos which means 'common'. When the Greek Bible uses the word koinos in relation to human beings, it means 'spiritually common' in the sense of defiled and unworthy—indicating a heathen, a pagan, an uncircumcised person, or racially a gentile, i.e. a non-Jew.[9] When the word is applied to animals, it does not and cannot mean unclean in any spiritual sense. It means 'common' in the same sense as St. Peter and St. Paul have used it, i.e. in the sense of 'inferior quality' or 'coarse fare'.

The reason given by Moses in the above quotations for the prohibition of pork is, on the face of it, not very convincing. One wonders what difference it makes whether or not an animal has its hoofs cloven or whether it chews the cud or not. However, when one studies this Biblical statement in the light of modern scientific classification of animals, the significance of this condition becomes obvious.

There are certain factors which are common among that suborder of mammals which have been proved by thousands of years of practical human experience to be suitable for eating. Those factors have been accepted as the distinguishing physiological features which determine their hereditary characteristics. Let us try to understand those distinguishing features. In the modern biological definition of this suborder of edible mammals, they are artiodactyl (even-toed) ungulates whose hoofs are cloven and who regurgitate food; ruminate and masticate it. In simple words, the animals which belong to this class have the following two features in common:

(a) Their hoofs are cloven and split and not solid like the hoofs of some other animals.

(b) They chew the cud, which means that, to begin with, they throw the food into one of the compartments of their stomach without chewing it, so that it may be acted upon by bacteria in the rumen (first stomach) and the otherwise indigestible fibre broken down until it is fit to be brought back into the mouth to be chewed and swallowed and then digested in that compartment of the stomach which is equipped by nature with enzymes formed by living cells.

Somehow a biological distinction had to be made by the prophets between those species of animals which may be used for food and those which are hygienically unsuitable for consumption. The criterion of cud-chewing happens to be one of the obvious discriminative factors between pigs and other cloven-footed animals. All the other domesticated animals which are allowed by the Mosaic Law are the ones which chew the cud, such as oxen, sheep, goats, and deer. Otherwise, pigs have quite a few other features in common for which they are liable to be confused with them. The Bible equates the eating of their flesh with the eating of mice and other rodents, in the following words:

> They that sanctify themselves, and purify themselves in the gardens behind one tree in the midst, eating swine's flesh, and the abomination, and the mouse, shall be consumed together, saith the Lord.[10]

It is for this and other such reasons that the Law of Moses accentuated the prohibition of this animal as food. Perhaps the great Hebrew Prophet and the Lawgiver could not or would not explain in scientific terminology the difference between the pigs' flesh and that of animals which human experience of thousands of years has found to be acceptable as food. In the words of Rev. Vories:

> The Bible so clearly and definitely forbids the eating of pork that all who love the word of God and would follow its teachings have no question at all as to whether or not they should abstain from feasting on the unclean creature.[11]

Muslims too believe that the authentic Mosaic Law was divinely inspired and that it is capable of maintaining its validity even under modern scientific scrutiny. All the Biblical prophets who followed Moses, until the advent of Jesus Christ, endorsed this prohibition which is being observed by most Jews even today. The prohibition of pork is one of the dietetic laws of Moses which have much in common with those of Islam. For example, according to both, all those animals which die a natural death or are killed by beasts have been forbidden as food; and so is blood forbidden.[12] There are, however, quite a few differences of detail between the two codes of law, which shall be discussed later in the book.

CHRISTANITY

According to Muslims, as they understand the teachings of Jesus Christ, he did not rescind the law of Moses in this respect nor did he declare the Mosaic prohibition of pork as revoked. In the Sermon on the Mount, he declared: "Think not that I am come to destroy the Law, or the prophets: I am not come to destroy, but to fulfill."[13]

Muslims understand this and from various other declarations of Jesus that the Law of Moses remains valid except for those parts of the Rabbinical law which were specifically altered, amended, or repealed by Jesus.

It is believed by some Christians that Jesus was born in a family of Essenes who belonged to a monastic order among the Jews of Palestine from the 2nd century B.C. to the 2nd century A.C. They were a community which observed strict moral laws and stringent austerity. It is claimed by such Christians that Jesus, as an Essene, was a vegetarian. We are not concerned here about this as it is a controversial subject among Christians. What we know for certain is that no record of his life mentions him as eating swine flesh, or indeed any other meat. On the contrary, according to the New Testament, he considered pigs as unclean.

Muslims regard Jesus as a great messenger of God. According to the Qur'ân he was born as a result of his mother Mary's immaculate conception and his mission was assisted by the Holy Spirit.[14] Like the Christians, those Muslims who accept some *Hadith* on this subject, too are hoping and praying for his second Advent. It is natural, therefore, that Muslims attach great importance to his teachings. This is what he had to say about pigs: ". . . neither cast ye your pearls before swine, lest they trample them under their feet, and turn again and rend you."[15]

The incidence of Gergesenes or Gadarenes has been recorded in both the Gospels of St. Matthew[16] and St. Mark[17]. According to them one or two madmen were possessed by unclean Spirits or Devils. Jesus, in order to exorcise those Spirits out of the madmen, transferred the Spirits from them into a herd of about two thousand pigs. The pigs became so possessed with the evil Spirits that the whole herd jumped over the edge of a cliff into the sea or a lake and perished.

If the above version of the Gospels were to be taken literally, one cannot help drawing two conclusions: firstly, that Jesus valued the health of two madmen more than the lives of about two thousand innocent pigs; secondly, that in the eyes of Jesus pigs were such despicable and insignificant creatures that he filled them with unclean Spirits without any compunction and caused them to jump over the cliff and die.

Muslims, however, hold Jesus Christ in such reverence that they find such an act of cruelty to animals out of character of one who devoted all his life to teaching that love was all-embracing and the greatest salvation of mankind. His compassion for all living creatures, which would include pigs as well, was such that St. Luke records him as saying: "Are not five sparrows sold for two farthings, and not one of them is forgotten before God."[18]

We believe that if Jesus were saying the same thing in our modern English, he would have conveyed this message in words such as: 'Even the smallest and the humblest of living creatures have their place within the circle of God's love'.

The observance of the Sabbath has always been so important to the Jews that its violation is considered to be a major sin. When Jesus wanted to heal the withered hand of a man in a synagogue on Sabbath day, he was told that it was unlawful to do so. His reply to them is indicative of the importance he attached not only to human life but also to the life of animals. He said:

> What man shall there be among you, that shall have one sheep, and if it falls into a pit on the sabbath day, will he not lay hold on it, and lift it out.[19]

Some Christians believe that, according to a vision of St. Peter, pigs have been cleansed by God and, therefore, the Jewish prohibition of pork has been rescinded. Let us study the vision in detail to see how far their interpretation is correct:

> Peter . . . fell into a trance, and saw heaven opened, and a certain vessel descending unto him, as it had been a great sheet knit at the four corners and let down to the earth: wherein were all manner of four-footed beasts of the earth, and wild beasts, and creeping things, and fowls of the air. And there came a voice to him, rise, Peter; kill, and eat. But Peter said, 'Not so, Lord; for I have never eaten any thing that is common or unclean.' And the voice spake unto him again the second time, what God hath cleansed that call not thou common. This was done thrice: and the vessel was received up again into heaven (Acts Chapter 10).[20]

The argument advanced in favour of pork is that all manner of animals, including pigs, have been cleansed by God according to this vision and, hence, are lawful to eat. If this interpretation were to be accepted, then it would mean that all living creatures, without exception, are lawful to eat. But we know that there are certain animals, creeping things and insects which are hygienically unsuitable and even noxious for human consumption. Obviously, this interpretation of the vision is fallacious. However, it is gratifying to know that most of the Christian theologians give this vision a metaphorical interpretation. According to the common Jewish belief in those days, all the non-Hebrew peoples of the world were unclean and unfit for the Biblical teachings. This vision of St. Peter was meant to put this fallacy right and to explain to the Christians that the blessings of the mission of Jesus Christ were meant for all humanity. When the voice in the vision told St. Peter to eat those animals, it was meant in a spiritual sense to embrace all creation within the fold of the divine message through Jesus Christ, irrespective of caste, colour, or race.

The metaphorical interpretation of St. Peter is also borne out of the events directly connected with his vision, both before and after the vision. A Roman Soldier, named Cornelius of Caesarea, was considered to be 'unclean' as a gentile. Yet he was a pious and charitable man. God inspired him to contact Peter. He sent three of his servants to Joppa to invite Peter to his place. When St. Peter was having this vision, the three so-called unclean men were on their way to convey to him the invitation of Cornelius. St. Peter went to see Cornelius where he found many other 'unclean' gentiles waiting for him. St. Peter said to them:

> Ye know that it is an unlawful thing for a man that is a Jew to keep company, or come unto one of another nation; but God hath showed me [in a vision] that I should not call any man common or unclean

The fact that St. Peter refused to eat unclean animals in his vision ten years after Jesus Christ shows the biblical dietary laws were still being observed by the Christians at large and that pork was considered by them as forbidden; until St. Paul made it lawful, some believe, as a concession to the Romans' relish for it. Some Christians, however, reject the very assertion that he sanctioned the consumption of pork at all. According to them, what he said was that "there is nothing unclean of itself", meaning that no creature of God should be considered common and ordinary."[21]

Notwithstanding the fact that Christians, by and large, have become large consumers of pork, there are quite a few of them who are still adhering to the original Biblical dietary laws in general and abstinence from pork in particular. One comes across some prominent Christians, even among the Chinese who are renowned as pork-eaters, who strongly believe that Christians should not eat pork. A Chinese Christian priest, Lin Hung Pin, writes in his book entitled *Tai Chu Yo Tao*:

> Not only pork should be shunned, but anything harm-
> ful to health should be altogether avoided . . . I dare to bear
> witness that anyone who obeys the teachings of health
> of the true God, his health will surely improve. Anyone
> who disbelieves will always suffer from sickness . . . God
> Forbids His people from rearing and trading in pigs. They
> should not eat pork nor should they touch it. It is clearly
> said in the Bible that the whole body of the pig is dirty and
> so ham, which is pork, is equally dirty.[22]

Another clergyman writes about pigs:

> See the brute as he wallows in the mud. See him in
> the very height of his glory, on top of a manure pile, with
> his head in the dung from which exalted site he gives
> expression to his joy and satisfaction by his rhythmic
> grunts.[23]

A Christian anthropologist, Dr. Marwin Harris, describes the pig's unhygienic habits: "it will cover its skin with its own urine and faeces."[24] H.L. Hastings, a learned authority on the Bible, has this to say about pigs' eating habits:

> "Swine were designed to be scavengers, to eat up
> filth and abominations; but when they had done their
> work it was not designed that men should turn around
> and eat the swine."[25]

ISLAM

In line with the verdict of Judaism and some Christians, Islam too has declared swineflesh as unclean and unsuitable for human consumption. The Qur'ân declares pork as Haram in these words:

He [Allah] has forbidden you what dies a natural death, and the swineflesh. . . . (Qur'ân 2:173)

Forbidden to you is that which dies a natural death, and blood, and the swineflesh. . . . (Qur'ân 2:173)

Say [O Prophet]: 'In all that has been revealed unto me, I do not find anything forbidden to eat, if one wants to eat thereof, unless it be . . . and the flesh of swine—for surely that is unclean . . . but if one is driven by necessity, neither coveting it nor exceeding the limit of one's want, then thy Sustainer is much forgiving and merciful. (Qur'ân 6:145)

The words 'if one wants to eat it' are meant to leave the option open for a Muslim to become vegetarian, if one opts to do so. The same message is repeated in these words:

He [Allah] has forbidden you only what dies a natural death, and blood, and the swineflesh . . . but if one is driven by necessity, neither coveting it nor exceeding the limits of one's want—then Allah is much forgiving and merciful" (Qur'ân 16:115)

In the last two verses, it is significant to note the exception to the rule by allowing the Muslims the freedom of infringement under necessity and in leaving the decision to the judgement of the individual's conscience. Had the prohibition to the eating of pork been on the grounds of fanaticism in the sense of excessive religious enthusiasm; or pantheism in the sense of irrational and doctrinal belief in deities; or occultism in the sense that this animal possesses some mysterious and magical powers to destroy those who eat it; or had the prohibition been on the ground of superstition in the sense of belief in the supernatural—then the Qur'ânic Law would not have given permission to eat pork even in the circumstances of absolute biological and natural necessity.

What these verses are trying to tell the believers is that pork is not good for your health; but, if you ever find yourself in a situation where no other food is available, then do not endanger your life by starvation and eat it without relish and only as much as is necessary to keep yourself alive. It should be understood that the Qur'ânic prohibition of swineflesh applies to all the parts of its body and its by-products. The Arabic word *lahm* means flesh but stands for all the parts.[26] The verses bring out two important points: firstly, that swineflesh is hygienically unsuitable for consumption and detrimental for physical health (*rijs*)[27]; secondly, that is sinful to eat pork because it is spiritually harmful (*fisque*). Keeping in mid the overall Qur'ânic concept of sin, it should not be difficult to appreciate that the sins by way of physical transgression of the laws of nature result in physical retribution in the form of pain, suffering and disease in this life. Sins by way of deviation from rectitude, on the other hand, are punishable in the life hereafter. The reason why physical transgressions are also classified as sins, and not merely as mistakes, is that they are conducive to moral and spiritual dereliction. This inter-connection between physical and spiritual sins has been explained by Jesus Christ also in these words:

> For from within, out of the hearts of men, proceed evil thoughts, adulteries, fornications, murders, thefts, covetousness, wickedness, deceit, lasciviousness, an evil eye, blasphemy, pride, foolishness: all these evil things come from within, and defile the man.[28]

The point cannot be over-emphasized that prohibition of pork in Islam and Judaism (and depending on interpretation, in Christianity) only because it is unhealthy to eat and not because of any superstition or bias against the animal. One often hears the arguments that the proverbial pigsties or the dirty hovels of the olden days have been replaced by clean pens; that the pigs' diet is now healthier and that the standard of general farming conditions has been improved; and hence, this animal has become much more suitable for our tables. But all scientific evidence shows that no hygienic improvements in breeding and rearing can change the built-in metabolism of an animal. According to a saying quoted by St. Peter: "the dog is turned to his own vomit again; and the sow that was washed to her wallowing in the mire."[29] The Oxford Dictionary gives figurative description of the pig as "a greedy, dirty, sulky, obstinate or annoying person."

It will not be amiss here to inform the readers of the various names and terms used in English for different kinds of pigs and their meat, as most Muslims are not conversant with them. It is interesting to note how the experts of physiological science (physiologists) explain the very name 'swine'. According to their definition, swine is an "ungulate, non-ruminant, omnivorous mammal." Let us see what do these unfamiliar terms mean: 'ungulate' means a hoofed animal, 'non-ruminant' is one who does not chew the cud. The most relevant to the subject under discussion is the word 'omnivorous'. It is made up of 'omni' and 'vorous'. Omni means all or everything; and vorous is one who is greedy and voracious in eating. Although Omnivorous is usually used to denote someone or some animal who eats both meat and plants, it can have a further meaning denoting greed. 'Mammal' is a word derived from 'mamma' which means the milk-secreting organs of a female. Thus, a mammal belongs to that order of animals whose females suckle or breastfeed their young. So, in simple words, a swine is a hoofed animal who does not chew the cud, is a greedy, voracious, and indiscriminate eater of anything on offer, even if it is unclean or unhygienic.

These days the name 'pig' is used more commonly for swine. A fattened pig raised for food is called a 'porker'; a young uncastrated pig is a boar; a castrated pig, especially reared for food is called a 'hog'; an adult female is a 'sow'; and a young female is called a 'gilt'.

Flesh of swine in general is called pork; cured back and sides is 'bacon'; the bottom of bacon including the hind legs is 'gammon'; salted and dried thigh of hog is 'ham'; smoked or cured ham is called 'gammon of bacon'; clarified fat of pigs from the internal parts of the abdomen is called 'lard' and 'to lard' is a term used for inserting strips of bacon in other meats before cooking for which a 'larding needle' is used.

THE NOSOLOGY OF PIGS

Let us see what our veterinary scientists and dieticians have to say about swineflesh as food, in the light of modern medical research. However, before reading the undermentioned long list of diseases, it must be understood that all other food animals are also prone to most of these diseases and that their flesh too can pass those diseases onto the meat eater. The reason why these diseases are being listed below in the context of pigs is that, according to the modern veterinarians, pigs have far more predisposition to these diseases and are a greater hazard to health than other animals through parasitical infestation. It is fallacy to think that pork can be made safe for consumption by prevention and sanitation. This is what a learned veterinarian, Dr. Dykstra, tells us about this problem.

> Theoretically, all of it [parasitical infestation] is controllable by sanitation. But who is to solve the practical problems, such as keeping pigs away from the pastures which have been infected by their own kind, or stop them from eating rubbish, dead worms, insects, and other infected carcasses? The problem is that most of the parasitical food which pigs eat, if they can lay their snouts on it, contains germs which are resistant to normal and economical anti-toxins, especially when they are in the stage of single cells as spores."

Dr. Dykstra goes on:

> Man should convince himself that the pork products he consumes have been well cooked . . . it hardly seems that cooked worms could be appetising, but it is clearly evident that many do not cook pork sufficiently to kill trichinae. In a series of 24 cases of trichinosis reported recently, 22 were said to have resulted from cooked pork.[30]

Perhaps it is due to the fact that they eat far more and the wrong kind of food than is good for their health. As a result, they become more prone to infection which they pass on to those who eat or handle them. There are quite a few diseases which have been named after swine and pigs, such as: swine-fever, swine-plague, swinepox, swine-influenza, swine-erysipelas, swine-variola, lung disease of swine, pig-paratyphoid, and measles of pork etc. It is a medical fact that pigs are liable to suffer from all these and many other diseases besides, although other species of food-animals suffer from some of them. Let us go through the list of some of the pigs' diseases:[31]

PARASITICAL DISEASES

1.   **Trichinella:** There is a hairlike parasite in the body of swine which is introduced in the human body by eating pork when not cooked properly. The parasite is called Trichinella, and the disease is called Trichinosis. Another animal which is infected with this parasite is the rat—an equally unclean animal. After lodging in the intestines, the larvae enter the muscles of the pigs and infect those who eat the infected flesh. The disease starts with severe pain in the muscles, nausea, diarrhoea, swelling of the face and often proves fatal. It is generally believed that pigs get this infection by eating infected dead rodents. These worms are very small and attach themselves to the intestinal wall. Those who have these worms pass them out through their stools, each parasitical segment containing as many as 75,000 eggs.[32] These eggs mature and are ready to reproduce within 40 hours. Each parasite larva or cell (cyst) contains up to seven worms which continue living for about 30 years after infection. All such scientific facts were not known during the periods when the Qur'ân and the other revealed scriptures before it declared this animal as unfit for consumption. It was only in 1828 A.C. that medical science discovered the trichina worm.

A famous authority on the subject, Dr. Glen Shephard, says:

> One in six people in the United States of America and Canada have germs in their muscles—Trichinosis— from eating pork infected with Trichina or Trichina-worms. Many people who are so infected, have no symptoms. Most of those who have, recover very slowly. Some die, some are reduced to permanent invalidity. All were careless pork eaters. No one is immune from this disease and there is no cure. Neither antibiotics nor drugs, nor vaccines affect these tiny deadly worms. Preventing infection is the real answer. Fully grown Trichina worms are about 1/8 inch long and about 1/400 inch broad. They remain alive for up to 40 years, curled up in lemon shaped tiny capsules between fibres. When you eat infected meat, those dormant worm capsules are digested but their contents grow into full-sized worms each of which has about 1,500 offspring. They get

into your blood one to two weeks after you have eaten their parents. Because many organs can be invaded by the worms, symptoms can resemble those of 50 other diseases. This makes diagnosis difficult. Ordinary methods of salting and smoking do not kill those worms; nor can government inspection of meat at packing houses or abattoirs identify all inspected pork.[33]

Many other medical experts have expressed similar opinions about trichinella spiralis. For example:

Next to fat, pork—the 'second curse' on the image of pork—is trichinosis. It is a common opinion among consumers that there is something wrong with pork.[34]

The infected pork eaten by man will liberate the worms [Trichinae] which develop quickly and multiply rapidly into young generations; some leave the human bowel and some travel via the blood to the muscles of man. The symptoms of the disease produced may be an acute abdominal pain and diarrhoea; twitching in various muscles, the face becoming puffy, and eyelids swell, and the patients become weak. Then comes the stage of fever like typhoid and at this stage the younger generation of worms are going about the blood trying to settle in the muscles, they cause intense rheumatic and muscular pains. Breathing may be interfered in some cases asthma actually develops. The skin develops a rash and if the stress falls on the lungs, it may be fatal to man at this stage and the mortality rate has been as high as 30 percent of the infected cases. The disease is never recognised in the living swine or even the dead ones. The inspection is unsatisfactory. Out of 6,239 cases of this disease in man which occurred in Germany, 32 percent were traced to meat which had been inspected as free of Trichina.[35]

In a series of 24 cases of trichinosis reported recently, 22 were said to have resulted from 'cooked pork'.[36]

It has been estimated that for man, ingestion of 5 trichinae larvae per gram of body weight is fatal, for hogs 10 and for rats 30. In the year 1945 it was found that the incidence of human infection was high where examinations were made in routine autopsies. The infection ranged from about 5 percent in New Orleans to 18 percent in the entire U.S. Even these figures are apparently below the actual incidence. No other country in the world had (and still has, to the best of my knowledge) an incidence as high as America. 'Several years ago, the government abandoned the microscopic examinations of meat as impractical, so that meats are no longer certified as free from Trichina'.[37]

2. **Taenia:**[ii] They are a genus of tape worms commonly known as 'Pork Tape Worms' and are of two kinds. Those which infest cattle are called 'Taenia Saginata', which complete their life cycle in the intestines. They can, therefore, be removed from the body by drugs. The other kind, however, infest pigs and are called 'Taenia Solium'. They pass through the intestines into the bloodstream and affect the various vital organs such as the heart, lungs, brain, liver, eyes, muscles, and can cause insanity, hysteria, loss of consciousness, and possibly coronary thrombosis. Once the eggs have developed into the stage of cells containing embryos and have become cysticerci, the patient becomes incurable. It is medically confirmed that pigs are the main carriers of these worms in their flesh—which is eaten by humans. Pigs generally get infested by eating excreta expelled from bodies which contain eggs of this worm. According to the

---

ii **Editor's Note:** Taenia Solium causes neurocysticercosis which is a major disease worldwide; millions are affected but the exact figure is unknown. Aside from death, it can cause epilepsy and also hydrocephalus. The tapeworm burrows into the person's bloodstream and ends up in the brain, forming cysts. The cysts can cause muscular convulsions, and if the worms die in the brain they can cause coma due to inflammation. Calcified cysts can trigger immune response for years. (Zimmer, Carl. May 15, 2012, (June 2012 Issue), "Hidden Epidemic: Tapeworms Living Inside People's Brains," *Discover Magazine*.)

There is no known cure for the disease; some drugs that have been tried have serious or fatal side-effects. It is ranked no. 1 by the United Nations Food and Agricultural Organization, among parasitical diseases. Although it is so prevalent in the poorer countries in the world, it is also a problem in Western nations. Experts on this disease are urging that human cysticercosis be made a notifiable disease and to develop a register for it. ("Taenia solium in Europe: Still endemic?" https://doi.org/10.1016/j.actatropica.2015.08.006)

CDC website: "Note that cystecirosis is only acquired from the fecal-oral route, not via . . . undercooked pork, which is associated with intestinal taeiasis."

3. **Cysticercus Tenuicollis:** Caused by the larval form of a certain species of tapeworms (*Taenia hydatigena*), also called bladder-worms. The larvae live in the liver, the intestinal wall and in the membranes.

4. **Cysticercus Cellulosae:** Caused by another species of tapeworm (*Taenia solium*). They live in the flesh, heart, and tongue of pigs. Most remain asymptomatic.

5. **Hydatid:** A cyst found in various parts of the body, filled with watery fluid caused by *Echinococcus Granulosus*. These tapeworms infect the intestines and are considered to be one of the most dangerous and often fatal parasites. It is a very common disease in pig-breeding and pork-eating counties.

6. **Echinococcus Polymorphus:** It is the larval stage another small tapeworm (*Taenia Echinococcus*). The adult infests the intestines while the larvae develop in various tissues. It is a dangerous and often fatal parasite. The cyst or hydatid (see above) formed by the larvae becomes very large. secondary cysts develop within it, from the walls of which numerous tapeworm heads (scoleces) grow. These, if eaten by a hog or other animals, may develop into adult worms.

7. **Round Worms:** They are a genus of nematode worms, from the family *Ascaridae*, distinguished by the three-lipped mouth. They grow to a length of 9 to 10 inches, resembling an earthworm in size and appearance. They travel to almost all the organisms in the body and are thus also called 'travelling worms.' Since they live in the flesh of food-animals, especially pigs, the human consumers of flesh get infected by them. It has been microbiologically established that these parasites, found both in the swine and the human body, are identical and belong to the same family.[38]

8. **Ascaris Lumbricoides:** Also belong to the same family of worm as round worms, except that they are parasites in the intestines and can grow to 14 inches. The minute microbes of this worm enter the lung through the bloodstream, after passing out

of the intestines, and then return to the intestines again after a stay of ten days in the lung. It takes them about ten weeks to reach maturity. Their average lifespan is five years.

9.   **Arduenna Strongylina:** They are a kind of roundworm also of the species of nematodes, constituting the family of *strongylidae*. They are parasitic that live in the mucous membrane of the pig's stomach walls, causing catarrhal gastritis.

10.   **Hookworms:** These worms, like other parasites, are found more in pigs than in other animals. They enter the body through the skin, especially if it is open by a wound, or orally. Pigs are prone to infection more than other animals because of their eating habits. These worms thrive in a tropical climate.

11.   **Macracanthorhynchus Hirudinaceus:** They are another leech-like hookworm living in the small intestines of pigs. Heavy infections may induce a catarrhal enteritis and, rarely, penetration of the intestinal wall, which can result in a fatal peritonitis.

12.   **Kidney Worms:** They are a species of nematode worms with elongated bodies and pointed extremities. They are parasitic in kidneys, lungs, liver, and anywhere in the blood vessels outside the digestive system of pigs. They are also called 'lard worms,' i.e. the worms of the pig-fat, and are very common and extremely injurious. Their eggs are expelled by pigs in very large numbers through urination, and hatch within 24 hours. These parasites generally become embodied in the loin muscles.

13.   **Clonorchis Sinensis:** They are a kind of fluke parasite most commonly found in the bile passage of the pig's liver as well as the liver, gallbladder, and bile duct in humans. Through the wounds caused by these parasites, secondary bacterial infections may also enter the body causing tuberculosis, typhoid, etc. They are found mostly in Asia and typically transferred by eating raw or undercooked fish carrying the parasite.

14.   **Coccidiosis:** It is a disease of the liver cells commonly found in piglets. The parasites, called coccidia, live and multiply inside the host's intestinal tract. There are three types: Eimeria, Isospora, and Cryptosporidia. The adult germ is a minute intracellular parasite, which becomes encysted for the falciform young to develop. The

liver becomes enlarged, and the parasite may cause diarrhoea, inflammation of the bile ducts (called Cholangitis), jaundice, stones in the liver, cancer, and general debility. This disease sometimes proves fatal, and no effective treatment has been discovered once symptoms appear.

15. **Paragonimus Parasites** (Lung Fluke): They are very common parasites living in the lungs of pigs, causing pneumonia. The disease was discovered in 1880 by Dr. Masson, but Triclabendazole (one of two available treatments) was only approved by the FDA in 2019. Human beings are liable to be infected even by contact with pigs, though it is more commonly associated with eating infected crab or crayfish. This disease does not occur in countries where excessive pig-breeding is not practised.

16. **Metastrongylus Apri:** They, too, are small parasites infecting pigs' lungs. They are a "worldwide lungworm, infecting domestic pigs, wild boars, and peccary"[iii] which cause pneumonia in pigs (metastrongylosis).

17. **Tubercle Bacillus:** Refers to several types of tuberculosis-causing vegetable organisms (bacterium), discovered in 1882 by the German physician and bacteriologist, Robert Knoch: Mycobacterium avium, Mycobacterium bovis, and Mycobacterium tuberculosis. Mycobacterium avium is the most common variant found in pigs.

18. **Giganthorinchus Gigas:** They inhabit pig as well as human intestines and were discovered in 1782 by Dr. Coexe. They are now known as Macracanthorhynchus hirudinaceus and cause Acanthocephaliasis.

19. **Fasciolopsis Buski:** They are parasites which remain latent for a long time in the small intestines of pigs. On leaving the pigs, they infect water snails through which the disease may be transmitted to other pigs as well as human beings.

20. **Oesophagostomum Dentatum:** They are nodular worms that infest the small intestine or the alimentary canal, causing lesions. Secondary infections are common.

---

iii Alan A. Marchiondo MS, PhD in *Parasiticide Screening* 2, Elsevier, (2019), pp. 135-335 https://doi.org/10.1016/B978-0-12-816577-5.00007-7

21. **Setaria Bernardi:** They are nematode parasites that live in the bowels of pigs.

22. **Physocephalus Sexalatus:** They too are nematode parasites; they live in the mucous membrane of the stomach and are often asymptomatic.

23. **Simondsia Paradoxa:** They also attach themselves to the mucous membrane of the pig's stomach. Paradoxes are a genus of parasites having three lobes, called trilobita, with 17 of 20 free segments and a large headshield (cephalic).

24. **Gnathostoma Hispidum:** Also live in the mucous membrane of the stomach, forming tumors in the gastric wall. Gnathobdellida are an order of leeche-like spirurid nematodes, with three-toothed jaws in which there is no trunk or snout (proboscis). They have stiff hairs and minute spines and lay their eggs in cocoons.

25. **Sarcoptes Scabiei** var. Suis: More commonly called "scabies" or sarcoptic mange, it is a kind of parasite of compound organism (mite), having water-conducting cells like a jelly fish enclosed in a capsule. They enter the skin of pigs and give them a variety of rashes; symptoms include itching, sores, scales, and blisters. Sarcoptes Scabiei has different varieties based on the host: *suis* for swine, *hominis* for humans. Though zoonotic, it will not change hosts across species.

26. **Haematopinus Suis:** Also known as the hog louse or "sucking lice", *H. suis* lives on the surface of pigs' skin and feeds on their blood. It is also a known vector of many swine diseases including swine pox, African swine fever, and eperythrozoonosis.

27. **Fusiformis Necrophorus:** Now called *Fusobacterium necrophorum*, this is a bacterium which causes necrosis—mortification of gangrene. They occur mainly in pigs, who can pass them on to humans. It can cause a variety of infections in humans, including postanginal sepsis, meningitis, and sinus thrombosis.

28. **Choerostrongylus Pudendotectus:** They are lungworms which infest the respiratory and circulatory systems of mammals.

29. **Spirometra Mansoni:** They live in pigs' flesh and muscles and cause Sparganosis. These worms may settle anywhere, with symptoms varying based on the final location.

30. **Stephanurus Dentatus:** They are worms infesting the stomach, liver, and fat of pigs. They create lesions at many different sites, as the larvae migrates, causing severe damage such as phlebitis and interstitial hepatitis.

31. **Trichuris Suis** (whipworm): They are worms which live in the caecum (blind gut) and in that part of the large intestine (colon) of pigs which extends from the caecum to the rectum.

BACTERIAL DISEASES

1. **Salmonella:** Food poisoning can be caused by various organisms. Different sources can be responsible for it, but the main source has been traced to be contaminated meat— including pork. Salmonella is considered to be the most common infections caused by meat, having as many types as one thousand. Kaufman Mutsui was the first to isolate its bacteria in 1930. In 1963 there occurred a Salmonella epidemic in England, involving more than 72 cases and the source was traced to be a slaughterhouse of pigs. Statistics show that the majority of cases occur through pork sausages. In 1963, there occurred a Salmonella epidemic in England, involving more than 72 cases and the source was traced to be a slaughterhouse of pigs. One often hears of similar outbreaks in pork-eating countries. According to the scientists who study epidemics (epidemiologists), the most common source of this disease is swine-flesh. In England alone, a country which is considered to be one of the most hygienically administered countries in the world, about one thousand people fell victim to Salmonella food-poisoning in 1976, out of which 48 died.[iv]

2. **Botulism:** This is also a serious kind of food-poisoning. Its bacteria belong to organisms of Clostridia group. It is very common in pork-eating countries. It is true that all kinds of meat could be contaminated and carry the germs or spores of food-poisoning diseases, but swineflesh has been found to be the major source of bacterial organisms of Clostridia group. The results of a survey show that 10 percent of pigs are the carriers of this bacteria as compared to 6.79 percent of other food-animals and 4 percent of poultry.

---

iv **Editor's note:** In 2016, there were 95,430 human cases of salmonellosis in the European Union.

3. **Brucellosis:** It is a fever of two kinds, one of which is caused by organisms called the Abortus group, found in pigs, and is called *Brucella Suis*. It was first discovered in the Mediterranean coastal towns, and hence, is also known as Malta fever. It is more common in the American countries and is not, therefore, much known in Europe. Cattle, too, suffer from it. Mostly pig-breeders, farmers, and those who handle dead or live pigs are prone to this infection. The general effects of this fever are enlargement of the spleen, high temperature for long periods, and general aches and pains.

4. **Melioidosis:** This is another disease caused by contact with pigs and other animals of Rodentia order such as rats, mice, porcupines etc. Melioidosis has a wide range of symptoms, as they depend on the location of the infection.

5. **Tuberculosis (T.B.):** It is a well-known disease all over the world. In pigs it generally takes the form of abdominal T.B. One of the sources of infection in humans is meat, including that of pigs. Tubercle Bacillus is very common in pigs and even the pastures on which pigs graze become infected with this bacterium.

6. **Anthrax:** This is a bacterial infection which usually proves fatal. It affects all animals, both domestic and wild (including pigs), who then communicate it to humans by contact or consumption.

7. **Foot and Mouth Disease:** It affects all cloven-hoofed animals and pigs are one of its easy victims. Physical contact is the source of transmission of its virus to humans, although this is uncommon.

8. **Septic Arthritis:** This is an infection in synovial fluid and joint tissues. It can be caused by various types of bacteria, viruses, and fungi commonly found around pigs.

9. **Swine Fever:** Commonly called 'Classical Swine Fever' (CSF), it is caused by a virus of the genus *Pestivirus* of the family *Flaviviridae* It is also known as Hog Cholera, and is a fatal infectious disease specific to swine causing hemorrhagic septicemia. The CSF virus can survive in pork and processed pork products for months when meat is refrigerated and for years when it is frozen.

10. **Bacillus Choleraesuis:** Now called *Salmonella choleraesuis*, this bacterium shows the highest predilection to cause systemic infections in humans, out of more than 2,000 serotypes. It causes

ulceration of the mucosa (mucous membrane), diarrhoea, and haemorrhages in the skin.

11. **Swine Plague:** It resembles Hog Cholera but shows a greater tendency to pneumonia. It is an infectious disease caused by *Pasteurella multocida*. The swine-specific bacterium was formerly classified as *Past. suiseptica*.

OTHER PATHOGENS

1. **Swine Influenza:** as the very name suggests, this kind of influenza is believed to originate from pigs—a fact which was medically established in the early thirties, after millions of people had died of it all over the world. It is estimated that more people lost their lives by the Swine Influenza epidemic which swept throughout the world in 1918 than were killed in the actual fighting during the First World War. Again in 1957 this pandemic influenza took its toll of human lives. The pathologists believe that the deadly virus is always present in pigs and lies dormant, waiting for suitable weather conditions to become active periodically. It is not a mere coincidence that, whenever there is an epidemic of influenza among pigs, the human population also starts suffering from it. The epidemic 1976 is another example of this pattern.

2. **Swine Variola:** Also known as Swine Pox, it is a contagious disease characterised by vomiting, intense lumbar pains in the loin, and peculiar pustular eruption (containing pus) of thick crusts which slough off as dead tissues, often leaving a pit or scar. It is communicable to man by eating flesh of an infected pig. The *Variola Suilla* virus is one of the filter-passing viruses and difficult to investigate. The disease often proves fatal. Smallpox, a close variant, was eliminated from the human population in 1980.

3. **Swine Vesicular Stomatitis:** It is a kind of fever which affects those who come in contact with pigs. Its virus affects the lungs, produces inflammation of the mouth (Stomatitis), and lesions or cysts (vesicles). Another variation of this disease is called 'Japanese B Vesicular Stomatitis.'

4. **Endemic Hemoptysis:** It is another lung disease caused by lung flukes, which is very common in pig breeding and pork

consuming countries such as China, Japan, and Taiwan. Patients suffer from a cough with rusty sputum, profuse bleeding of lungs, and other secondary infections such as bronchitis, pneumonia, and abscess of the lungs.

Skin And General Diseases

1.   **Yellow Ulcers:** It is a disease of pigs, similar to common ulcers, which discharge pus and occurs on the external or internal surface of the body.

2.   **Swine Erysipeloid:** It is a serious skin infection, transmitted to those who handle pigs and their by-products. It takes the form of compact, unshapely masses and reddened or cyanotic skin, and often affects the limbs of the patient as arthritis. The accompanying fever often goes as high as 104-105 degrees Fahrenheit or more, resulting in various other complications.

3.   **Viral Encephalitis:** It is a disease also passed onto man by pigs. Its infection takes place by contact and causes the inflammation of the brain parenchyma. This infection is very common among the pig-breeding farmers.

4.   **Actinomycosis:** This disease becomes very serious if not controlled in the early stages. It is caused by a kind of fungus called *Actinomyces Bovis* through contact with pigs. Farmers call it 'pig-jaw,' 'lumpy jaw,' or 'wooden tongue' because it starts with swelling and ulcers around the mouth. The kind that affects humans is called *Strephtothrix Actinomyces*. The pus that spreads from the ulcers affects the internal organs of the body, especially the lungs and intestines, causing chronic cough, and often ends up as a very serious illness which generally needs surgical treatment to remove infected tissue.

5.   **Balantidiasis:** This is a kind of dysentery also found occasionally in other food-animals. It is so common in swine that it is generally known as 'pig-disease'. It is caused by tiny single-cell organisms or protozoa called Balantidium Coli and occurs mostly in pork-eating countries with, sometimes, serious consequences.

6.   **Wen:** It is an indolent, painless, encysted tumour of the skin—especially a sebaceous cyst secreting oily matter (pilar cyst).

This disease is very common in the Far East where pork has been eaten for thousands of years. The very word 'wen' means in Latin a 'pigling'.

7. **Pig-paratyphoid:** It is a disease resembling typhoid fever in its symptoms, caused by *Salmonella choleraesuis*. However, through the wounds caused by these parasites, secondary infections may lead to typhoid fever.

In addition to the diseases mentioned above, there are many other diseases which are generally associated with pigs, but as of yet, medical opinion is neutral about them. Let us give some of them a cursory glance-over:

1. **Diarrhoea:** When pork containing Cysticercus (parasites living in a cyst or capsules) is eaten, the worms are set free from the cyst and cause the tissues under the skin to swell by a process called inflammation. This causes a 'ground itch' leading to digestive disorders, fever, and persistent diarrhoea.

2. **Myopathy:** Pathy (or pathia) denotes suffering and disease in general. The combination of 'myo' and 'pathy' is applied to a group of diseases affecting the muscles, to which pigs are very susceptible. Cardiomyopathy is a group of diseases of the heart. Diseases of this kind are more prevalent in pork-eating countries than in others, although all red meat is suspected of being involved.

3. **Pneumonia** and **Pancreatitis:** If Micrococcus Lanceolatus (parasites) infect the lungs, it causes their inflammation, leading to pneumonia; if they infect the intestines, it causes their obstruction and pancreatitis resulting in jaundice; if they infect the respiratory tubes, it causes breathing problems and suffocation. It has been mentioned before that pigs are easy prey to such diseases.

4. **Scrofula:** It is a glandular disease with a tendency to consumption.

5. **Necrotic Enteritis:** It is a serious disease with a tendency to consumption.

6. **Neuropathy:** It is an affliction of the nervous system

7. **Multiple Sclerosis:** It involves the degeneration of nervous tissues in the body. The medical science is not sure what causes it, and intensive research is being carried out.

8.   **Cancer:** It is a malignant tumour—a purposeless growth of abnormal cells—eating the parts of the body which goes on spreading and may recur even when surgically removed.

9.   **Dermatitis:** It is the inflammation of the skin, caused by bacteria, virus, parasite, allergy, etc.

HEART DISEASES

Lastly, let us discuss the most dangerous diseases which has become the scourge of our modern lifestyle, especially in those affluent countries where they have built up so many surplus meat-mountains that they no longer know what to do with them—and that scourge is heart diseases. There are various names for the heart diseases according to the parts which are affected and according to their causes. In general, the disease may affect adversely the essential function of the heart.

In 1984 the National Institute of Health convened a panel of fourteen experts in Bethesda. Md., to discuss this issue. According to their findings, the leading cause of death by heart-diseases in the United States of America was the high level of cholesterol and fatty food. Their statistics confirmed that one in every four persons in U.S. was in danger of having heart disease. Cholesterol is a crystal like white, fatty compound of alcohol which is found in animal products such as meat. Some people mistakenly believe that a joint of meat from which visible fat has been scraped is free of fat and consists of muscular tissues only. But the fact is that even a piece of lean meat contains within it a large quantity of fat. That is why doctors generally advise the heart-patients to eat less meat and avoid high-fat and high-cholesterol diets. The latest advice by the dieticians is that saturated fat should not form more than ten percent of a balanced diet.

A comparative study of fat contents in the meat of various food-animals shows that pig-meat contains far more fatty acids than others. The types of fat which are most dangerous in connection with heart diseases are called saturated fats. All animal fats are saturated, but pig-meat is more saturated than other meats, as the following figures show: The clarified pig-fat or lard which is used in cooking and frying has more than six times the content of fatty acid than the oils extracted from vegetable seeds. In uncooked meats: bacon has 40.5% fat; beef 17.1% and poultry 6.7%. In roasted meats: pork has 40% fat; lamb 20% and corned beef 15%.

In cooked meats: bacon has 38.8% fat; ham 18.9%; beef 11%; lamb 22.1% and poultry 5.4%. Pork sausages have 32.1% fat and beef sausages 24.1%.

The dieticians' statistics show that, while pork takes an average of four hours to cook, beef takes three. Beef and mutton are digested in the stomach in three hours while pork takes four hours. If pieces of beef, mutton, and pork are put in the sun, the pork will rot first, then mutton and then beef—the difference in time being one hour between each. Blood pressure is another factor which plays a major role in our health. The thickness (viscosity) of our blood, among other factors, determines its pressure and regulates the beating of our hearts. Higher than normal pressure is a serious disease and can cause strokes. The normal blood pressure of a healthy person should be 120/80 mm of mercury. Compared to that: pigs have 170/108 mm, cows 134/88 mm, and sheep 114/68 mm.

This unfortunate animal is so apt to spread diseases that even the plot of land on which it is put to pasture often becomes sick. The farmers call it 'pig-sick-land' which has to be given a rest period of at least two years to recover.

Pigs's Sex Life And Behaviour

The main purpose of discussing these diseases of swine is to stress the point that the characteristics and the intrinsicality of the animals we eat work upon our own physical as well as mental ethos. Pigs' sexual behaviour and the diseases associated with it is very relevant to the point of inter-relation between our diet and character formation. As mentioned before repeatedly before, it is true that all other animals are susceptible to various kinds of diseases which are liable to be passed on to those who eat them. However, the essential point to note is that pigs carry far more diseases than the other animals we eat and, therefore, are a greater danger to our health. Poultry too are subject to many diseases. It is pigs and poultry which are the most commonly intensively farmed farm animals globally.

Each species of animals has been created by nature with certain traits and characteristics. Cats, for example, have a very clean habit of covering their faeces or excreta with soil while other animals, and even some human beings, do not bother to do so. Some animals are carnivorous and eat flesh only of other species while pigs, are cannibals and do sometimes eat their own kind. Some animals abstain from eating foul-smelling, decomposed, and rotten food while others, such as pigs, are not so selective. Some animals keep their habitat clean while others, such as pigs, do not. Modern pig breeders claim that, if given space and opportunity, pigs will keep their sleeping quarters clean and will muck outside. Even if it were true, the pertinent point here is that pigs, unlike most other domesticated animals, are not deterred by the dung of their own species. All animals in the wild enjoy equal freedom of the environment. Those who had a chance, as the writer has had, to study them in their natural habitats will bear out the fact that pigs take swinish delight in wallowing in their own muck and filth. There is a natural reason for this kind of dirty behaviour. They have to keep their bodies moist and cool and they have no sweat-glands to do so. It must, however, be pointed out that we humans have no right to claim superiority over other species of animals in this respect. Even in this age of hygienic advance, there are still some of the human species who would eat anything that moves and hygienically have lower standards and dirtier habits than some animals living in the wild.

There is no denying that there is a strong link between animal's physical and its metaphysical natures, including those of man. Modern science confirms the religious concept that our diet and general lifestyle not only influence our physical health but also play a large part in the formation and development of character and ethos. Unfortunately, our reaction these days against the ritualised religious institutions has created in us an attitude of rejection— even against those of the religious teachings which are obviously logical. The latest psycho-physiological study of man by science leaves no doubt that there is a constant interaction between the elements of man's mental and physical existence. And this is exactly what religion has been trying to explain for thousands of years. The only difference is that science defines these things in scientific terminology; while religion uses spiritual, moral, and ethical terms.

It is not intended to deal with this subject here, as it is highly scientific and would involve the use of many medical and scientific terms which an average reader will find difficult to follow. For example, the modern theories will have to be explained about the patterns and their influences on genetic inheritance; how do the laws of inheritance determine genetic factors and control the function of each cell; how do the chromosomes work in our bodies as carriers of inheritance; how has the genetic research led up to the Sheehan's Chart of Genes' Test; how all the tissues in our bodies are made up of cells; what is DNA (Deoxyribonucleic Acid) in the centre of each cell; how is all this elaborate and highly complicated mechanism affected by the kind of nourishment we give to our bodies and, finally, how does the physical nature of our bodies affect the psychic forces in our personalities, comprising our soul, spirit and mind.

In the foregoing pages a few cursory remarks have been made about the pigs' dirty eating habits. However, a little more information about their diet is called for to understand why this animal is a carrier of more diseases than most other food-animals and how its diet contributes to the formation of its character and behaviour, especially as it has been mentioned earlier, pigs would eat anything and everything that comes their way, dead or alive, fresh or rotten. They would eat dead rats, mice, squirrels, and other rodents full of disease-infested maggots, and human or animal excreta. It is a common practice among the small-scale breeders who keep a few pigs in their backyards in the rural areas to feed them the rubbish and leftovers such as meat and bone waste which they collect from butchers, fishmongers, and restaurants; the swill from the drinking houses or breweries; and chicken droppings and poultry muck. In some countries this feeding of swill to pigs has been banned. Even the dirty sink waste has been given the name of 'hogs' 'wash' because, instead of draining it down the pipes, it is given to pigs o drink. The large-scale breeders, too, feed their pigs waste-products and cheap fertilizers. The very word pig has become synonymous with gluttony and voraciousness, so much so that a person who eats too much and indiscriminately is said to be 'eating like a pig'. Let us see how this has affected its character, behaviour, and metabolism.

By nature, pigs can be vicious, aggressive and ill-tempered. The current cramped cruel conditions in which they are generally bred are making their temperament even worse and their behaviour toward each other sometimes ends up in serious and even fatal injuries. It is not uncommon among them to start chewing off and eating each other's tails. Sows sometimes start eating their own piglets after farrowing. Of course, these behaviours are incited by the barren conditions in which many pigs are kept. Even the piglets may start biting the teats of their mothers while suckling. It is a common practice among the breeders to have both the upper and lower sharp teeth of the piglets removed. One of the most labour-consuming chores of the pig-breeders is to keep their pens clean and hygienic—a battle the farmers have to fight against longer odds. No wonder, in the English language, an ill-tempered and obdurate person is called a 'hog' or 'pig-headed'.

There are certain biological processes which build up the food we eat into living organisms to form the metabolism of a body. If left on their own, all living creatures learn how to cope with the peculiarities of their metabolism and adjust their behaviour accordingly. The maladjustment, however, occurs when man starts tampering with their food and environment. The modern methods of intensive farming are not only lowering the quality of their meat by feeding them on chemical compounds, but are also changing their normal and natural behaviour. Pig-farming has become a multi-billion-pound business in the world today. Apart from large sums of money being spent by the 'hidden persuaders' on advertisements to convince innocent consumers, no expense is spared to make the sows produce bigger litters and to fatten the porkers as fast as possible. All this economic onslaught on the poor animals has not improved their nature. Instead, it seems that the characteristics of this species are changing for the worse. A brief study of this animal's sex-life will serve as a good example.

Pigs are the most prolific and the most sensual of all farm-animals with the exception of rabbits. The gestation period of sows is only 114 days as compared to 336 days of mares, 282 days of cows, and much faster than they would do in the wild. A boar can serve sows four times a week.

Apart from the numerous diseases mentioned earlier to which they are susceptible, they have more than their share of venereal diseases:

1.   **Streptococcus:** The process of the procreation does not run smoothly in pigs as it normally does in other animals. The only thing the piteous sow seems to be apt at is to get herself impregnated without much fuss. After that she may develop all sorts of obstetrical complications during the whole period of gestation. Most of them start having farrowing fever which is an infection due to a variety of germs, such as streptococcus which cause the inflammation of the womb and almost always leads to offensive discharge. The source of this disease is known to be the serving boar.

2.   **Post-Parturient** (After-birth) **Fever:** Another fairly common trouble with sows is that their womb gets turned inside-out. Quite a few sows lack certain parts of the genital tract. Sterility is not infrequent among them. Due to all these malfunctions in the genital organs, the death of the foetus in the womb is not uncommon. Many piglets born of a sow suffering from post-parturient fever, which is quite common, have to be taken away from mothers and hand-fed. It is not surprising that the sows who suffer so much during the ante-natal as well as the post-natal periods refuse to accept their offspring after giving birth to them and start biting them or even eating them.

3.   **Hermaphroditism:** The male pigs have their own sexual maladjustments and abnormalities of sexual behaviour. Some boars are born sexually deformed and imperfect and are called 'rigs'. The most common malfunction in such cases is that one of the testicles is not functional enough to descend. Nature has played another cruel joke on this poor animal—some pigs are born with double sex. This is called Hermaphroditism and is genetic in origin.

4.   **Copulatory Organ Diseases:** Another common complaint among boars is the swelling and enlargement of the penis for which the only cure is surgical operation. Among the other allied

complaints is that the penis starts bleeding which generally, renders the boar unfit for breeding.

In addition to the above abnormalities peculiar to the male and female pigs, there are quite a few other diseases connected, directly and indirectly, with their sexual behaviour, such as:

5.   **Prolapse of Rectum:** This disease causes the putting out of the back passage and is very common among pigs. If not treated at the early stages, it becomes so serious that the affected animal has to be destroyed.

6.   **Rhinitis:** It is a disease which causes inflammation of the turbinate or nasal bones. This also is very common in pigs, especially in America, and it is contagious. Even piglets under eight weeks show severe symptoms of it.

7.   **Blindness:** Those who live in the pig-farm areas cannot help noticing blind pigs; pigs constantly shaking their heads due to mange or lice parasites in their ears and brain abscesses or water on the brain. These are mostly genetic ailments and are passed on from generation to generation.

Is it any wonder that Islam has declared the flesh of this animal as unhealthy to eat—except in an emergency—in terms of *rijs* and *fisque* (unclean and spiritually morbid)?

REFERENCES AND NOTES (CHAPTER 3)

1. I Corinthians, 3:16,17.
2. Narrated by Anas. Mishkat al-Masabih, 3:1392. Quoted from Bukhari. (See footnote 1;21).
3. The Book of Rites; Ch. 'Shao Yi'; Translation based on Chinese-English Dictionary; by Mathew, R.R.
4. Cf. Sheh Shen Lu (The Record of Health). The author himself lived for 100 years and was held in high esteem in the Royal Court, Cir.10th century A.C.
5. Yan Show Tan, a famous 'Longevity journal' of China.
6. Thukalpiam, Ch. 163. Siva is one of the gods of Hindu Triad representing various attributes and powers and has more than 1,000 titles
7. Deut. (The Fifth Book of Moses), 14:8.
8. Levit. 11:7,8. (Chapters: Deut. 14 and Levit.11 deal in detail which animals are lawful or unlawful to eat).
9. The Acts, 10:28.
10. Isaiah, 10:28
11. The Hog; Rev. Vories, C.L. ; p.26. (A booklet).
12. Levit. 7:26; and the Qur'an, 2:173; 5:4; 6:145; 16:115.
13. Matthew, 15-19.
14. The Qur'an, 3:45-47; 2:87.
15. Matthew, 7:6.
16. Matthew, 8:28-34.
17. Mark, 5:1-20.
18. Luke, 12:6.
19. Matthew, 12:11.
20. The Acts, 10:1-28
21. Romans, 14:14.
22. Tai Chu Yo Tao ("There is a Way in the Very Beginning"); as quoted in the translation of the Qur'an, 6:145, by Ilias Wang Chang Ch'ai; Muslim Welfare Organization, Selangor Mansions, Kuala Lumpur, Malaysia.
23. As n Ref. No.12.
24. The Human Strategy; Dr. Marvin Harris; A well-known Christian anthropologist.
25. Will the Old Book Stand; Hastings, H.L.;p.92.
26. The Qur'an, 2:259; 16:14; 23:14.
27. The word Rijs has been used in the Qur'an eight times not only for pork but also for intoxicants, games of chance, sacrifices to idols and other evil practices and manners—in the sense of unclean, filthy, abominable, disgraceful, etc. See: 5:93; 6:125,145; 7:71; 9:95; 10:100; 22:30; 33:33. In verse 7:157 all such prohibited things are called Khabuitha, i.e. impure and loathsome.
28. Mark, 7:21-23.
29. II Peter, 2:22 (False Teachers).

30. *Animal Sanitation and Disease Control*; Dr. Dykstra, R.R., Dean of Veterinary Medicine, Kansas State College; 1942.

31. Individual references for all the diseases mentioned in the book will make the list too long. For details and authentication, refer to the following books:

    a. *All About Pigs*—800 Questions Answered; Pig Publications Ltd., Lloyds Chambers, Ipswich, England; 1955;

    b. *Trichuris, Trichinella & Their Allies*; Chapt.18 (Introduction), pp.399-415; Wiley & Sons, New York; 1961;

    c. *Nutrition & Behaviour & Learning*; J. Cravato & E.R. Del'Cardie; Vol.16, pp.80-96; M. Recheigl, New York; 1973

    d. *Nutrition & Your Mind*; George Watson; Harper& Row, New York; 1972

    e. *Modern nutrition in Health & Diseases—Dietotheray*; R.S. Goodhart & M.E. Shil; Lea & Feberger, Philadelphia; 1974;

    f. *Dietary Fatty Acids: Their Metabolic Fate and Influence on Fatty Acid Biosynthesis*; (The Journal of the American Oil Chem. Soc. 42;1124, 1965);

    g. *Diseases of Metabolism*; G.G. Duncan; W.B. Saunders Co., Philadelphia; 1964;

    h. *Pork*; Syed Akhtar Rizvi; Box 2245, Tehran, Iran; 1972;

    i. *The Hog; Should it be Used for Food?*; Rev. C.L. Vories; College Press, Washington; 1971.

32. cf. *Cestoda* in *Encyclopedia Britannica*.

33. Dr. Glen Shepherd; *Washington Post*; 31st May 1952.

34. Neal Black; Managing Editor: *National Hog Farmer* (Magazine)

35. *Preventive Medicine*; Dr. Milton J. Rosenav.

36. *U.S.D.A. Leaflet, /-/34*, p.8.

37. *Illinois Health Messenger*, 15th October 1938.

38. cf. *Still's Parasitology*; Dr. Ramson.

4

ANIMAL SACRIFICE

PREAMBLE

THE CONCEPT OF ANIMAL sacrifice goes as far back as recorded history. During the early stages of man's awareness of a psychic force within himself, the primordial concept of sacrifice was that of thanking the supernatural forces and to appease their anger by atonement, while the archaic concept of the supernatural was that of astral beings which could take physical forms and, like human beings, had corporeal needs which had to be satisfied. In order to express obeisance to these beings, man started making tangible and visible symbols to represent these imaginary beings in the form of idols. The deities and spirits had to be kept happy by offerings of gifts, such as food and drink, or other prized possessions of man.

The concept of sacrifice in the name of gods and deities has passed through various stages and forms of development. The fear of the unknown and the unsubduable elements of nature created feelings of frustration and helplessness which, in turn, demanded submissiveness and self-denial. Primitive man could think of no other way of keeping the astral spirits happy except by offering them the things he prized in his own life. The sentiment of sacrifice, however, remains unfulfilled unless it is enacted ostentatiously in the form of ritual and ceremony. The history of religion shows that, during the early stages, ritual was considered to be the most important part of worship—mostly through sacrifice.

Most commentators of the Scriptures, especially modern theologians, have tried to explain away their respective sacrificial traditions in terms of symbolic worship of God. Some religions have declared animal sacrifice as a means of atonement by transferring one's sins to an animal as if God was incapable of forgiving man's sins without punishing someone, even though it were an innocent substitute for the sinner. In this day and age there are still people who believe that blood is the sacred token of life. Primitive man used to shed human blood as an offering to his gods, deities, and numerous other astral spirits. Modern man claims that he has become more civilised and rational. He offers to his God animal flesh and blood instead.

ANCIENT ASIA

For the last six thousand years the Vedic doctrine of *Ahimsâ* has played a very significant role not only in the matter of sacrifice, but also in the general attitude towards animals. *Ahimsâ* is generally translated as 'non-injury', but it means much more than that. It covers the negation of animosity (*Avera*) and ill will (*Abyapajja*) as well as positive feelings of fraternity (*Mettacitta*). However, this doctrine has not succeeded in abolishing animal sacrifice to the same extent as it has promoted vegetarianism, which has already been discussed in Chapter Two.

CONFUCIANISM

According to Taylor, sacrificial feasts used to be officially celebrated in China during the time of Confucius.[1] Confucius rejected the suggestion of a disciple, Tzu-Kung, that the practice of offering a sheep as a sacrifice at every new moon be discontinued. His verdict was that ritual (*li*) was more important than sheep and said to Tzu-Kung: "you grudge sheep, but I grudge ritual".[2] Again he has been recorded in the Analects as saying: "I believe in and have a passion for [the ways of] the ancients".[3]

HINDUISM

Numerically Hindus form the majority of the followers of Vedic Scriptures, although it is suggested by some that Hinduism is only a derivative branch of the original Vedic religion. Every act in the life of a Hindu, whether religious or secular, is governed by some sort of prophetic signification of omens and portents through ritual, some of which even involve animal sacrifice. The Mogul Emperor Akbar attempted to stop the practice of human sacrifice when Hindu widows were burned alive on the funeral pyres of their husbands as *suttees* or *satees*. Later the British Raj had to pass strict laws to abolish the custom. Since independence, the Government of India has been trying to ban the practice of animal sacrifice, yet the traditional custom still continues in certain places. The notorious horse sacrifice, known as *Asva Mehda*, is still being practiced in parts of India.[4] In Nepal, animal sacrifice is a regular feature of religious festivals.[5]

The writer once happened to witness a bull-sacrifice some sixty years ago in an Indian State called Chumba, in the Himachal Pradesh range of mountains about 25 miles north of Dalhousie. It was an ultra-orthodox Hindu State, so much so that even to boo a cow or bull in the street was considered sacrilegious. Paradoxically, however, the same cow-worshippers used to throw a bull once a year down the cliffs into the tributary of a river as a sacrifice to the goddess of water. On this occasion the garlanded bull was led to the cliff-edge by a choir of laudative pundits, followed by a fanfare of trumpets and horns. After a long session of intonations and incantations, the legs of the bull were strapped, and the poor animal was shoved over the cliff. The bull started tumbling down, the cascade of water knocking it about from boulder to boulder, until a bend in the gorge hid it from view. Everyone present raised his hands and eyes upwards as if to say to the goddess above the clouds: "See, how good we are! We have done our duty. Now it is up to you to look after us until this day next year—*Om, Shanti, Hari Om*—Great is the Trinity of Vishnu, Siva and Brahma, Peace; Long live the Trinity".

JAINISM

As mentioned earlier, Jainism is supposed to be an offshoot of Hinduism but with much more stringent dietetic laws than those of the general body of Hinduism. Being staunch vegetarians and believers in *Ahimsâ* to the letter, they totally reject the very concept of animal sacrifice. Their verdict can best be summed up in these words from the Yogasastra: "Those inconsiderate people who sacrifice animals as an offering to gods are devoid of tender feelings and mercy and are doomed to destruction".[6]

BUDDHISM

The Buddhists too do not believe in animal sacrifice as such. Some of them do eat meat, but it does not involve any ritualistic killing, nor do they make animals into scapegoats for atonement. Their concept of sacrifice is based on reciprocity by way of voluntary interchange of life between man and beast, as discussed previously. Some examples of this kind of mutual sacrifice are found in their scriptures.[7] In spite of many differences, Buddhism has one very significant principle in common with Islam: not to lay down any categorical laws which cannot be observed; and to follow the "Middle Path", known in Islam as "tarîque al-wusta".

CHRISTIANITY

The Christian concept that Christ allowed himself to be sacrificed at the Cross, as the "lamb of God", to redeem the world of its sins leaves no scope for any scapegoat to take over the Christians' sins nor the sacrifice of any animal for atonement.

The doctrine of 'Cosmic Christ', although based on a very different theology from that of the Buddhist and the general Hindu *Vedanta*, has led to the Christian belief in the presence of God even in animals. Certain passages in the Old Testament do give the impression that all animals have been created merely for the benefit of human species and that man has the divine-given right to sacrifice them at the altar of his needs. However, Christians have started interpreting such passages in the context of Cosmic Christology. The practical examples set by the Christian saints have been greatly responsible for the creation of a sense of affinity between man and other sentient beings.

The very image of the baby-Christ lying in the manger of a stable cements that sense of affinity. St. Hubert, the hunter, saw the image of Christ in a stag and refrained from shooting it. The 'little poor man', St. Francis of Assisi (12th. Century), used to talk to animals and preach sermons to the birds—although it is said that he used to eat meat. Many of the Christian saints were such fervent animal lovers that they have gone down in history as their patrons. St. Benedict has been associated with ravens; St. Ulrich with rats; St. Bridget with ducks; St. Menas with camels; and so on. The British Government passed the first law against cruelty to animals in 1822. It is not generally known, however, that six hundred years earlier St. Francis had entreated the Roman Emperor to pass a similar law. About four centuries ago St. Martin de Porres, opened a hospital for animals. He was born to a Spanish nobleman and a freed African slave and lived in Lima, Peru. St. Paul, while talking of suffering in the world, talks of all creation and not of mankind alone in these words: "for we know that the whole creation groaneth and travaileth in pain together until now. And not only they, but ourselves also, which have the first fruits of the Spirit, even we ourselves groan with ourselves. . . ."[8]

Judaism

Muslims in general know very little about Judaism as a religion. Their general impression is that Islam is a continuation of Prophet Abraham's creed; that both Islam and Judaism are the true monotheistic religions; that marriages with Jewish women are allowed; and, most relevantly, that Jewish food is lawful for Muslims. It is intended in this chapter to try to put right some of their mistaken notions about Judaic theology in matters related to animal sacrifices.

The Biblical Concept Of God

Islam came at a period of history when Judaism was well established in the Arabian Peninsula. One of the reasons why Judaism was better organised than Christianity was that all the tribes of Israel had one common ethnic origin and, hence, one common traditional source of Aramaean culture. Christianity and Islam, as opposed to that, were non-ethnic religions with their doors open to the whole world irrespective of race or colour. The Hebrews are originally

Semites who were spread out as Babylonians, Assyrians, Aramaeans, Phoenicians, Edomites, Ammonites, Hebrews, and Abyssinians. It is only for the last 3,000 years that the history of the Jewish people can be identified. Before the Davidic (Dawûd) period (from about 1,000 B.C.) the religion of this tribe of Hebrews which is now known as Israelites was greatly influenced by the cults of other Semitic tribes. This influence shows itself very markedly during the Hammurabi period (Cir. 2,000 B.C.). Later on, Zoroastrianism also played a part in the development of Judaic theology.[9]

The most conspicuous feature of the concept of God in the Hebrew Bible is His physical existence, as if He were a corporeal being whose bodily needs have to be satisfied—the same as the needs of animals and human beings. He needs food and drink and enjoys the savoury smell of roasting meat. Many passages ask believers to offer to Him drink (libation) and food or bread; and depict Him as a saber-rattling parochial God of Zion who commands His people to "subdue nations":

> Thus said the Lord to his anointed, to Cyrus [Kûrush], whose right hand I have holden, to subdue nations before him.[10]

> Proclaim ye this among the gentiles; Prepare war. . . The Lord also shall roar out of Zion . . . So shall ye know that I am the Lord your God dwelling in Zion, my holy Mountain: then shall Jerusalem be holy and no strangers pass through her any more.[11]

Originally simple water used to be offered to God at the altar, but later wine was substituted.[12] In some versions of the Bible even the word 'strong wine' has been used. It is interesting to note that the wine was not wasted by splashing it against the altar like the blood of sacrificial animals. The wine-jars were waved symbolically at the altar and the wine saved to be drunk by the priests.

It was only at a later stage that the Deuteronomic law sanctioned the consumption of meat, otherwise, before that all slaughter was a sacrifice as God's food.[13] The Bible calls the portions of meat burnt on the altar as the 'Lord's food or bread';[14] the altar as the 'Lord's table'.[15] Even the utensils used for the rites in the tabernacle are called the 'Lord's vessels and pots'. According to Leviticus, only the male children of Aaron could eat portions of some offerings and the rest was God's share.[16] Whenever a burnt offering is mentioned, it is clear that the Lord enjoys the 'sweet savoury smell' of burning meat. Out of numerous such quotations, one about Noah (*Nûh*) would be of more interest to Muslims:

> And Noah builded an altar unto the Lord; and took of every clean beast, and of every clean fowl and offered burnt offerings on the altar. And the Lord smelled a sweet savour. . . [17]

Another interesting definition of God is that of the Cabalist Jews. According to them *Sekinah* represents the masculine and the feminine natures of the divine world. Talmud, Midrash and the Targums[18] speak of *Sekinah* as an intermediary between God and the world of nature, including mankind, through which God rules the world. It also works as the uniting force between God and the priest who performs the sacrifice. *Sekinah's* feminine gender is represented by *Sefirah Malkhut* while *Sefirah Tiferet* is her husband. The union between husband and wife, or between the masculine and feminine in the divine world is brought about through the blood of sacrificed animals. More importantly, slaughter is a sort of favour to the animal because it releases its spirit and enables it to return to its origin.

The Cabalists believe that sacrifices help 'good' to overpower 'evil' in the universal struggle between the two. This is carried still further in their belief that sacrifices are shared between Satan (*Sitra Ohra*) and God. The flesh serves as food for the evil powers of cosmos, while God receives the good intentions of the person who offers the sacrifice. The scapegoat sacrifice on the Day of Atonement, however, is meant exclusively to placate the evil powers.[19]

Before Israel, the Babylonians and Mesopotamians used to call their chief deity *Yahwe*. The word 'Yah' stands for the supreme astral being. Later the Israelites adopted this name for their God and by reading the Hebrew Bible it would seem that some of the attributes assigned to the pre-Israelite *Yahwe* have influenced their concept of God.

CONCEPTS OF GOD

Monotheism and polytheism are separated by a hair's breadth. An earnest study of the Hebrew Bible leaves no doubt that its revealed text has been so mixed up with the Rabbinical appendages that the two have become inseparable. In Judaism, at every step and on every occasion Divine worship had to be augmented with offerings—especially burnt offerings of animals. This kind of symbolism and ritualism appealed to the Israelites not because it was convincing to them theologically, but because their minds could not discard the pre-Judaic image of the blood-thirsty *Yahwe*—just as some Muslims have not yet been able to shake off the influences of their respective pre-Islamic cultures, even after fourteen centuries.

ATONEMENT

The Old Testament goes to great lengths to explain that atonement can be achieved through animal sacrifice and that the blood of sacrificed animals has the potency to cleanse sins. Another suggested way of getting rid of sins is by the use of a scapegoat. For example:

> And when he hath made an end of reconciling the holy place, and the tabernacle of the congregation, and the altar [with blood], he shall bring the live goat: and Aaron shall lay both his hands upon the head of the live goat, and confess over him all the iniquities of the children of Israel and all their transgressions in all their sins, putting them [the sins] upon the head of the goat, and shall send him [the goat] away by the hand of a fit man into the wilderness: and the goat shall bear upon him all their iniquities unto a land not inhabited: and he shall let go the goat in the wilderness.[20]
>
> And Aaron shall cast lots upon the two goats; one lot for the Lord, and the other lot for the scapegoat.[21]

These and many other such passages give the impression that sins are like a bundle of nettles which can be transferred from one's back onto that of a goat. The very word 'scapegoat' owes its origin to this practice.

THE JUDAIC THEOLOGY OF SACRIFICE

The Jewish belief in the importance of animal sacrifice goes as far back as the two sons of Adam. Both Cain and Abel (*Qâbêl* and *Hâbêl*) brought their offerings to the Lord; Cain offered fruit and Abel offered animals. The result is very significant: "And the Lord had respect unto Abel and to his offering; but unto Cain and to his offering he had no respect".[22] Since then all the Biblical prophets have been recorded as offering animal sacrifices at the altars:

> And Noah builded an altar unto the Lord; and took of every clean beast, and of every clean fowl and offered burnt offerings on the altar. And the Lord smelled a sweet savour; and the Lord said in his heart, I will not again curse the ground any more for man's sake.[23]

Job (*Ayyûb*) of Uz was a "perfect and upright" man who "feared God and eschewed evil". He had seven sons and three daughters. In order to sanctify them he continually offered 'burnt offerings' of one animal for each child.[24] God's "wrath was kindled" against three people named Eliphaz, Bildad and Zophar. By way of punishment the Lord commanded these three people: "take unto you now seven bullocks and seven rams, and go to my servant Job, and offer up for yourselves a burnt offering; and my servant Job shall pray for you".[25] Jacob (*Ya'qûb*) is also recorded as having made a sacrifice called *Zevahim* to seal a promise which he had given to Laban that he would not "afflict" his daughter in his absence.[26] Another occasion when he offered *Zevahim* sacrifices was at Beer-Sheba.[27] Whenever Prophet Abraham migrated to a new place, he did two things: "he called upon the name of God" and "there he builded an altar unto the Lord".[28] He is recorded as having made not ordinary but burnt offerings on those altars.[29] Many other patriarchs are also recorded as following the same practice. Isaac (*Ishâque*) glorified the name of the Lord and built altars for burnt sacrifices.[30] Building altars and offering animal sacrifices was an integral part of the prophets' worship, wherever they went.[31]

THE CULTUS OF SACRIFICE

All the Biblical books, starting from the patriarchal scriptures, lay great emphasis on ritual and ceremony. The very word used for Judaic worship is derived from the Latin word 'cultus' which generally means the worship of a deity in the form of external ritual and ceremony, as distinguished from the intrinsic spirit of worship.

This subject deserves more than mere academic interest because of the enormity of carnage this mode of worship resulted in. Animals not in thousands but in millions; not for food but to appease—were slaughtered and turned to cinders.

The Jewish festivals are divided into many categories. Some are Proprietary for the appeasement of the offended God, such as the guilt and sin offerings ('Asham and Hall'at). Some are Dedicatory, mostly in the form of communal sacrifices.[32] Then there are burnt-sacrifices (ha-tamid and olah) to God. They have to be continual—one in the morning and one in the evening, with additional weekly sacrifices on Sabbaths, and monthly sacrifices on New Moon and other moon-festivals and holy days.[33]

BIBLICAL CONDEMNATION OF SACRIFICE

There are many antitheses in the Hebrew Bible about sacrifice. There are numerous passages accentuating the importance of sacrifice as a means of atonement while, at the same time, the following passages speak in terms of condemnation of it:

> To what purpose is the multitude of your sacrifices unto me? saith the Lord: I am full of the burnt offerings of rams, and the fat of the fed beasts; and I delight not in the blood of bullocks, or of lambs, or of the goats. . . . Bring me no more vain oblations. . . I am weary to bear them. Your hands are full of blood. . . . [34]

> O Ephraim, what shall I do unto thee? O Juda, what shall I do unto thee? for your goodness is as a morning cloud, and as the early dew it goeth away . . . For I desired mercy, and not sacrifice; and the knowledge of God more than burnt offerings.[35]

> Woe unto you that desire the day of the Lord! to
> what end is it for you? the day of the Lord is darkness,
> and not light. . . . I hate, I despise your feast days, and
> I will not smell in your solemn assemblies. Though ye
> offer me burnt offerings and your meat offerings I will
> not accept them: neither will I regard the peace offerings
> of your fat beasts.[36]

In the following verse, a very clear-cut message is conveyed, laying down the basic principles about animal sacrifice that God does not disapprove of sacrifices provided the meat is put to some good use; that He disapproves of the wastage of meat which is mistakenly believed to be God's share; that God does not feel hungry and does not eat flesh, nor does he drink blood; and finally, that the only sensible way to offer thanks to God for His bounties is by living up to the vows you have taken unto Him through the Covenant:

> O Israel, and I will testify against thee: I am God,
> even thy God. I will not reprove thee for thy sacrifices or
> thy burnt offerings, to have been continually before me.
> I will take no bullock out of thy house, nor the goats out
> of thy folds. For every beast of the forest is mine, And the
> cattle upon a thousand hills. I know all the fowls of the
> mountains. And the wild beasts of the field are mine. If I
> were hungry, I would not tell thee: For the world is mine,
> and the fullness thereof. Will I eat flesh of bulls, Or
> drink the blood of goats? Offer unto God thanksgiving;
> And pay thy vows unto the most High.[37]

This message of the Hebrew Bible was repeated centuries later in the Qur'ân in these words:

> It is not their flesh, nor their blood, that reaches God;
> it is your righteousness [piety and spiritual volition] that
> reaches Him. . . . (22:37)

The Islamic concept of sacrifice will be discussed in some detail later in this chapter. Meanwhile, the following Biblical quotation emphasizes the same message:

> Thus saith the Lord of hosts, the God of Israel; Put
> your burnt offerings unto your sacrifices, and eat flesh. . . .[38]

Maimonides[39] and other classicists have expressed the view that the Israelites at the time of Moses were not ready to give up sacrificial practices, therefore God allowed them to continue with them. In spite of all this disapprobation and reproof, the Israelites continued the sacrificial tradition—each new generation of priests adding to the involved intricacies for ritual.

After the fall of Jerusalem and the destruction of the Temple in 70 A.C. it was no longer possible to continue with the daily *Tamid* and other sacrifices. Instead, special prayer services, called *Shaharit, Minha,* and *Musaf* were introduced.[40] However, the Jewish tradition of animal sacrifice was so strong that a special prayer was added to the Amidah prayer for the re-introduction of sacrifice. Joseph Hertz, while explaining the reason, says "Moderns do not always realize the genuine hold the sacrificial service had upon the affections of the people in ancient Israel."[41] Orthodox Jews still go on saying this additional prayer. Michael Friedlander advocated the views of the orthodoxy in 1913: "The revival of sacrificial service must, likewise, be sanctioned by the voice of a prophet. . . ."[42]

Liberal Jews believe that:

> the decline which Jewish life has suffered in the last 200 years has been due in large measure to the refusal of its 'orthodox' leaders to come to terms with the modern world.[43]

Perhaps this kind of censure on Jewish orthodox leaders would inspire Muslims to take stock of their own 'orthodox' leadership. It is mostly due to its schismatic tendencies and lack of spiritual volition (*taqwa*) that irresponsible movements have sprung up in Islam.

THE RABBINATE (PRIESTHOOD)

One of the main reasons why Jews clung onto the mode of worship through sacrifice was the influence of priesthood on their religion. When salvation and atonement became attainable more through law than worship, the worship itself became difficult to follow without the guidance of priests. The shift of emphasis from the spiritual worship of God to the ever-increasing list of ceremonial rituals in the temple was responsible to a large extent in making the Jews seek atonement through sacrificial offerings—animal sacrifice claiming the highest place. A mistake in the observance of a ritualistic detail would nullify the sacrifices. Who else is there to guide a simple layman through the elaborate sacrificial procedure than the priests who are the hereditary beneficiaries of the sacrifices? In a situation like this, who can blame the Jewish laity if they unwittingly fell into the trap and got themselves entangled in the web of rituals and ceremonies?

MEANING OF SACRIFICE

According to the occult theosophy of the Jewish Cabalists, every letter, word, number, and accent of the Hebrew Bible contains a hidden meaning. The symbolic acts associated with sacrifice have special esoteric significance for the Jews in general and for the Cabalists in particular. Some of their views throw light on the enormity of the problem which the reformers within Judaism have had to face and are facing today. According to the Cabalists, sacrifices are a link between man and God and serve as the physical media of expression for spiritual worship. Jews attach great importance to the condition that the animal must be without blemish, not only for sacrificial animals but also for those for daily consumption. Their concept of 'blemish' is very different from that of Muslims. This condition has a great bearing on the controversial issue of the method of slaughter and the use of stunners.

Man's inhumanity to man in the name of religion and God is psychologically in the historical sequence of his atrocities against the rest of the animated world. The theologians have always found some passage or other in their respective Scriptures to support their conduct both against man and beast. The Holy Office of Rome dug up enough ecclesiastical excuses in the New Testament to justify the torture of so-called heretics during the Spanish Inquisition.[44] The slave traders found their justification in the Bible to the effect that the station in life of the so-called "Negroid races" was to remain hewers of wood and drawers of water.[45] Even these days there is hardly any part of the world where wars are not being fought in the name of religion—each faction soiling the pages of their Scriptures with thumb-marks to prove that theirs is the 'holy' cause. All this has happened in the past, is happening, and will go on happening, unless man starts respecting life as a whole in its entirety. For centuries prophets and sages have been warning the human species that their cruelty to animals would have a psychotic effect on their own mentality and that this would, ultimately, rebound on themselves. All the evidence in the world today shows that the reaction of cruelty to animals has started taking mankind on the rebound.

With what pathos George Bernard Shaw (1856—1950) echoes these sentiments in the following poem:

> WAR—LIVING GRAVES
>
> We are the living graves of murdered beasts,
> Slaughtered to satisfy our appetites.
> We never pause to wonder at our feats,
> If animals, like men, can possibly have rights.
> We pray on Sundays that we may have light,
> To guide our footsteps on the path we tread.
> We're sick of War, we do not want to fight-
> The thought of it now fills our hearts with dread,
> And yet—we gorge ourselves upon the dead.
>
> Like carrion crows, we live and feed on meat,
> Regardless of the suffering and pain
> We cause by doing so, if thus we treat
> Defenceless animals for sport or gain,
> How can we hope in this world to attain
> The PEACE we say we are so anxious for.
> We pray for it, o'er hecatombs, of slain,
> To God, while outraging the moral law.
> Thus cruelty begets its offspring.[46]

Islam

The utilitarian value of animals and the Islamic concern for them has been discussed in Chapter One. It has been explained why Islam has not prohibited meat-eating altogether, and has left it to individual choice, needs and circumstances. In this chapter an attempt has been made to explain the Islamic concept of animal sacrifice. In order to understand that, it is necessary to deal with the subject on two levels. One is the Scriptural or canonical level, i.e. the concept of sacrifice as contained in the Islamic law or *Sharîah*. The second level is how that scriptural concept is being understood and practised by the various strata of Muslim society in different parts of the world. Those who feel that Islam should not have allowed animal sacrifice at all should read this chapter in conjunction with Chapter Two in which the subject of vegetarianism and meatarianism has been discussed. Accepting the fact that Islam has allowed the consumption of meat, even if wrongly from their point of view, this chapter should be read to appreciate how much Islam has tried to change the primordial concept of sacrifice by channelling it into an institution of charity. At the same time, those Muslims who are not used to taking self-criticism in good spirits should appreciate the fact that Islam is a spiritual ideology and all Muslims as its followers need not necessarily be capable of comprehending that ideology intellectually.

Islam is not a new or isolated religion. It is a continuation of all the previous monotheistic theologies which, according to the Qur'ân, have been revealed throughout the ages in all parts of the world.[47] Belief in all of them is one of the terms of faith in Islam.[48] This conception is taken so affirmatively that the creed of Prophet Abraham, for example, is believed to be the religion of Islam. Similarly, a Muslim's faith in Islam, remains incomplete unless they accept Jesus Christ also as a Messenger of God and The Messiah (*Al-Masîh*).[49]

THE PRELUDE TO ISLAMIC SACRIFICE

It was with this kind of religious background that Islam continued with the tradition of animal sacrifice. First, it is important to study the Qur'ânic version of Prophet Abraham's sacrifice, which is the basic source of the Islamic concept of sacrifice. Prophet Abraham saw a vision of the future, where he was on the verge of sacrificing his beloved son, Ishmael.¹ Both father and son interpreted this as a command, but at the last moment, God called out to Abraham to stop, saying:

> You have indeed fulfilled the vision [by showing your willingness to sacrifice your son]. Thus do We reward the righteous. This was obviously a great trial— and We ransomed him with a momentous sacrifice, and left him, thus, for posterity to say in laudation: "Peace be upon him." (Qur'ân 37:100-111)

Muslims understand from this incident that:

a. It serves as a supreme example of man's submission to the will of God.

b. During that period of history, human sacrifice was quite a common practice all over the world. All the races of ancient Greece, such as the Minoan, the Mycenaean, and the Pelasgians of the Mediterranean race, used to offer human sacrifices regularly. The practice remained persistently in vogue during the much later period of their partial domination by the Achaean and the Dorian tribes throughout the mainland of Greece. Even the Hellenic period from the first Olympiad (776-5 B.C.) to the death of Alexander (320 B.C.) was not free from this abominable practice.⁵⁰ The same was the case with the Babylonians and the other Semitic tribes, including the Hebrews.⁵¹ God's act of ransoming Abraham's son with a ram was meant, according to Muslims, to serve as a prohibition of human sacrifices.

---

i **Editor's Note:** There has been an inconsistency concerning the story of Prophet Abraham, which has not been resolved satisfactorily for centuries. A solution has been presented in the article "Prophet Abraham and the Causal Loop: A New Perspective on a Landmark Historical Event & its Universal Implications" (*Scientific God Journal* 2, No. 8, 2011, pp. 740-752), by Nadeem Haque, where it has been proven that Prophet Abraham saw a vision of the future event in which he was on the verge of sacrificing his son, Ishmael. He interpreted the vision as a command, though it was not in reality, as God cannot command an evil act since it contradicts the nature of God and the Qur'an (hence the 'inconsistency'). However, this vision compelled Prophet Abraham to act on his own misinterpretation; it forms what Haque calls a 'future to present causal loop": a true vision of a future act, causing the envisioner to move towards committing the act. It then served all the purposes mentioned by Masri.

c. Most Muslim commentators of the Qur'ân suggest that the word 'momentous' (*Azîm*) in the verse "We ransomed him with a momentous sacrifice" and the promise that posterity will always send blessings on Abraham signify the commemoration of that great man's willingness to cut the throat of that son for whom he had prayed so earnestly to get. It is to celebrate this that the Festival of Sacrifice (*'Eid al-Adzhâ*) is held annually and animals are sacrificed for distribution among the poor. The Prophet Mohammad was once asked by his companions why animal sacrifice was allowed to be continued in Islam. He replied: "This is a commemorative tradition (*Sunnah*) of your patriarch Abraham."[52] The invocation of God's blessings on Prophet Abraham has since been an integral part of the prescribed mode of worship during the ten days of pilgrimage in the form of the following oft-repeated prayer:

> O God! Exalt Mohammad and the posterity of Mohammad, as you did exalt Abraham and the posterity of Abraham: You are Praiseworthy and Glorious. O God! Bless Mohammad and the posterity of Mohammad, as You did bless Abraham and the posterity of Abraham; You are Praiseworthy and Glorious.

The importance that Muslims attach to Prophet Abraham and his sacrifice can be appreciated from the fact that the above prayer is also repeated many times a day by all Muslims in their congregational as well as in other individual prayers. There is another association between the animal sacrifices during the pilgrimage and Prophet Abraham. It is based on a prayer of Abraham recorded in the Qur'ân. When he took abode in the valley of Mecca with his wife and son, he prayed:

> Our Lord! I have settled some of my offspring in a barren valley near Thy sacred House so that, O our Sustainer! they might keep up their prayers. Cause you, therefore, people's hearts to incline towards them and provide them with fruitful sustenance, that they may be grateful. (Qur'ân 14:37)

THE ISLAMIC THEOLOGY OF SACRIFICE

The tradition of animal sacrifice in Islam is based mainly on the following verses of the Qur'ân:

When We assigned unto Abraham the site of this House [of Ka'bah], We said 'Do not ascribe divinity to aught beside Me, and sanctify My House for those who walk around it, who stand upright and bow down and prostrate themselves in it to pray'. (Qur'ân 22:26)

Hence, O Mohammad! proclaim among people the pilgrimage: they will come to thee on foot and on every kind of nimble-footed mounts from far and wide. (Qur'ân 22:27)

That they may avail themselves of many benefits of it and call to mind the name of God on the appointed days of pilgrimage over the sustenance He has provided for them in the form of flocks and herds. Eat, then, of them and feed the unfortunate poor. (Qur'ân 22:28)

And accomplish the pilgrimage (Hajj) and the Visit of the sacred places (Umrah) for God: but if you are prevented from doing so, then send instead whatever offering is feasible. And do not shave your heads until the offering has reached its destination. He among you who is ill or suffers from some ailment of the scalp, [necessitating the shaving of the head before the appointed time], should expiate either by fasting or almsgiving or by any other form of worship. In times of peace and security—one who avails oneself of combining a Visit to the sacred places and the Pilgrimage—shall make an offering such as one can easily afford. (Qur'ân 2:196)

... All cattle have been made lawful for you [as food], save those already mentioned to you [as forbidden]. ... (Qur'ân 22:30)

And for all people We have ordained acts of devotion that they might mention the name of God on what He has given them of the flocks and herds [for food] ... And give glad tidings to those who are ... humble. ... (Qur'ân 22:34)

Whose hearts are filled with awe at the mention of
God . . . and who expend in charity out of what We have
bestowed upon them as sustenance. (Qur'ân 22:35)

. . . So pronounce over them the name of God . . . eat
yourselves thereof and feed those poor who are resigned
to their lot, as well as those who beg with humility. It
is to this end that We have subjected animals to your
needs that you may be grateful. (Qur'ân 22:36)

[Know that] neither their flesh nor their blood
reaches God; it is only your righteousness that reaches
him. It is to this end that We have subjected animals to
your needs that you may glorify God for His guidance to
you: And give thou glad tidings to those who do good [to
others]. (Qur'ân 22:37)

Declare [O Mohammad]: 'As for me, my Lord has
guided me onto a right path through an ever-true
religion—the creed of Abraham who was a man of pure
faith and was not one of the polytheists. Say: 'My prayer,
my service of sacrifice, my living and my dying—surely
all are for God, who is the Lord of all the worlds'. (Qur'ân
6:161.162)

Muslims generally believe that the above verses lay down a
canonical law to offer animal sacrifices during the festival of
pilgrimage and that replacement of animals with any other kind of
offering would be wrong. However, a close study of these and other
such verses makes it abundantly clear that the Qur'ânic approach is
not meant to take animal sacrifice as an end in itself; it is meant to
be used as a means to serve a social need.

SACRIFICE AS CHARITY & ALTERNATIVE OFFERINGS

One salient point that emerges from these verses is that the main
purpose of allowing the Muslims to continue with animal sacrifices
was to turn this age-old tradition into an institution of charity.
Even the literal annotations which some Muslim theologians
put on these verses to the effect that animal sacrifice is an act of
worship and thanksgiving to God becomes valid only if sacrifice
ends up as an act of charity. All the verses of the Qur'ân which deal

with the subject wind up with the proviso that the meat be fed to the poor, the needy, those who are too modest to beg as well as the mendicants—those who beg openly.[53] In some cases the offerers of the sacrifice are allowed to consume a portion of the meat themselves, while in others the whole of the carcass is to be given in charity. Sacrifice is meant to be an act of worship and thanksgiving to solicit the approbation of God neither in the sense of atonement nor in the sense of transposing one's sins onto a scapegoat; but it is meant to be an act of benevolence (*Ihsân*) to fulfil a social obligation. After reading the Qur'ânic version of sacrifice, there remains no doubt in one's mind that any sacrifice that is allowed to go to waste is a sinful as well as a criminal violation of the Islamic law (*sharia*). Verses 22:36 and 37 make this proviso abundantly clear.

The original purpose of offering gifts (*hâdy*) at the sacred house of *Ka'bah* was to succour the ancient Meccans who were the descendants of Prophet Abraham in response to his prayer in verse 14:37. In those days the supply of provisions, such as meat, was their most essential need. The whole area was an arid desert. Under those circumstances it was a very sensible and practical proposition for Islam to ask pilgrims to offer gifts in the form of sacrificial animals. Today the Meccans are in a position to import their food without anybody's help, while there are millions of people in the rest of the Islamic world who are undernourished. Sending food to the Meccans these days is no more than an abstract rapport. Gifts are meant to express one's love and adoration, and are appreciated the more if they are to the recipient's taste and need and serve some useful purpose. Gifts of meat to the Meccans are certainly not serving any purpose at all these days. On the contrary, it has become a problem for the Saudi Government how to dispose of the carcasses. So, why not think of some kind of gifts which could be put to some use? If gifts of cash, for example, were to be substituted for animals, the money could be used for various advantageous and needed services of Islam.

The Qur'ân does mention animal sacrifices, but at the same time it mentions alternative offerings and alternative acts of devotion. Verse 2:196 suggests fasting or almsgiving or whatever kind of offering is feasible. These alternatives have been suggested for those who are prevented from attending the pilgrimage not only because of ill health, but for other reasons. In the following verse the Qur'ân does not even mention any reason and leaves the choice of alternatives to the individual. The precincts of Mecca are declared as an animal and bird sanctuary during the period of pilgrimage in the following verse:

> O believers! Slay no game while you are in a pilgrim-sanctity. Whosoever of you slays it intentionally, shall pay the penalty by offering to the Ka'bah a domestic animal the like of that which he has slain—as determined by two persons of equity among you; or he shall expiate by feeding the indigent; or by keeping equivalent fasts: so that he may taste the dire consequences of his offence. . . .[54] (Qur'ân 5:98)

In this verse three options for restitution have been left open for the offender to choose from: payment in kind out of livestock; feeding the poor; or fasting. It is true that the alternative offerings and punitory payments are there in consideration of the individual's circumstances. However, the important point to note is that all these verses lay down a principle—and that the same principle should equally apply to the circumstances of a community as a whole.

Various reasons for the prohibition of hunting during the pilgrimage period have been suggested by commentators. One rational reason which the writer can think of is that, during that period, there is enough meat for all to eat and that the additional meat of game would run to waste. This would, obviously, be against the most important Islamic concept that the killing of animals is sinful, except for the bare necessities of life. For example, in the following verses, the Qur'ân mentions two necessities of life for which cattle may be used:

> Of the cattle there are some as beasts of burden and some for meat. Eat of those which God has provided for you as sustenance, and follow not the footsteps of Satan; surely he is your manifest foe. (Qur'ân 6:142)

By the 'footsteps of the Devil' is meant, in this context, the then current practice of offering meat to deities and to the misconceived god who was thought to relish the savoury smell of burning flesh and blood. The Qur'ânic injunctions are so exacting on the point of not taking the life of an animal without a justifiable cause (be-ghair-e-haqqin) that wasting meat, even by offering it to deities and gods is called here a devilish act. The Qur'ân urges them in remonstrance in verse 6:141 not to waste food by overeating (lâ tusrefû). In verse 6:138 this malpractice of wasting meat has been censured more directly and with a touch of sarcasm, where it is stated that they set aside as God's share a portion out of the agricultural produce and cattle which God has created, saying fancifully that only what they will allow can be eaten.

A learned Muslim scholar, Sheikh Farîd Wagdi, says in his *Wagdi's Encyclopaedia*—Article on Sacrifice:

> Islam sanctioned sacrifice and expounded its wisdom and purpose; the wisdom being to induce the rich to spend, the purpose being to feed the poor unfortunate –for thus saith the Lord 'Eat of it and feed the poor unfortunate'.

Sheikh Wagdi even goes so far as to suggest that there might come a day when Muslims shall have to substitute the rite of animal sacrifice with other methods of giving alms.

An important conference was held in Cairo in 1966 under the auspices of The Academy of Islamic Research in which the famous Muslim scholar, Dr. Mahmoud Hoballah—The Secretary General of The Academy—and His Eminence The Grand Imam Rector of al-Azhar read their papers.[55] Another member of the Academy, Sheikh Abdul Rahman al-Kalhud, said in his paper:

> The Holy Qur'ân states in clear terms that the Creator wants the sacrifice not as such but as a symbol of the sacrificer's devotion to God, as is evident from the verse: 'Their flesh will never reach God, nor yet their blood, but your devotion will reach Him'. (Qur'ân 22:37)

This verse expressly indicates that the sacrifice is not meant in itself as an essential part of the religion but as an act of charity to enrich the poor.

> At present time, however, sacrificial offerings are thrown away . . . thus defeating the original purpose of *Hady*, namely, to feed the poor and needy. Thus does all this animal wealth run to waste. There is no doubt that this waste is a sort of mischief, 'And God' as the Qur'ân puts it, 'loveth not mischief'. (Qur'ân 2:205)

It is for this reason that a great number of scholars and reformers have urged that this problem must be solved, and a system chalked out to ensure the effective use of sacrificial offerings in the public interest which is supposed to underlie all the ordinances of the canon law. Another member of the Academy, Sheikh Muhammad Noor el-Hassan, expressed the following views in his paper:

> Anyone who witnesses the sacrifices slaughtered during the time of pilgrimage, cast away on the ground, unselected by their owners who desist from making them useful to others and afterwards left to decay and putrefy until offensive smell comes out of them, causing the Muslims much discomfort and danger to their health; in short anyone who witnesses the disgraceful state of affairs, will be immensely grieved about Muslims' mismanagement and their unawareness of Islamic rules misleading them to squandering and lavishment regarded as reproved by both Islam and usage. We implore God the Almighty to save Muslims from this ignorance and to guide them to the right path.

> I mention with great regret what aggravates the problem of sacrifices, because a considerable number of pilgrims slaughter their animals and cast them on the ground; they do that thinking that they are offering sacrifices. However, the sacrifice is a Sunnah, an example set by the Holy Prophet to the resident and not to a newcomer pilgrim as had been stated by Malik [93-179 A.H.—673-759 A.C.] who had been the Imam of Medinah, the town of the Emigration. If we admit for

the sake of a disputed point that it is Sunnah for the pilgrim also and that the offering of these sacrifices will certainly lead to disadvantages and misuses, which we witness occurring from them, we ought to give up this harmful usage, because to prevent harmful misuse is prior to seeking benefit deemed to be useful. So, if pilgrims follow Malik's view as regards sacrifices, they will satisfy themselves and gratify others.

We pray to God to direct the learned [people] of every Muslim town and country to enable them to guide their people and to impart to them what is most righteous and advantageous to them in their worldly life and the life to come. I believe that if Muslims conformed with the guidance we have elucidated, they will never face such complications termed as the problem of sacrifices that arise during the season of pilgrimage.

The Conference concluded by passing the following resolution No. 4-2:

> The Conference appeals to all Muslim people and governments to check the dangers which might arise during the pilgrimage from sacrificial offerings, to put them to a good use as is permitted by the Law-giver, to adopt the ways wherewith to accomplish this object.

One could quote many more authorities who have been deploring the Muslim lassitude in solving the problem associated with the senseless killing of animals as sacrifices. Perhaps one more piece of advice by a great scholar might help. Sheikh Tantawi Gowhary quotes Ibn Qaiyim in his book *Zad el Ma'ad* under the Title: "Legal Rulings Change according to Varying Places, Times and Customs":

> The canon law is based on wisdom and public interest. It is all justice and all mercy. Any case which changes it from justice to injustice, from mercy to cruelty, from good to evil, from wisdom to nonsense is alien to the common law even if it [the injustice, the cruelty, the evil, or the nonsense] has been introduced into it through misinterpretation.

> The [sacrificial gift] *Hady* offered at Mina is meant to achieve a public interest, but in fact, it has involved a harm and a loss of wealth and lives. The chief purpose of that rite is to sustain not to destroy human life. It behoves Muslims to get rid of this disease, ignorance and shame. Indeed, it is a folly which Muslims should give up. . . . Many a solution to this problem may be offered. The most practical one is to preserve the sacrificial offerings and distribute their flesh to the needy.[56]

In case the suggestion made above to offer cash instead of animals as sacrifice seems to be too unconventional or unconformable to the Tradition (*Sunnah*), there are other ways to stop this pointless carnage of innocent animals in the name of the Merciful God—while still remaining within the bounds of Tradition. Surely it is much more sinful to butcher animals cold-bloodedly, year after year in their millions just to throw their carcasses away, than to regulate the Tradition to suit the present conditions prevailing in the Islamic world. During the early period of Islam, the traditional offerings of animals made some sense. Meat was then an important ingredient of human diet and not even a scrap of it was wasted. Today we have made their killing an empty ritual and forgotten the intent.

It is understandable that a canning factory or a freezing plant cannot be an economical proposition, but monetary considerations should not be allowed to take preference over moral principles—especially when the principle of humaneness and mercy is involved. One of the titles of the Prophet Mohammad is that he was sent as 'a mercy to all creation' (*Rahmatun lil-âlamin*) (Qur'ân 21:107) and not to human species only. Any of the above proposed reforms can be workable only if the authorities of the Islamic governments and the Muslim leaders in the various countries take the initiative and organise a 'Hâdy Trust'. In case they fail to do that, then the moral responsibility lies with individuals. After all, each individual will be answerable on his or her own on the Day of Reckoning." . . . No soul earns [evil] but to its own detriment; No heavy laden soul shall be made to bear another's burden. . . ." (Qur'ân 6:164)

SACRIFICE BY PROXY

One way out of this quandary is for pilgrims to offer their sacrifices in countries of their domicile. Before starting for the pilgrimage, they can leave the needed funds with someone at home to offer the sacrifice on their behalf on the appointed days. It will be more in line with the spirit of sacrifice. In almost every part of the world wherefrom the pilgrims come, there is no paucity of poor people who would be overwhelmed with gratitude for every pound of meat they would get. It is a common sight in those countries to see a queue of men, women, and children at the door of a house where an animal is slaughtered as a sacrifice. Even the skins are donated to charitable organisations. The offering of a sacrifice by proxy for general charity (*Sadaqah*. i.e. other than the pilgrimage sacrifice) has always been an established convention among Muslims. People sick in hospitals, or away from home for any other reason, often ask their families to offer a sacrifice in their name and distribute the meat among the poor. So, why could not the same be done with the sacrificial offerings of the pilgrimage? It is the same in principle as the performance of the pilgrimage itself by proxy (*Hajj-e-badal*), which is quite a common practice. Many people who are unable to go personally for *Hajj* pay someone else to go on their behalf. Similarly, those pilgrims who feel that their sacrifices in Mecca are not fulfilling the stipulated purpose and are infringing the intrinsic spirit of the Tradition (*Sunnah*) can have their sacrifices offered on their behalf in their respective countries by proxy as *Qurban-e-badal*.

Muslims living in Western countries are in a similar predicament as the pilgrims. Thanks to the laws in the West, no animal can be slaughtered for trade except under supervision and only in licensed abattoirs. When a Muslim in these countries has to offer a sacrifice, they buy a carcass from a meat-shop. The real problem starts after that. In the Welfare States of Europe there are no 'poor' to be found. Even if there are some, they often cannot be reached easily. What happens then is that a sacrifice which was initially meant to be a charity, ends up as a feast for the family and friends. Millions of carcasses are brought by Muslims in Western countries as sacrifices and as general charity (*Sadaqah*) while not a morsel of meat reaches the poor—and thus the well-intentioned ideal of feeding the indigent ends up as a farcical pretence. Such Muslims in the West, if they are really earnest about it, should either donate an equivalent amount of cash to some charitable institution or have their sacrifices offered by proxy in their countries of origin. As it is, to name their family feasts or social banquets as *Qurbani* or *Sadaqah* is nothing short of making a mockery of the Islamic concept of charity and sacrifice.

Some years ago, a scandalous incident happened in London which, rightly, roused the indignation of the general public. A member of an Islamic Embassy was reported by the media to have slaughtered a sheep in a London street, in full view of the neighbours, supposedly as a sacrifice. It would not be wrong to assume that, being a responsible officer of an Embassy, he was an educated man and well-versed in at least the fundamentals of the Islamic law. He should have known, for example, that it is not necessary for an offerer of a sacrifice to slaughter the animal with his own hands; there are no such poor people in London as to qualify for this kind of charity; and that the poor in his own country are more in need of nourishment than here.

In order to derive real knowledge and inspiration from the revealed Scriptures, our aim should be to grasp the spirit of the message rather than to give undue devotion to the letter. These discussions on the positive and revealed theology might look to some as pedagogic, but there are millions of people, even in this age of agnosticism and cynicism, who still seek guidance in their respective Scriptures and try to discipline their lives according to their teachings. A misunderstood and misinterpreted doctrine not only defeats its purpose but can sometimes result in harmful consequences. Almost all modern Muslim scholars have expressed their concern at the way the Islamic tenet of sacrifice is being interpreted and practised. Allama Yusuf Ali, the distinguished translator of the Qur'ân says:

> ... the meat then killed is meant to be eaten for food and distributed to the poor and the needy. In present conditions, where much of it is wasted on the spot, it would be a good thing if the surplus meat were canned and utilised for export, or if the sacrifices were performed

in some other form approved by due authority." Then he adds: "This is the true end of a sacrifice, not propitiation of higher powers, for God is One, and He does not delight in flesh and blood, but a symbol of thanksgiving to God by sharing meat with fellow-men.[57]

Another distinguished translator of the Qur'ân into English, Muhammad Asad, gives his views as follows:

> Whereas the pilgrims are merely *permitted* to eat some of the flesh of the animals which they have sacrificed, the feeding of the poor is *mandatory* (Tabari and Zamakhsahrî) and constitutes, thus, the primary objective of these sacrifices.[58]

It is generally argued that animal sacrifices during the pilgrimage are 'God's symbols' (*Sha'âir God*), symbolising the worshipper's devotion and gratefulness to God for His bounties to man. This view is based on verses 5:3 and 22:32, 36. What is overlooked, however, is that these verses speak of God's symbols in terms of all the rites of pilgrimage and not exclusively of sacrifices. Many learned scholars, including Tabari, hold the same view. If these verses are studied in their full context, it becomes clear that sacrifice is one of the many other symbols of God and that it becomes a symbol of worship only if the proviso of charity if fulfilled. Otherwise, it becomes a diabolical ritual of immolation. Another very important point to note in this respect (verses 22:34,35) is that the act of sacrifice becomes a symbol of worship only when it is done by those who 'submit' (*Aslimû*); who do it in 'humility' (*Mukhbetîn*); and whose hearts tremble (*Wajelat Qulûbohum*) at the time when they are invoking the name of God to slaughter an animal, and 'expend on charity out of what We have bestowed on them'. (For the position of Eid sacrifices in Mecca, see Appendix A at the end of this chapter).

THE THREE KINDS OF SACRIFICES

The code governing the procedure of pilgrimage does not fall within the preview of this book. There are comprehensive books available on this subject in almost every language. Then there are officially appointed guides (mu'alims) to instruct pilgrims at every step. However, the following brief information is relevant to the subject of pilgrimage sacrifice (hâdy) and to sacrifice in general:

There are only three occasions when Muslims offer sacrifice. The first is during the three special days of the pilgrimage (ayyâm-e-tashrîk) which fall on the 8th, 9th, and 10th of the month of dzul-Hajj. This sacrifice is called hâdy (plural of hadyah or hadiyah) meaning gifts. In the context of pilgrimage, it means the sacrificial animals or any other kind of gifts offered to the sacred house of Ka'bah in Mecca. The sacrificial animals named in the Qur'ân are of eight kinds of cattle out of three categories, viz. camels, cows or bulls, and sheep or goats.[59] As mentioned earlier, the offerers are allowed to eat of their sacrifices, "but the primary objective is to feed the poor."[60] There is, however, one kind of sacrifice which the pilgrim is not allowed to eat at all and should give the whole carcass in charity. When one goes to perform the pilgrimage only and does not combine it with a visit to the holy places ('Umrah or the minor pilgrimage), it is called Hajj-al-Ifrâd, meaning singular or exclusive pilgrimage in the sense of major. If a pilgrim violates any of the prescribed rules during the major pilgrimage, they become liable to a sort of fine of a special offering called dhamm al-gobran. This sacrifice is solely for charity and the offender, including the family and friends, cannot eat even a morsel of it.

The rule that the sacrifices must be made within the three days mentioned above has been misunderstood by some Muslims to mean that the meat must be consumed within those three days and that it should not be preserved any longer. There is no authority for this stipulation in any sources of the Islamic law. On the contrary Sahîh Bukharî quotes the Prophet in Hadith 25:124 as having suggested to his companions, including Jabir bin Abdullah, to take some left-over sacrificial meat with them as a provision for their journey back. Perhaps this misunderstanding arose originally because of the Biblical rulings limiting the period during which the sacrificial meat could be consumed, the surplus after that period being thrown away.

The second occasion for sacrifice is at the birth of a child, whether male or female, and is called akikah. Putting the female issue on a par with the male might look to be in the natural order of things these days, but in the pre-Islamic period, female infanticide was quite common. The Qur'ân not only stopped the killing of infants after birth, but also gave equal status to both sexes.[61] The birth of a child is a festive occasion for the family and usually friends and the dignitaries of society are invited to a feast. Yet, even on this occasion, the Islamic convention of sacrifice is to share the meat with the poor. Traditionally Muslims distribute half the carcass among the poor, keeping the other half for themselves.

The third kind of sacrifice is a pure and simple charity (sadaqah). There being no special occasion for it, it is offered by individuals at will as a meritorious act of feeding the poor. Neither the offerer of this sacrifice, nor their family or friends have any share in the meat. So much so, that if any of them consumes even a morsel of it, it is considered to be baneful for them. Even the professional butcher who is called in to slaughter and flay refuses to take his due share of meat. The skin, as is the case with all sacrifices, is given to some charitable institution. This kind of sacrifice is very common among Muslims all over the world and fulfils a great social need in countries where the normal diet of the poor people lacks in food-essentials.

It is significant to note that there is no ritual involved in the sacrificial slaughter. Those Muslims who have started changing this plain matter-of-fact act into a ritual should know better. The two conditions of invoking the name of God and using a sharp knife are the same in sacrificial slaughter as in the normal slaughter for food. The only differentiating stipulation in the case of sacrificial animals is that they should be healthy and free from any perceptible sign of illness. The expression 'free from blemish' is liable to be misunderstood in the Jewish sense of the word 'blemish'. The Islamic definition of 'blemish', according to the Prophet Mohammad is that the sacrificial animal should not be: obviously diseased; raw-boned lean; blind even in one eye; or lame.[62] With the exception of a diseased animal, which people do not eat anyway, the other three are the only additional conditions laid down for sacrificial animals. One plausible reason for these additional conditions is to make sure that the poor people for whom these sacrifices are offered get reasonably good quality meat.

APPENDIX TO CHAPTER 4

The following letter from the Islamic Development Bank, Jeddah, Saudi Arabia, dated August 1986, is self-explanatory:

To: Al-Hafiz B.A. Masri . . .,

Dear Sir,

The Government of the Kingdom of Saudi Arabia, keeping in view the wastage of meat during Eid Al-Adha, has established a Sacrificial Meat Utilization Project in 1983 on an experimental basis and devoted particular attention to this project as it does regarding all matters related to the Hajj.

Following several studies carried out by the concerned authorities in the Kingdom of Saudi Arabia regarding the optimal use of the sacrificial meat, a special committee has been set up to supervise the implementation of the project. The committee includes the Islamic Development Bank (IDB), which co-operates with the Saudi competent authorities.

The first experiment took place in the 1403H. [1983 A.C.] Hajj season. The meat of 63,000 heads was utilised, most of which was airlifted to refugees in Sudan, D'jibouti and to Afghan refugees in Pakistan. For purposes of the project, the al-Moaisim Slaughterhouse was designed by the Saudi Government and fully equipped with the most modern installations.

In the light of the first year's experience, it was decided to expand the project. In 1404H. [1984 A.C.] Hajj season, the meat of 186, 195 heads of sheep was utilized, of which about 144,000 heads were airlifted and distributed to the poor Muslim communities in D'jibouti, Bangladesh, Chad, Yemen Arab Republic, as well as to Afghan refugees in Pakistan and Palestinian refugees in Jordan, besides what was distributed at Al-Harm.

In the light of the project's success in 1403H. and 1404H., thanks be to God, it was envisaged to expand the project in 1405H. Hajj season. The programme for the 1405 H. Hajj season aimed at utilizing 300,000 heads of sheep, but due to the growing response and support which the project received from the pilgrims, the number of coupons sold exceeded the target figure by over 7,000.

In 1405H. a complete unit with all necessary equipment was added to the Al-Moaisim Slaughterhouse to make use of some of the offals of the sacrificed animals. Moreover, two cold rooms, each with a capacity of 50,000 heads, were added for freezing the meat.

The expansion in the programme can be gauged from the fact that in its first year, i.e. 1403., 63,000 sheep were utilized. In the second year (1404H.) the number of sheep utilised was 186,195 and the number in 1405H. was 307,266.

In 1406H. [1986 A.C.], 350,000 sheep have been utilised and the meat has been distributed on the same lines as in 1405H. in Sudan, Pakistan D'jibouti, Bangladesh, Jordan, Chad, Yemen (DR), Mauritania, Mali, Burkina Faso, Egypt, Senegal, Gambia, Syria, and Niger.

The Muna Development Office is presently preparing studies on the financial allocation required for the second model slaughterhouse.

When the second slaughterhouse is completed, the project will be extended to include camels and cattle as well as sheep. It is intended in future years also to utilise the parts of the slaughtered animals other than their meat.

As far as sacrifices by proxy are concerned, I would like to inform you that there is no objection to the authorisation of slaughtering the animals. The upright Islamic Shariah allows the Muslim, in carrying out the slaughtering of his sacrificial offering, to authorise whoever he deems as a trustworthy representative. The representative is expected to fulfil such authorisation in accordance with the requirements of the Shariah. You in turn should fully observe these requirements. Any offering given as an atonement for committing a prohibition or as a reparation for failing to observe a required duty must be distributed to the poor in Makkah. As for any other type of sacrificial offering, the meat can be distributed to the poor in Makkah or to other pilgrims or to anyone else as provided by the Shariah.

Hoping that this can meet your requirements as mentioned in your letter.

Best regards.

Yours faithfully,

(Abdul Fattah Kiswani)

Head: Sacrificial Meat Office

The Government of the Kingdom of Saudi Arabia deserve felicitations on their resolution to solve this problem. Let us hope that soon their efforts will succeed in the utilisation of every ounce of meat and the by-products of every sacrificial animal for the purpose of charity for which the institution of animal sacrifice was originally established by Islam.

It is very encouraging to note in the above letter that the accredited theologians of Saudi Arabia also endorse the two suggestions I have made in this chapter, namely: the option of offering sacrifices by proxy; and the offering of cash in lieu of an animal. As I understand from this letter, the pilgrims pay cash to the authorities for which they are given coupons.

The word 'atonement' used in this letter should be read in the sense of a fine by way of penalty for breaking some rule. The concept of atonement for the expiation of sins by killing scapegoats does not exist in the Islamic *sharia*.

REFERENCES AND NOTES (CHAPTER 4)

1. cf. *The Way of Heaven*; Taylor, R.L.; E.J. Brill, Leiden; 1985.
2. *Lun-Yu*, 3:17, as recorded in *The Analects of Confucius*; Arthur Waley; Vintage, New York; 1938; p.98.
3. *Lun-Yu*, 7:1, as recorded in *Sources of Chinese Tradition*; S.J. de Bary; Columbia University Press, New York; 1960; p.25.
4. cf. *Brhadaranyaka Upanishad*, 1:1, 2
5. cf. *Samkhya Karika, Isvarakrisna*.
6. *Yogasastra*, 11:39.
7. cf. *The Bodhisattva Doctrine in Buddhist Sanskrit Literature*; Har Dayal; Kegan Paul & Co., London; 1931; also cf. *Avadana Kalpalata*.
8. *The Epistle of St Paul the apostle to the Romans*, 8:22,23.
9. Zoroaster (Zarathustra) was the founder of the religion in Persia, cir. 1,000B.C. It is also called Magianism, Parseism or Mazdaism.
10. *Isa*. 45:1.
11. *Joel*. 3:9-17.
12. *Exod*. 29:40.
13. *Deut*. 12:20-28.
14. *Lev*. 3:11; 21:21; *Num*. 28:2.
15. *Ezek*. 44:16. *Malachi*, 1:7.
16. Lev. 6:16; 7:6.
17. Gen. 8:20, 21.
18. *Talmud* is the body of Jewish civil and canonical law, consisting of *Mishna* and *Gemara*. The final version was completed in the 5th century. *Midrash* is the haggadic scriptural exegesis, especially that which was made during a period of about 1,800 years after Exile. *Targums* (Hebrew: *Targumim*; Arabic: *Tarâjim*) are the translations of some portions of the Old Testament in Aramaic Judea.
19. For full details of the Cabalist concept see: *Zohar*; *Sefer ha-Bahir*; *Issac the Blind*; *Egra*; and *Azriel of Gerona*.
20. *Lev*. 16:20-22; 4:20; 5:10
21. *Lev*. 16:8
22. *Gen*. 4:3-5.
23. *Gen*. 8:20,21.
24. *Job*. 1:1-5.
25. *Job*. 42:7, 8.
26. *Gen*. 31:45-54.
27. *Gen*. 46:1.
28. *Gen*. 12:7, 8; 13:3, 4.
29. *Gen*. 22:13.
30. *Gen*. 26:25.
31. *Gen*. 33:20; 35:7.

32. For details see: *Leviticus, Numbers, II Kings.*
33. *Lev.* 12:6-8; 15:14, 15, 29, 30; 16:3, 5, 24. *Exod.* 29:38-42. *Num.* 6:10, 11, 14-16; 28:1-14, 19-29; 29:2-4, 8, 12-38.
34. *Isaiah,* 1:10-17.
35. *Hosea,* 6:4-6.
36. *Amos,* 5:18-22.
37. *Psalm of Asaph,* 50:7-14.
38. *Jer.* 7:21.
39. Moses ben Maimun, the famous Spanish Jewish Rabbi, philosopher and writer (1135-1204 A.C.).
40. *Ber.* 4:1; 7:266.
41. *Hertz Prayer Book;* Joseph Hertz; 15:7. Also cf. 33,34.
42. *The Jewish Religion;* Michael Friedlander; 1913; p.417.
43. *Facts and Fallacies about Liberal Judaism,* originally by Rabbi Hooker; revised by Sidney Brichto, London; 1972; p.14.
44. A general tribunal, called the Holy Office, was developed by the Roman Catholic Church under Pope Innocent III and Pope Gregory IX (1198-1241) to make inquisitional examination of the so-called heretics. The Spanish Inquisition has gone down in history as the most torturous of them all, during the 15th and the 16th centuries. The Inquisition was abolished in France in 1772 and in Spain in 1834.
45. *Joshua.* 9:21.
46. *War—Living Graves;* Shaw, George Bernard; Irish dramatist and scholar; (1856—1950).
47. *The Qur'ân:* 4:164; 10:47; 13:7; 16:36; 35:24; 40:78.
48. *The Qur'ân:* 4:150, 151.
49. There are numerous passages in the Qur'ân about Prophet Abraham and Jesus Christ. The following few references will give a general idea: About Abraham: 2:124, 130; 3:33; 16:120; 21:69; 22:78; 38:45-47. About Christ: 4:171; 43:57; 61:14.
50. cf. *Encyclopedia Britannica—Article on Sacrifice.* Also cf. The Origins of Sacrifice; James, E.O.; pp. 84-86.
51. cf. *The Religion of the Semites;* Robertson Smith. Also cf. *Encyclopedia of Religion and Ethics;* Hastings.
52. cf. *Ibn Kathir;* Vol III; p.221.
53. *The Qur'ân,* 2:196; 22:28, 35-37.
52. *The Qur'ân,* 5:98. Also cf. 5:2, 97.
55. *The Third Conference of the Academy of Islamic Research;* G.O. Government Printing Offices, Cairo, 13810-1966-3,000 ex., 1966; pp. 115-130.
56. Sheikh Tantawi Gowhari in his book entitled *Al-Gawahir,* as a Commentary on Chapter 22 of the Qur'ân.
57. *The Holy Qur'ân;* A. Yusuf Ali; Sh. Muhammad Ashraf, Kashmiri Bazar, Lahore, Pakistan; footnotes Nos. 2802 and 2810 to verses 22:28, 34.

58. *The Message of the Qur'ân*; Muhammad Asad; Dar-al-Andalus, Gibraltar; footnote No. 42 to verse 22:28.

59. *The Qur'ân*, 6:143. Also cf. *Bidayet al-Mujtahid*; Ibn Rushd.

60. cf. *Tabari* and *Zamakhshari*.

61. *The Qur'ân*, 6:151; 17:31.

62. *Al-Muwatta*; Imam Malik on the authority of al-Bara'bin Azil.

5

HALAL MEAT:
THE BONE OF CONTENTION

PREAMBLE

SOME LIGHT HAS BEEN thrown in previous chapters on the emphasis which Islam lays on an all-embracing relationship with the environment—each creature and element working as a coefficient agent of nature. All species of sentient beings are covenanted to be complementary in the utilisation of each other's intrinsic potentialities. Those who take undue advantage of other species break the Divine Law of equilibrium in nature—and nature never forgives. The Qur'ân dwells on this theme recurrently, such as:

> Allah has not created all this without truth [*haqq*] (Qur'ân. 10:5;) for it is He who created everything, and ordained it with due potential [*taqdir*] (Qur'ân. 25:2;) not to allow any change to corrupt what Allah has created (Qur'ân. 30:30)." Then a warning is given to those people who are guilty of infraction, in these words; "Do they not know how many We have annihilated before them— those whom We had established on earth as more powerful than We have established you...." (Qur'ân. 6:6)

Anyone who tries to understand the Islamic teachings on this subject will find that, even in his relentless search for food, man has to keep himself within the bounds of humanity, compassion, and mercy so as not to cause any unnecessary and avoidable pain to the victims of his needs. Muslims generally know what is *halal* and *harâm*. They also have a general idea about the method of slaughter as prescribed by Islam. However, it cannot be denied that there does exist some confusion in matters of detail among some Muslims. This is mostly due to the fact that the various aspects of the Islamic dietary laws are presented to the Muslim public as isolated and incohesive excerpts from the Qur'ân and *Ahadith*. This sketchy information does not help laymen sort out their priorities in a given situation.

An overall study of the law leaves no doubt that Islam does not want us to be uncompromisingly austere in our dietetic regimen. It does not want us to end up like the orthodox Hindus who would throw away their food if it gets even touched by a non-Hindu. Mahatma Gandhi's clan strongly opposed his parents' decision to send him to England for education on the grounds that the child would lose caste by crossing the waters and eating non-Hindu food. Orthodox Jews have imposed on themselves segregation by their over-exacting laws of diet. However, the writer has come across quite a few Muslims who would not eat even at other Muslims' houses because they are not prepared to take on trust the orthodoxy of the host. This has started happening to the followers of that Prophet who repeatedly emphasised the socio-cultural importance of mutual exchange of hospitality. For example, he says: "Eat in company, not alone, for congregation inspires Divine Grace", or "One who is invited to a meal and does not respond, gives offence to Allah and His Messenger."

Those living in Islamic countries have little idea of the dietary problems which Muslims in the West have to face. During the past few decades millions of Muslims have migrated to Western countries. Until a few years ago, *halal* meat shops were few and far between. Even these days people have to travel long distances in some areas to get *halal* meat.

An attempt has been made in this chapter to discuss some problems which are confronting the oncoming Muslim generations in their daily lives. Questions such as the lawfulness or unlawfulness (*halal* or *harâm*) of meat slaughtered by Christians and Jews and the question of pre-slaughter stunning, are not only important from the theological point of view but they have also become emotive ethnological issues. The purpose of this discussion is to present bare facts in the light of Islamic teachings, leaving the inference to the reader's judgement. However, the writer has availed himself of the liberty of conscience to express his personal views on some of the controversial issues, in the hope that readers would find them helpful. After all, the new generations of Muslims are to live all their lives in countries of non-Islamic culture and religion. Not only they, but in time all their succeeding generations too, will have to live in similar situations. They will be able to keep up their heritage not by shutting themselves up into their own cultural ghettos but by an educated sense of compatibility and integration—as opposed to assimilation.

Lawful And Unlawful Meat

The Qu'ran has laid down general guidance about what kind of animals are lawful (*halal*) or unlawful (*harâm*) to eat, while *Ahadith* and the jurists (*Fuqaha'a*) have elucidated those laws. The important point to note in this respect is that the prohibition of certain foods is solely for hygienic reasons. Keeping in mind the long-term influences of diet on the consumer's ethos, the dietetic laws are meant to be taken seriously, albeit not so seriously as to jeopardize one's very health or life. That is why all restrictions are lifted in circumstances of genuine need and distress. Summarily the following animals are lawful as food in Islam:

The cud-chewing animals (ruminants) such as cattle, sheep, goats, camels, buffaloes, wild ruminants; animals which live permanently in water (aquatics) such as fish and members of the mammalian order (cetaceans) such as whales; and most birds. It is taken for granted that every species of animal and bird is permissible as food unless specifically prohibited in the Qur'ân or *Hadith*. Some of the prohibited so named are: pigs; some of those living both on land and in water, though not able to breathe under water (amphibia) such as frogs and crocodiles; all the flesh-eating mammalia (carnivores)— whether domesticated or wild—such as cats, dogs, wolves, jackals, foxes, lions, tigers; animals which are zoologically human in form (anthropoids or simiods) such as monkeys and apes; most of the creeping creatures (reptiles and amoeba) such as snakes and toxic lizards; animals feeding on carrion or refuse (scavengers) and birds that prey with their claws or talons such as kites, crows, eagles and hawks. Asses, donkeys, and mules are prohibited, but there is a difference of opinion about wild asses, zebras, and quaggas. Blood is prohibited, but only that which pours forth at the time of slaughter. (Qur'ân 6:145). That which is left in the body as residuum is washed off before cooking.[1]

THE QUR'ÂNIC DIETARY ORDINANCES

It is noteworthy that the four Schools of Thought in Islam, mistakenly called 'sects' by some, are agreed on the quintessence of Islamic dietary laws, except on some points of detail.[2]

The Qur'ân speaks of 'sin' not only in terms of dereliction of moral rectitude, but also in the sense of violation of the physical laws of nature. All its dietary laws are based on the principle that both the physical and the metaphysical existence of man are inversely correspondent. Those who seek to interpret these laws as merely ritualistic symbols benefit from them neither spiritually nor physically. These days the real problem in understanding the true spirit of those laws is that most of the classical literature on this subject was written some centuries ago, when human lifestyles and its contingencies were different. What is needed now is the reappraisal and reinterpretation of those laws—of course within the bounds of the Divine code (sharia)—to keep religion a dynamic force. There are quite a few verses laying down the law on food, which will be discussed later.

First, it is important to discuss the following verse which is the most comprehensive of them all:

> Forbidden to you is that which dies of itself; blood; flesh of swine; that on which any name other than that of Allah has been invoked; the strangled animals; that beaten to death; that killed by a fall; that gorged to death with the horn; that [parts of] which wild beasts have eaten—except those which you [are able to] slaughter; that which is sacrificed on stones set up [as idols]; and

that on which you draw lots by arrows. This day have
I perfected your religion for you . . . However, if one is
compelled by hunger—not inclining wilfully to sin—
then surely Allah is Forgiving, Merciful. (Qur'ân 5:4)

A careful analysis of this verse shows that the prohibited food
falls into four categories, viz. carrion, blood, pork, and animals
killed idolatrously. A further analysis shows that the prohibition is
based on two considerations, viz. physical as well as metaphysical
welfare. Pork, blood, or the flesh of animals which are dead (*maitat*)
for any reason before being cleansed of blood (*tadhkiyyah*) are
physically unhealthy (*rijs*) to eat. Animals killed idolatrously or
even heretically—such as sortition by arrows—are detrimental to
spiritual health (*fisq*). However, here again, Islam qualifies this law
with reservations for exceptional circumstances. The extenuatory
clause at the end of the verse applies to everything listed as
unlawful (*harâm*).

'Animals slaughtered on stones' refers to the stone altars on
which sacrifices used to be offered to deities and idols by pagans.[3]
'The drawing of lots by arrows' refers to the pagan practice of
portioning out the sacrificial meat among themselves by shooting
flat and featherless arrows (*al-azlam*) at them.[4] This verse was
revealed to the Prophet Mohammad 81 or 82 days before his death,
which makes it the final word on the Qur'ânic dietary law.[5]

Another significant point to note in this verse is that all injured
animals—such as those mutilated by wild beasts and partly eaten
by them, beaten up, strangulated, or gorged—are allowed to be eaten
provided they are live enough to be bled.[6] This Qur'ânic ruling is of
great significance in relation to the Jewish objection to causing an
injury and a blemish to the animal by stunning it before slaughter.
The Islamic approach in this respect is in sharp contrast to that of
Judaism. The Islamic prohibition imposed on all the above categories
of animals is abrogated *ipso facto* in cases where they can be bled by
slaughter—irrespective of the extent, nature or cause of their injuries.
The point cannot be over-emphasised that the Islamic dietetic law
is based on the utility value of all the resources of food in general
and of food-animals in particular. The very survival of a living being

depends on nutriment. That is why even pork has been allowed to be eaten in case of exigency, with the qualifying clauses of not relishing it (*ghaira bâgh'in*) nor consuming more than necessary (*lââd'in*). The Islamic juristic rule is: "what is not declared as unlawful is lawful." The Qur'ân repeatedly upbraids the fanatical zealots who add their own pedantic doctrine to the straightforward Divine Law. It criticises those who take their theologians as gods in Chapter 9, verse 31. When requested by a companion named 'Adi bin Hatim to explain, the Prophet replied that such people declare some lawful things as unlawful and some unlawful things as lawful and thus act as if they were the Lords (*Arbab*). The pith of the Qur'ânic message in this respect is not to impose on oneself unnecessary abstinence and to thankfully enjoy all the good and pure bounties (*tayyibât*) of nature. The following few verses will serve as an example, and would perhaps help Muslim readers in resolving some of their dietetic problems in the West:

> O you messengers! Eat of the good things [tayyibât] and do righteous deeds. Surely, I know what you do. (Qur'ân 23:51)

> O believers! Eat what We have provided for you of lawful and good things, and give thanks for Allah's favour, if it is He whom you serve. (Qur'ân 2:172; 16:114)

The word '*tayyib*', translated as 'good', 'pure', 'wholesome', etc. has already been explained to mean pure both in the physical and the moral sense. For example, food obtained by any illegal or unethical means, such as by subjecting the animals to cruelties in their breeding, transport, slaughter, or in their general welfare would be impure and unlawful to eat (*harâm*) food even if they had been slaughtered in the strictest Islamic manner.

> ... He [Mohammad] enjoins them to good and forbids them evil and makes lawful to them the good things and prohibits for them impure things, and removes from them their burden and the shackles which used to be on them.... (Qur'ân. 7:157)

> Say [O Mohammad!] I find not in what has been revealed to me any food [meat] forbidden to those who

234

wish to eat it, unless it be dead meat, or blood that pours forth, or the flesh of swine—for it is unclean [rijs]—or the sacrilegious [fisq] meat which has been slaughtered in anybody's name other than that of Allah. However, if one is stressed by necessity [one may eat any of the above-mentioned things] without wilful disobedience and without transgressing the due limits. [In that case, know that] thy Lord is Forgiving and Merciful. (Qur'ân 6:145)

It is significant to note that meat-eating is neither encouraged nor even recommended by Islam. According to the above verse, these laws have been laid down for those "who wish to eat it" (Tâimin yat'amohu).

The message of the above verse is repeated in other verses to lay stress upon the point that it is only those categories of food which have been named which are unlawful to eat and that the rest is lawful (Qur'ân 2:173; 16:115). The reason for this repetition and emphasis seems to have been to liberate Muslims from the then prevalent pre-Islamic interdicts on food, most of which were superstitious and superfluous. The Qur'ân puts a question in these words:

And what reason have you that you should not eat of that on which Allah's name has been pronounced, when He has already explained to you in detail what is forbidden—excepting that which you are compelled to eat under necessity? Yet there are those who lead people astray by their low desires out of ignorance. Surely your Lord—He knows the transgressors. (Qur'ân. 6:119)

Of the cattle there are some for burden and some for slaughter as food. Eat what Allah has provided for you as sustenance, and do not be led by the devil—he is your manifest foe. (Qur'ân 6:142)

By the devil in this context is meant those who take the law into their own hands by declaring lawful things as unlawful and vice versa. Arbitrary taboos in religion make its laws unconformable and the life of its followers unnecessarily difficult. The Qur'ân declares the final judgement in these words: "Today [all] things good and pure have been made lawful for you. . . ." (Qur'ân 5:6)

The general counsel of the Qur'ân regarding food is of moderation in eating and of a well-balanced discernment between the lawful and the unlawful. Out of many verses on this theme, the following would suffice here:

> O believers! make not unlawful the good things which Allah has made lawful for you, and exceed not the limits—for Allah does not hold dear those who overpass the limits. (Qur'ân 5:90)

Many commentators have elucidated the Qur'ânic wording 'Lâ-ta'tadû' (do not exceed the limits) and 'Lâ tuharrimû' (do not declare as forbidden). It is generally agreed that the injunction 'do not exceed the limits' means that one should not indulge in gluttony. However, the counterpart of the true sense often remains unappreciated that this injunction also qualifies the preceding injunction of 'do not declare as forbidden' and therefore can be taken to mean: 'do not exceed the limitations by declaring lawful things as unlawful'. In this context the latter interpretation is more in accord with the general drift of this and other verses on this theme. The next verse further supports this interpretation by laying stress on the counsel to eat of all good and pure things. Some illustrious authorities, such as Zamakshari, Tabari, and Razi, opine that these verses are meant to dissuade people from the monastic tendencies of self-mortification by denying themselves legitimate creature comforts and by unnecessary abstinence from good food.

FOOD OF THE "PEOPLE OF THE BOOK"

The verse 5:6, while declaring all good and pure things as lawful to eat, continues to declare: "And the food of those who have been given the Book is lawful for you and your food is lawful for them. . . ."

The learned commentators believe that the Arabic word 'Ta'âm' used for food means 'meat' in this context. According to Abd Allah bin Abbas, who was a companion of the Prophet, 'Ta'âm' here means slaughtered meat (Dhabihah).[7]

By the "People of the Book" is meant the followers of those scriptures which are historically acknowledged to have been revealed by God. Muslims generally apply this term (Ahl al-Kitab or

Kitabi) to Christians and Jews. However, during the early days of Islam, the Persians also were included. Originally Sabians too were included in this term, but this religion does not exist anymore.[8]

It is a latent condition in this verse that only that kind of the *Kitabis'* food which is permissible to Muslims is that which is lawful (*Halal*) according to Islamic law. Until recently the question whether or not the meat slaughtered by Christians was lawful used to be more or less of academic interest. These days, however, it has started posing itself with all its pragmatical implications. Although the above verse puts the Christians and the Jews in the same bracket, many Muslims have been feeling an aversion to Christian food since the time when St. Paul declared the flesh of swine as lawful. For Muslims leading a quiet and religiously conventional life within Islamic countries, the question does not warrant a serious discussion. However, for Muslims living in Christian countries it affects not only their daily diet but also their social life and has to be thrashed out.

THE PARADOXICAL ENIGMA OF PORK

It is generally argued that, at the time when the above-quoted verse (5:6) was revealed, Christians used to observe the Mosaic prohibition of swine-flesh; which they no longer do. However, this line of reasoning is based on the false premise that, while revealing this verse, Allah did not know that there would come a time when Christians and Jews would start to ignore some of the Biblical dietetic laws. According to Muslim credence Allah is All-Knowing; His knowledge is above the limitations of time and space. Surely, His knowledge did comprehend all this. Had it been within the design of His wisdom to allow Muslims to eat the meat slaughtered by the *Kitabis* as a transient expediency, He would have put in some sort of a caveat in this verse to the effect that Muslims should stop eating meat slaughtered by them when they started eating pork. It is not the Muslims' concern what Christians and Jews eat. They should be concerned only to the extent that they themselves do not eat those items of their food which have been specifically named as forbidden by the Islamic law (*sharia*) and that they should not impose on themselves any restrictions beyond that. The famous Kufi theologian—Sha'bi (d.722 A.C.), while commenting on this verse, says that Allah knows what the *Kitabis* do and it is He who allowed us to eat meat slaughtered by them.

It is imperative to keep in mind throughout this discourse, the ruling (*Fatwa*) of the Imams Abu Hanifah and Hanbal.[9] According to them the Qur'ânic permission to Muslims to eat the food (meat) of the People of the Book is restricted to those things which have been declared as lawful. Things declared as unlawful for Muslims are not to be eaten in any case. The opinions of Muslim authorities, quoted below, take for granted this postulate:

One of the early authorities to pronounce an edict (*Fatwa*) on this issue was Ma'bad al-Juhani (d.660 A.C., 80 A.H.). According to him, meat slaughtered by Christians is lawful for Muslims. Ata bin Yassar (d.721 A.C.) who was the Judge (*Qadhi*) of Medina, endorsed his views. Similarly, al-Laithi and Rabi'ah (both d. 791 A.C.) have expressed their verdicts to the same effect.[10] Syed Sabiq also adds in *Fiqhus-Sunnah* that meat slaughtered by Christians and Jews is lawful.[11] Sarakhsiî (d. 899 A.C.) even went so far as to say: "the flesh of an animal slaughtered by a Christian or a Jew is ALWAYS lawful for Muslims to eat. . . ."[12] It is significant to note that such edicts started being issued within a few years after the death of the Prophet when there were many learned authorities still alive who had direct knowledge of the Prophet's sayings and deeds, and yet none of the Muslims contradicted these verdicts. Below are the edicts of some very prominent succeeding theologians: The first and *prima facie* view is that their (*Kitabis'*) foods are lawful for the Muslims. . . .[13]

The Mufti of Jordan says:

> The jurists have agreed that a Muslim is allowed to eat meat offered by a man of the People of the Book. It is not right for him to suspect the method of their slaughtering and whether or not the name of God has been invoked at the time of slaughtering. It is not even good to make an enquiry on the subject, because the verses in the Qur'ân are absolute without any restrictions (*mutlaw*). A considerable number of religious doctors have

said that animals cut by a man of the 'People of the Book' are permitted for Muslims to eat, whatever may be the method of slaughtering. . . .

Those who do not eat their meat in Europe and U.S.A., according to opinions held by some who are against the above-mentioned opinion, have no reason for doing so, save illusion (*waham*). This opinion [supporting the prohibition of the Jewish or Christian-slaughtered meat] goes against the majority view, which allows meat cut by Christians and Jews for Muslims.[14]

Maulana Sa'îd Ahmad Akbarabadi, the celebrated Muslim theologian of India, has endorsed the views of the Mufti of Jordan.[15] An eminent Egyptian scholar and theologian, 'Khallaf, says:

The cattle and all other animals which the Christians and Jews slaughter in a manner which makes it lawful for them to eat according to their religions, are lawful for Muslims to eat.[16]

Another prominent Muslim scholar, El-Abbadi, bases his views on the Qur'ân 5:6 to say that the most important point is whether or not the slaughter has been carried out in accordance with religious prescript, and that it makes no difference whether or not the slaughterer is a Muslim or one from among the People of the Book.[17]

The following Muslim scholars of great authority have opined that, according to the Qur'ânic verse 5:6, the meat sold in Christian and Jewish shops in the West is lawful for Muslims: 1, Sheikh Muhammad Abduh, former Mufti of Egypt. 2, Sheikh Rashid Reda, a colleague of Sheikh Muhammad Abdu. 3, Sheikh Mahmoud Shaltoot, former Rector of Al-Azhar. 4, Dr. Yusuf al-Qardawe of Qatar.

The verdict of another authority from Jordan, El-Khayyat, is that such meats are lawful for Muslims and that "we are not required to consider the way in which animals have been slaughtered, and whether or not Allah's name has been mentioned on them . . . Foodstuffs imported from countries of the People of the Book are lawful unless there is evidence that they are unlawful for themselves, such as carrion, blood or swine-flesh."[18] The Director of Islamic affairs, Qatar, also agreed with the above verdicts.

The great Indian Muslim educationalist and commentator of the Qur'ân 'Sir Sayyid Ahmad Khan (d. 1898 A.C.)' was on his way to London and ate the meat provided on the ship. He says in one of his letters describing his voyage: "After an inquiry we came to know that the process of slaughtering animals, such as sheep and lambs is to cut their jugular veins with a sharp knife—for their blood is unlawful to Christians . . . The meat is, according to our religion, lawful for Muslims."[19]

Thousands of Muslim businessmen, diplomats, tourists, and professional people travel to Western countries every day and stay in hotels where they eat meat supplied by Christian butchers. Many such dignitaries are personally known to the writer as good practising Muslims. They instruct the Management not to serve them any food which contains swine-flesh or lard, and their wishes are complied with. Many of the Islamic organisations in the West are dependent for their very existence on the donations from such so-called unorthodox Muslims. However, in the light of the following incident recorded in *Hadith*, they are not guilty of violation of any Islamic law in eating meat in Western hotels: "Some companions of the Holy Prophet Mohammad, during their travels in Syria, ate the meat supplied by Christians without enquiring as to how the animals were slaughtered." An Islamic Magazine of Geneva has also supported this conclusion.[20]

Is Jewish Food *Halal*?

Some Muslim theologians have recently started advising that the meat slaughtered only by orthodox Jews is lawful. This poses the unsolvable problem of ascertaining who is or is not an orthodox Jew. Once such a principle is accepted, there is no reason why it should not apply to the Muslim slaughtermen as well. What it amounts to in practical terms is that a customer should ask at the *Halal* and *Kosher* shops, before buying the meat, whether or not the animal was slaughtered by a practising orthodox Muslim or Jew. One wonders what would be the advice of such theologians if the shop-owner says that he does not know. People who bandy such pieces of advice succeed only in making religious discipline insufferable and act against the spirit of the Qur'ânic axiom that religious discipline should be easy to follow and not a source of hardship (Qur'ân 2:185). Again the Qur'ân declares this maxim in these words: ". . . Allah does not desire to make [religious discipline] any impediment to you; but He does desire to purify you. . . ." (Qur'ân 5:7)

Those Muslim theologians (*Ulama'a*) who recommend *Kosher* meat as *Halal*, while the Christian-slaughtered meat as *Harâm* should make their assurance doubly sure in the light of the following statements by independent authorities:

> A high proportion of Shechita meat which has been rejected by the Jewish Inspectors as being non-Kosher [*Harâm*] is therefore distributed to the open market [mostly to individual Muslim customers as well as to the Muslim meat shops].[21]

> Most poultry going for religious slaughter comes from the spent hen trade [hens which have stopped laying eggs] . . . For Shechita slaughter, only those birds which are completely healthy and good specimens are selected. This selection is often carried out on the lorry (truck) before the crated birds are off-loaded. We have seen such a practice and noted in this instance that those birds which the handler considered unsuitable for Shechita slaughter were re-crated for despatch to other outlets such as street markets [and Muslim shops] . . . We found that on retail premises where slaughter of poultry is carried out by the Muslim method, live birds (some of which are 'rejects' for Shechita slaughter) are kept in crates or pens. . . .[22]

> It has been drawn to our attention that animals (particularly poultry) are being slaughtered by religious methods when it is known at the time of slaughter that the meat is to be sold on to the alternative markets.[23]

BLOOD

It has now been scientifically established that blood contains toxic substances which the body discharges through urine, after being filtered in the kidneys. From the Islamic point of view, it is a symbol of life only in the sense that it supplies nutrients to the tissue-cells.

The Qur'ân has very judiciously circumscribed the prohibition only to that blood which flows out of the body after slaughter (*daman masfûhan*) (Qur'ân 6:145). By this qualification, Islam has freed the Muslims from the practice of removing every particle of blood from the flesh in order to make it *kosher* or *halal*. The reason for this liberality in the law is that Islam rejects the concept of any symbolic sacredness of blood. It is to be considered of paramount importance only because it keeps a body alive—and all life is to be considered as sacrosanct. Otherwise, Islam attaches no sacrificial or mysterious significance to it. Islam's prohibition of blood is solely on the grounds of hygiene. Muslims generally wash and rinse the meat before cooking and take it for granted that the residual particles on the flesh would be neutralised by the heat of cooking.

THE INVOCATION OF GOD'S NAME (*TAKBIR*)

Islam has laid down two covenants on the act of slaughter in order to make the meat permissible to eat (*Halal*). One is the covenant regarding the method of slaughtering and cleansing the carcass (*dhabh* and *tadhkiyyah*). The second covenant of invoking the name of God at slaughter is often confused with the Jewish ritual of slaughter. This invocation consists of a short sentence comprising two pithy phrases; viz *Bi-smi-llah*, meaning "in the name of God" and is called *tasmiyyah*, i.e. "to call the name". The second phrase is *Allahu Akbar*, meaning "God is the greatest" and is called *takbir*, i.e. "the glorification of God". In short, both phrases are called *takbir*. No other prayer or supplication is required to be added to the wording: "*Bi-smi-llah-Alahu Akbar*". There is no authority to support the mistaken impression of some Muslims that it should be uttered more than once at each slaughter. It seems that some pietistical Muslim butchers have given a wrong impression to a prominent writer about the Islamic law of slaughter. He says:

> As the Muslim ritual requires that, during the ceremony, a prayer must be repeated three times, some Muslims apparently think that the throat should be severed in three stages as opposed to the rapid single, to and fro, movement of the Jews.[24]

Takbir is meant to be much more than a mere ritual. In view of the sanctity Islam attaches to life, the invocation of God's name at the time of slaughtering an animal is meant to remind the slaughterer that:

> He has no right to take this life without Allah's permission; that, except for Allah's permission, the meat of this animal would have been unlawful (*harâm*) for him to eat; that a Muslim accepts the authority of no god other than of One God who is the Greatest Authority; that he thanks Allah for making it lawful for him to use animals for his sustenance; and that the act of slaughter should be performed in a spirit of humility with a trembling heart at the mention of God's name. (Qur'ân 22:34, 35)

Marmaduke Pickthall explains the significance of *takbir* at slaughter in his commentary on these verses in these words:

> In order that they may realise the awfulness of taking life, and the solemn nature of the trust which Allah has imposed on them in the permission to eat animal food.[25]

Killing a living being is after all an act of iniquity. Those who feel justified in killing animals for food are expected to remind themselves at the time of cutting each throat that God is the only One (*wahid*) authority Who can grant dispensation from the penalty of this iniquitous act. The invocation of God's name (*takbir*) is meant to be an avowal of that Authority as well as a benediction by way of thankfulness to God. The real spirit and sentiment of God's glorification at the time of slaughter remains an expression of thankfulness to Him only if the remains of the slaughtered animal are put to the use for which God has granted the dispensation and are not wasted. Any waste amounts to ungratefulness of His bounty; and the invocation of any other god, deity, idol, or patron saint (*walî*) makes a mockery of God's Authority—the one and only God who is the Creator (*khalique*) and the Owner (*malik*) of that animal. Human beings in general and Muslims in particular must realise that, in the eyes of the Creator, an animal is worth much more than its weight in flesh.

Taking the teachings of Islam on this subject in their entirety leaves one with the impression that the Islamic Law lays much greater emphasis on the invocation of *Takbir* than on the method of slaughter (*dhabh*). The following verses of the Qur'ân and *Ahadith* establish the fact that, under certain circumstances, the meat of an animal becomes lawful to eat (*Halal*), even if its blood has not been drawn out by slaughter—but the stipulation of *Takbir* stands in all circumstances. Apparently, the issue seems to be plain enough not to need any involved discussion. However, there are certain details on which Muslim savants are not unanimous. One serious point of concern in this respect for Muslims in the West is whether or not meat slaughtered by Christians is lawful. The Qur'ânic approbation of their meat has been mentioned earlier (Qur'ân 5:6). In spite of this, the objectors give three main reasons for rejecting Christian-slaughtered meat. The question of pork has already been discussed. The second reason is the Christian method of slaughter in general and use of stunners. The third reason, which concerns us here, is that Christians do not invoke the name of God at slaughter. This issue has to be discussed in the light of the following verses:

> He (Allah) has forbidden you . . . the flesh of that animal over which any name other than that of Allah has been invoked. . . ." (Qur'ân 2:173)

This verse was repeated in 16:115, while verse 5:4 contains the additional prohibition of flesh of that "which has been slaughtered on the idolatrous altars." These prohibitions do not apply to Christians, as they do not invoke the name of any deity when they slaughter their food animals, neither do they make any idolatrous offerings. The moot point of this issue revolves round the following verses of the Qur'ân:

> So, eat of meats on which Allah's name has been pronounced, if you have faith in his revelations. And what reason have you that you should not eat of that on which Allah's name has been pronounced—when He has already distinguished for you the things which are forbidden . . ." (Qur'ân 6:118, 119).[26]

Hence eat not of that on which Allah's name has
not been pronounced, for this would be an infraction
[*Fisque*]. . . . (Qur'ân 6:121)

Verses 118 and 119 give Muslims permission to eat meat of
those animals on which Allah's name *has been* pronounced; and
verse 121 categorically forbids the eating of that on which it *has
not been* pronounced. We know that Christians generally do not
invoke God's or anyone else's name at the time of slaughter. Hence,
according to the above verses, meat slaughtered by them must be
unlawful for Muslims. However, verse 5:6, quoted earlier in this
chapter, declares their meat as lawful, and this has been posing
a serious theological problem for Muslims. It is inconceivable for
Muslims even to think of any contradiction in the revealed word of
God or to acquiesce to any suggestion that any passage of the Qur'ân
abrogates another. Even the explanation that the meat slaughtered
by Christians was made lawful in verse 5:6 because they used to
invoke the name of God during the early days of Christianity and
that it was only later that they stopped doing so, does not hold good.
Firstly, there is no conclusive evidence that they used to invoke the
name of God in those days. Secondly, as stated earlier in connection
with pork, God's comprehension of the future is for perpetuity.
This obviously, is a serious theological subject of inquiry for those
millions of Muslims who wish to discipline their lives according to
the tenets of Islam.

The question of whether the meat of an animal slaughtered
without pronouncing the name of God is lawful or not has been
under discussion since the early days of Islam. Erudites such as
Ata'bin Yassar, Qasim bin Mukhaimarah, Sha'bi, Zahri, Mak'hul
and Rabi'ah opine that it is lawful. Opposed to that is the opinion
of savants such as the Imam Ali, 'Aishah, Ibadah bin Samit and Abi
Darda. However, the majority of classical doctors of law (*Fuqaha'a*)
believe that such meat becomes lawful by pronouncing the name
of God before eating. Until recently the problem used to be, more
or less, of theoretical concern but, with the current migration of
millions of Muslims to Christian-dominated countries, it has
become a quandary of practical implications which cannot be

solved by popular sentiment. Perhaps a discussion, in the light of the following Qur'ânic commentaries and *Ahadith*, would help readers in finding their own answers:

The Imam Ali bin Abi Talib[27] said, on the authority of the Prophet: "May God curse those who slay without repeating the name of God, in the same manner as the polytheists did in the name of their idols."[28]

Imam Malik holds that the invocation of God's name is obligatory for Muslims only. If a Christian or Jew does not invoke the name, the meat is still lawful for a Muslim. Ibn Abbas also believes that the law to invoke God's name is not obligatory for Christians and Jews.

'Ata, Auza'i, Mak'hul and Laith bin Sa'd hold that the verse 'the food of those who have received the Scripture is lawful for you' has rendered lawful 'that which has been immolated to other than Allah'. Auza'i says that one may eat of the game hunted by a Christian even if one hears the Christian taking the name of Christ over his dog as he sets it off. Mak'hul says that there is no harm in eating of the animals which the People of the Book slaughter for their churches and synagogues and religious ceremonies.[29]

> . . .the reciting of Tasmiyyah at the time of slaughtering of the animal [for reasons other than food] is not a necessary concomitant, although a desirable one. The reciting of the Tasimiyyah described in the above-mentioned verses refers only to the slaughtering of animals for the sake of food. . . .
>
> It should be observed that if someone has eaten the meat of an animal slaughtered for food without reciting the name of God on it, no learned doctor of religion has ever considered this a transgression or sin (*fisq*).
>
> It is related from the Imams Shafi'î, Ibn Hanbal and Malik that the Tasmiyyah is not necessary [for non-Muslims]. The Imam Abu Hanifah held that it was essential. Nevertheless, he also says that, if the slaughterer forgot the Tasmiyyah then the meat was quite all right and permissible to eat.[30]

Meat slaughtered by the People of the Book without reciting the name of God is, according to the Imam Abu Hanifa, undesirable or hateful to eat. This view is supported by various Imams, such as Nawawi, Abu Yusuf, Zufar, Muhammad, and Nakhi'i.[31]

Imam Shafi'i opines that the food of the People of the Book is lawful for Muslims whether they have invoked the name of God or not. However, he believes that, if it were known that the slaughterer has invoked the name of someone other than God, the food becomes unlawful for Muslims.

Zuhri (a companion of the Prophet) said:

> there is no harm in [eating the meat of] an animal slaughtered by a Christian. If you hear him [the slaughterer] invoking the name of someone other than Allah, do not eat it, but if you do not hear him, then Allah has made it lawful for you and He knew of their *Kufr*, i.e. Allah knew that they [the Christians] did not believe in Islam.

Ibn Abbas, a prominent authority on Islam, while commenting on verse 5:6, confirms the above verdict and explains in clear words that this verse means that the animals slaughtered by the People of the Book are lawful for Muslims to eat provided the name of anyone other than that of Allah has not been invoked at the animal.[32]

According to Ibn Kathir the People of the Book also consider as unlawful the meat of an animal slaughtered in the name of idols or deities, even though their concept of God may be different in certain details from that of Muslims.[33]

According to the greatest authority of them all on *Hadith*, Imam Bukhari, the meat becomes unlawful only if the name of anyone other than that of God is invoked. However, he goes on to add that it becomes lawful if God's name (*Takbir*) is pronounced afterwards, i.e. before eating.

> If the slaughterer was heard invoking a name other than that of Allah, the meat was not to be eaten; but if it was not so heard, then it was lawful for Muslims to eat.[34]

Imam Fakhr al-Din Razi, commenting on verse 6:121 says:

> that over which any name other than that of Allah
> has been invoked means the animals slaughtered by the
> worshippers of idols, which they used to slaughter as
> offerings to their idols.[35]

Qazi al-Baidawi agrees with this interpretation of this verse and
says that it means "that meat over which the name of an idol has
been invoked at the time of slaughter."[36]

It is obvious that, while some Imams and doctors of law (*fuqaha'a*)
differ with each other in matters of detail, they are agreed on the
point that the meat of any animal on which the name of an idol or
deity has been invoked is unlawful for Muslims.

There is another point of detail on which Muslim authorities
are not unanimous. What is the position if a Muslim slaughterer
omits to pronounce *takbir*? The majority of jurists (*fuqaha'a*) agree
that the meat is lawful if the omission is unintentional. Imam
Shafi'i is of the opinion that, although it is not lawful to omit the
takbir intentionally and that the eating of such a meat is undesirable
(*makruh*), yet it cannot be declared as unlawful (*harâm*), provided
that the other conditions of slaughter have been carried out rightly.
Imam Malik believes that the meat of such an animal is unlawful
even if the omission of *takbir* is unintentional. Imam Abu Hanifah
takes the mid-course that such meat is lawful, if the omission is
unintentional; and unlawful, if it is intentional.

According to the following *Hadith*, the meat of an animal which
has been slaughtered without invoking God's name becomes lawful
for Muslims if the consumer pronounces the name of God before
eating—whatever the circumstances and reasons for the omission
may be:

> A group of people said to the Prophet: 'some people
> bring the meat and we do not know whether they have
> mentioned Allah's name or not while slaughtering the
> animal'. The Prophet said, 'mention Allah's name on the
> meat and eat it'.[37]

It is argued by some that the people who are mentioned in this *Hadith* as selling meat to Muslims were recent converts to Islam and, although Muslims, were of doubtful faith. If this kind of principle were to be accepted, then one should scrutinise and ascertain the probity, the faith (*Iman*), and proficiency in the Islamic Law of every Muslim butcher and slaughterman before eating the meat of an animal slaughtered by him. It is not easy to imagine what kind of world it would become if religious discipline were to be imposed in that spirit. There is a precept in Islam that, in case of unintentional omission of God's name before any act, one should mention it whenever one is reminded of it after the event in these words: "In the name of God—both for the antecedence and the subsequence" (*Bi-smi-llahe awwaleha wa akhareha*). However, these days it is a practice more honoured in the breach than the observance.

Muslims are supposed to invoke Allah's name before eating, drinking, or doing anything. It is what they call in English "saying grace" in these words: "In the name of Allah Who is Beneficent and Merciful" (*Bi-smi-llahi-r-Rahmani-r-Rahim*). Some people have misunderstood the significance of the above *Hadith* by equating the normal grace with the invocation of God's name before slaughter which comprises two phrases. One is the invocation of Allah's name (*Bi-smi-llahi*), i.e. "in the name of Allah" and the second is the glorification of Allah (*Allahu Akbar*), meaning "God is the Greatest." When the Prophet was asked by his companions in the above *Hadith* about the meat slaughtered by people who might not have carried out the act of slaughter (*Tadhkiyyah*) and the recitation of God's name (*Tasmiyyah* and *Takbir*) according to the Islamic prescript, his advice was not to discard the meat because of that reason but to eat the meat after invoking God's name in the same phraseology which is used at the time of slaughter. This *Hadith* implies that: when a Muslim is in doubt whether the animal was slaughtered according to the *sharia* law or not, he should make it lawful by pronouncing God's name (*Tasmiyyah* and *Takbir*) before eating it.

THE RELATIVE SIGNIFICANCE OF BLEEDING AND THE INVOCATION OF GOD'S NAME

It was mentioned earlier that the invocation of God's name (*takbir*) is considered more important than the act or method of slaughter. There is no disputing the fact that, according to the dietetic laws of *sharia*, the flesh of game hunted for food is lawful (*halal*) if the *takbir* has been pronounced before shooting or setting the dogs and birds of prey after it—even though the animal dies before the hunter has had a chance to slaughter it. Islam has laid great emphasis on bleeding the animal to render the meat hygienically pure as food. In the Islamic terminology, the very act of slaughter (*dhabh*) is called 'the process of purification and cleansing' (*tadhkiyyah*). In spite of all this emphasis on bleeding, the law of slaughter is mollified in the case of hunting, while the hunter still remains bound by the covenant of *takbir*. It is very important for Muslims to appreciate the reason underlying this relaxation of the law. In the case of animals slain by hunting, Islam is more concerned with the fundamental requirement that no life should be allowed to go to waste, rather than with the formalistic enactment of decrees.

There is a large number of Muslims living in the tropical and subtropical savannahs where their main source of meat is hunting. Many a time and oft such people do not get a chance to bleed the animal and carry out the normal *tadhkiyyah* before it is dead. Unlike Mosaic law,[35] Islam allows Muslims to procure their food by hunting. It cannot, therefore, be said that the relaxation of the law of normal slaughter is by way of an exception—it is a regular feature of the law as the following Qur'ânic passages would show:

> They ask you [O Mohammad!] what is lawful to them as food. Tell them: 'lawful unto you are [all] things good and pure; and what your trained animals and birds of prey catch in the manner directed to you by Allah. So eat of that which they catch for you and pronounce the name of Allah over it—Allah is Swift in reckoning. (Qur'ân 5:5)

> And you are allowed to hunt the aquatic game; its use as food is a provision both for those of you who are at home and those who are on a journey.... (Qur'ân 5:99)

There is a consensus among Muslim theologians that hunting is allowed in Islam only for the basic necessities of life and that it may be done with animals or birds of prey, with bows and arrows, or with other weapons including firearms.

> "Abu Th'labah, a companion of the Prophet, narrates that the Prophet said, in reply to some questions, that you can eat an animal which you have hunted with your bow or with your dog, whom you have trained as a hunting dog, provided you have mentioned the name of Allah on it and provided it has no stench."[36]

> "Adi bin Hatim told that Allah's Messenger said to him: 'When you set off your dog, mention Allah's name, and if it catches anything and you come up to it while it is still alive, cut its throat; if you come up to it when the dog has killed it but not eaten any of it, eat it' . . . For further clarification, Adi bin Hatim told Allah's Messenger that he set off trained dogs, and the Prophet replied, 'Eat what they catch for you.' Adi asked if that applied even if the dogs had killed the game. The Prophet replied that it did."[37]

Many other such *Ahadith* leave no doubt that a hunted animal is lawful to eat, even if it dies unslaughtered and that it makes no difference how long it has been dead—as long as its flesh has not putrefied and is hygienically edible. For example:

> Adi bin Hatim narrates that he said to the Messenger of God: 'I shoot at game and find it dead the next day with my arrow in it.' The Messenger of God replied: 'When you know that your arrow killed it and you see no mark of a beast of prey on the animal, you may eat it.'[38]

It has never been the purport of Islamic laws to be observed as ceremonial rites. Great care has been taken to keep them within the bounds of practicability—to make them congruous with all situations and circumstances of human needs. Muhammad Asad, the learned translator of the Qur'ân of this century, while commenting on verse 6:119 which allows the eating of any lawful meat on which God's name has been pronounced says:

The purpose of this and the following verse is . . . a reminder that the observance of such laws should not be made an end in itself and an object of ritual: and this is the reason why these two verses have been placed in the midst of a discourse on God's transcendental unity and the way of man's faith. The "errant views" [fancies = 'ahwa'ihim] spoken of in 119 are such as lay stress on artificial rituals and taboos rather than on spiritual values.[39]

REFERENCES AND NOTES (CHAPTER 5)

1. For details cf. *Al Halal wa al-Haram ft al-Islam* (in Arabic); Yusuf Al-Qardawi; Mektebe Whaba, Cairo; 1977. English translation: *The Lawful and the Prohibited in Islam*; Kamal El-Helbawy and others; American Trust Publications, 10900 W. Washington Street, Indianapolis, IN 46231, USA. Also *EI-Fikh* (In Arabic) (The Islamic Jurisprudence); Abdul-Rahman Khallaf; Maktabe al-Sa'ab, Cairo.

2. The four Schools of Thought were established by the following Imams within the first about one and a half centuries of the Islamic era. The only purpose of the establishment of these Schools was the codification of the Islamic jurisprudence (*Fiqh*):
   i. Imam Abu Hanifa Nu'man bin Thabit, Born at Basra, (699-767 A.C.).
   ii. Imam Malik bin Anas, Born at Madinah (713-795 A.C.)
   iii. Imam Abu 'Abd-Allah Muhammad bin Idris al-Shafi'i. Born in Palestine (767-821 A.C.)
   iv. Imam Ahmad bin Hanbal. Born in Baghdad (781-858 A.C.)

3. cf. *Commentary of the Qur'ân* by Ibn Juralj. Also cf. *Al-Tafsir al-Kabir* by Imam Fakhral–Din Razi. (Hereafter referred to as Razi).

4. For the literal meaning of Istaqsimu and Azldm, cf. Shaikh Abu-al-Qasim al-Hral-Raghib in *Al-Mufradat fi Gharib al-Qur'ân* (hereafter referred to as 'Raghib'), dictionary of the Qur'ân entitled: *Arabic-English Lexicon* by Edward William Lane.

5. cf. Razi (See Ref. No. 3).

6. cf. Raghib (See Ref. 4).

7. *Bukhari,* 72:22.

8. The Sabians mentioned in the Qur'ân as *Sdbe'fn* in three places (2:62; 5:72; 22:17) are different people from the Biblical Sabians, perhaps deriving their name from *Sheba*. The Qur'ânic Sabe'in were an offshoot of Christianity. *Encyclopaedia Britannica* describes them as "Christians of St. John the Baptist." In the early Arab literature, they have also been called as 'those who wash themselves' (Mughtasilah). The Biblical Sabians seem to be a people of Southern Arabia whose kingdom was at its height in the 5th. centruy B.C. They were prosperous businessmen, very rich and worshipped heavenly bodies. As polytheists, they could not have been called by the Qur'ân as the possessors of Scripture or the People of the Book (*Ahl-e-Kitab*).

9. See Ref. No. 2.

10. Sayyid Sabiq; *Fiqh al-Sunnah* (Islamic Jurisprudence based on the practice of the Prophet). Vol.3, p.264 (hereafter referred to as "Sabiq"), Dar al-Kitab al-Arabi, Beirut 1971.

11. See "Sabiq", Ref. No.12; p.298.

12. Sarakhsi'i has gone down in history with the title of Shams *al-A'immah* (the sunshine of Muslim nations); *Al-Mabsut.* (The word 'ALWAYS' capitalised by the writer).

13. Abu Hayyan Gharrati (the famous 14th century A.C. commentator of Qur'ân; *Al-Bahr al-Muheet*, Vol. III, p.431.

14. The Mufti of Jordan as quoted by: *Al-Muslimoon*; Geneva, June 1964, pp.108-111.

15. *The Urdu Magazine*; Burhan; Pakistan, 1964.

16. Shaikh Abd-al-Wahhab Khallaf, as quoted in the Arabic Magazine: *Lewa al-Islam*, Cairo, April-May, 1949.

17. Dr. Abdullah el-Abbadi; *"Corbans in Islamic Law"* (in Arabic); pp.64-67.

18. Dr. Abdul Aziz el-Khayat, Dean of the Faculty of Islamic Law, University of Jordan; *Report on Food and Slaughtered Animals in Islam*; pp.35-44.

19. Sir Sayyid Ahmad Khan; *Musafiran-e-London*; Lahore, Pakistan; 1961; p.74.

20. *Al-Muslimoon*; Geneva; July 1964; p.53.

21. *Report on the Welfare of Livestock when Slaughtered by Religious Methods*; Farm Animal Welfare Council, H.M. Stationery (London) Book Ref. 262, 1985, Para 27, p.9. (hereafter referred to as *"Report-FAWC"*).

22. *Report-FAWC* Book Ref. 262; (See Ref. No. 33) paras 66-69, pp.17, 18.

23. *Report-FAWC* Book Ref, 262; (See Ref. No. 33) para 90, p.34.

24. Ritual Slaughter of Food Animals; H.E. Bywater, M.R.C.V.S.; as quoted in *Veterinary Annual* of the Farm Animal Dept., England; John Right & Sons Ltd., Bristol; 1968; p. 4.

25. *The Meaning of the Glorious Qur'ân*; Marmaduke Pickthall; 1957; footnote 2, Chapt. 22, verse 34, p.342.

26. Verses 5:4,5, preceding the verse 5:6, explain in some detail what is unlawful to eat and what is lawful (*Tayyibat*).

27. Imam Ali was the son-in-law of the Holy Prophet and the fourth Caliph (656-661 A.C.).

28. Narrated by Abu Tufail. *Mishkat al-Masabih*, Book XVIII, Chapt. 1, as quoted in *The Dictionary of Islam* by Patrick Hughes, p.697. As quoted by Abu A'la Maududi, *Tarjumanul Qur'ân*, 1959.

29. *Al-Taaj fi Usool al-Hadith*, Cairo, Vol. III, p.110. (For details about the four Imams, see Ref. No. 2.)

i. cf. Abu Hayyan Andlusi; *Bahre-Muheet*; Vol. IV; p.131.

30. *Musnad of Ahmad*; Vol. 1. p.302. so. *Ibn Kathir*, Vol. III, p.19.

31. Bukhari, 72: 20-22 Abu 'Abd Allah Muhammad Bin Ismail al-Bukhari (774-836 A.C.) is the compiler of the most authentic book of Hadith named after him as *Sahih al-Bukhari*.

32. cf. "Razi" (See Ref. No. 3.).

33. cf. *Anwar al-Tanzil wa Asrar al-Ta'wil* (Commentary of the Qur'ân) in Arabic; Qazi Abu Sa'id Abdullah bin'Umar al-Baidawi.

34. Narrated by A'ishah, the wife of the Holy Prophet. *Bukhari*, 72:22 English translation Vol. VII, p. 302.

35. cf. *Landau*, 1770, p.104.

36 *Bukhari*, 72:4. Also Muslim.

37 a) *Bukhari* 7:2 and 7:7, *Muslim* and *Abu Dawud*. Also: James Robson's English translation of *Mishkat al Masabih*; Sh. Muhammad Ashraf, Lahore, Pakistan; 1963; Vol. 3, p. 873. (hereafter referred to as "Robson") Also: *Kitab-us-Said wa'l-Dhaba'ih wa ma Yu'kalu min al-Hayawan*; English translation: *Book of Game and the Animals Which May be Slaughtered And the Animals that May be Eaten*; Chapt. DCCCX on "Hunting with the Help of Dogs"; Hadith No. 4732.

b) For details about the training of hunting dogs etc. see: *Hidayah 'Umar*; Vol. IV, p. 86.

38. *Abu Dawud*, as quoted in *Mishkat al-Masabih*; "Robson", p.873 (See Ref. No. 57.).

39. *The Message of the Qur'an*; Muhammad Asad; Dar al-Andalus, Gibralter, 1980; Footnote No. 104, p.190, Chapter 6.

6

The Islamic Method Of Slaughter[i]

Preamble

SLAUGHTERING AN ANIMAL FOR food is just a functional act—to drain the blood out. There is not, and should not be, any ritual involved in it—not even in sacrificial slaughtering. The spirit of sacrifice lies in offering the animal as charity to the indigent IN THE NAME OF GOD AND NOT TO GOD. God has no stomach for this kind or any other food. However, the reverence for life demands that all slaying, whether it is a slaughter for own consumption or an immolation for sacrifice, should be done in due form and with a sense of accountability to God. It is a grave responsibility and, hence, the need for religious discipline to make this hurtful act as painless and humane as possible. The greatness of religion is this concept that taking the life of an animal to quench human hunger is acceptable only if the animal is slaughtered in the name of God because only God has the will and power to forgive people who take the life of another animal, even for food, which has been grossly misinterpreted.

Most of the Western orientalists confirm that the Prophet of Islam, as a religious law-giver, has left detailed instructions for the humane treatment of animals used either in the service of man or for food. In the words of an animal-welfare worker:

---

i **Editor's Note:** This Chapter has been updated by Compassion in World Farming (CIWF) from the original version published in 1989 to render it up to date in terms of technological enhancements and legislation. The focus is on the Islamic permissibility or non-permissibility to use various stunning methods; the few sections in the original edition that were considered side-issues on this subject by CIWF, with respect to Masri's views Judaism, have been excluded. **The reader should note that any references post 1992 are by CIWF.**

There is no religion that has taken a higher view in its authoritative documents of animal life, and none wherein the precept has been so much honoured by its practical observance.[1]

It needs to be repeated here, especially for the benefit of general Muslims, that Islam neither recommends nor forbids the eating of meat. For those who choose to eat it, there are comprehensive laws and directives regulating the pre-slaughter treatment of animals, which have already been discussed in some detail. The directives concerning the humane method of slaughter shall be referred to again while discussing the religious stance on the use of stunners. At this stage it seems necessary to understand the intrinsicality of the Islamic directives on the method of slaughter. To do that, it is important to explain some terminology which has been used in the prescribed code of practice. The Qur'ân uses three words for 'slaughter'.

1. DHABH: (Old Hebrew *zebech* or *zabakh*, now called *shechita*). It signifies killing by cutting the throat of an animal for food or sacrifice, as different from the word '*qatal*' which means killing in the general sense, such as murder. In the Qur'ân, *dhabh* is used in respect of an animal slaughtered according to the method prescribed by Islam which makes the meat lawful (*halal*). (Qur'ân. 2:71; 5:4) A slaughterer is called *Dhâbih*, *Jazzar* or *Qassab*. However, a meat-seller is also called a *Qassab* in common parlance, as most of them used to slaughter animals themselves.

2. DHAKA: from *Dhakat*. It means to augment the number or size of a thing, or to enhance its quality by purification in a general sense (Qur'ân. 19:13). In the context of 'slaughter', the derivation of this word is *Tadhkiyyah*, which stands for the purification of the body of a food-animal by allowing the impurities to flush out with the blood. (Qur'ân *dhakkaitum*, 5:4)

3. NAHR: Literally this word means the lower part of the neck or the uppermost part of the breast. It is used in the general sense of slaughter by stabbing or sticking through the neck. The Qur'ân has used this word in the context of immolation as a sacrifice. (Qur'ân 108:2)

Here are a few other Arabic words that need to be defined:

HALAL: means a thing sanctioned and made lawful or permissible. It is the antonym of *harâm*. *Harâm* is a word used for a thing which is forbidden for being wrong or bad. This word is often confused with the word *Haram*, but without the diacritical mark on the second 'a'. The word 'Hareem', often used derisively in English as a bevy of wives, is a derivation from the same word *Haram*. *Hareem* actually means the precincts and members of a household whose honour is too sacred to be violated—with the same connotation as "an Englishman's house is his castle." The two words—*Harâm* and *Haram*—mean two different things.

MAKRUH: means unpalatable or hated. It applies to those foods which, though not forbidden in law, do not agree with the taste or metabolism of an individual and are bad to eat.

MASHBUH (from *Shubha*) or **Mashkuk** (from *Shak*): These terms are used for things suspected or doubtful. If one is not certain about the lawfulness or unlawfulness of an item of food and there is no explicit directive to be found in the Law about it, the advice of the Prophet is to abstain from eating it "as a matter of faith and conscience."

It is almost impossible these days for a Muslim to totally avoid consuming unlawful (*harâm*) things in ignorance. Even some of the items of everyday consumption, which are taken for granted as lawful (*halal*) contain forbidden ingredients. For example, bread, cakes, biscuits, confectionery, frozen foods, dairy products, tinned fruits and vegetables, soups and a hoard of other items contain additives and preservatives extracted from meats, bones and fats of unlawful animals and are of doubtful (*mushkuk*) origin. The technology of modern food-sciences is no respecter of any religious discipline. Even those items which are labelled as using vegetable extracts may contain 10 to 20 percent of animal fats and extracts— and no-one knows of which animals. There are more than 2,000 kinds of additives used for enhancing the flavour, colouring, and preserving food chemically.[2]

The Islamic Law makes a distinction between two kinds of slaughter, namely:

1. **Optional Slaughter** (*Dhabh Ikhtiyari*): when the animal's throat is cut under controlled and normal conditions.

2. **Peremptory Slaughter** (*Dhabh Idhtirari*): when the normal slaughtering cannot be done due to some fortuitous mishap. It often happens in such situations that the proper implements of slaughter are not available, or the animal is constrained in a posture where its throat cannot be reached. In such emergencies, Islam allows the bleeding of the animal to death by any available means so that it is put out of its misery and at the same time its flesh is not wasted. According to Imam Bukhari, in an emergency slaughter, any sharp implement could be used and the meat is lawful to eat.[3] The following *Ahadith* make it clear that any method of slaughter could be used in an emergency:

> During the battle of Dhul-Halaifah the Holy Prophet allowed the slaughter of food-animals with the edge of a cane as an emergency and said; "Slaughter with whatever makes the blood to flow, except tooth or nail, and eat it provided that the name of Allah has been pronounced on it."[4] A shepherdess found a goat dying in pain due to some accident while she was pasturing the flock of Ka'b bin Malik. To put it out of its misery, she slaughtered it with a sharp stone. When the Prophet was asked what to do with the meat, he said; "eat it." (Narrated by Muâd bin Sa'd Bukhari, 47:3)

Most of the Muslim Doctors of Law and Imams, except Imam Shafi'î, hold that the meat of an animal slaughtered unconventionally in an emergency with a crude implement is lawful to eat.[5] The following *Hadith* further confirms that view that the meat of such animals is lawful to eat:

> The Holy Prophet was asked: 'Is the emergency slaughtering to be done only in the throat and the upper part of the breast?' He replied: 'If you pierce its thigh, that would serve you'.[6]

This Islamic Law about emergency slaughter has a significant bearing on the issue of pre-slaughter stunning and will be discussed later. First the Islamic method of regular and prescriptive slaughter needs to be explained.

In theory, at least, the Islamic Law lays down very stringent regulations for the whole procedure of slaughter. For example: the slaughterer must be in possession of sound mental faculties; a Muslim, Christian or a Jew (*Ahl-e-Kitab*) of any sex, of age which is generally considered to be above 18 years; knowledgeable enough to know and follow all the Islamic directives of humane slaughter. The knife must be as sharp as possible. All the pre-slaughter care and comfort of the animal, such as transport, water, fodder, and general handling must be taken care of. What happens in practice, however, in places where attention to proper education, training and supervision is lacking, is anybody's guess. Most of the immigrants in the West will bear out the fact that neither the government officials nor the general public in these countries take any particular thought or care of the prevailing un-Islamic conditions in our abattoirs. Although Jews have meliorated their slaughtering conditions in recent times, originally, they too had similar attitudes to Muslims.

> Originally any Jew was allowed to perform shechita [slaughter] (Mishna,200) but since the operation is a very responsible task—the killing of an animal—only highly qualified persons are allowed to do it. (Issarlas, 1560b)[7]

There is no doubt, however, that Jewish abattoirs are far better organised than those of Muslims. Their *Shochets* (slaughtermen) have to undergo a training for about six to seven years, while there is no proper arrangement for the training of Muslim *Qassabs*. Experience shows that the Jewish treatment of animals during all the stages before a slaughter is much more humane than that of Muslims; their knives are sharper and of the right length according to the size of the animal—from 12 to 16 inches. In spite of all this, the findings of an independent Council appointed by the British Government had this to say about both Jewish and Islamic practices:

> In both Jewish and Muslim establishments we were very concerned at the rough way in which birds were removed from the crates. Also, their handling in the bleeding room left much to be desired. . . .

We observed that the 'single transverse cut' demanded by the Jews means, in practice, a backwards and forwards stroke. On one occasion, we observed a Jewish slaughterman make as many as seven backwards and forwards strokes with the knife, using a sawing action which was clearly in contravention of the Shochet's training. Indeed with both Jewish and Muslim slaughter the requirement for a single incision is open to different interpretation. Our observations suggest that the current procedure is in practice a single uninterrupted backwards and forwards motion.

Particular examples, seen in Muslim slaughter, included one occasion when a deep cut was made which almost severed the head of an animal; in another case the spinal column was severed. Sometimes the knife was not sufficiently sharp and there was difficulty in making the cut; the degree of sharpness varied from slaughterhouse to slaughterhouse; we also saw a curved skinning knife being used to slaughter sheep, although it was reasonably sharp. Although we have been told that the knife should be sharpened and sterilised before each animal is slaughtered, this was not the case.[8]

It is contrary to all reasonable expectation that members of this Council who are knowledgeable and conscientious people of professional probity, would pass judgements such as quoted above, just because they are "anti-Semites" or because they have banded together to disparage Judaism or Islam. Many of them have had opportunities of seeing what sort of conditions are prevailing in abattoirs in the East. Who can blame such critics if they fail to make a distinction between the Qur'ânic Islam and Islam in practice in some parts of the world?

It is one of the human weaknesses to respond emotionally to criticism and to seek self-vindication in counter criticism. The force of religion, or of any ideology, lies not in the sheets of paper on which its scriptures are written but in the mental and spiritual volition (*Taqwa*) of its votaries to follow the spirit of the message according to changing situations and circumstances, within the framework of its Law (*sharia*).

It has been mentioned above repeatedly that the only consideration from the Islamic point of view is that the meat to be used as food should be free from any disease that can be passed on to the consumer. As a precaution against such a possibility, great emphasis is laid on a mode of slaughter that allows the maximum amount of blood to drain out, carrying with it the germs and microbes that may be present in animal and therefore cause disease in humans. Except for this hygienic precaution, Muslims are allowed to eat all the unforbidden animals even if they are disfigured, bruised, or injured in any way. Both Jewish and Christian methods of slaughter fulfil the Islamic condition of bleeding the animal. It is the wrong impression of some Muslims that Christians decapitate the animal and sever the head by a single stroke with some sort of mechanical saw or machine. They too bleed the animals as Muslims and Jews do. They too take good care that the meat is hygienically free from any blood impurities The only difference is that the Christians make a stable incision, called sticking, in the major blood vessels anterior to the heart (more to the front), especially in cattle, while Muslims and Jews make a transverse incision across the throat posterior to the angle of the jaw to cut the same blood vessels. Nevertheless, all the methods of slaughter achieve the same end result, which is producing meat fit for human consumption.

The Qur'ânic verse 5:6, making the meat slaughtered by Christians and Jews lawful for Muslims, does not specify their or any other method of slaughter nor does it mention the exact spot where the blood vessels should be cut. Islamic laws are so accommodating that, if unintentionally and accidentally the animal's head is severed from the body while slaughtering, the meat still remains lawful to eat. Again, the Islamic law does not specify in which posture the animal should be slaughtered. It could be in any position most functional for the slaughterer and least uncomfortable for the animal. Traditionally, it has been the general practice to cast the animal down on its side. However, if it is found that the animal remains less perturbed standing in a slaughtering cradle and that the slaughterer can perform his function unencumbered, there is no reason why Muslim butchers should not start using the restraining pens which keep the animal upright. The chances of contaminating carcass surface with blood would also be greatly reduced if the animals were held in upright position and the blood was drained away from the restraining pens. There should be no objection to it at least from the religious point of view. As a matter of fact, verse 22:36 of the Qur'ân tells us to slaughter camels in a standing position. If it is lawful for large animals, it should be lawful for small animals too. Another misconception about the Islamic method of slaughter needs to be cleared. Some Muslims are under the impression that the animal to be slaughtered should be cast down facing the *Qiblah* in Mecca. Perhaps such people observe this practice out of compassion for the dying animal in the same spirit in which a dying Muslim is made to lie facing *Qiblah*. However, there is no authentic support in Islamic law or tradition for this practice. Although it seems to be a harmless practice, the real harm lies in the tragic historical fact that all such innovations in the religions of the world were started very innocently, but ended up as a millstone round the believer's neck.

The normal Islamic method of slaughter is to cut at vertical angles the soft structures of the neck, i.e. SKIN, TRACHEA, OESOPHAGUS, JUGULAR VEINS and CAROTID ARTERIES. The VERTEBRAL COLUMN of the CERVICAL SPINE is not to be cut and the head is not to be separated from the body. In the smaller and the medium sized animals, such as sheep and calves, the cut is made between the throat and the base of the neck or the head of the breast. In large animals, such as camels, it is made for convenience at the junction of the neck, where it meets the chest. (For the explanation of anatomical terms, written in capital letters, see Ref. No. 9.) It is expected to be a single to and fro cut by a sharp knife of suitable length, free from any notch or flaw. However, if the first oscillation of the knife fails to be effective for some reason, it is considered more humane to finish the job with an additional cut or cuts rather than to prolong the pain and suffering of the victim. It is significant to note that repetitious cuts, provided they are not intended, do not make the meat unlawful. If animals were to be wasted because of such unintentional mistakes, people would throw away the carcass of the wrongly slaughtered animal and slaughter another.[9]

A well-known veterinarian and writer on the subject of religious slaughter says:

> Mohammad upheld kindness to animals and it is said that he adopted ritual slaughter purely on humanitarian grounds as a result of the excessively cruel manner in which some animals were slaughtered by the faithful in the early days of Islam.[10]

It is distressing to see that some Muslims have started making a common cause with Jews in opposing the use of humane stunners. Jews believe that a tiny hole made by a penetrating stunner a few seconds before slaughter, violates the divine Law. If the Jewish literal interpretation of the Law were to be accepted, then the very act of cutting the throat also inflicts a blemish on the animal. After all, there is a lapse of time between the act of the cut and the ultimate death of the animal. In my view, the only sensible interpretation of the Jewish law of blemish is that the wound made by the stunner is part of the slaughtering process and not a blemish. Otherwise, even the wound made by the knife on the throat, prior to the animal's death, will have to be accepted as a blemish.

STUNNING LEGISLATION

Whereas Islam requires that due compassionate consideration must be given to animals used by man in general and slaughtered for food in particular, in the Western world too it is considered that animals are sentient (conscious) beings and that they should not be subjected to unnecessary and avoidable pain. There is an abundance of legislation governing this factor, particularly with regard to the method of slaughter. In the United Kingdom, for example, the Welfare of Animals (Slaughter or Killing) Regulations 1995[i] required that no animal may be slaughtered in a slaughterhouse unless it is either killed immediately or stunned

---

i   In spite of Brexit, at time of writing (September 2021), the EU regulation still holds good in the UK: Council Regulation (EC) No 1099/2009 of 24 September 2009, on the protection of animals at the time of killing. The EU Regulation is amplified by the Welfare of Animals at the Time of Killing (England) Regulations 2015—and similar regulations in other parts of UK .

prior to slaughter by a process "which causes immediate loss of consciousness which lasts until death".

Originally, the first Act in Great Britain to prevent cruelty to animals in slaughterhouses was contained in the Public Health Act of 1875. In 1904 a committee, set up under Lord Lee by the Admiralty, recommended to Parliament that "All animals, without exception, should be stunned" before slaughter. However, in 1908 the Local Government Board issued a circular to all Borough, Urban and Rural District Councils to the effect that "stunning should not be obligatory where slaughter was carried out by Jews". The first laws to implement humane slaughtering of food-animals in the UK originated from a private member's Bill, called "Slaughter of Animals (Scotland) Bill, 1927". In 1928, however, Jews were exempted from this law by another Scotland Bill and, later, Muslims too were included in the exemption. The main reason for the inclusion of Muslims was to facilitate religious slaughter by the East Indian sailors, called Lascars, who manned shipping in Scotland. The exemption was extended to England and Wales by the Slaughter of Animals Act 1933. Both Jews and Muslims were also exempted from stunning poultry under the Slaughter of Poultry Act 1967. The current position in the United Kingdom is that Jews and Muslims are exempt from the latest stunning laws of 1995. However, they are not exempt from the rest of the Welfare of Animals (Slaughter or Killing) Regulations 1995, one of which requires the restraint of bovines in a pen at the time of slaughter. At the time when Jews and Muslims were exempted from the laws requiring stunning some half a century ago, the legislature had in mind very small, almost negligible, minority communities. Today the slaughter by religious methods has escalated to large-scale proportions, both for local consumption and for export.

Although up-to-date statistics are not available, all the signs are that consumption of meat by Muslims in this country is on the increase. When one adds these figures to those slaughtered by Jews in Britain without pre-stunning, one can appreciate the concern of those who believe that slaughtering an animal without first stunning it into unconsciousness is inhumane. It is not in the United Kingdom alone that this concern has started becoming more and more vociferous. Throughout the Western world people have started lobbying their respective governments to make stunning compulsory for one and all. At present the European Union exempts Jews and Muslims from stunning. Similarly, the European Convention for the Protection of Animals for Slaughter has also exempted them from stunning. It is doubtful, however, if all these countries will be able to withstand the pressures of animal welfare campaigners for long. As it is, some countries have made stunning totally compulsory for Jews and Muslims and others are in the process of doing so.

Muslims in Western countries will have to decide, sooner or later, whether to give up eating meat or to accept the meat from animals slaughtered after stunning. The Jewish reasons for rejecting stunners are for completely different considerations from those of Muslims. There is no doubt, as far as Muslims are concerned, that the Islamic law (*sharia*) is immutable and not subject to variations in different cases, times, or places. However, the law is ignored by Muslims living in different parts of the world. The crux of the whole issue, however, is whether or not it is in keeping with the *sharia* law to render an animal unconscious and insensible to pain before cutting its throat. Then there are the hygienic requirements of the Islamic method of slaughter to bleed out the carcass. Does pre-slaughter stunning affect the flow of blood or not? The discussion that follows revolves around these and other allied issues from the Islamic point of view. Most of the objections to the use of stunners fall into these three categories: psycho-physiological, traditional, and theological. The psycho-physical aspect of the problem involves inquiry into animal morphology and anatomical structure in relation to their sensitiveness to mental suffering and physical pain. It should have been easy to explain away the objections based on traditional custom, but conventionalism has become so intertwined with the intrinsic values and revealed theology that it has become almost impossible to separate the chaff from the wheat. Notwithstanding all these problems, an attempt is being made below to explain some sober realities, in the hope of clarifying the prevalent misunderstanding about stunners.

STUNNERS MISUNDERSTOOD

It is only recently that Muslims in the East have started hearing about mechanical or electrical stunners. Generally, these are understood by most of them to be some sort of apparatus used in the process of killing animals for food. Few people have an exact idea what these instruments are and, fewer still, have had an opportunity of seeing how they function. A widespread denunciatory literature gives the impression that animals are KILLED by these MACHINES, instead of the fact that they are bled by cutting the throat as prescribed by Islam—after having been rendered unconscious by stunning. Then there is a general impression that a stunner decapitates the head or shatters the skull, while the fact is that the bolt of a mechanical stunner does not even make a hole in the head large enough to be called a gash. Some critical literature alleges that the killing of poultry is done by inserting a pike-like rod through the bird's mouth into the brain, which again is not true. In fact, such methods are prohibited by the law. Poultry are indeed stunned and immediately slaughtered by cutting the blood vessels in the neck.

These and many other similar misapprehensions have set in motion a wave of protests against the use of stunners on animals which are meant for Muslim and Jewish consumption. The protagonists of stunners, mostly being non-Muslims, have understandably failed to appreciate the latent theological implications involved in this controversy. To tell the followers of any religion that the code of practice, which they have been believing to be based on the revealed word of God, has now been superseded by modern science is to show a red rag to them. Westerners have made the mistake of putting Jews and Muslims in the same bracket.

The blame lies with both Muslims and non-Muslims. Both have failed to understand each other's point of view. Otherwise, the use of stunners, as far as the Islamic law is concerned, should never have become a controversial issue at all. In order to determine whether or not stunning an animal and rendering it immediately unconscious prior to cutting its throat is conformable to the prescribed Islamic law of slaughter, it is necessary to understand what these instruments called stunners are and how they function. They are instruments which will immediately render an animal unconscious and are mainly of three kinds—mechanical, electrical and gas.

MECHANICAL STUNNERS

They are either penetrating (percussion) or non-penetrating (concussion) stunners. Traditionally these devices look like a heavy barrelled pistol or, on the later designs, a heavy steel cylinder. Unlike a gun which could be used to fire a free bullet, cattle and sheep are stunned by firing a hardened steel bolt from the muzzle of the stunner at very high velocity on to the animal's head, which produces loss of consciousness on impact with the skull.

The bolt of a penetrating stunner penetrates the head to a depth of about 8 cm in the case of cattle, and rather less for sheep and goats. The point here is that, unlike a gun, the projectile or the bolt is held captive by a hardened steel flange at the end of its travel and is usually automatically retracted. That is why it is called a 'captive-bolt' pistol. This whole process is so swift that the movement of the bolt can hardly be perceived by the human eye. Pneumatically operated captive bolts, in which the energy from high-pressured compressed air is used to drive the bolt, have also been developed to perform the same function.

Concussion stunners work on the same principle as the above devices, except for the basic difference that, instead of a bolt which penetrates, they have been adapted to be fitted with a flat-headed mushroom-shaped bolt. This kind of bolt, instead of piercing the skull and penetrating the brain, delivers a very powerful blow to the head which knocks the animal unconscious for a period of time long enough to cut the throat and bleed the animal out.

Since Islamic law does not look at a pre-slaughter wound as a 'blemish', as the Judaic law does, there is no reason for Muslims to reject the penetrating type of captive-bolt stunners for that reason. However, for those who would not like to see a hole in the skull, the concussion stunners may be more acceptable as they have been specifically designed to meet such market requirements.

The most important point to note, from the religious point of view, is that both these types of stunners do not kill. They render animals unconscious and give enough time to slaughter them without causing pain or suffering. One overzealous manufacturer named a captive bolt 'humane killer' which, in the writer's opinion, is a misnomer—because it is neither meant to, nor does it kill. This anachronistic term has been partly responsible for giving the wrong impression to laymen that a stunner is used to kill without slaughtering the animal. Since its function is only to stun, it should have been called 'humane stunner'. The word 'humane' implies that it allows the killing of an animal compassionately and painlessly, while its brain is in a state of insensibility—in the same way as it would have become unconscious had it been shot in the head with a free bullet. It goes without saying that the use of these instruments, like that of any other mechanical instrument including the knife for slaughter, depends on the expertise of the user and the correct maintenance of the equipment.

Various other kinds of stunners have been developed in the search for means to render the animal unconscious before slaughter. They are:

ELECTRICAL STUNNERS

Electrical stunning relies on passing a sufficient electric current through the brain to induce unconsciousness and insensibility. The duration of unconsciousness would be sufficient to allow the animal's throat to be cut and to die without regaining consciousness. Under ideal conditions, especially where time-factors in the slaughter line are not involved, this system has proved very efficient on small animals such as sheep, goats, and young calves.

Correct positioning of the electrodes, the use of sufficient electric current and the application of the stunner for sufficient time are necessary to achieve a sufficient depth and duration of unconsciousness to allow time for the animal to be shackled, hoisted, slaughtered, and bled out before regaining consciousness. The minimum requirements to achieve humane slaughter are taken care of by appropriate legislation.

Mechanically, these devices are usually a large pair of scissor-tongs. In animals, such as sheep, which have a heavy fleece around the head, it is difficult to achieve a good electric contact which is the essential factor. To assist this, the tong-tips have a serrated edge and associated absorbent pads which must be kept wet with a conductive solution of water and salt or soap. In recent years there has been a great improvement in the development of lightweight but high voltage callipers which can be operated with one hand. They have also reduced dramatically the time in which the increased current has to flow. Many such devices automatically spray a conducting solution wetting the animal's head. The operator is given an indication when the current parameters have been automatically achieved—irrelevant to understanding the principles of electrical stunning.

In spite of all this sophistication in electrical stunning, however, there are certain drawbacks and problems to this system which technology has not yet been able to solve. The initial installation cost of the unit is very high, and its use is limited to places with a reliable and constant supply of A.C. electricity. Compared to the captive-bolt stunners, the electric stunners need more adequate inspection and supervision to ensure correct usage. Low voltage, and therefore inadequate current flow; incorrect positioning of the electrodes; and/or insufficient time can result in ineffective stunning and even in electro-paralysis which leaves the animal conscious or semiconscious and aware of pain. Another disadvantage of this system is the biological fact that each animal, though of the same species, possesses its individual measure of resistibility; this does not allow the technicians to set the instrument at a uniform voltage once and for all, irrelevant to understanding the principles of electrical stunning.

Another method of electrical stunning is to apply 300 to 400 volts from head to back which makes the animal unconscious and also stops the heart, killing the animal. It is scientifically claimed that even after cardiac arrest and death, the blood would still flow out normally if the animal is slaughtered as soon as possible. However, from the Islamic religious point of view, the animal is dead for all intents and purposes and has become unlawful (Harâm) as food.

There are so many uncertainties in electrical stunning, both from scientific and religious points of view, that it would not be honest to recommend its use to Muslims. As mentioned before, it is not always easy to assess how strong or for how long the current should be applied to each animal. A weak current would result in the animal regaining consciousness too soon, while too strong a current might kill the animal of oxygen deficiency in the brain (anoxia) before it is slaughtered for bloodletting (*Tadhkiyyah*). The minimum standards set in legislation are based on scientific data and they take care of animal welfare. In order to understand the technicalities of these problems, it should be kept in mind that electrical stunning should not be confused with Electro-Convulsive Therapy (ECT). This treatment of human patients is meant not to render them unconscious, while the electric current applied to animals is meant to make them stunned and lose their sensitivity. Similarly electrical stunning should not be confused with 'electrocution' which means KILLING by electricity.

GAS (CO2) STUNNERS

This method is used to anaesthetise animals with carbon dioxide gas (CO2). It is a mixture of 60 to 70 percent volume of gas and air. It became quite popular in the fifties, especially on pigs. However, scientific opinion on its use is very unfavourable. Each animal has to be shut up in a chamber and exposed to the gas for about one and a half minutes. The onset of unconsciousness is very slow, the animal becoming stressed and showing signs of distress. Moreover, this equipment is very expensive to install.

POULTRY STUNNING

The current methods of stunning chickens and other domestic fowls sometimes fall short of humanitarian standards. They are by their very nature small and delicate animals which can be easily injured. To meet the present commercial pressures and the ever-increasing demand of the poultry-eating public, they are being slaughtered in much larger numbers and without due attention to detail. The official figure of poultry killed in the UK is around 800 million every year. In the United Kingdom the process of their slaughter at the packing stations (poultry abattoirs) is regulated by the Welfare of Animals (Slaughter or Killing) Regulations 1995. On arrival at the processing centres, after having been transported from the rearing factories by very questionable means—surely chickens are not transported by hanging them on handlebars of bicycles and they are not deprived of food and water for prolonged periods as they happen in developing countries? The birds are hung upside down by their ankles on a moving conveyor. This carries them to an electrically charged water bath which, if operating properly, should pass sufficient current through the body to stun the bird.

However, by the very fact that this is a high-speed automatic process, no attention is paid to the individual. Some birds, while struggling to get free, miss the stunning bath and reach the point of slaughter while conscious. The slaughter is carried out so hurriedly that often the cut is not made complete. Often an automatic knife is used to cut the throat, with a 'back-up' slaughterman who cuts the throat if it has not been cut properly by the mechanical knife. As a result of poor stunning or neck-cutting, the birds can sometimes regain consciousness during bleeding-out. It is a common practice that the slaughtermen are paid by piece-rate wages and a bonus system, which tempts them to beat the clock—not in Europe where they are the highly paid workforce in the slaughterhouse, it is said. After the cut, the birds are dipped in nearly boiling water—not true, the temperature is 51°C—in a tank to loosen their feathers, while some of them are still alive—this is against the law in Europe. All this cruelty is being perpetrated in the name of supply and demand. The more dismal aspect of this problem is that many countries in the East have started similar methods of slaughter. Such inhumane methods of slaughter are absolutely un-Islamic and, perhaps, render the meat abominable (*Makruh*) to eat.

RESTRAINING PENS

Slaughterhouses by their very nature leave the animals in a highly stressed and excitable condition, especially after unfavourable travel conditions and insensitive handling. The only way to slaughter them safely, especially cattle, is to restrain their movements prior to slaughter and to this end a kind of metal crate, called a pen, is used. When an animal is finally persuaded inside a pen and positioned suitably for slaughter, its head sticks out of a hold and is held firmly with crossbars called a yoke. There is a plate inside the pen which is adjustable according to the size of the animal. They are also fitted with a moveable ramp to raise the animal to the required height and to support it. The pens are of two kinds:

ROTARY PENS

These come in different designs called Weinberg, Dyne or North British. The most commonly used, though highly condemned, are the Weinberg rotating pens. These rotary pens are now illegal in Great Britain. When the animal is positioned in it, one side of the crush is noisily pushed against the animal's side, restricting its leg and body movements. The clanging metal in this frighteningly strange environment further alarms the animal which tries to struggle itself free. The pen is rotated completely to 180 degrees to place the beast on its back—an extremely unnatural and uncomfortable position—so that its neck may be stretched out and cut from above. In the light of experience, experts have come to the conclusion that the rotary pens are not suitable for the purpose for which they were invented, i.e. to make the last moments of the poor victim a bit easier. Instead of lessening the stress and suffering of the animal, this kind of pen actually aggravates it. The animal feels completely disorientated by the rocking and swinging of the cradle-like pen; its head is still pinioned down in the traditional way by the foot of the slaughterman or kept tied by a rope. During all this process it goes on struggling in panic and often sustains flesh injuries and broken bones. Apart from the injuries, an animal slaughtered under such highly constraining and stressed conditions will automatically secrete an excessive amount of a hormone called adrenalin into the muscle tissues, which would produce a poor carcass for eating.

UPRIGHT SLAUGHTER

For slaughtering animals in a standing position, special pens have been invented, called 'Cincinnati' pens. They were originally manufactured by a company called Cincinnati and were approved by the American Society for the Prevention of Cruelty to Animals (ASPCA). Now some other variations of it have also come into use. After entering the pen, the animal is pushed forward mechanically until its head protrudes from an opening in the pen and is secured in a yoke. There is also an adjustable plate to support it from underneath the breast and a chin-lift to raise the head to the required height. The approach race is curved in some designs, which makes it easier for the animal to enter the pen. The most important feature of this design is that, throughout the operation, the animal remains standing without stress or panic. It is experienced that slaughtermen, once used to slaughtering a standing animal, find no difficulty in cutting the throat.

As stated earlier, the use of rotary pens has been prohibited in Great Britain. It seems that Jews have objected from their religious stance to slaughtering animals in a standing position and that some Muslims have followed suit. Again stated earlier, there is no law in Islam forbidding the slaughter of food-animals in a standing position. On the contrary, verse 22:36 of the Qur'ân sanctions the slaughtering of camels in an upright position, even though there were no breastplates in those days to restrain their fall after the cut. There is no reason why this Qur'ânic sanction for camels could not be extended to other animals. It is encouraging to see that Muslims in the Irish Republic have accepted the upright slaughtering pens and so have the Jewish communities there as well as in America.

According to the following explanation by scientists, slaughtering an animal in a standing position is no different from the lying down position:

> "The collapse of an animal following severance of major blood vessels in the neck is a manifestation of cerebral[ii] hypoxia / anoxia due to the sudden fall in pressure of the cerebrospinal fluid[iii] and is not due

---

ii Cerebral = of the brain

iii Cerebrospinal fluid = the fluid passing through the brain and the canal of the central nervous system called the spinal cord.

to anoxia[iv] following reduction in the flow of blood to the brain. Our observation of cattle slaughtered in the standing position in a 'Cincinnati' pen has shown this to occur on average five or six seconds after the cut. This is not scientifically sound: Nystagmus[v], which is an indication of commencement of loss of consciousness, follows 4 or 5 seconds later"[11]

ANIMALS' PSYCHO-PHYSIOLOGY

Islam has laid down the basic principles as a code of conduct. It is up to man to work out the details within the terms of those principles. For example, during the time of the Prophet, surgical operations used to be performed with the tools and techniques which were known to surgeons at that time. Today Muslims have accepted all the modern surgical technology and melioration—including the transplant of organs and heart surgery. When a dying Muslim is fitted with the heart of another person and gets a new lease of life, no one ever complains that this is an innovation and interference with the foreordination of the time of death. No Muslim refuses to be anaesthetised before a surgical operation on the grounds that anaesthetics have not been mentioned in the Qur'ân or *Ahadith*. However, when it comes to rendering an animal insensible before cutting its throat, it is taken as a scientific incursion on the Divine law and an attack on the immutability of the traditional practices.

When a human being is struck by lightning or dies of a sudden heart attack, he does not feel any physical pain or mental anguish except perhaps for a fraction of a second—and it is said that he died 'in peace'. As opposed to that, one who is told that he would be hanged the next day dies a thousand deaths before reaching the gallows. We know the feelings of other people because of our ability to communicate our abstract thoughts to each other. What happens to animals who are incapable of expressing their thoughts—or do they not have any thoughts? They are uprooted from their familiar surroundings; brought to an abattoir by an

iv Anoxia = deficiency of oxygen

v Nystagmus = to and fro movement (oscillation) of eyeballs uncomfortable means of transport; made to wait in a hostile environment where the bloody nature of the profession tends to make not only the slaughtermen callous-hearted but all those who are involved in this business; goaded unceremoniously into the slaughter hall and then cut across the throat. Apart from the physical discomfort and pain, do they suffer any mental anguish? Do they become aware of what is going to happen to them? Does physical pain touch them in mind and, if it does, to what extent? Is their apparent cool and calm due to their lack of cognition or is it due to resignation to the inevitable? No one, as yet, has been able to answer these questions categorically, not even scientists and naturalists. This is mainly because we do not have a scientific tool to measure mental state in humans and other animals. However, all of the life-saving drugs, anaesthetics and analgesics and drugs routinely used to treat humans with psychological (mental) disorders are tested on animals because they have anatomical, physiological, and psychological similarities to humans.

On the one hand scientists have not yet been able to measure conclusively the chronometrical relationship between the lapse of consciousness and physical insensitivity to pain. On the other hand the notaries of the religious mode of slaughter are inhibited against any change in their traditional ways based on religious authority. One of the main reasons for this confusion is that, until recently, man had taken it for granted that the rest of the species were less sensitive to pain than the human species. Even these days one of the arguments advanced against pre-slaughter stunning is that the nervous system of animals is different from that of humans. It is concluded, therefore, that animals are less sensitive to pain. The same logic is applied to their mental suffering.

During the past hundred years or so, great strides have been taken in the field of psychophysics. However, most scientists have confined their research in this field to human beings, neglecting the rest of the species. The three great contemporaneous psychoanalysts—Sigmund Freud, C. G. Jung, Alfred Adler—were interested only in the human species rather than in life as a whole. Even the human psychology related to cruelty to animals was not on their bill of research. Those anthropologists who devoted their lives to the science of man as an animal, in spite of making a valuable contribution to human knowledge, got their findings intervolved in the evolution of evolution. Charles Darwin's theory of the common origin of species, published 130 years ago, in 1859, whether right or not, should have created in man at least some feelings of affinity with animals. Instead, it has ended up as a target pad with concentric circles of polemics for academical archery. Scholars, such as Karl Popper, refuted it; it came into direct conflict with the Creationists; it has given birth to neo-Darwinism and to various other genetic theories based on animal fossils. All this scholastic talent and energy is being spent on ascertaining the genetic relationship between animals in general—anthropoids and homo sapiens—but only recently have scientists taken the task seriously of proving how long it takes an animal to become unconscious of pain after its throat has been cut, so that it could be determined on scientific evidence whether or not it is more humane to make an animal insensible to pain before the cut. It is worth noting that Charles Darwin believed and argued that we should look into nature open-mindedly and then form hypotheses (which he implemented successfully), rather than look into nature for evidence to support our preconceptions.

All this academic and anthropological debate is not of much help to a layman. An average person who feels that he is entitled to kill animals for food would like to know what is the most humane way of doing so. For Muslims it does not, or it should not, pose a problem. The Qur'ân puts all animals on a par with humans in every physical sense.[12] This means that their innate desire to live as well as their other corporeal needs are the same as those of human beings.[13] In case they were less sensitive to physical pain than human beings, Islam would not have insisted repeatedly on the use of the least painful mode of slaughtering. In case the sensory faculties of their brain were not developed enough to feel fear and mental trepidation at the time of slaughter, the Prophet Mohammad would not have forbidden the sharpening of the knife in the presence of the victims or to slaughter them within each other's range of vision. He was an unlettered man (*Ummi*), least of all in natural history and science. However, according to Muslims' firm belief, his knowledge was divinely-inspired. For Muslims, therefore, there should be no doubt that an animal has a degree of cognisance of what is happening around him in the slaughterhouse and that he does feel both physical and mental pain when his throat is cut—the same as a human being feels the pain of a surgical operation when not anaesthetised.

Many regions of the inner self-consciousness in animals are still unexplored territories. We know that consciousness needs a thinking brain. What we do not know is the range of animals' thinking capacity. Can an animal think in terms of "I think, therefore, I am"? The Qur'ân tells us that, when animals worship God, they KNOW their prayer and are CONSCIOUS of what they are doing.[14] Darwin believed that consciousness is something supernatural and, therefore, beyond the realm of science. Scientific psychology derives its data from the electrical impulses which pass through the brain. On the other hand, the Qur'ân tells us that animals are social communities, like humans.[15] This means that the consciousness of animals functions on the same principle of psychic forces as that of man. Animals are conscious of themselves and of their sub-conscious; they are aware of their communal existence and its altruistic responsibilities; otherwise they would not have been able to survive as communities so successfully as they have. According to the latest findings of natural science, consciousness is a prerequisite of physical as well as of mental awareness. Biologically, therefore, it can be safely syllogised from the scientific premises that animal behaviour and responses work on the same principles as those of humans and that they feel stress and pain as humans do.

The Qur'ân has been enunciating this proposition for the last fourteen centuries—albeit taking it beyond the realm of biology. It has been explaining persistently that consciousness, in its advanced stage, leads to spiritual awareness—a stage when the inner eye becomes the overseer not simply of the physique but of the whole personality, a stage of spiritual volition called in Islam *Taqwa*.

A Dutch team of scientists has found scientific evidence of mental suffering in animals. They have discovered that, like the human brain, an animal's brain too releases a substance called

'Endorphin' to cope with emotional distress and pain caused by frustration or conflict. This substance is 100 times more powerful than morphine.[16]

PHYSICAL PAIN

Pain is absolutely a personal and subjective experience which is confined to the creature in pain. The degree of pain depends on the susceptibility (anaphylaxis) of the sufferer and no one else can feel it. The human being can inform others where and how much it is paining or how they are feeling about it. An animal, however, cannot do so or we do not have the capacity to understand their language although animals in pain do vocalise when allowed to do so. It cannot even let out painful cries because, along with the blood vessels, the slaughterer has also cut its air passage in the throat (trachea) without which no sound can be produced. The animal does try to struggle itself out but cannot because it is restrained. Its 'escape reflexes' too, therefore, fail to give a measured indication of its mental suffering and physical pain both before and after the cut.

In the absence of conclusive scientific evidence various speculative theories are in circulation, with the result that laymen pick and choose the theories which support their preconceived traditional ideas. For example, some Jews and Muslims use the following arguments against the use of stunners:

(i) Animals do not feel pain when their throat is cut because the anatomical structure of their body and brain, especially that of the cud-chewing animals (ruminants), is designed to be less sensitive to pain than that of humans.

(ii) A cut in the skin gives pain only when the cut-ends of the wound meet each other, otherwise the incidence of bleeding is painless.

(iii) The convulsions during the throes of death are only muscular movements and not painful spasms of the last breaths. They are in the nature of automatic reflex reactions due to lack of oxygen in the brain (anoxia) and not a result of pain.

(iv) After the cut, the flow of blood from the four big vessels of the neck is so fast and profuse that the animal becomes unconscious IMMEDIATELY. When the carotids and the jugular veins are cut by *Shechita* method, the blood pressure in vessels and vertebral arteries which supply blood to the brain falls rapidly and causes a deficiency of oxygen (anoxia). It is claimed that blood pressure drops 25 percent within 3 seconds. The pressure of fluid which works as a link between the spinal cord and the brain falls even more rapidly than the blood-pressure. In anatomical science it is called the serous fluid which is contained in the subarachnoid space around the brain and spinal cord. The fall in pressure produces a state of shock and the animal loses consciousness within about three to five seconds. Some estimate the period to be a bit longer.

(v)   Animals are not aware of what is happening to them or around them and, therefore, they do not suffer any mental anguish and stress.

(vi)   Electro-Encephalo-Graph (EEG) and other techniques related to the physiology of the nervous system (neurophysiology) record only the electrical activity in the brain and are no criterion of consciousness. It has been scientifically proved now that measuring the "evoked responses", i.e. the electrical activity of the brain in response to various stimuli, is a more accurate indication of brain function than an encephalograph alone. At the same time it is claimed by some that stunning only paralyses into a condition of 'mixed-shock', leaving the animal fully conscious.

The modern science of psycho-physiology has dealt at great length with the inter-relation between human physiology and mental phenomena, but we know so little in this respect about animals. This ignorance is one of the main causes of human callousness towards animal suffering and of hypocritically double standards of morality in our dealings with them. People do everything within their means to alleviate the suffering of a human being and try to make the last moments of a dying person as congenial as possible. On the other hand, the same people would take the life of an innocent animal for sport without compunction. This morality is the result of quite a few mistaken notions about the psychophysiology of animals. They are supposed to have no soul, no mind, and no feelings. It is assumed that they have no mental awareness of their fate in the slaughterhouse. Even their anatomical structure, it is claimed, is different from that of the human species and that they become dead as a doornail immediately their throats are cut, without feeling any pain.

All such mistaken beliefs and popular myths have been refuted by Islam. Any Muslims who doubt it, should study the postulates as laid down in the Qur'ân and *Ahadith*, in the light of modern science and reorientate themselves with the spirit of the Islamic laws. The Qur'ân and *Ahadith*, quoted earlier in this book, clearly establish the fact that animals are endowed with the same mental, intellectual, and physical faculties as man, albeit to a lesser degree, and scientists are trying to find out the degrees of comparison between the two. It is true that their findings are at variance with each other, in certain points of detail, but most of them are agreed on the broad principles as enunciated by Islam. It has now been scientifically proved that animals are not less sensitive to physical pain than human beings. Their physique is made up of similar structure as that of the human species. The only difference is in the development of the brain. It is true that they are less developed mentally than the human brain, but this is no yardstick to measure physical sensibility. A human baby has no mental awareness of its existence. Does it mean that the baby does not feel physical pain or that they would not feel the agony of torture, even if the torture lasts for a short period. The fact that an animal cannot articulate the words "I am" does not mean that it does not know that "it is". Its desire to live, its struggle for existence and its wit to survive is in some cases better planned and more co-ordinated with nature than the lifestyle of the human species.

Another sophistical argument advanced against stunning is that pain does exist there whether the animal is in a state of consciousness or of unconsciousness. It is argued that the paralysis of the sensorium only incapacitates the faculty of expression, while an animal goes on feeling pain all the same. Does this fine distinction between the actual existence of pain and the feeling of it apply only to animals and not to humans? It is a fact of common occurrence that, when a human being is knocked senseless, he stops feeling pain. If biologically the pain is still there, he is not sensitive to it—and this exactly is the purpose of stunning. The same purpose is achieved by anaesthetisation before surgical operations. The reasons why animals are not anaesthetised before the operation of throat-cutting are that this method is time-consuming, uneconomic and requires medical expertise. It is only for these reasons, otherwise there would not have been any religious objection to pre-slaughter anaesthetisation—the same as there should not be any objection to captive-bolt or concussion stunning.

Another point in this respect which needs scientific investigation is to determine the sensibility to pain during semi-consciousness. As laymen, we know that during a fully unconscious state one does not feel any pain, such as during surgical operations under anaesthetics or when the brain has been smashed by a bullet. What we do not know, however, is the reason *why* one does feel pain, even physical pain, during a nightmare when the subconscious mind is still working. If nightmares are brought in sleep by digestive or nervous disorders in human beings, resulting in extremely frightful and oppressive activity of the subconscious mind, then how can it be justifiably assumed that the subconscious or semiconscious minds of animals do not feel fright, oppression, and pain during the period when their whole nervous system is passing through gradual disorder after their throats have been cut without stunning?

TIME FACTOR

It has not yet been established scientifically exactly how much time it takes after the cut for an animal to lose consciousness to a degree where it stops feeling pain—consciously or even subconsciously. I think the existing scientific data would help estimate this. To a casual observer the animal seems to be dead when it collapses 'immediately' after its carotid arteries and jugular veins have been severed. In this respect too, scientists have not yet been able to say definitely whether this collapse is due to cerebral shock, i.e. the fall in the fluid which normally flows between the brain and spine (cerebrospinal fluid), or whether it is due to the reduction of oxygen-carrying blood in the brain (anoxia). The majority of scientists believe that the supply of oxygen to the brain is cut off gradually and not immediately after the throat has been cut. What it means in other words is that, although the animal does collapse and appears to have died, its brain-sensitivity takes much longer to be completely dead.

In assessing the suffering involved in not stunning animals, the central question is: how long after throat-cutting do animals stop feeling pain? In attempting to answer this question, scientists have tried to determine the time required for animals to lose brain responsiveness by measuring at what point after throat-cutting the brain loses its ability to respond to certain external stimuli. This involves measuring the interval from the throat-cutting to loss of visual and/or somatosensory evoked responses. The absence of such responses reflects a profound disturbance of the brain and indicates a point at which it is safe to assume that the animal is insensible to pain. The consensus of scientific experts in this field is that loss of visual evoked activity of the brain is a very reliable index of brain failure.

Scientists have found that there can be a relatively long time-lapse between throat-cutting and loss of responsiveness in the brain, i.e. when the animal can clearly no longer feel pain.

Scientists have found that with sheep, if both carotid arteries and jugular veins are severed, it takes on average 14 seconds to induce loss of brain responsiveness. They found, however, that this interval was five times longer—70 seconds—where only one carotid artery and jugular vein were severed. Where only the jugular veins were severed, the time to loss of brain responsiveness rose markedly to about 5 minutes.

A number of studies have shown that calves can take a much longer time than other species to lose their brain function following throat-cutting. A recent study found that responsiveness can be present in the brains of calves for as long as 104 seconds after neck-sticking.[16] As a result, some calves show clear signs of recovery after sticking.

Another study reported on the slaughter of a number of fully conscious lambs, sheep, calves and one young bull . The researcher concluded that severing the carotid arteries without prior stunning does not result in a rapid loss of consciousness in calves. He found that on average with the calves, 171 seconds elapsed between throat-cutting and the cessation of apparently co-ordinated attempts to rise. He also reported that the young bull made such attempts to rise for 20 seconds.

Another study using adult cattle found that the duration of brain function after slaughter without prior stunning is very variable. This found that it took an average 55 seconds for brain responsiveness to be lost after throat-cutting.

It can take a very considerable time for a chicken to lose brain responsiveness following neck-cutting; the amount of time involved varies enormously, depending on which blood vessels in the neck are cut. The time[vi] between neck-cutting and loss of brain responsiveness in chickens varies between 163 and 349 seconds, depending on the method of neck-cutting used.[16]

This scientific fact cannot be refuted, it has been proven that there is a period of interval between the cut and complete unconsciousness. Even if it is just a few seconds, the animal does remain conscious or semiconscious during that period and does feel both the mental pangs and physical pain. On the other hand, every hunter would bear witness to the scientifically proven fact that a direct shot in the brain with a bullet or a bolt renders an animal unconscious instantaneously without giving it time to realise what has happened to it—and there lies the real advantage of stunning that, during that period of unconsciousness, the act of slaughter can be performed exactly according to the religious law. In the light of the Islamic teachings in this respect Muslims should not need any scientific facts and figures to convince them that the best method of slaughter is the method which inflicts the least possible pain to the victim. The Islamic concern is so great against cruelty to animals that it has declared the infliction of

---

vi **Editor's note:** Since Al-Hafiz B.A. Masri wrote this book, a major scientific report published in 2004 concluded that "Without stunning, the time between cutting through the major blood vessels and insensibility, as deduced from behavioural and brain response, is up to 20 seconds in sheep. . . up to 2 minutes in cattle, up to 2½ or more minutes in poultry".

any unnecessary and avoidable pain "even to a sparrow or any creature smaller than that" as a sin for which the culprit would be answerable to God on the Day of Judgement.

EXSANGUINATION (Drawing Out Of Blood)

All the religious objections to stunning centre round the one major objection that it does not allow all the blood to drain out of the carcass. People generally have been fed with information which is not easy to understand for a layman without some knowledge of anatomy. Then they have been told some stale scientific facts which have now been superseded by new knowledge. In a nutshell, they have been led to believe that stunning has a paralysing effect on the muscles of the heart and disconnects the central nervous system by damaging the Circle of Willis (arteries).[17] This disruption affects the heartbeats which, in turn, affect the pumping out of blood. They argue that this convulsive action of the muscles after the cut accelerates the squeezing out of blood from the meat-tissues into the blood stream. Convulsions are possible only if the brain is alive, the nervous system functional and the heart pulsating. It is wrongfully believed that all these functions are stopped by stunning.

Scientists, however, have shown that the heart does not stop beating and pumping after stunning. Provided that the right current is used, the heart's beating is not stopped by stunning. Indeed, electrical stunning is reversible; in other words, the animal would recover from the stun if its throat was not cut. It is the letting out of the blood by throat-cutting which causes death. Another scientific finding is significant in this respect. They have found out that stunning does not affect the flow of blood. Experiments done for this very purpose have shown that exactly the same amount of blood remains in the meat, whether the animal has been stunned or not, as long is *rigor mortis* has not set in, i.e. it has not become cold and stiff.[20]

Some professionals even claim that stunners make the animal's brain free from mental stresses and strains which allows the heart to perform, physiologically, at the normal pace and to pump more blood out of the body than otherwise.

The same point, however, is being used by some to support the argument that all the excitement, discomfort, and fear during the preparatory arrangements for slaughter increase the heartbeat. During the incision, they say, it increases still more and that the increased palpitation increases the flow of blood.

All such arguments have been proved wrong by laboratory tests of meat by extracting the minute matter of the corpuscles which give colouring to blood (haemoglobin). The reason why the colour of meat slaughtered without pre-stunning is lighter than the colour of meat slaughtered after stunning is not that there is less blood in it. The real reason is that an animal, when slaughtered while it is conscious, breathes more gaspingly. This produces a greater amount of oxyhaemoglobin (a combination of oxygen and haemoglobin) in the blood and lightens the colour of the meat.[18] Much scientific research has been done in this respect. According to Gotze an authority on the subject (Gotze 1974), animals that die from natural causes have much higher levels of haemoglobin in the diaphragm than those slaughtered as an emergency in moribund condition, i.e. when they are at the point of death. *Haemoglobin* is the matter of the red corpuscles of blood; corpuscles are the minute bodies which constitute a large part of the blood. His experiments further showed that the emergency-slaughtered animals had higher levels of the red corpuscles than the animals normally slaughtered. He concludes that "it is likely that these different amounts of residual haemoglobin reflected the degree of stimulation of the sympathetic nervous system."[19] Similarly, experiments done by using the neuromuscular blocking drug, curare, show that the muscle spasm and spasmodic leg and body movements do not make the body expel more blood from the muscles.[20]

The concentration of haemoglobin in the muscles of meat animals slaughtered using normal commercial practices range from 0.2 to 1 mg/g. Based on a concentration of haemoglobin in the blood of sheep and cattle of 100g/litre, this is equivalent to between 2 and 9 ml blood/kg muscle.[21]

Another scientist explains the change of colour in meat in these words:

> Dark cutting beef . . . is caused by a deficiency of glycogen in the muscles of an animal at slaughter which prevents the normal decrease in pH postmortem. As a result there is an increase in enzyme activity which uses up the oxygen which would normally convert the dark myoglobin into pink oxymyoglobin, and the meat appears dark; it also tends to be dry because of the high water-binding capacity of muscle protein at higher pH. The stores of glycogen are depleted principally by muscular exhaustion and stress and these two factors must be avoided in the 48 hours before slaughter in order to minimise the risk of dark cutting beef.[22]

Although some business concerns are promoting the consumption of blood as a source of protein, dieticians in general agree that blood is unsafe as food. The Scriptural religions have, right from the beginning, declared it as unhygienic and have forbidden its consumption. Where the protagonists and the antagonists of pre-slaughter stunning differ is the moot point of whether stunning impedes the flow of blood or not.

The Jewish objection to stunning has the additional point of 'blemish', which is not one of the conscientious or religious objections of Muslims. It has been discussed in previous chapters that the Islamic law allows the consumption of an animal even though it has been injured in any way, provided its flesh has been cleansed by bleeding (*Tadhkiyyah*).

There are some Muslims who object to stunners on the grounds that it is an additional cruelty to injure the animal twice—once by shooting it with a bolt and the second time by cutting its throat. This moral issue has been discussed under mental stress and physical pain. If the Islamic law had looked upon this issue in that light, it would not have allowed the hunting of animals in which they are first shot and then slaughtered. The question of blood and bleeding is not so much a religious issue for Muslims. It is, in fact, a hygienic and hence a scientific issue which should be understood as such. For Muslims the slaughter of animals for food has no ritualistic, ceremonious or any kind of symbolic significance. Even the animals killed as a sacrifice are in reality for food by way of charity to provide sustenance to the indigent—IN the name of God and not FOR God.

There is no doubt that great advances have been made in meat science. For example, the Foss Super-scan IRT meat analysis can measure within about ten minutes the amount of protein, fat, carbohydrate, water, and meat—both in raw materials and in finished products, whether fresh or frozen. In spite of all this knowledge, it would be wrong for anyone to feel that the Islamic method of slaughter was based on antiquated food hygiene practices of some fourteen centuries ago and that it has now been outmoded; and it would be wrong to assume that the Islamic proviso of bleeding the animal, while it is still alive, could be dispensed with. Even the latest knowledge derived from the modern science of meat confirms that more blood is retained in the body when an animal is slaughtered (or stuck) after its death, whether stunned or not.

There are some scientists who claim that stoppage of the heart does not affect the bleeding out. Others claim that most of the residual amount of blood remains only in the organs of the thorax and abdominal cavities. According to the Farm Animal Welfare Council:

> About 70 percent of the total blood loss occurs in the first two minutes following sticking. It is estimated that the blood loss represents 60 percent of the animal's blood with 20—25 percent remaining in the viscera and 15—20 percent in the muscle and bone.[23]

However, there is enough contrary evidence of the fact that more blood does remain within the body of an animal which is slaughtered after death than of one that is slaughtered live. From the point of view of the religious concepts of bleeding it makes no difference which parts of the body contain that residual blood and explanations, such as quoted below, fail to satisfy the Muslims on this point:

> The blood not lost at sticking was partially accounted for. Some was lost after the two-minute recorded collection period and a small fraction could be accounted for in an increased weight of abdominal

viscera [the interior organs in the great cavities of the body], heart and lungs. It was concluded that if methods of stunning which stopped the heart were developed some blood would be retained in the carcass or offal but no decrease in meat quality would result.[24]

Another animal physiologist, P. D. Warris, says:

> Blood not lost at sticking is probably largely retained in the viscera rather than the carcass. The residual blood content of lean meat is 2 to 9 ml/kg muscle. There is no evidence that this amount is affected by different slaughter methods or that large amounts of residual blood influence the microbiology of meat.
>
> Warris (1977) concluded that there was no unequivocal evidence that large quantities of residual blood were detrimental to the quality of meat. The factors which influence the process of exsanguination [draining out of blood] can be classed as either physiological or mechanical. Physiological factors are those which influence the distribution of the total blood volume between peripheral vascular beds [bases of the external surface of vessels or ducts conveying blood], while mechanical factors influence the drainage of blood from the vessels at sticking [slaughtering].
>
> The amount of blood in the small vessels, arterioles [small arteries], venules [small veins] and capillaries [minute thin-walled blood vessels] is controlled principally by the physiological state of the vascular beds. . . . the main factor determining the residual blood content of muscles is the degree of physiological stress experienced by the animal at slaughter. (Warris 1978)
>
> The stress inherent in stunning and exsanguination would normally produce peripheral vasoconstriction through the action of catecholamines released from the adrenal medulla and sympathetic nerve endings. Adrenalin is a vasodilator in muscle capillaries at low concentration but vasoconstrictive at all concentrations. (Goodman and Gilman 1975) The action of these hormones would result in minimal retention of blood.[25]

In simple words, what this amounts to is that an animal is under stress both during the preparatory stages and at the time of the cut. This stress releases in its body certain chemical substances which have a soothing effect on it. However, if those substances are allowed to be produced in higher than required levels, the degree of stress becomes more than normal, resulting in a greater amount of residual blood within the body after slaughter. On the other hand, making an animal insensitive to mental stress and physical pain by stunning helps the animal's body to produce the right amount of those chemical substances to keep it relaxed and to eject more blood after the throat is cut.

At the same time it has been established scientifically that spear-struck animals, in which only blood vessels are cut, lose about 12 percent less blood than those slaughtered with a gash cut, such as the Islamic method, which severs practically all the soft tissues in the neck.[26] In view of the above stated facts about bleeding and concomitant implications or religious convictions, it is imperative that the animal be alive, even though unconscious, at the time of slaughter. Without this proviso it would be neither possible nor correct for Muslims to accept pre-slaughter stunning.

Islamic law forbids the consumption of blood, but it does not want Muslims to be prudish about it. While prohibiting blood the Qur'ân has taken good care to restrict the prohibition to that blood which pours forth naturally at the time of slaughter.[27] That which still remains within the viscera organs can be washed off. If still there are some minute corpuscles left, it is expected that the antibodies in the consumer's metabolism would counteract their unhygienic properties. It is an inevitable biological fact that there are certain very small blood vessels in the body which cannot be emptied of blood by any manner of slaughter.

Surely the Islamic prohibition of blood was never meant to override the other more peremptory and positive laws of compassion for animals. Many such laws have been quoted earlier in this book. For example, there are laws declaring the flesh of animals which have been killed by cruel methods (Al-Muthlah) as carrion (Al-Mujaththamah) and unlawful to eat (Harâm). Muslims should consider carefully whether animals which are kept conscious during the time of slaughter fall into the category of *Al-Muthlah*. If they do, because of the avoidable pain and suffering involved, surely they are either unlawful as food (*Harâm*) or, at least, undesirable to eat (*Makruh*). It has scientifically been measured now that the amount of blood left over within the body after slaughter (*Tadhkiyyah*) is very small. For example:

> It is estimated that the musculature in the carcass of an ox contained blood equivalent to 1 and 4 percent of the total blood volume of the live animal, a relatively small proportion.[28]
>
> No evidence has been found for any influence of different slaughtering procedures in normal use on the residual blood content of meat.[29]

After reading such facts and figures of modern science there remains no doubt that the Qur'ân was divinely inspired. Otherwise, the Prophet Mohammad could never have thought on his own fourteen hundred years ago to make allowance for practicability by circumscribing the prohibition to that blood only which "poureth forth" at the time of slaughter in verse 6: 145.

(Some biological terms used in these passages are explained in Appendix A.)

THE JINX OF BLEMISH

> And the Lord spoke unto Moses, saying . . . Ye shall offer unto the Lord a burnt offering . . . without blemish . . . . But whatever hath a blemish, that shall ye not offer: for it shall not be acceptable for you. . . . it shall be perfect to be accepted; there shall be no blemish therein. . . . Ye shall not offer unto the Lord that which is bruised, or crushed, or broken, or cut. . .[30]

The above is just one of many such verses of the Hebrew Bible emphatically forbidding the offering of animals with a blemish. Based on this, one of the main objections of Jews to stunners is that the tiny hole which the penetrating stunner makes in the skull causes an imperfection tantamount to a blemish. However, all the Biblical verses on 'blemish' occur only in the context of sacrificial animals. Why is it, then, that the law of blemish is applied with all might and main to food animals as well? One explanation by Jewish theologians is that, since animal sacrifice in the temples is no longer allowed, the killing of animals to eat them is considered by Jews as an act of worship in the spirit of sacrifice. However, the following verse in the Bible clearly advises the Israelites to eat animals EVEN IF THERE BE A BLEMISH IN THEM:

> And if there be any blemish therein, as if it be lame, or blind, or have ill blemish, thou shalt not sacrifice it unto the Lord thy God: THOU SHALT EAT IT WITHIN THY GATES [in your homes]: the unclean and the clean shall eat it alike. . . .[31]

Blemish is not one of the Islamic proscriptions on food. It has been explained earlier that Islam makes a clear distinction between animals for general consumption and those sacrificed for charity (*Qurban* or *Sadaqah*). It is only animals killed to feed the indigent which are required to be free from any physical deformity, so that the poor recipients do not get inferior quality meat. Otherwise, animals for general consumption can have any sort of blemish—as long as they are normally healthy. So at least Muslims do not have any reason to reject pre-slaughter stunning on the grounds of 'blemish'. There is nowhere in the Qur'ân or *Ahadith* that an animal should be physically uninjured or mentally conscious before slaughter. It is true that the Qur'ân or *Ahadith* do not mention stunners or other methods of rendering the animal unconscious before slaughter. There are many modern practices which Muslims have adopted and numerous technological aids and appliances which have not been mentioned either in the Islamic statute law (*Fiqh*) or its convention (*Sunnah*) and yet Muslims have started using them, justifiably, without any sense of guilt. The Islamic juristic maxim in such cases is the same as the principle that "What things God doeth neither command nor forbid . . . He permitteth."[32]

Another prejudice against stunning is the taste of meat. One often hears the immigrant communities complaining that meat in the West does not taste as savoury as in the East and they lay the blame on the slaughter and stunning techniques. While their complaint is right, the reason they ascribe to it is not. There are other reasons why meat in Western countries is comparatively insipid and less tasty. Animals in the West are reared under unnatural conditions by factory-farming methods and fed on drugs to make them grow fast. For example, broiler chickens become ready for slaughter at 6 weeks old. Most animals are reared by intensive farming, without any freedom of movement and exercise. All their miserable lives, they seldom get a chance to bask in the sun or revel in grassy fields. The flesh of such animals is generally deep-frozen and reaches the shops long after slaughter. Imported meat, in particular, is months old. It is obvious that this kind of meat cannot compare in taste and texture with that of free-range animals in the East, reared and fed as nature intended them to be.

It is true that modern extensive and intensive methods of animal husbandry and conveyor-belt slaughtering techniques used to be alien to Eastern and Islamic aesthetics and taste. However, the current increase in demand for animal products and meat has driven the international markets to adopt such methods of production and distribution. Islamic countries are importing huge quantities of both live animals and meat from other parts of the world. For example, each year around 5 to 6 million live sheep are exported from Australia to Muslim countries in the Middle East. Each year, according to Australian government statistics, 45,000-75,000 of these animals die during the long sea journeys from other parts of the world. The total figures of livestock internationally exported and imported are more than one can tell. It is farcical to blame Western exporters alone for the cruelty to animals involved in this multi-million-pound trade; the importing countries are equally blameworthy—it is the inevitable law of commerce that 'demand' actuates 'supply' and its ways and means.

The impression that Western commercial interests are promoting the fast slaughtering techniques is wrong. It is the current increase in demand for meat which is responsible for the present state of affairs and the abominable cruelties that go with it. The least the Islamic countries can do is to stop importing live animals. They can always make adequate arrangements in the exporting countries to have animals slaughtered by their own slaughtermen, preferably after being stunned in their presence so that consumers in Islamic countries can have no doubts about the lawfulness of that meat.

CONCLUSION

It is generally claimed that the Islamic method of slaughter without pre-stunning is an important part of the Muslims' CULTURE AND RELIGION and to ban it would be against the basic human rights of religious freedom. This mix-up of culture and religion has been mainly responsible for the current confusion in the minds of some Muslims on this issue. The word 'culture' implies, among various other things, the characteristic enlightenment acquired by mental and moral training. In spite of the fact that the moral side of this enlightenment is attained through religious discipline, the use of mental faculties plays an equally important part in this process That is why the Qur'ân persistently exhorts man to use his brains (Aql) even in matters spiritual. While the basic laws of religious discipline are immutable, cultural traits and habitudes are subject to mutability and modulation according to the social and environmental evolution. There are many practices, customs, and usages among Muslims all over the world which are taken for granted as part of religion while in reality they owe their origin to pre-Islamic cultural roots—as distinct from tradition based on the Islamic common law. It is not always easy to draw a line between culture and religion. Similarly, it is rather a dubious undertaking to decide how far to use common sense in the practical rendering of those tenets about which religion has laid down no detailed injunctions. The following explication of this theme by an acknowledged Muslim theologian of the 20th century, Maulana Abu A'la Maududi, is very helpful in the understanding of this problem.

> In certain matters the Qur'ân and the *Sunnah* [practice of the Prophet] have laid down clear and categorical injunctions and prescribed specific rules of conduct. In such matters no jurist, judge, legislative body, not even the *Ummah* [the collective body of Muslims] as a whole, can alter the specific injunctions of the *sharia* [the Islamic law] or the rules of behaviour expounded by it. This does not mean, however, that there is no scope

left for legislation in this sphere. The function of human legislation in relation to such matters lies in:

a) finding out exactly and precisely what the law is, its nature and extent.

b) determining its meaning and intent.

c) investigating the conditions for which it is intended and the way in which it is to be applied to the practical problems.

d) working out minor details in the case of such laws as are too brief for an immediate application in actual life.

e) determining the extent of its applicability or non-applicability in cases of exceptional circumstances.

Then there are those types of problems about which although no specific injunctions have been laid down in the *sharia*, but provisions have been made about some analogous situations.

There is yet another category of human affairs about which the *sharia* has prescribed no specific guidance but has laid down broad principles or indicated the intention of the Law-giver as to what is to be encouraged and what is to be discouraged.

Apart from these, there is yet another vast range of human affairs about which the *sharia* is totally silent... This silence is by itself indicative of the fact that the Supreme Law-giver has left it to human beings to decide such matters in their own discretion and judgement. Hence independent legislation can be resorted to in such cases but it must be in consonance with the real spirit of Islam and its general principles. ...

The whole of this legislative process, which makes the legal system of Islam dynamic and makes its development and evolution in the changing circumstances possible, results from a particular type of academic research and intellectual effort which, in the terminology of Islam, is called 'Ijtihad'.[33]

It has already been established in this book that the main counsel of Islam in the slaughter of food animals is to do it in the least painful manner and numerous Qur'ânic and *Ahadith* injunctions have been cited to that effect. However, stunners have not been specifically mentioned in any of these injunctions. The judicious guidance of Maulana Maududi is that, in such cases, God has left it to human beings to use their own discretion and judgement "in consonance with the real spirit of Islam and its principles." After reading this book, there should remain no doubt in anyone's mind that all the Islamic laws on the treatment of animals, including the method of slaughter, are based in all conscience on "the spirit" of compassion, fellowship, and benevolence. Let us study the following *Hadith* in the light of the above-quoted criteria:

> Allah, Who is Blessed and Exalted, has prescribed BENEVOLENCE towards everything and has ordained that everything be done in the right way; so when you must kill a living being, do it in the proper way— when you slaughter an animal, use the BEST METHOD and sharpen your knife so as to cause as little pain as possible.[34]

The *Hadith* ends up by emphasising that the knife should be sharp. The question arises whether the specific mention of a knife is meant to preclude the use of any other instrument in addition to a knife. The simple answer to this question is that it does not preclude the use of other instruments such as stunners, the reason being that they had not been invented at that time—just like hundreds of other technological objects which we have started using these days in spite of the fact there is no direct or indirect mention of them in the Qur'ân or *Ahadith*. The crucial test, according to Maulana Maududi's definition, is whether or not the stunning techniques are "in consonance with the real spirit of the broad principles and the intention" of God the Law-giver. It has been repeatedly explained earlier that pre-slaughter stunning is not meant to kill, but only to render the animal unconscious. It must be understood clearly that stunners are an instrument in addition to the instrument of the knife, and do not replace it. After the animal has been rendered unconscious by a stunner, the act of slaughter could still be carried out in accordance with the religious rectitude of *Tasmiyyah* and

Tadhkiyyah in every detail. The scientific fact has already been mentioned that the process of *Tadhkiyyah* is not affected in any way and stunning makes no difference in bleeding.

The exceptional risk that a stunned animal might be already dead, before the slaughterer gets a chance to bleed it, is no sound reason to reject the very principle of stunning. A slaughterman is expected to be experienced enough to notice if a stunned animal is alive or dead. Of course, there is always a possibility of erroneous stunning, just as there is always a possibility of human error by a Muslim slaughterman in making the cut on an unstunned animal. If a Muslim slaughterman finds a stunned animal dead, he can, and should, leave it alone and reject the carcass as *Harâm*. The whole principle of *Halal* meat is based on this postulate. Verse 5:4 of the Qur'ân allows the meat of the following dying animals on the condition that they should have at least a flicker enough of life left in them to be bled (*Illa ma Dhakkaitum*):

> The strangled (*Al-Munkhaneqah*): beaten up or dying of a blow (*Al-Mauqudhah*); fallen from a height (*Al-Mutaraddiyah*); gored by horns (*Al-Natiha*) and savaged by beasts (*Ma Akala al-Sabuo*).

Surely the wound inflicted on an animal by a captive bolt under controlled conditions is less unhygienic than the injuries it receives by: strangulation; beating up and blows; a fall; goring by other animals whose horns are known to be virulent; or torn up and mutilated by beasts of prey whose teeth and claws are also known to be virulent. There is only one dissimilarity between the analogous situation of the two kinds of wounds. The wounds mentioned in the above verse are generally accidental, while the wound made by a captive bolt is intentional. This dissimilarity however should make no difference in the intrinsicality of the general principles—especially because the stunning wound is made in the spirit of being cruel to be kind.

The writer has been directly involved in animal welfare work for the last half century and has been studying the use of stunners in conjunction with various religious aspects of the issue. Only as recently as August 1986 he visited an abattoir to see the effect of electrical as well as captive-bolt stunning both on sheep and cattle.

The details of his views about various kinds of stunners have been given earlier in this chapter. In conclusion, he has no doubt in his mind that stunning prior to slaughter does not interfere with the prescribed Islamic method of slaughter (*dhabh*); it does not affect the flow of blood (*tadhkiyyah*); and it certainly is the most humane way known so far by rendering the animal unconscious before cutting its throat. In his considered opinion, had pre-slaughter stunning been invented during the time of the Prophet Mohammad, he would have given the inventor a commendation and declared their use as obligatory. This analogical inference is logically in complete "consonance with the real spirit and intent" of Islamic laws of slaughter (*dhabh*). Who can say that the stunners currently in use might be replaced in future by some still better instruments and techniques to render an animal unconscious before slaughter? There is no finality in science and knowledge. Even at present scientists are experimenting with the possibilities of employing ultra-sound and laser techniques.

A great Muslim scholar of the 19th century who is acknowledged in the Muslim world as an authority on theology—Sheikh Muhammad Abduh, the great Grand Mufti (Jurist) of Egypt, Dar al-Iftah, (d.1905 A.C.)—expresses the same view in these words:

> I believe, that, if the Holy Prophet had knowledge of any method of slaughter which could make it easier for the animal to die without affliction—such as slaughter after being given electric shock—he would have declared such a method an improvement upon the direct method.[35]

While discussing the same question in detail, he opines that

> the modern method of slaughter is near to the Islamic method, because it is less painful to the animal, and it was for this very reason that the Prophet adopted the best method of his time.[36]

The following salient points in the above verdicts (*Fatawa*) of Sheikh Abduh, are worthy of note:

He approved of stunning on the grounds that it is a less painful method of slaughter than the direct cutting of the throat in spite of the fact that in his time, almost a century ago, stunning techniques were only rudimentary. Today they have been much improved in performance and the risk of an animal dying as a result of stunning before slaughter has been greatly reduced. His approval lays down the basic principle that stunning does not interfere with the Islamic method of bleeding the animal before death. He has very advisedly used the Arabic wording "*Tadhkiyyah be-l-Kahrubaiyyah*", meaning "slaughtering according to the method as prescribed by Islam, after the electric shock."[37]

His reasoning that the Prophet adopted the method of direct slaughter because that was "the best method OF HIS TIME" allays the emotional fears of some Muslims that a suggestion of any improvement upon the method adopted by the Prophet would be an acknowledgement of his (May God forbid) inadequacy as a Messenger of God. His views are meant to keep the door open for any scientific and technological advance on the traditional methods and practices, provided it does not infringe upon the intrinsic values and prescripts of Islam. It is in this sense and spirit that stunners should be taken as an additional aid to lessen the affliction of the poor animal, in the real spirit of Islamic compassion (*Rehm*) for animals— and not as a repudiation of the traditional method of slaughter.

Many other scholars, theologians and accredited authorities in the Islamic world have expressed their views in favour of stunning, yet the general Muslim public (*Ummah*) has failed to take up the matter seriously. One plausible reason for this apparent apathy seems to be that the general public is not aware of the enormity of cruelty that is being inflicted on animals in this age, when the mouths to feed have increased manifold. The religious reason for the Muslim reluctance to accept stunners is the absence of edicts (*Fatawa*) on this subject by early classical authorities. Obviously, they could not give their verdicts on an issue which did not exist in their time. The views and verdicts of authorities of the 20th century, when stunners came into use, do not carry the same classic weight. In spite of this drawback, it will help to see what some of the modern theologians of renown have to say about stunning.

Dr. Faz-ar-Rahman, the Director of the Research Institute of Islamic Studies in Pakistan during the Presidency of Field

Marshal Muhammad Ayub Khan, believed that the meat of animals slaughtered after stunning was lawful (*Halal*) for Muslims. He wrote to Al-Azhar Seminary in Cairo for guidance. Al-Azhar appointed a special committee, consisting of representatives of the four acknowledged Schools of Thought in Islam, i.e. Shafi'i, Hanafi, Maliki and Hanbali. The unanimous verdict (*Fatwa*) of this Committee was:

> Muslim countries, by approving the modern method of slaughtering, have no religious objection in their way. This is lawful as long as the new means are 'sharp' (*ahadd*) and clean and do 'cause bleeding' (*museelah al-damm*).
>
> If new means of slaughtering are more quick and sharp, their employment is a more desirable thing. It comes under the saying of the Prophet 'God has ordered us to be kind to everything' (*inna'l-laha kataba-'l'ihsan 'ala kulle Shay'in*).[38]

Another great Muslim scholar of this century, Sheikh Ahmed Hassan el-Baqouri—the then Rector of Al-Azhar Seminary and whom the writer has the honour of knowing as a personal friend—concludes his verdict about stunners in these words:

> . . . I have reviewed the Islamic principles concerning this subject. . . . One of the *Ahadith* says: 'God asks of everyone, who undertakes something, to do it properly. When you kill an animal, you should do it properly (as quickly and humanely as possible)'. It is obvious that the stunning knock on the forehead causes far less suffering than the methods now used by the slaughterman. . . . No one can deny that this new method [of pre-slaughter stunning] is merciful, otherwise consciousness would linger on (in a dying animal); THEREFORE THE TWO NECESSARY CONDITIONS PREVAIL, namely: the required Islamic method of slaughter combined with mercy towards the animal.[39]

The following opinion is from the scientific point of view by a Muslim, Dr. M. Abd-us-Salaam. He is a Public Health Veterinarian, specialising in the Socio-Cultural science of food, working at a German Institute:

301

The writer believes that modification of the method of slaughter is possible if it makes it really more humane and does not infringe the basic concept. [The basic concept being that blood should drain out in the normal way, i.e. *Tadhkiyyah*].

In discussions with doctors of Islamic law in different countries, the writer was greatly impressed by their concern for humane treatment of animals and for avoiding unnecessary pain before and during slaughter. They were also willing to consider the use of modern methods directed by this purpose as long as they did not infringe the basic concepts. For example, they were generally agreeable to the use of those methods of pre-slaughter stunning which would not kill the animal, even if it is not slaughtered. The writer is of the opinion that there is room for further discussion and consideration of the use of stunning, especially if non-fatal methods of reducing pain can be proposed.[40]

There is one very important theological point in the above quotation which needs clarification. The proviso in the quotation that only that method of pre-slaughter stunning would be acceptable to Muslims "which would not kill the animal, EVEN IF IT IS NOT SLAUGHTERED" is not borne out by any Islamic law. On the contrary, there is evidence in the Qur'ân that such a condition would be superfluous. While laying down the law about slaughter of injured animals in verse 5:4, it makes it abundantly clear that they become lawful (*Halal*) if slaughtered while alive; and unlawful (*Harâm* and *Metat*) if they die before slaughter. There is no reason whatsoever why the same law should not be applied to animals injured by stunning. This point has already been discussed in some detail: the Muslim slaughterman could always reject a stunned animal if he finds it dead. People who express unauthorised opinions such as the Doctors of Law as quoted by Dr. Abd-us-Salaam do not realise that, though inadvertently, they are still making the law (*sharia*) unnecessarily complicated—while Islam has gone to great lengths to make it simple and practicable. Many Muslim theologians, both classical and modern, have tried to curb this tendency.

The Qur'ân too, has repeatedly discouraged the tendency to split hairs in matters of law. The bases of moral and ethical laws should be the 'intention'; and the only judge for intention, apart from God the All-Knower, is the conscience of the individual himself. The Islamic maxim lays down this golden principle in these words: "Actions shall be judged on intention (*Innamal A'amalo bin-niyyah*)." The Qur'ân gives an example of the tendency to complicate law by citing the story of the Israelites, when they were commanded by Moses to kill a heifer which they had started worshipping. The Israelites were reluctant to kill it and started asking Moses paltry details about the cow with the intention of confusing the issue. The following commentary on these verses (Qur'ân 2:67-71) by Muhammad Asad, the learned translator of the Qur'ân into English, is very relevant here:

> It would appear that the moral point of this story points to an important problem of all (and, therefore, of Islamic) religious jurisprudence: namely, the inadvisability of trying to elicit additional details in respect of any religious law that had originally been given in general terms—for, the more numerous and multiform such details become, the more complicated and rigid becomes the law. This point has been actually grasped by Rashid Rida, who says in his commentary on the above Qur'ânic passage (see Manâr 1,345f.): 'Its lesson is that one should not pursue one's [legal] inquiries in such a way as to make laws more complicated. . . . This was how the early generations [of Muslims] visualised the problem They did not make things complicated for themselves—and so, for them, the religious law (*dîn*) was natural, simple and liberal in its straight-forwardness. But those who came later added to it [certain other] injunctions which they had deduced by means of their own reasoning (*ijtihad*); and they multiplied those [additional] injunctions to such an extent that the religious law became a heavy burden on the community.[41]

Great Muslim savants, such as Ibn Abbas, Tabari, Zamakhshari and many others, have expressed similar disquiet on the tendency of making religious law more and more complex and unconformable.

The present rigidity which has been grafted into the pristine and natural simplicity of the Islamic law is nowhere more disturbing than in matters of food and methods of slaughter.

To crown all verdicts (*Fatawa*), here is the 'Recommendation' of a pre-eminent Muslim organisation of this century—The Muslim World League (*Rabitat al-Alam al-Islami*). It was founded in Makkah al-Mukarramah in 1962 A.C. (1382 A.H.), with 55 Muslim theologians (*Ulama'a*), scientists and leaders on its Constituent Council from all over the world. MWL is a member of the United Nations, UNESCO, and UNICEF. In January 1986 it held a joint meeting with the World Health Organisation (WHO) and made the following 'Recommendation' about pre-slaughter stunning (No.3:1 WHO-EM/FOS/1-E, p.8):

> Pre-slaughter stunning by electric shock, if proven to lessen the animal's suffering, is lawful, provided that it is carried out with the weakest electric current that directly renders the animal unconscious, and that it neither leads to the animal's death nor renders its meat harmful to the consumer.

The implications of the provisos laid down in the above 'Recommendation' have already been discussed at length in this chapter. The most encouraging thing is that an organisation which represents the current thought and opinion of the Muslim world has approved of pre-slaughter stunning in principle.

In order to appreciate fully the significance of this 'Recommendation', it is important to see the list of Muslim participants in this meeting in Appendix B.

FINAL DESIDERATUM

Muslims living in Western countries have an opportunity to make a comparative study of animal welfare work in those countries and pass on that knowledge to their respective countries of origin. People all over the world have acknowledged present-day Western superiority in all fields of technology and science. Students go to their academies for training and qualification and are benefiting from them in every aspect of life. So, why should they not appreciate and benefit from all those technical aids in the business of slaughtering food animals which do not infringe upon fundamental religious laws? According to the sayings of the Prophet Mohammad; "Knowledge is like a stray camel, catch it wherever it is found" and "Acquire learning, even if you have to go for it as far as China." There should be no complex of inferiority in accepting the fact that, like all other tools and instruments, Western science and technology has also improved the tools and techniques of slaughter. They should be accepted in the knowledge and with the conviction that they are nothing but a confirmation of the Islamic directives of compassion for animals.

There are always two sides of a coin. It is true that many people in the West have started neglecting their religious dietary discipline, with the result that cruelty to food-animals has increased in new forms and guises. Animals are skinned alive, such as eel-fish; many are boiled alive, such as lobsters; frogs are dismembered live just to eat their weazen legs. Geese are force-fed up to 2.5kg of salted maize every day for three to four weeks by pushing the food down their throat by a funnel. During all this period they are kept confined in 25 x 38cm cages. As a result, their liver increases by 371 percent and at this stage they are bled to death. Why? Because, according to a French recipe, the crammed livers of such geese make tastier 'pâté de foie gras'. All these and many other inhumane abominations in the food trade are the inevitable result of the breakdown of religious discipline.

At the same time, the obverse of the coin is that there are more conscientious people in Western countries who are genuinely concerned for animal rights and welfare than in Eastern countries. Thousands of Western voluntary organisations have declared a "Jihad" against cruelties to animals as a natural sentiment and a spontaneous reaction against any source of cruelty—be it commerce, science, or religion. They come in conflict with religion only when religious dogmatism starts violating the principles and the spirit of its own revealed theology. The following court case is just an example of the fact that the current sentiment of animal welfare is no respecter of any religious bigotry, be it Islam, Christianity, Judaism, or any other religion.

In 1984, Peter Roberts, the founder and then the Director of Compassion in World Farming, prosecuted the Prior of Storrington Priory in Southern England together with the Manager of the Priory veal unit. The prosecution claimed that certain "Welfare Codes" published by the British Ministry of Agriculture had been breached and that in consequence cruelty was proven. About 650 calves were kept in the unit, each confined within a crate barely 61cm wide, tethered on a 51cm chain, lying on bare wooden slats with no bedding and separated from the other calves on either side by high solid wooden partitions. The calves were unable to develop their ruminant nature because they were kept on an all-liquid feed and with no solid fibrous food. They were in virtual solitary confinement for life.

This test case was the first of its kind. The cruelty of brutality and that of neglect had led to numerous prosecutions in the past. But the cruelty due to deprivation in factory farming had never before been challenged through the Courts.

Evidently the implications of a successful prosecution were in the minds of the judges. It could mean not only an end to the individual veal crate system but would soon lead to the battery cage for hens being challenged, as well as other modern farming methods. The judges refused to convict, and awarded heavy costs to the Priory, but the Priory veal farm did not survive local opinion and soon closed down.

The welfare society sought a meeting with the Minister and claimed that it was now proven that the Codes were not capable of being enforced. Later the Minister announced that he saw the need for Regulations instead of Codes and he decided to ban this cruel rearing method.[42]

In 1981 the World Society for the Protection of Animals invited the representatives of some responsible Muslim organisations in the United Kingdom to a demonstration of stunning organised by the Humane Slaughter Association.

> A sheep was first stunned and then lifted up to a cradle and transversely cut. Immediately it was plain that the animal's heart was continuing to beat and

the blood to pump, effecting a satisfactory bleeding out. The sheep was dead after five minutes. The same procedure was then carried out on a heifer, after first being restrained. For this animal, the pumping blood and continuing heartbeat proved even more dramatic and conclusive. The heifer was dead six minutes after the cut. The demonstration was filmed and recorded on video tape to enable its viewing by religious leaders all over the world.[43]

This kind of humanitarian sentiment should have been the prerogative of those who believe that every word about the welfare of animals in the Qur'ân is the revealed word of God and that every saying and action of His Messenger was divinely inspired. Muslims in the West should have been the first of the immigrant communities to join such organisations, playing an active role in them. If nothing else, it would have given them a chance to reappraise their Islamic values in the field of welfare work. There is a lot which needs to be done in Eastern, especially in Islamic, countries in this field. For example, those who know what is happening in our abattoirs in the East would agree that proper education and professional training is urgently needed—of all the personnel engaged in them—not only in the physical act of slaughter but also in the mental and intellectual understanding of the Islamic instruction regarding all the procedures of this profession. Slaughtermen and other workers should be engaged with diligent scrutiny to make sure that they are well versed in the Islamic laws about the compassionate and humanitarian treatment of animals before, during and after slaughter. Stringent supervision in abattoirs by qualified and religiously educated inspectors should be arranged. Muslims owe these and many other such reforms not only to those animals whom they kill for food, but also to that great Prophet who went to unprecedented lengths to establish the rights of animals.

There are sins of 'commission' and sins of 'omission'. A sin of commission is doing something which is forbidden by God to do, such as inflicting pain upon others; while a sin of omission is omitting to do something which should have been done, such as alleviating the pain of a sufferer. In the words of Addison; "The most natural division of all offences is into those of omission and those of commission."[44]

After reading this book there should remain no doubt in anybody's mind that the modern apparatus and techniques of slaughter, including stunners, cause no impediment to the normal flow of blood which is the most important hygienic requirement of the Islamic laws of slaughter (*Tadhkiyyah*). At the same time they do mitigate the pain and grief of the animal. In the spirit of the Islamic teachings, the use of such aids and techniques is not merely a matter of choice and preference; it is for Muslims a moral imperative and religious obligation. Refusal to use them and not to spare the animal avoidable pain is, without doubt, a SIN OF OMISSION.

APPENDIX A

SOME MEDICAL TERMS IN CHAPTER 6 EXPLAINED

VAGUS NERVE: It is the tenth cranial nerve. Arising from the brain it passes downwards into the chest and abdomen, supplying branches to the throat, lungs, heart, stomach, and other abdominal organs. It contains motor, secretory, sensory and vasodilator fibres.

PERIPHERAL: Towards the periphery, i.e., away from the centre of the body.

VASO CONSTRICTION: Vaso means vessel. It means constriction or contraction of a vessel. Every vessel wall is supplied by nerves. Stimulation of nerves can bring about either constriction or dilatation of a vessel. Dilatation of a vessel is called vasodilatation. When a nervous stimulation causes vasoconstriction, the narrowing of the vessel leads to increased pressure of the blood flowing in that vessel and the animal is thus put under stress. However, vasodilatation brings about relative slowing in the flow of blood due to decreased pressure and the animal feels relaxed.

CATECHOLAMINES: Impulses in the nerves are transmitted from one nerve cell to another through junctions, which are called SYNAPSES. These impulses are transmitted in the form of chemical substances, some of which are:

ADRENALIN AND NORADRENALIN. (Additionally, there are certain other substances as well.) Both these transmitters of impulses are called catecholamines. Catecholamines are also released from autonomic neurons and are also secreted from the adrenal gland.

ADRENAL GLAND: It is an endocrine gland which secretes adrenalin and noradrenalin. As this gland lies over the upper pole of the kidneys, (kidneys are also called renals), so it is called supra renal gland.

CENTRAL NERVOUS SYSTEM

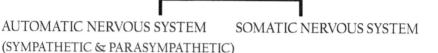

AUTOMATIC NERVOUS SYSTEM   SOMATIC NERVOUS SYSTEM
(SYMPATHETIC & PARASYMPATHETIC)

SOMATIC NERVOUS SYSTEM: Deals with impulses arising from the skin and some other parts of the body to the central nervous system. These include pain and proprioception.

AUTOMATIC NERVOUS SYSTEM: Relays impulses from the viscera (organs lying deep in the body as liver, kidneys, spleen, intestines, stomach etc.) to the central nervous system. It also regulates the function and normal physiological mechanisms of visceral organs. Impulses from visceral structures reach the central nervous system via the sympathetic and parasympathetic pathways and vice versa.

SYMPATHETIC NERVE ENDINGS: the nerve endings of the sympathetic nervous system.

ARTERIES: Blood vessels that carry oxygenated blood from the heart to cells, tissues, and organs of the body (except the pulmonary artery, which carries deoxygenated blood from the heart to the lungs).

ARTERIOLES: Smallest arteries.

VEINS: Blood vessels which carry deoxygenated blood from the cells, tissues, and organs of the body to the heart, from where the blood is pumped to the lungs to be oxygenated.

VENULES: Smallest veins

CAPILLARIES: Are the smallest vessels in the body which form a communicating network between arteries and veins and are present everywhere in the body.

MUSCLE CAPILLARIES: Are capillaries lying in a muscle.

VISCERA: Internal organs of the body as explained above.

GLYCOGEN: Is the storage form of glucose in the animal tissues. When glucose is needed in the body, glycogen is acted upon by certain enzymes and broken down to glucose.

MYOGLOBIN: Is an iron- and oxygen-binding protein found in skeletal muscle.

OXYMYOGLOBIN: When myoglobin binds oxygen.

APPENDIX B

LIST OF MEMBERS OF THE MUSLIM WORLD LEAGUE RECOMMENDING PRE-SLAUGHTER STUNNING.

1. Dr. Abdullah Naseef, Secretary General LMW, Mecca, Saudi Arabia.
2. Sheikh Lahbib Balkhouja, Secretary General, Islamic Fiqh Academy, Islamic Conference Organisations, Mecca, Saudi Arabia.
3. Sheikh Abdel-Kader Abdalla Khalaf Al-Anani, Researcher, Ministry of Awkaf, Kuwait.
4. Mr. Badr Nasser Al-Mattiri, Inspector, Islamic Affairs Department, Ministry of Awkaf, Kuwait.
5. H.E. Professor Dr. Abdel Aziz Al-Khayat, Minister of Awkaf and Professor of Comparative Fiqh, University of Jordan, Amman, Jordan.
6. Dr. Talal Omar Bafakih, Director of the Fiqh Academy, LMW, Mecca, Saudi Arabia.
7. Sheikh Mohammad Tijani Jawhari, Director, Religious Affairs Department, LMW, Mecca, Saudi Arabia.
8. Mr. Mohammad Mazhar Hussaini, Executive Director, Islamic Food & Nutrition Council of America, Chicago, U.S.A.
9. Sheikh Mohammad Alouini, Director: Islamic Cultural Centre; Secretary-General: Continental Council for Mosques, Brussels, Belgium.
10. Dr. M. Hawari, Islamisches Zentrum, Aachen, West Germany.
11. Dr. Mohammad Abdel Monem Abul-Fadl, Professor of Medical Analyses, Zamalek, Cairo, Egypt.
12. Sheikh Abdallah Al-Bassam, Judge, Western Region, Mecca, Saudi Arabia.
13. Sheikh Abdel Kader Mohammad Al-Amari, Judge, First Islamic Court, Doha, Qatar.
14. Mr. Fouad Zeini Koutbi, Director General of Branch Ministry of Commerce, Mecca, Saudi Arabia.

15. Mr. Yahia Sanbol, Director of Jeddah Branch, Standardization Organisation, Jeddah, Saudi Arabia.

16. Mr. Tewfik Ibrahim Tewfik, Under-Secretary of State of Provisions, Ministry of Commerce, Riyadh, Saudi Arabia.

17. Mr. Yahia Ahmed Motahhar, Director-General: Organisations and Government Foreign Relations, LMW, Mecca, Saudi Arabia.

18. Mr. Badr Obeid Al-Saad, Director, Nutritional and Agricultural Products, Standardization Organisation, Riyadh, Saudi Arabia.

19. Sheikh Abdallah Al-Sheikh Al-Mahfouz Arbeih, Professor: Faculty of Arts, King Abdul Aziz University, Jeddah, Saudi Arabia.

20. Dr. Mohammad Abdussalam, Director: FAO/WHO Collaborating Centre, Robert von Ostertag Institute, Bundergesundheitsant, Berlin, Federal Republic of Germany.

21. Dr. Hussein A. Gezairy, Regional Director, WHO Regional Office for the Eastern Mediterranean, Alexandria, Egypt.

22. Dr. H. A. El-Uafi, WHO Representative, Riyadh, Saudi Arabia.

23. Dr. M. H. Khayat, Manager, Regional Programme and Publications, WHO/EMRO, Alexandria, Egypt.

24. Mr. T. Zeribi, Regional Adviser: Environmental Hazards and Pollution Control WHO/EMRO, Alexandria, Egypt.

References And Notes (Chapter 6)

1. David Whiting (the then General Secretary of Compassion in World Farming, England) in his letter to a Local Authority published in their magazine *Agscene*, dated 27 March 1984.
2. For details of food ingredients: cf (1) *A Muslim Guide to Food Ingredients* (2) *Shortening in Foods* (3) *A Manual of Food Shortening*; All by Ahmad H. Sakr, Ph.D., Professor of Nutritional Biochemistry; Laurence Press Co., Cedar Rapids, Iowa, USA.
3. *Bukhari*, 72:17.
4. Narrated by Rafi bin Khady; Bukhari 47:3.
5. cf. Hidâyah and Dur-'ul-Mukhtâr.
6. Narrated by Abul Ushara (Usama bin Malik bin Qatham) on the authority of his father. All the following books of Hadith have quoted it: *Tirmidhi, Abu Dawud, Nassai, Ibn Majah*, and *Dârimî*.
7. *Jewish Attitude Towards Slaughter*; I.M. Levinger; p.107; Animal Regulation Studies; 1978; Elsevier Publishing Co., Amsterdam. (Hereafter referred to as "Levinger").
8. "Report on the Welfare of Livestock when Slaughtered by Religious Methods". Farm Animal Welfare Council, H.M. Stationers, (London). Book Ref.262; 1965 paras 68, 70, 71, pp.18, 19. (Hereafter referred to as "FAWC Report".)
9. Terms explained:
    1. SKIN: The point between the throat and the head of the breastbone, where the cut is made, is called in Arabic: *Labbah*.
    2. TRACHEA: Principal air passage of the body. Arabic: *Al-hulqûn*.
    3. OESOPHAGUS: The canal from mouth to stomach. Arabic: *Al-Mârî*.
    4. JUGULAR VEINS: Great veins of the neck or throat conveying blood. Arabic: *Al-waridain*.
    5. CAROTID ARTERIES: The two great arteries carrying blood to the heart. ARTERY is a tube which forms a part of the system by which blood is conveyed from heart to all parts of the body. Arabic: *Sharyân*.
    6. VERTEBRAL COLUMN: The column of backbone made up of segments or parts called vertebrae (singular: vertebra). Arabic: *Al-silsila-tul-fekriyyah*.
    7. CERVICAL SPINE: The series of parts of vertebrae forming the neck-column. Arabic: *Rawasat* or *'Unq*.
10. See Bywater (Ref. No. 24, Chapter 5); p.6.
11. "FAWC Report", Book No. 262, pp. 19-20. (See Ref. No. 8)
12. *Qur'ân* 6:38. The full verse has been quoted earlier.
13. Narrated by Ibn Abbas, *Muslim*.
14. *Qur'ân*, 24:41; 22:18. Full verses have been quoted earlier.
15. *Qur'ân* 6:38 Full verse has been quoted earlier.

16. The Dutch scientific team comprising Gregory M. Cronin and Piet R. Wiepkema of the Ethology Section, Agricultural University, Wageningen; and Jan M. Van Ree, Medical Faculty of the University of Utrecht; (as reported in the Newsletter of Compassion in World Farming Agscene, August 1985, formerly at 5a Charles Street, Petersfield, Hants, England.)

17. Circle of Willis is the complete circle made up of branches of the carotid and the basilar arteries at the base of the brain. It is named after the English anatomist, Thomas Willis (D.1675 A.C.).

18. cf. *Bywater*, p.5 (see Ref. No. 24, Chapter 5).

19. Gotze U. 1974; cf. *(British) Veterinary Record* (1984); 115, 292-295.

20. cf. B.B. Chrystall and others (1981); *Meat Science* 5,339; cf *(British) Veterinary Record* (1984); 115, 292-295.

21. cf. P.D. Warris & D. N. Rhodes (1977 *Journal of the Science and Agriculture*, 28, 931; P.D.Warris & T.M. Leach (1978), *Journal of the Science and Agriculture*, 29,608; R.A. Field, L.R. Sanchez, J.E. Kunsman, W.G. Kruggel (1980), *Journal of Food and Science* 45, 1109; B.B. Chrystall, C.E. Divine, K.G. Newton (1981), *Meat Science* 5, 339; D.L. Doxey (1977), *Veterinary Record* 100, 555; as quoted in *(British) Veterinary Record*, 22 September (1984) 115, 292-295.

22. M.E. Cooke (1968); *Meat Hygienist* 49,24.

23. "FAWC Report", Book No. 248; para 91. p.24 (See Ref. No. 8): viscera means the interior organs, such as: liver, heart, brain and abdominal.

24. *(British) Veterinary Record* (1984) 115, 292-295.

25. P.D. Warris, B.Sc., MI. Biol.; Animal Physiology Division, AFRC Meat Research Institute, Langford, Bristol, England.

26. This statement is based on the findings of A.H. Kirton & E.G. Wood (1977); *New Zealand Journal of Agricultural Research*, 20, 449; as mentioned in the *(British) Veterinary Record* (1984) 115, 292-295.

27. *Qur'ân* (6:145) The full verse has been quoted earlier.

28. P.D. Warris and D.N. Rhodes (1977); *Journal of the Science of Food and Agriculture* 28.931; as quoted in the *(British) Veterinary Record* (1984) 115, 292-295.

29. P.D. Warris and T.M. Leach (1978) *Journal of the Science of Food and Agriculture*, 29,608; P.D. Warris and S.B. Wotton (1981), *Research in Veterinary Science*; 31, 82; B.B. Chrystall, C.E. Divine and K.G. Newton (1981), *Meat Science*, 5,339; as quoted in *(British) Veterinary Record* (1984) 115, 292-295.

30. *Lev.* 22:17-24.

31. *Deut.* 19-23 (Capitalisation of letters by the writer).

32. Richard Hooker, 1554-1600 A.C.

33. *Islamic Law and Constitution*; Abu'Ala Maududi (1903-1979); Islamic Publications Ltd., Karachi; 1960; pp. 77-79; English translation by Kurshid Ahmad M.A. LLB.

34. *The Sahih Muslim*, 2:156. Also *Al-Taaj fi Jaami al-Usool*, Vol.3, p.110, Cairo edition. Also *Al-Faruo min-al-Kafi*, p.2., and others. (Capitalisation of letters by the writer).

35. *Tafsir al-Manar* (in Arabic); Cairo; Vol.6, p.144.

36. *Tafsir al-Manar*; Vol. 6, p.133 or the Second Edition; Vol. 8. p.147-170, Cairo, 1929.
37. *The Rooznamah Mashrique* (Daily Newspaper), Lahore, Pakistan, 29 September 1967.
38. *The History of Azhar*, Cairo; 1964; pp. 361-363.
39. Sheikh Ahmed Hassan el-Baqouri, "The Rector of Al-Azhar University", as quoted in *The Annual Report.*, 1975-6, of Brooke Hospital for Animals, 2, Bayram el-Tonsi (Sikket el Mazbah), Sayeda Zeinab, Cairo, Egypt.
40. *Muslim Attitudes to Slaughter of Food Animals*; M. Abdussalam; Institut für Veterinârmedizim des Bundesqesundheitsamtes, 1000 Berlin 33, Germany; 1981; pp. 217 and 221.
41. *The Message of The Qur'ân*; Muhammad Asad; Dar al-Andalus Ltd., 3 Library Ramp, Gibraltar, Morocco; 1980; Footnote No. 55 on verses 2:67-71. For the sociological effects of this problem and the reasons why "The genuine ordinances of Islamic Law are almost always devoid of details", see his book *State and Government in Islam*; pp. 11ff passim.
42. Roberts v Ruggerio, Div. Ct. March 1985.
43. "Animals International"; For details of this video, contact: WSPA, 2 Langley Lane, London SW8; Vol. V, No. 16, Spring 1985, p.4.
44. Joseph Addison, English poet and essayist. (1672-1719).

About the Editor

Nadeem Haque is a philosopher of science, author and practicing civil engineering in Canada, with a degree in this field from King's College, University of London, and an earlier degree in Economics from University of Toronto. Nadeem has written numerous books and articles/papers (over 50) at the intersection between Islam and Science/Philosophy, tackling major areas such as evolution, consciousness, extraterrestrial life/Quran, the environment/ animals, science/religion unification, pre-ancient history, history of science, physics (its unification), philosophical science fiction and futurism and poetry. He has presented talks internationally at: ESSSAT (Poland and France), Harvard University, Paris (on a book launch for Masri's translation of Animals in Islam into French), Oxford Centre for Animal Ethics (concerning animal experimentation), and most recently, Norway. Nadeem has been on a number of podcasts and national television in Canada. He was the co-founder of King's College Islamic Society in 1985 and is currently the Director of the Institute of Higher Reasoning (IHR). Nadeem is the grandson of Al-Hafiz B.A. Masri, whose pioneering research he continued after Masri's demise. His latest book is *Ecolibrium: The Sacred Balance in Islam*, published by Beacon Books in Manchester, England. He may be reached at: nhaque@mail.com.

INDEX

A

abattoirs (slaughterhouses), 261–62, 272–73, 298–99, 307. *See also* slaughter

Abd Allah bin Abbas, 236, 246–47

Abduh, Muhammad, 239, 299–300

Abdullah, Jabir bin, 221

Abd-us-Salaam, M., 301–2

Abel, 201

Abi Darda, 245

Abraham, 145, 201, 207–9, 210

Abû A'la Maudadi, Sayyid, 110

Abu Bakr, Hazrat, 144–45

Abu Hanifa, 238, 246–48

Abu Th'labah, 251

Abu Yusuf, 247

Academy of Islamic Research, Cairo conference, 214–17

Addison, Joseph, 307–8

additives, in processed foods, 259

Adi bin Hatim, 234, 251

agriculture, 99–101, 126

Agscene (magazine), 257–58

Ahadith: on acceptance of other religions, 144; on animal sacrifice, 209, 221; on animals' feelings, 108; animals' sentience in, 146; on beasts of burden, 107; on communities of animals, 55, 70–71; on conservation of species, 73, 75, 90; dietary laws and, 230–31, 240, 246, 247, 248–49, 251, 259, 260; on dogs, 21; on furs and skins, 94; on *harâm* (unlawful) food, 95, 97, 233; on hunting, 13, 36; inferences about, 31, 299–300, 305; Islamic juristic rules and, 87– 88; on pigs, 54, 158, 163; on rights of animals, 22; *sharia* law shaped by, 38, 87–88, 94, 95, 97, 106–7; on slaughter, 56, 57, 109, 249, 260, 282, 293, 297–298, 301; on suffering, 36, 42, 97; *takbir* and, 244, 247–49; on unjustified killing of animals, 56, 94, 106; on utility-value of animals, 73, 79; on viceregency, 70; on vivisection, 95, 96, 97. *See also* Mohammad; Qur'ân

Ahadith, on treatment of animals, 146; accountability to God for, 56, 90; humane, 158, 257–58, 307; just, 13–14; kind, 4–5, 12, 36–37, 70, 104, 106, 158

ahimsa (non-harming) principle, 16, 135, 137–39, 194, 195–96

A'ishah (wife of Prophet Mohammad), 96

Akbar, Emperor, 195

Akbarabadi, Maulana Sa'id Ahmad, 239

akikah (animal sacrifice after birth of a child), 221–22

Al-Azhar seminary (Egypt), 40

Al-Azhar University (Egypt), 54, 301

Ali, Allama Yusuf, 219–20

Ali, Hazrat, 70, 72, 107, 109

Ali bin Abi Talib, 245–46

American Society for the Prevention of Cruelty to Animals (ASPCA), 275

anaesthetisation, 276, 283

Analects, the, 132

anatomical terms, related to slaughter, 264, 281, 309–11, 314n9; Circle of

Willis, 286, 315n17; viscera, 289–90, 291, 315n23. *See also* slaughter, Islamic method of

anatomy of man, 124–25

animal blood. *See* blood

animal experience: communities of animals, 4, 10, 11, 20, 26, 55, 70–71; conflicting and questionable views about, 24–30; egalitarianism and, 24–27; faculty of speech, 73, 79; human exceptionalism and, 25–26, 27–30; individuality, 103; kindness to animals, 4–5, 12, 36–37, 70, 106, 158; as kindred spirits, 19; mental capacity, 28, 29, 277, 282; sentience, 12, 19, 20–21, 28–29, 146, 265; unjustified killing of animals, 56, 94, 106; utility-value of animals, 73, 79. *See also* emotional capacity of animals

animal experimentation, 89–91

animal fighting, 98–99

animal hospitals, 38

animal husbandry, 99–101

animal rights: to resources of nature, 34, 73, 84–86; in *sharia* law, 38–41, 71

animal sacrifice, 193–225; Abraham and, 207–9; after birth of a child (*akikah*), 221–22; *Ahadith* on, 209, 221; in ancient Asia, 194–96; Bible on, 197–204; in Buddhism, 196; as charity (*sadaqah*), and alternative offerings, 211–17, 222, 223–25; in Christianity, 196–97; in Confucianism, 194; in Hinduism, 194–95; Islamic theology of, 210–11; in Jainism, 195–96; pilgrimage (*hâdy*) and, 210–17, 218, 221–22; by proxy, 218–20, 224; Qur'ân on, 203, 208–9, 210–11, 214–15; ritual slaughter, 6, 14–15, 56; *sharia* law and, 207, 212, 215, 216, 219. *See also* Judaism, animal sacrifice in

Animals and World Religions (Kemmerer), 33

Animals & Nature First (Fox), 18

animals' relationship with Allah, 4, 10, 25

animal welfare, Islamic teachings and, 54–56

animal welfare, related to slaughter, 257–58, 265, 285–86, 291–92, 294, 298–99, 304–8; pain, physical, 264, 277, 280–83; psycho-physiology, of animals, 276–80, 281–82; stunning legislation, 266–67. *See also* slaughter, Islamic method of

antibiotics, 5, 43, 102

ants, 4, 20–21

anymals, 33–45; dietary choice and, 41–45; meaning of term, 33ni; Mohammad as moral exemplar and, 36–37; nature and, 34–36; *sharia* and, 38–41; viceregency and compassion, 37–38

Asad, Muhammad, 220, 251–52, 303

Asoka, Emperor, 134

Ata bin Yassar, 238, 245–46

atonement, 193, 199, 200, 202–3

Attar, Farid ud-Din, 11

Auza'i, 246

Azad, Maulana Abul Kalam, 143

B

bacterial diseases, in pigs, 178–80

al-Baidawi, Qazi, 248

al-Banna, Gamal, 6

Barth, Karl, 141

beasts of burden, 107

bees, 10, 25

Berry, Thomas, 11

Bible, Hebrew (Torah): on animal sacrifice, 202–3, 205; concept of God in, 198, 199, 200; dietary laws and, 160, 292–93; vegetarianism and, 141–42, 147, 150

Bible, the, 140–41, 142, 147–48, 166; on animal sacrifice, 197–204; on body as temple, 156–57; God, concept of, 197–200; hidden meaning in, 205

bin Mukhaimarah, Qasim, 245

bin Sa'd, Laith, 246

birds, 10–11, 21

blemish, prohibition against, 265, 269, 288, 292–95

blood, 241–42; animal sacrifice and, 200; hunting of game animals and, 250–52; prohibition on consumption of, 148–49, 162, 242, 244, 288, 291–92. See also exsanguination

blood, slaughter laws on, 22, 232–33, 241–42, 258, 260, 263; in both Judaism and Islam, 147, 148–49; exsanguination and, 263, 286–92; stunning and, 268, 271; tadhkiyyah (bloodletting), 233, 272, 288, 292, 297–98, 300, 302, 308. See also slaughter, Islamic method of

blood pressure: in animals, slaughter and, 281; in humans, 43, 120, 123, 184

blood sports, 96

Brahmins, 134–35

breathing beings (nafs), 106

Buddhism, 83, 135–39, 160, 196

buffalo, 17

Bukhari, Muâd bin Sa'd, 260

al-Bukhari, Abd Allah Muhammad Bin Ismail, 247, 254n31

C

Cabalists, 199, 205

Cain, 201

camels, Mohammad and, 4, 22, 36

carnivores, 157. See also meatarianism

carrion-eaters, 15

Case of the Animals versus Man before the King of the Jinn, The, 40–41

caste system, Indian, 16

cattle, 43, 101–2, 128, 213; health and welfare of, in India, 16–17. See also dairy

charity, 211–17, 222, 223–25

chickens, 5, 184–85; eggs, 36, 102, 104; factory-farming, 102, 103, 104; poultry stunning, 268, 272–73

China, 132, 159

cholesterol, effect of diet on levels of, 183–84

Christianity, 140–41, 156–57, 162–66, 196–97; Jesus Christ, 21–22, 140–141, 168, 196, 207; slaughter laws and, 237–41, 243–44, 247, 263. See also Bible, the

Cincinnati pens, 274–76

Circle of Willis (arteries), 286, 315n17

Cobb, John B., 13

cognition, scientific argument for human exceptionalism and, 28–29

communication, animals' faculty of speech and, 25, 73, 78–79

communion, realization of Self-in-Other, or One-mindfulness, 10–11

communities of animals, 4, 10, 11, 20, 26, 55, 70–71

compassion, 37–38, 300, 305

Compassion in World Farming (CIWF), 3, 56, 257, 306

Conference of the Birds, The (Attar), 11

Confucianism, 83, 132–33, 159–60, 194

consciousness: psycho-physiology, 276–80, 281–82; sentience, 12, 19, 20–21, 28–29, 146, 265. See also stunning, of animals for slaughter

cows. See cattle

Creationism, 278

Creatures of God (video), 58

Cronin, Gregory M., 315n16
crop rotation, 99
culture, as distinct from religion, 295–97
Cumhuriyet (Turkish newspaper), 89
cynophobia (fear of dogs), 15

D

dairy, 16–17, 43, 101–2, 119, 129–30
Dalai Lama, 139–40
Darwin, Charles, 278, 279
degenerative disease, 120, 124
DeMello, Margo, 28
Dhabh (slaughter), 258, 299
Dhaka (slaughter), 258
diet, health and, 43, 119–20, 184
dietary choice, 41–45; *halal* foods, 33, 41–43, 147; *tayyib* (good) food, 5–6, 43–45, 234; veganism, 42–45, 43, 57–59, 119, 122, 142. *See also* meatarianism; vegetarianism
dietary laws, 131; *Ahadith* on, 230–31, 240, 246, 247, 248–49, 251, 259, 260; on consumption of blood, 148–49, 162, 242, 244, 288, 291–92; in Hebrew Bible, 160, 292–93; Qur'ân on, 5, 166–69, 232–36, 238. *See also halal* (lawful) food; *harâm* (unlawful) food; Judaism and Islam, dietary laws compared
al-Din Razi, Fakhr, 248
disease. *See* health; nosology of pigs
Divine Law of equilibrium, 229
dogs, 15, 21
dominion, of humans, 67, 70, 71–72
Dowding, Hugh, 54

E

economics of food, 125–31
egalitarianism, 24–27
eggs, 36, 102, 104

Eid-ul-Adha festival, 6, 209, 223
El-Abbadi, 239
electrical stunners, 270–72, 299–300, 304
Electro-Convulsive Therapy (ECT), 272
Electro-Encephalo-Graph (EEG), 281
elephants, 122
emotional capacity of animals, 28, 37–38, 96, 108, 130; humans, compared, 25, 103. *See also* animal experience; suffering
Essenes community, 140–41
European Convention for the Protection of Animals for Slaughter (1979), 267
European Union, 102
evolution, 278
experiments on animals, 89–91
exsanguination, 263, 286–92; meat, color of, 287–88; sticking (stable incision), 263, 284, 289–90; *tadhkiyyah* (bloodletting), 233, 272, 288, 292, 297–98, 300, 302, 308. *See also* blood; slaughter, Islamic method of

F

factory farming, 99–104; *sharia* and, 39–40, 41–42, 58
Farm Animal Welfare Council, 289
fars (blood-milk secretion), 80
Fatawa (verdict), 299–300, 304
fat consumption, 183–84
feathers, 36
fireworks, 10
fish, 43–44
Foss Super-scan IRT meat analysis, 289
four Schools of Thought, 253n2
Fox, Matthew, 14
Friedlander, Michael, 204
fur, 36, 94

G

Gandhi, Mahatma, 16, 139, 230
gas stunners, 272
Gautama Buddha, 137
Gilmore, William, 122
God: Abraham and, 208–9; Biblical concept of, 197–200
Golden Rule, 12–13
Gotze, U., 287
Gowhary, Sheikh Tantawi, 216
grain consumption, 43–44
grazing animals, 5
Great Britain, 126–27
Gyatso, Tenzin, 139–40

H

Hadith. See Ahadith
haemoglobin, 287
Haitham, Hasan bin, 112n1
Hajj/hâdy (pilgrimage), 210–17, 218, 221–22
halal (lawful) food, 229, 250–51, 301, 302; defined, 259; dietary choice and, 33, 41–43, 147; Judaism influence on, 143; *kosher* foods as, 241. *See also sharia* (Islamic law)
halal (lawful) meat, 41–42; blood and, 242; definitions and understandings, 5, 22, 41, 230–31, 242, 298; from Muslim countries, 22, 57; non-Muslim slaughter and, 237–41, 244; People of the Book, meat offered by, 236, 238–239, 246–247; permissible animals, 231–32; pork and, 155; *takbir* and, 242–49, 250–51. *See also harâm* (unlawful) food; meat; slaughter, Islamic method of
Haque, Nadeem, 208ni
harâm (unlawful) actions, 92
harâm (unlawful) food, 232–34, 259, 271, 291–92, 298, 302; Judaism

influence on, 143. *See also sharia* (Islamic law)
harâm (unlawful) meat, 271, 291–92, 298, 302; *Ahadith* on, 95, 97, 233; animal fighting and, 98–99; blood and, 242; definitions and understandings, 229, 230–31, 259; non-Muslim slaughter and, 230, 241; pork declared, 155, 166–67; *takbir* and, 247–48. *See also halal* (lawful) food; slaughter, Islamic method of; swine consumption
Harris, Marwin, 166
el-Hassan, Sheikh Muhammad Noor, 215–16
Hassan el-Baqouri, Ahmed, 301
Hastings, H.L., 166
Al-Hazen, 112n1
health: diet and, 43, 119–20, 184; human anatomy and, 124–25; meatarianism and, 117, 118, 119–20, 124; vegetarianism and, 119–20, 128–29; vitamins, importance of, 121–24
heart diseases, 183–84
Hebrew Bible. *See* Bible, Hebrew (Torah)
Heracleus, 144
herbivores, 157
Hertz, Joseph, 204
Hinduism, 16, 51–52, 133–35, 137, 159, 194–95
Hoballah, Mahmoud, 214
hormones, 43
horses, 18
Hsun-Tzu, 83
human-animal relationship, 72–86; animals' faculty of speech, 73, 78–79; animals' right to resources of nature, 73, 83–86; balance in nature, 73, 74–75; conservation of species, 73, 75–78; metaphysics of animal mind, 73, 80–83; utility-

value of animals, 73, 79–80. *See also* animal experience

Humane Slaughter Association, 306–7

humane treatment of animals, 158, 257–58, 307. *See also Ahadith,* on treatment of animals

human exceptionalism, 25–26, 27–30

human experience: human emotions, compared with animal, 25, 103; human needs and interests, 91–94, 95. *See also* animal experience

hunting, 13, 36, 213, 250–52

Hunzakuts people, 124

I

ibn al-Khattab, Hazrat 'Omar, 96

Ibn 'Arabi, 38

Ibn Hanbal, Ahmad, 238, 246

Ibn Kathir, 247

ijtihâd (law by inference and analogy), 88, 91

India, 16–17, 43, 134, 135, 195

individualism, 11

International Association Against Painful Experiments on Animals (IAAPEA), 54–55

International Association for Religious Freedom, 53

Inuit people, 123–24

Ishmael, 208

Islam, moral appeal of, 105–6

Islam and Judaism, dietary laws compared. *See* Judaism and Islam, dietary laws compared

Islam and Judaism, slaughter laws and practice compared. *See* Judaism and Islam, slaughter laws and practice compared

Islamic Concern for Animals (Masri), 56

Islamic Development Bank (IDB), 223–25

Islamic juristic rules. *See sharia* (Islamic law)

Islamic law. *See sharia* (Islamic law)

Islamic Review, The (journal), 53

Islamic teachings. *See Ahadith;* Qur'ân

ivory, 36

J

Jacob, 148

Jainism, 16, 135–37, 138, 139, 160, 195–96

Jesus Christ, 21–22, 140–41, 168, 196, 207

Job, 201

Journal of the American Medical Association, The, 122

Judaism, 140, 141–51, 160–62, 168, 226n18. *See also* Bible, Hebrew (Torah)

Judaism, animal sacrifice in, 143, 197–206; atonement and, 199, 200, 202–3; Biblical condemnation, 202–4; concept of God and, 197–200; cultus of sacrifice, 202; Judaic theology of sacrifice, 201; meaning of sacrifice and, 205–6; rabbinate influence on, 204–5. *See also* animal sacrifice

Judaism and Islam, dietary laws compared, 141–51; Abraham and, 145; Christianity and, 145; Hebrew Bible, contradictory statements in, 142; Hebrew Bible supports vegetarianism, 141–42, 147; Judaism's influence on Muslims, 143–45, 151; meatarianism as choice in Islam, 145–47; meatarianism as concession in Judaism, 147–48, 150; slaughter methods compared, 145–46, 147, 148, 151; spirit *vs.* letter of the law, 148, 149; war ethics compared, 144–45

Judaism and Islam, slaughter laws and practice compared, 147, 237–

41, 261–63, 275; blemish and, 269, 288, 292–93; blood and, 148–49; People of the Book, meat offered by, 236, 238–239, 246–247; stunning, 265–67, 269, 280–81, 288. *See also* slaughter, Islamic method of

al-Juhani, Ma'bad, 238

justice, 13–14

K

al-Kalhud, Sheikh Abdul Rahman, 214

Keshani, Hussein, 31

khalifa or *khalifah* (successor or representative), 30, 67

'Khallaf, 239

Khan, Sayyid Ahmad, 240

kindness toward animals, 4–5, 12, 36–37, 70, 104, 106, 158. *See also Ahadith,* on treatment of animals

Kiswani, Abdul Fattah, 223–25

Koran. *See* Qur'ân

kosher foods, 241

Krantz, Deanna, 16

L

Land, Food and the People (Wokes and Vesey), 127

Lascars (East Indian sailors in Scotland), 266

'Lâta'tadû' (do not exceed limits), 236

law, secular, 91; against animal cruelty, 197, 273; Roman, 88; stunning legislation, 265–67. *See also sharia* (Islamic law)

laws of nature, 69, 75, 103, 139, 157; violation of, 13, 82, 168, 232

leather/skins, 36

Lee, Arthur (Lord of Fareham), 266

Lin Hung Pin, 166

lions, 52

M

Mahavira, Vardhamana, 137

maitri (loving kindness toward all beings), 18

Mak'hul, 245–46

Makruh (unpalatable/abominable), 259, 273, 292

Malik, 215–16

Malik, Imam, 246

Manu Samhita (ancient Indian code of law), 133

Masai people, 51, 123–24

Mashbuh/Mashkuk (suspect or doubtful), 259

Masri, Al-Hafiz B.A., 3–4, 8–9, 10, 14; biography of , 51–60; on human exceptionalism, 24–25, 27; meatarianism, experience of, 117–18

Masri, Salima, 52, 54

materialism, 11

Mathnawi (Rumi), 35

Maududi, Abu A'la, 295–97

meat, 22–23; colour of, 287–88; Foss Super-scan IRT analysis, 289; import and export of, 294–95; taste of, 293–94. *See also halal* (lawful) meat; slaughter, Islamic method of

meatarianism, 109, 117–51; Buddhism and, 135–39; carnivore species, 157; Christianity, 140–41; Confucianism and, 132–33; degenerative diseases and, 120, 124; economics of food and, 125–31; health and, 117, 118, 119–20, 124; Hinduism and, 133–35, 137; human anatomy and, 124–25; Islam and Judaism, compared, 141–51; Jainism and, 135, 137–38, 139; Masri's experience of, 117–18; vitamins and, 121–24. *See also* dietary choice; vegetarianism

mechanical stunners, 265, 269–70, 288, 292–95

Mencius (Confucian sage), 132–33

mental capacity of animals, 28, 29, 277, 282. *See also* emotional capacity of animals; stunning, of animals for slaughter

mental cruelty, 38, 108. *See also* suffering

mercy killing, 16–17

Message of The Qur'ân, The (Asad), 303

Mir Taki Mir, 35

Misri, Abdul-Rahman, 51–52

Mohammad: education *vs.* divine inspiration of, 278–79, 292; as moral exemplar, 36–37; Qur'ân dictation by, 149; titles of, 217. *See also Ahadith*

moral appeal of Islam, 105–6

Moses, 22, 86

Muslim countries: factory farming in, 104; *halal* assumptions about meat from, 22, 57

Muslim jurists (*fuqaha'a*), 87

Muslims, working in cattle slaughter facilities, 16–17

Muslim World League (Rabitat al-Alam al-Islami), 304, 312–13

Al-Muthlah (killing by cruel methods), 291–92

N

Nahr (slaughter), 258

Nakhi'î, 247

Native Americans, 10, 11, 15

naturalists, 73, 78

Nawawi, 247

neo-Darwinism, 278

Nepal, 195

Noah, 147, 199

Noah's Ark, 77

non-intervention, attitude of, 16

nosology of pigs, 169–84, 188–89; bacterial diseases, 178–80; heart diseases, in humans, 183–84; parasitical diseases, 170–78; pathogens, other, 180–81; skin and general diseases, 181–83. *See also* swine consumption

O

Objectivism, 11

Obote, Milton, 53

Omar, *Hazrat'*, 109–10

omnivores, 169

optional (non-emergency) slaughter (*Dhabh Ikhtiyari*), 259, 260–65

Ozdemir, Ibrahim, 34

P

paganism, 14

pain, physical, 264, 277, 280–83

parasites, in pigs, 170–78

pathogens, in pigs, 180–81

patriarchal authority, 70

People of the Book, meat offered by, 236, 238–39, 246–47

peremptory (emergency) slaughter (*Dhabh Idhtirari*), 260, 287

PETA, 60

pets and companion animals, 39, 78, 108

Pickthall, Marmaduke, 243

pigs. *See* swine

pilgrimage (*Hajj/hâdy*), 210–217, 218, 221–222

planetary CPR (conservation, preservation, and restoration), 12

plant-based diet (veganism), 42–45, 57–59, 119, 122, 142

polytheism, 200

Popper, Karl, 278

pork. *See* swine consumption

posttraumatic stress disorder, 10

poultry stunning, 268, 272–73. *See also* chickens

Prophet Mohammad. *See* Mohammad

proxy, animal sacrifice by, 218–20, 224

psycho-physiology, of animals, 276–80, 281–82

Q

al-Qadi, Wadad, 30

al-Qardawe, Yusuf, 239

Qassabs (slaughterers), 258, 261

Qiblah (direction, towards Mecca), 264

Qur'ân: on animal sacrifice, 203, 208–9, 210–11, 214–15; on animals' faculty of speech, 73, 79; on animals' right to resources of nature, 34, 73, 84–86; animals' sentience in, 20–21, 146; on balance in nature, 73, 74–75; on blood consumption, 242, 291; on communities of animals, 4, 11, 20, 70–71; on conservation of species, 73, 75–78; as continuation of monotheistic texts, 143–45, 197, 207; dictation of, 149; dietary laws and, 5, 166–69, 232–36, 238; Divine Law of equilibrium, 229; dogs in, 21; on *harâm* actions, 92; hunting of game animals and, 250; on individuality of animals, 103; on metaphysics of animal mind, 73, 81–83; on non-compulsion in religion, 156; non-Muslim slaughter and, 239, 244; on resource exploitation, 72; scribing of, 149; *sharia* and, 38, 87–88, 92–93, 157–58; on swine consumption, 166–69; *takbir* and, 244–45; on upright way of life, 69–70; on utility-value of animals, 73, 79–80; on viceregency, 30, 68–69; on vivisection, 97–98; on war, 144–45. *See also Ahadith*

Qur'ân, regarding slaughter, 147, 282, 293, 295, 303, 307; on animals found dying, 298, 302; on animals'

psycho-physiology, 276, 278, 279, 282; on blemish, 293; blood and, 242, 291, 292; on Christians and Jews slaughtering meat, 263; on position of animals, 264, 275; terminology used in, 258–60. *See also* slaughter, Islamic method of

R

Rabi'ah, 245

rabies, 15, 21

Raghib, Imam, 70

Rahman, Faz-ar, 300–301

Ramadan, Tariq, 42

rationality, 28–29, 69

Reda, Rashid, 239

religious education on animal welfare, 66–67, 86

Research Institute of Islamic Studies, 300–301

restraining pens, 273–76; rotary pens, 274; upright slaughter, 263–64, 274–76. *See also* slaughter, Islamic method of

Rida, Rashid, 303

ritual slaughter, 6, 14–15, 56

Roberts, Peter, 3, 306

Roberts v Ruggerio (1985), 305–6

Roman law, 88

rotary pens, 274

Rules for Judgment in the Cases of Living Beings (legal treatise), 39

Rumi, Jalal al-Din, 35, 38

Rusabhdev, 137

Russell, John, 128

S

Sabiq, Syed, 238

Sahîh Bukharî, 221, 254n31

Saleh, Prophet, 86

Samit, Ibadah bin, 245

Sarakhsi'i, 254n12

Saudi Arabia, 223–25

scapegoats, 196, 199, 200, 212, 225

Schools of Thought, in Islam, 301

science, human exceptionalism and, 27–29

science, swine consumption and. *See* nosology of pigs

Sdbe'fn (Sabians), 253n8

secularism, 13–14

Sekinah, 199

sentience, 12, 19, 20–21, 28–29, 146, 265

servitude of animals, 87

Sha'bi, 238, 245

Shafi'i, Abu 'Abd-Allah Muhammad bin Idris al, 246–47, 260

Shah Jahan Mosque (Woking, England), 53, 60

Shaltoot, Mahmoud, 239

sharia (Islamic law), 10, 72, 291–92, 295–97, 302; *Ahadith* and, 38, 87–88, 94, 95, 97, 106–7; animal (anymal) rights under, 38–41, 71; animal sacrifice and, 207, 212, 215, 216, 219; code of laws *(din-al-fitrah),* 157–58; complicating, 303–4; education on, 145–46; factory farming and, 39–40, 41–42, 58; interpretation and inference of, 87–89, 90–91, 92, 105, 149, 262, 267, 282; Islamic juristic rules, 87–89, 91–92; Qur'ân and, 38, 87–88, 92–93, 157–158; treatment of animals under, 55–56, 145–46, 258, 307; vivisection and, 94, 95, 97; on war, 144–45. *See also* dietary laws; *halal* (lawful) food; *harâm* (unlawful) food; Judaism and Islam, dietary laws compared

Shaw, George Bernard, 206

Shephard, Glen, 171–72

sin, 106–7, 307–8

skin diseases, in pigs, 181

slaughter, 151; of cattle, in India, 16–17; Christianity and, 237–41, 243–44, 247, 263; God's name invoked in *(takbir),* 146; Judaism influence on Muslim thought, 143

slaughter, Islamic method of, 22, 41, 109–10, 146–48, 257–308; *Ahadith* on, 56, 57, 109, 249, 260, 282, 293, 297–98, 301; blemish, prohibition against, 265, 269, 288, 292–95; culture, as distinct from religion, 295–97; optional (non-emergency) slaughter *(Dhabh Ikhtiyari),* 259, 260–65; pain, physical, 264, 277, 280–83; peremptory (emergency) slaughter *(Dhabh Idhtirari),* 260, 287; psycho-physiology, of animals, 276–80, 281–82; restraining pens, 263–64, 273–76; ritual slaughter, 6, 14–15, 56; terminology, 258–60; time factor, 270, 283–86; unintentional mistakes, 263, 264, 298; in United Kingdom, 261–62, 265–67, 272–73, 274, 306. *See also* anatomical terms, related to slaughter; blood, slaughter laws on; exsanguination; *halal* (lawful) food; Qur'ân, regarding slaughter; restraining pens; stunning, of animals for slaughter

soya beans, 129, 159

spiritual volition *(taqwa),* 70, 262, 279

"sport" animal fights, 39

starvation, 43–44

statute law *(Fiqh),* 293

sticking (stable incision), 263, 284, 289–90

Storrington Priory, 306

stunning, of animals for slaughter, 3, 6, 22, 57–58, 268–73; electrical stunners, 270–72, 299–300, 304; gas stunners, 272; Judaism and, 265–67, 269, 280–81, 288; legislation of, 265–67; mechanical stunners, 265, 269–

70, 288, 292–95; misunderstandings about, 268–69, 270; opinions on, by Islamic authorities, 300–304, 312–13; poultry stunning, 268, 272–73. *See also* restraining pens; slaughter, Islamic method of

suffering, 90, 197; *Ahadith* on, 36, 42, 97; *ahimsa* on, 139; of cows in India, 16, 17; dietary choice for minimizing, 59; ending, as act of compassion, 16, 139; factory farming and, 58; slaughter laws and, 22, 270, 277, 279–81, 284, 292, 301, 304. *See also* emotional capacity of animals

Sufism, 34–35, 38

Sunnah (convention), 293, 295

swine, defined, 169

swine consumption, 89, 155–89, 237; *Ahadith* on, 54, 158, 163; in ancient Asian religions, 159–60; in Christianity, 162–66, 168; circumstantial, 234; declared *harâm*, 155, 166–67; factory-farming, 102; hatred of pigs, 158; in Islam, 166–69; in Judaism, 160–62, 168; nosology of pigs and, 169–84, 188–89; pigs seen as unclean, 15, 54; pigs' sex life and behavior, 184–88; Qur'ân on, 166–69; swine, defined, 169. *See also* nosology of pigs

T

al-Ṭabarī, Ibn Jarīr, 27

tadhkiyyah (bloodletting), 233, 272, 288, 292, 297–98, 300, 302, 308. *See also* blood; exsanguination

Tai Chu Yo Tao (Lin Hung Pin), 166

takbir (invocation of God's name), 146, 242–49, 250–51

Tanganyika SPCA (Society for the Prevention of Cruelty to Animals), 52

target practice, 96–97

Taylor, R.L., 194

tayyib (good) food, 5–6, 43–45, 234. *See also* halal (lawful) food

Thamûd tribe, 86

time factor, of slaughter, 270, 283–86

Torah, the. *See* Bible, Hebrew (Torah)

al-Tostari, Sahl ibn Abd Allah, 38

treatment of animals, 17, 31, 40, 72, 110; accountability for, 36; cultural relativity, 15; other religions on, 12, 67–68, 151, 261; *sharia* on, 55–56, 145–46, 258, 307

trichinella and trichinosis, 170, 171–73

turkeys, 6

Tzu-Kung, 194

U

Uganda People's Congress, 53

Uganda SPCA (Society for the Prevention of Cruelty to Animals), 52

unintentional mistakes, during slaughter, 263, 264, 298

United Kingdom, 123; religious slaughter in, 261–62, 265–67, 272–73, 274, 306

upright slaughter, 263–64, 274–76

V

Van Ree, Jan M., 315n16

veal cattle, factory-farming, 102

Vedas, the, 133, 159, 194–95

veganism, 42–45, 57–59, 119, 122, 142

vegetarianism, 42–45, 57–59, 109, 117–51; Buddhism and, 135–39; Christianity, 140–41; Confucianism and, 132–33; economics of food and, 125–31; health and, 119–20, 128–29; Hebrew Bible and, 141–42, 147, 150; herbivore species, 157; Hinduism and, 133–35, 137; human anatomy and, 124–25; Jainism and, 135–37, 138, 139; Judaism, 140; vitamins and, 121–24. *See also* Judaism and Islam, dietary laws compared; meatarianism

Vesey, Cyril, 127

viceregency *(khalifah)*, 20, 30, 37–41, 67–69, 70

viscera, 289–90, 291, 315n23

vitamins, 121–24

vivisection, 94–99

Vories, Reverend, 162

W

Wagdi, Sheikh Farîd, 214

Wagdi's Encyclopaedia, 214

war, *sharia* on, 144–45

War—Living Graves (Shaw), 206

Warris, P. D., 290

Wasserman, Edward A., 28

water supply, 101

Weinberg rotating pens, 274

Whiting, David, 257–58

Wiepkema, Piet R., 315n16

Willis, Thomas, 315n17

Wokes, Frank, 127

wolves, 10, 142

World Health Organisation (WHO), 304

World Organisation for Animal Health, 6

"World Poultry" gazette, 104

World Society for the Protection of Animals, 60, 306–7

World Wildlife Fund, 60

Wynne-Tyson, Jon, 127

Z

Zahri, 245

Zentall, Thomas R., 28

Zuhri, 247

ABOUT THE PUBLISHER

LANTERN PUBLISHING & MEDIA was founded in 2020 to follow and expand on the legacy of Lantern Books—a publishing company started in 1999 on the principles of living with a greater depth and commitment to the preservation of the natural world. Like its predecessor, Lantern Publishing & Media produces books on animal advocacy, veganism, religion, social justice, humane education, psychology, family therapy, and recovery. Lantern is dedicated to printing in the United States on recycled paper and saving resources in our day-to-day operations. Our titles are also available as e-books and audiobooks.

To catch up on Lantern's publishing program, visit us at www.lanternpm.org.

facebook.com/lanternpm
twitter.com/lanternpm
instagram.com/lanternpm